Running a Restaurant

FOR

DUMMIES®

2ND EDITION

by Michael Garvey, Heather Dismore,
and Andrew G. Dismore

WILEY

John Wiley & Sons, Inc.

Running a Restaurant For Dummies®, 2nd Edition

Published by
John Wiley & Sons, Inc.
111 River St.
Hoboken, NJ 07030-5774
www.wiley.com

Copyright © 2011 by John Wiley & Sons, Inc., Hoboken, New Jersey

Published by John Wiley & Sons, Inc., Hoboken, New Jersey

Published simultaneously in Canada

For general information on our other products and services, please contact our Customer Care Department within the U.S. at 877-762-2974, outside the U.S. at 317-572-3993, or fax 317-572-4002.

For technical support, please visit www.wiley.com/techsupport.

Wiley also publishes its books in a variety of electronic formats and by print-on-demand. Some content that appears in standard print versions of this book may not be available in other formats. For more information about Wiley products, visit us at www.wiley.com.

Library of Congress Control Number: 2011936928

ISBN 978-1-118-02792-9 (pbk); ISBN 978-1-118-15258-4 (ebk); ISBN 978-1-118-15259-1 (ebk); ISBN 978-1-118-15257-7 (ebk)

Manufactured in the United States of America

10 9 8 7

WILEY

About the Authors

Michael Garvey was at one time an unassuming if not innocent soul from Brooklyn before he was grabbed by the clutches of the evil shadow known simply as the restaurant business. Starting as a resort waiter in the Poconos of Pennsylvania, he quickly became smitten by his new work and found himself a genuine masochist at heart. Garvey delved into other facets of the industry, from bartending in saloons to waiting in fine dining atmospheres. He also found time to volunteer in the kitchen of the Marist Brothers in Esopus, NY, manufacturing meals for handicapped and underprivileged children and adults. In 1994, he returned to New York City for some real brutality. He latched on to a small three-unit outfit by the name of Mumbles as a manager. After seeing action in their other locations, Michael landed a job as floor manager at The Oyster Bar in Grand Central Station owned by famed restaurateur Jerry Brody.

The Oyster Bar was a wonderland for the then medium-rare manager. Garvey took advantage of many opportunities including wine cellar stewarding which led to sommelier certification. He was part of the management team that rebuilt the institution in 1997 after a devastating fire. In 1998, he was offered the General Manager position and added President to his titles in 2000. Today, in addition to running the day-to-day operations in Grand Central, Michael has led efforts to franchise The Oyster Bar concept. While writing this book, he organized the first franchise in Tokyo, half a world and a culture away. At the time of printing, it is surpassing the franchisee's sales projections by over 100 percent. Garvey currently resides in Long Beach, NY, with his beautiful (and understanding) wife Vicki and their ridiculously cute daughter Torrance.

Heather Heath Dismore is a veteran of both the restaurant and publishing industries. She has published works including such titles as "Indian Cooking For Dummies," part of the compilation *Cooking Around the World For Dummies All-in-One; Jewelry Making and Beading For Dummies;* and the award winning *Running a Bar For Dummies* (all published by John Wiley & Sons, Inc.). Additionally, she's published Start Your Restaurant Career in the Entrepreneur Pocket Guide series from Entrepreneur Press.

A graduate of DePauw University, she succumbed to the restaurant business in Denver, Colorado while applying to law school. She rapidly rose to management at such regional and national chains as The Italian Fisherman, Don Pablo's Mexican Kitchen, and Romano's Macaroni Grill. She orchestrated the openings of 15 new restaurants and developed the training, procedural, and purchasing systems that were used as the gold standard in numerous concepts throughout her tenure.

Andrew Dismore has forged a meteoric 16-year career marked by creativity, critical acclaim and the consistent introduction of unique, ownable products onto the national palate.

Since 2010, Andy has been the Senior Director of Foodservice Product Innovation and Development for the Schwan Food Company. In this capacity, he has led the custom development of insights-driven, strategically-grounded new products for leading national restaurant chains including Subway, Yum! Brands, Dunkin Donuts, Buffalo Wild Wings, Red Robin, and the Target Corporation among others.

From 2007 to 2010, Andy served as Senior Director of Product Innovation for the Denny's Corporation. In this capacity, he lead the Culinary, Food Science & Technology, and Operational Integration teams aligned against Denny's overall product and brand innovation strategy.

In this capacity, Chef Dismore and his team created a robust pipeline full of innovative and ownable new products, including the *$2 $4 $6 $8 Value Menu, Pancake Puppies, The Grand Slamwich,* the critically acclaimed *Rock Star Menu* for which he was awarded the 2009 Menu Master Award by Nation's Restaurant News, and many, many more. You can read his complete bio at www.andydismore.com.

Dedications

Michael Garvey: To Pat Tillman, a true American hero.

Heather Heath Dismore: To my sweetest loves Riley and Lucy. You are my greatest joy and my greatest inspiration.

Andrew Dismore: To everyone who ever gave me a chance and the support to succeed . . . especially Heather.

Authors' Acknowledgments

Michael: The crews I've worked with over the years, big and small, for standing together in the trenches. Jerry Brody for acting on a feeling and giving me an opportunity. Marlene Brody for continuing to give me opportunities. The night manager who chopped open the door that pointed to the future. Craig Harrison for being a kind and understanding chef while still kicking ass. Jonathan Young for taking the training wheels off and making me laugh whenever I fell (even now). Wine salespeople for walking the tightrope of keeping me up to date without nagging. My Mother for giving me my first For Dummies book. Hiro Nagano, Ai Ito, Ishii Hideo, Master Toda, and all of the WDI staff for showing me while I showed you. Mark Abrahamson for letting a cellar rat run with it. Don and Debbie Richter for keeping me behind the bar and adjusting on the fly. Austin Power for showing me how to have fun waiting tables. My coauthors for keeping me up at night and bringing back a lot of memories. My current staff for helping through another gut checking year. Vicki for leaving the light on so many nights.

Heather: A special thank you to Tim Gallan, one of the best Project Editors in the business. And to everyone else at Wiley who made this book a success, including Diane Steele, Kristin Ferguson-Wagstaffe, Tracy Boggier, Danielle Voirol, Megan Knoll, Jennifer Ehrlich, Christy Beck, and many other behind-the-scenes folks in the editorial and production departments. Thanks for the opportunity to work with the best in the business. Thanks to Mike Garvey, who once again added some great stories and insights to this book. Finally, thanks to my incredible family for their patience and support during the never-ending writing schedule.

Andrew: This second edition would not have been possible had it not been for the dedication, drive, and tireless patience shown every day by Heather. If it had not been for Heather's persistence, this book would still be a well-intentioned manuscript. Additionally, I want to recognize the contribution to this book made by my daughters Riley and Lucy, for without their undying love, genuine support, and endless motivation I would have never accomplished anything in this career or in this life worth writing about.

Publisher's Acknowledgments

We're proud of this book; please send us your comments at http://dummies.custhelp.com. For other comments, please contact our Customer Care Department within the U.S. at 877-762-2974, outside the U.S. at 317-572-3993, or fax 317-572-4002.

Some of the people who helped bring this book to market include the following:

Acquisitions, Editorial, and Vertical Websites

Senior Project Editor: Tim Gallan

Acquisitions Editor: Tracy Boggier

Senior Copy Editor: Danielle Voirol

Copy Editor: Megan Knoll

Assistant Editor: David Lutton

Editorial Program Coordinator: Joe Niesen

Technical Reviewers: Keith and Kate Brown

Editorial Manager: Michelle Hacker

Editorial Assistants: Rachelle S. Amick, Alexa Koschier

Cover Photos: © iStockphoto.com / Hande Guleryuz Yuce and © iStockphoto.com / sunygraphics

Cartoons: Rich Tennant (www.the5thwave.com)

Composition Services

Project Coordinator: Sheree Montgomery

Layout and Graphics: Joyce Haughey, Corrie Socolovitch, Laura Westhuis

Proofreaders: BIM Indexing & Proofreading Services, Lauren Mandelbaum

Indexer: Ty Koontz

Publishing and Editorial for Consumer Dummies

    Kathleen Nebenhaus, Vice President and Executive Publisher

    Kristin Ferguson-Wagstaffe, Product Development Director

    Ensley Eikenburg, Associate Publisher, Travel

    Kelly Regan, Editorial Director, Travel

Publishing for Technology Dummies

    Andy Cummings, Vice President and Publisher

Composition Services

    Debbie Stailey, Director of Composition Services

Contents at a Glance

Table of Contents

Introduction

The restaurant business is an exciting one, full of challenges and opportunities. We're glad you're interested in finding out more about it, and you've definitely come to the right place to get started. Years ago, going out to eat was truly an event — reserved for weekends or special occasions. Today, however, even a Tuesday, just another day, can be an occasion to eat out, especially when busy careers and overloaded family schedules leave little time to cook. Fortunately, consumers have more restaurant choices than ever before. And opportunities in the industry have never been greater. This book can help you minimize the challenges and overcome the obstacles before they overcome you.

We've managed, worked, eaten, mopped floors, tended bars, learned to repair equipment midshift on a Saturday night, hired, fired, trained, and done inventory in some of the best (and worst) restaurants in the world. We've worked in ultrafine dining, fast food, catering, and everything in between. We've worked dining rooms that sat 30 and catered events that fed 50,000 diners in a single day. Sure, each of these situations is somewhat different, but many aspects of running a restaurant transcend restaurant size, location, or dining style and fall under the category of universal restaurant truths. We do our best to bring all that information to you in this book.

Whether you're a seasoned restaurant veteran or just out of cooking school, we believe that if you're reading this book, you have the desire to run a restaurant. After reading it, you should know whether you have a passion for it — or what we sometimes call The Sickness.

About This Book

Success in the restaurant business is the dream of many and the achievement of few. Often, would-be restaurateurs have misconceptions about what running a restaurant is really like. Some folks are quick to see the glitz and glamour without also seeing the anxiety and effort that accompany it. Others have seen the business from the inside and are sure that they can do it better than the people they've worked for, without feeling the true weight and complexity of the tasks and decisions that face The Boss everyday. On the other side of the coin, you find people who could do very well in the restaurant business but stay out because of the horror stories they've heard.

We want you to see the full picture — the good, the bad, and the absurd — so you can make an informed decision about your place in this business.

We wrote this book because no Bureau of Restaurant Operators exists to test your knowledge and skills to determine whether you have what it takes to get into the business. After you've read the pages between these gorgeous yellow and black covers, you'll have a good idea of whether this is the racket for you — and the knowledge to get started on the right foot.

Plenty of books tell you how to open a restaurant, but you don't find many on how to *keep* it open. This book does both. Why? Because you can never stop improving your service, evaluating your product, scoping out the competition, and researching opportunities in the marketplace. Change is the only constant in the restaurant business. To succeed, you must anticipate and act on new trends, new pressures, and whatever else the market throws your way. The spoils go to those who see opportunities before they happen.

Please don't mistake our realism for cynicism. We want you to be in the business. But we're going to make sure that you have the information you need to be a success. We show you many everyday realities that people don't always consider but should. We hope you take the information and use it to be wildly successful. You can do this, but you have to look at this business the right way. If you do, save us a table!

Conventions Used in This Book

To help you navigate through this book, we use the following conventions:

- *Italic* is used for emphasis and to highlight new words or terms that we define.
- **Boldface** indicates keywords in bulleted lists and the action parts of numbered steps.
- `Monofont` is used for Web addresses.

What You're Not to Read

Sidebars, which appear as text enclosed in shaded gray boxes, consist of information that's interesting but not critical to your understanding of the chapter or section topic. You can skip them if you're pressed for time. You can also bypass bonus material marked with the Technical Stuff icon.

Foolish Assumptions

Just as restaurant owners have to make assumptions about the customers who will be eating there, authors have to make assumptions about their readers. If one or more of the following descriptions hits home, you've come to the right place:

- ✔ You're thinking about opening your own restaurant, and you want practical, how-to advice to accomplish your goals.
- ✔ You've worked in the business, and now you're thinking about getting in on the ownership or management end of things.
- ✔ You've never worked in a restaurant, but you've met with success in other professional endeavors and possess skills that may be applicable to this business.
- ✔ You're fresh out of cooking school and are thinking about putting those skills to work in your own place.
- ✔ You buy every book that sports a yellow and black cover.
- ✔ You currently own or operate a restaurant, and you're seeking advice, tips, and suggestions to keep things running smoothly and successfully.

How This Book Is Organized

This book is organized into five separate parts. Here's what's on the menu.

Part 1: Getting Started

In this part, we give you a crash course in the restaurant business, including tips for getting started, understanding your options, creating your concept, and picking your name. We help you research the marketplace to determine whether your concept has a shot at success, and we provide information on how customers approach buying decisions. We take you through the critical step of writing a business plan. We also help you figure out whether you have what it takes to make it in the business.

Part II: Putting Your Plan in Motion

In this part, we focus on acting on your idea. We go through the ins and outs of finding the right location or making an existing location work for you. We give you tips on finding financing for your new business. And we wrap up by dotting some *i*'s and crossing some *t*'s, including help on getting the right permits and licenses, getting up to speed on local laws, and legally protecting yourself the right way.

Part III: Preparing to Open the Doors

Here, we detail all the tasks you need to do to get up and running. We walk you through hiring and training your staff and developing your menu and beverage program. We show you how to set up your kitchen and dining room for the best flow of food and people. We also give you concrete tips for purchasing and managing your inventory, which can take you a long way toward profitability. And finally, we cover two often-neglected areas of the business: operating your office and promoting your business.

Part IV: Keeping Your Restaurant Running Smoothly

This part is for anyone running a restaurant today or tomorrow or considering doing it in the future. We show you how to maintain and build on your current operation, including tips for managing employees, keeping your diners coming back, and handling customer service situations. We explain how to keep your place spick-and-span and ensure food safety. We show you how to get great information about what your customers want. And we wrap it up with a lesson in watching your numbers, with tips on which reports to run, how to analyze the numbers, and how to make changes to your business when necessary.

Part V: The Part of Tens

Here, we dispel ten common myths about running a restaurant, and we give you some of our favorite only-in-the-restaurant-business stories.

Icons Used in This Book

Icons are the fancy little pictures in the margins of this book. Here's a guide to what they mean:

The Tip icon marks ideas that can make your job a bit easier. The tips are often hands-on ways to improve your business today.

The Remember icon points out ideas that sum up and reinforce the concepts we discuss. In fact, if you're in a time crunch and can't read everything, you may want to go straight to this icon.

The Warning icon to alert you to potential pitfalls and to give you a heads-up on mistakes to avoid. Pay particular attention when you see the lit fuse.

Think of the paragraphs marked with the Technical Stuff icon as bonus material. Usually, the info gives you some noncritical background on the subject. We think the info is interesting, so we include it, but you don't have to read it to get the essential ideas and concepts.

We use the Mock Concept icon to highlight information related to our imaginary restaurant, Urban Forge Pizza Bar, which we create in Chapter 2. We use Urban Forge as an example throughout the book to help you see in concrete, easy-to-understand terms exactly how to create sales forecasts, write marketing copy, and more.

Where to Go from Here

We think that you'll find the information in this title valuable enough that you'll want to read it all. Doing so provides you with a strong, general foundation for starting and running a restaurant.

But one of the great things about a *For Dummies* book (among the hundreds that we can count) is that you don't have to read it word for word, front to back, cover to cover. If you're more interested in one particular topic than another, that's fine. Check out the corresponding part, chapter, or section and read up on that issue. You can find out about your topic of choice without first having read the information that precedes it, giving you get-in-and-get-out convenience. Interested in tips to create or improve your menu? Turn to Chapter 8. Are you currently looking for a location to plant your new shop? Check out Chapter 6. Is sanitation your thing? Chapter 17 has your name written all over it. Need help understanding how to make social media work for your restaurant today? Hop on over to Chapter 15.

You can jump around, start wherever you want, and finish when you feel like it. So tie on your apron and get going.

Part I
Getting Started

The 5th Wave   By Rich Tennant

"I just don't think asking for extra virgin
ketchup on your hamburger reflects
a full appreciation of Italian cuisine."

In this part . . .

You're standing on square one. In the chapters that follow, we introduce you to the restaurant business and help you determine whether you have what it takes to make a go of it in the restaurant world. We help you choose the kind of restaurant that fits your geographic area and your expertise. We help you understand that in order to be successful, you have to create food that people want to buy, again and again. We also help you nail down your concept, come up with a name, and start researching everything from your potential customers to the competition. And we show you how to develop a restaurant-specific business plan.

Chapter 1

Grasping the Basics of the Restaurant Business

In This Chapter

▶ Understanding the basics of the business

▶ Deciding whether you have the necessary skills

*R*estaurants are fun. Whether you stop by to celebrate a special occasion, grab a quick bite for lunch, meet friends for a drink, or pick up dinner for the family on the way home from work, the experience is usually enjoyable. (At the very least, it's more enjoyable than not eating or being forced to cook!). Just about everyone associates restaurants with having a good time. So it's natural for people to think, "I enjoy going to restaurants, so I may as well get paid to do what I enjoy — hang out in bars and eat at great restaurants."

And you know what? Living the restaurant life is fun. We've been doing it for many a year, and we love it. But the problem comes when people see only the fun and never the struggle. Viewed from the dining room or barstool (or from the kitchen, stockroom, or anywhere else other than the seat marked "Proprietor"), it's difficult to see the 95 percent of the picture that's pretty tough work. In the restaurant business, you have so much fun that you can hardly stand it. It's kind of like wishing every day was Christmas and actually getting your wish. You get tired of wrapping the presents, preparing the eggnog, and checking that the elves are on time for their shifts, and if you have to look at any more roasted chestnuts, you'll die. The restaurant business quickly becomes more work than fun, so don't be fooled.

In this chapter, we take you on a quick tour of the business. We introduce you to all the upfront work that you must do on paper before you can even think about picking up a pan or laying down a place setting. We move on to the physical preparations that will consume your every waking minute on the way to opening your doors. Then we remind you that when you first open your doors, the work has only begun. Finally, we help you examine your motivations and expectations for pursuing your dream to determine whether both are rooted in reality.

Getting a Feel for the Restaurant World

The restaurant world is more than glitz and glamour. It's truly a business, and if you don't look at it that way, you won't succeed. Ultimately, being a restaurateur is being a manufacturer. You're producing a product (food) from raw materials (your ingredients) and selling it to a customer (your diner). You're competing with lots of other manufacturers for that same diner. So you'd better do it better than the other guy, or you'll be out of business.

In this section, we discuss planning your restaurant, hiring experts to help you set up shop, and attracting customers.

Laying the foundation

Sometimes the business of *the business* is tough for people to relate to. Your product is packaged in many layers, including your exterior, your lobby, your staff's attire, the music playing, the aromas emanating from the kitchen, the friendliness and knowledge of your staff, your silverware, your china, and your glassware. All these things make up your packaging, affect the costs of doing business, and influence your diners' decision to come in and, ultimately, to come back.

As with any business, the planning stage is crucial, and you have to survive it before you can enjoy any of the fun. Right off the bat, you have to develop your restaurant's theme and concept (see Chapter 2), research the market (Chapter 3), develop a detailed business plan and use it to find and secure financing (Chapters 4 and 5), and find the best location for your new restaurant and get the right licenses and permits (Chapters 6 and 7).

Buy your products at the right price and sell them at the right price. This simple tenet can make or break your business. Check out Chapter 13 for tips on getting the best price and look to Chapter 8 for pricing your food and beverage menus right from the start.

Setting up shop (with a little help)

Depending on how new you are to the restaurant biz, you may need accountants, attorneys, contractors, and a host of other characters, all at the ready and working with you at various stages of the project.

Hire an accountant early in the process of setting up your business. She can help you get your numbers together for your business plan, which is a must-do if you're trying to get financing for your venture. (Chapters 4 and 5 can give you the details.) After you're up and running, you analyze your monthly financial reports and look for ways to improve the numbers. A good accountant, preferably one with restaurant experience, can help.

When starting any new business, you need to review contracts, file your permits, or maybe incorporate your business. Depending on how you set up your business, you may need to draft a partnership agreement or two. Before you sign franchise agreements or vendor contracts or fire your first employee, make sure that you're working with a good attorney, who can help you with all these tasks and more. Watch for details in Chapter 7.

Most people starting a new restaurant or taking over an existing one change a few things (or a few hundred things) at their new location. Maybe you need to set up a new kitchen from scratch or improve the airflow of the hood over the range. Maybe you want to upgrade the plumbing or install air filtration in your bar. Contractors can save you lots of time and trouble. Don't hesitate to ask them questions and check their references.

Check out Chapters 9 through 11 for the scoop on designing your exterior, dining room, kitchen, and bar — with or without the help of contractors, designers, and architects. Interior designers and architects come in very handy around renovation and revamp time. Sometimes they can give your place a face-lift for much less than you imagine.

Welcoming the world to your restaurant

All the hard work you do to get to the point where you can open the doors means absolutely nothing if no one shows up. Start thinking about how to draw customers way before you open your doors (and every day after that). Develop your marketing plan based on what's special about your restaurant. Maybe it's the food, ambience, price, or value. Study your competition, watch what they're doing well (and not so well), and understand where you have the advantage.

Different groups respond to different messages, so figure out what works for the diners you're going after. Check out Chapter 15 for details on telling the world about your place and getting them to beat a path to your door. After you get the customers in the seats, you have to keep them there. We've heard that you can't use restraining devices in most states and municipalities, so you do have to let diners go and hope they come back. We want you to do more than hope. Chapter 18 gives you concrete tips for building your clientele and ensuring that most of them come back — and bring their friends.

To be successful in this or in any business, you need to take care of your business today, tomorrow, and years from now. Stay up on trends in your sector and the restaurant business as a whole. Watch for information about shifting dining preferences and behavior in trade magazines, print publications, television news (and the not-so-news magazine shows), the Internet, or anywhere else you get information. And always keep an eye on your competition. Don't copy them, but know what they're up to. See Chapter 3 for information on how to conduct a market analysis, and check out Chapter 19 for ways to maintain what you create, using feedback from financial analysis and operational reports.

Finding Out Whether You Have What It Takes

Culinary prowess, a charming personality, and an ability to smile for the cameras — that's about all you need, right? Wrong. Take a step back. Running a restaurant successfully takes a lot more. Anyone can run a restaurant, but not everyone can run one well. (In fact, we should've titled this book, *Running a Restaurant Really Well For Dummies,* 2nd Edition, but the publisher wouldn't go for it.) In this section, we help you evaluate your motivations and expectations, and we identify the key traits of a successful restaurateur.

Monitoring your motivations

The restaurant business is a tough business, and if you want to succeed, you have to have the inner motivation — the drive — to sustain you through all the downs that accompany the ups. This isn't a venture for the faint of heart. If you want to own a restaurant to have a place to hang out with your friends and get free drinks, we say take the bar bill and avoid the hassles.

The first thing you need to do, before you invest any additional time or money in this venture (besides purchasing and reading this book, of course), is to examine and understand the factors that motivate you. Be honest with yourself.

There are lots of great reasons to want to run a restaurant. Here are a few of our favorites:

- ✔ You love an ever-changing work environment.
- ✔ You love taking on a challenge.
- ✔ You're passionate about the business.

✔ You have a passion for food.

✔ You hate having any free time (including the holidays).

✔ You're continuing the family tradition.

The following list contains a few reasons for running a restaurant that should send up a red flag in your mind:

✔ You think it'll be fun.

✔ You want to be a celebrity chef.

✔ You want a place to hang out.

✔ If Emeril can do it, so can you.

✔ You're tired of having a "real" job.

✔ You've always wanted to run a restaurant after you retire.

If one or more of these red-flag reasons sounds familiar, don't be completely discouraged. Just make sure that motivations such as these aren't your only, or even your primary, reasons for wanting to get into the business. Do some further investigation before making the financial, personal, and professional commitment to the business.

Evaluating your expectations

Running a restaurant, either yours or someone else's, is a huge commitment. It requires long hours, constant vigilance, and the ability to control potentially chaotic situations — on a daily basis.

Think about *Cocktail,* the great (or not-so-great, depending on your point of view) '80s movie in which a salty old bartender marries a rich lady and uses her money to open his own place. Just before he kills himself, he pours out his soul to his younger bartender friend, played by Tom Cruise, about what it's really like to own your own place. He confesses, "The only thing I know about saloons is how to pour whiskey and run my mouth off. I knew nothing about insurance, sales tax, or building code, or labor costs, or the power company, or purchasing, or linens. Everyone with a hand stuck it in my pocket."

Running a restaurant shouldn't be a leap of faith. You need to go into this venture with your eyes open. Just as you should carefully consider your motivations (see the preceding section), you also need to make sure that your expectations are firmly planted in reality.

Take out a pen and some paper and divide the paper into two columns. In the first column, list all your expectations for the future business. List everything from the profits you expect to the lifestyle you hope those profits will support to newspaper reviews or the customer views you hope to elicit. This is your chance to put your dreams on paper. In the second column, write down what you expect out of yourself to make this thing happen — your contribution in terms of time and money, sacrifices you'll have to make, and anything else that you can think of.

Then determine whether the expectations on your lists reflect the reality of the situation. Reading this book is a great place to start — our goal is to present a balanced look at the joys and pains of running a restaurant. (If you want an instant reality check, skip over to Chapter 20, where we confront ten common myths.) But don't stop there. As we state in Chapter 2, you have to start researching every aspect of the business on Day 1, and you don't get to stop until you close your doors for the very last time. So you may as well start now. Minimize the mystery by getting out in the restaurant world — talk to owners, managers, waiters, and suppliers about their experiences and what you can expect.

Tracking key traits of successful restaurateurs

Based on our experience in the restaurant business, successful restaurateurs exhibit a few common traits. We list them here. Don't worry if you possess more of some traits than others. Just being aware of them is a great step toward making them all part of your world and succeeding in the business.

Business sense

Business sense is probably the single most important trait for restaurateurs. For all that the restaurant business is, it's still basically a business, subject to the same pressures as any other. Keep that thought in mind going into your arrangement. Skills that you've learned, developed, and honed in the real world can apply in this business, like buying skillfully, managing tactfully, and negotiating shrewdly. But many different facets of this business are tough to pick up, so you need good business sense.

Tolerance

The ability to keep your cool under pressure, thrive in chaos, and handle multiple points of view and personalities serves you well in the business. Whether you're dealing with customers, employees, purveyors, changing trends, or a fickle clientele, you have to develop a thick skin. The inherent stress of the restaurant makes for short fuses. Your job is to dampen those tempers, smooth the rocky waters, and calm the storm.

Flexibility

The restaurant environment changes from minute to minute, so you have to be able to adjust and think on your feet. Seek a good balance of process- and product-motivated people. *Process-motivated* people micromanage what's going on in their organization. *Product-minded* people focus on the end result. Sometimes you'll wear both hats.

Creativity

Infuse creativity into every facet of your business, from how you approach your customers and your food to how you promote your business. That creativity affects how your business performs.

Positive energy

Whenever you're in the restaurant, you have to be "on" — all the time. Restaurants that have a positive vibe are the ones that survive. Positive energy is *key*, as intangible as it is, and your restaurant can't have positive energy if you don't.

Ability to hold (or hold off) liquor

Coveted by many, achieved by few, the ability to handle one's liquor has been the downfall (physically, financially, and spiritually) of many a restaurateur. Per capita, no industry drinks more than the restaurant business. For some people, managing a restaurant is like getting the keys to the grown-up candy store, and the temptation is too much to resist. As a restaurateur, you often drink as part of your job. No matter what the circumstances, you still have to count the money at the end of the night, and you have to be ready to go first thing in the morning.

Leadership skills

> **Restaurateur** /res-tuh-ruh-TUR/: n. doctor, babysitter, marriage counselor, bail bondsman, parent, mediator, conscience, seer, sage. *See Patton, George; Ghandi; et al.*

Being a leader in this industry means being able to balance an entire range of different management approaches, knowing when to lead by example, and knowing when to give the troops their marching orders. Most importantly, a successful restaurant leader is able to find her own leadership style and deal with employees fairly, consistently, and respectfully.

Schmoozability

Pucker up. People like to feel important. They want to be part of the inner circle of the restaurant, no matter how large that circle may be. It's cool to say, "I know the manager" or "The chef's a friend of mine." Nothing gets return business like calling a diner by name. That's why you put up with the pictures of grandkids, complaints about big projects at work, and not-so-interesting travel tales. Always make the customer feel welcome, at home, and at ease. Turning a good mood into a bad one is incredibly easy. Turning a bad mood into a good mood is exponentially more difficult.

Passion

We call it The Sickness. To succeed, you have to have passion. Running a restaurant is a business that eventually chooses you; you ultimately can't choose it. If you don't have passion for the business, you can't sustain, maintain, and overcome the obstacles that crop up.

You have to connect *everything* to your passion. You have to get the wait staff wired with it, because they're selling your vision to the customers. You have to get the prep guys pumped, because they're cranking on a tough schedule, without the natural excitement of a restaurant full of people. You have to get the dishwashers psyched about cleaning the dishes, because the dishes frame the experience for the customer. Diners should experience a buildup of expectations for their experience from the first time they come into contact with anyone from the restaurant (whether on the phone, in person, or online). Imagine doing all that without a passion for your restaurant, and you see why passion is mandatory.

Presence

Being in the restaurant day in and day out has no substitute. Absentee landlords need not apply. Just stopping in to say hello or giving off an aura that you know what's up ultimately won't allow you to run the restaurant. If you're not there, those who are there in your stead will be the de facto rulers. If you're not physically present in the building most of the time, the schmoozing, the energy, the passion, and so on can't get to your staff and ultimately to your diners. You can't positively impact your restaurant if you're not there.

Chapter 2

Deciding What Kind of Restaurant to Run

In This Chapter

▶ Finding the right starting point

▶ Picking the right restaurant for you

▶ Selecting your concept and restaurant name

*I*f you're like most folks who are thinking about getting into the restaurant business, you have an idea of what kind of restaurant you want to run and are looking for a way to get started. But before you run out and print your menus, think about your options. Better yet, take the time to research your options to set up the best plan for you and your restaurant.

Think about your reasons for wanting to get into this business. Money? Prestige? Are you buying a franchise as an investment or creating your dream restaurant just as you visualized it? The more you can understand your motivations for getting into the business, the more you can define the type of restaurant you should open and what rewards, hazards, and trade-offs come with each individual choice.

In this chapter, we show you different ways you can get your business started, and we give you some pros and cons for each. We walk you through the different styles of services you can offer. We introduce a mock concept restaurant that we use as an example throughout the book, and we help you finalize the theme and concept for your new restaurant. Your concept ultimately shapes all your research, planning, and design, so spend some time developing it.

Figuring Out Where to Start

For most restaurants, you have several possible starting points, including going with a franchise, taking over an existing restaurant, or starting from scratch. We give you the pros and cons of each in the following sections.

Buying into a franchise

In the restaurant business, buying a franchise is buying a license to sell a restaurant's food and use its brand, logos, and name. Wendy's, McDonald's, Burger King, and KFC are examples of restaurants often sold as franchises. The company who sells its franchises is called a *franchisor*.

Not all chains are franchises, but all franchises are chains. A *chain* of restaurants simply means that there's more than one just like it. Many chains, such as In-n-Out Burger, Starbucks, and Hard Rock Cafe, are owned by a parent company, not by independent *franchisees,* people or companies who buy into a franchise.

Buying into the franchise is a relatively safe investment in the risky restaurant business, but it's not without some limitations. Here are the pros of buying into a franchise:

- ✔ Franchises typically have a proven track record and have worked out the bugs.

- ✔ Franchises have a consistent product, have a set menu, and usually have product developers on staff to handle menu updates.

- ✔ Franchises have built-in brand recognition and established customer loyalty.

- ✔ Franchises help you with marketing, realistic sales projections, market research, and market analysis.

- ✔ You get a jump-start on all human resources (HR) and administrative issues because franchises come equipped with all their own forms, policies, and scheduling philosophies.

As good as all that sounds, most of the cons of buying into a franchise are closely associated with the pros:

✔ You have to pay franchisors potentially hefty initial franchise fees and significant royalty fees monthly, usually a percentage of sales.

✔ You have to follow their rules, meet their numbers, and serve their menu. If you're the creative type, the franchise mold may be the wrong size or shape for you. Love it or hate it, when people see the golden arches, they know what to expect, and they don't want you messing with it.

✔ Because franchises are fairly lucrative, franchisors are very selective about whom they franchise to. Often you have to have a significant amount of money to invest and agree to open multiple units.

Obviously, this info is only a snapshot look at the world of franchising. If you decide that a franchise is the path you'd like to take, we suggest you check out *Franchising For Dummies,* 2nd Edition, by Dave Thomas and Michael Seid (John Wiley & Sons, Inc).

Taking over an existing restaurant

You may have an opportunity to take over an existing operation, either one you've been a part of or one that you're completely new to. Maybe your boss wants out and you're going to buy into it. Maybe you're walking by and see a for-sale sign in the window of your favorite diner.

The primary positive and negative aspects of taking over an existing restaurant are relatively straightforward, but it all boils down to discerning the owner's motivation for selling. If the restaurant is relatively successful and the owner is retiring or moving or has health concerns, taking over may be a head start. It presents you with an instant client base that you can build upon. Often, though, restaurants are sold for reasons that paint a much bleaker picture of future success. The owner may be trying to pass along a loser or is facing a significant investment to remodel the restaurant to bring it up to code or compliance with local regulations.

Your job is to figure out which of these scenarios is more likely. Before signing on the dotted line, work your way through the following list:

✔ **Open up the books and get the full financial picture.** Chapters 4 and 19 cover which numbers to look at and what information to gather.

✔ **Find out the history of the space and the current concept.** Just knowing it was a restaurant isn't enough. If it was a shop before that, why did it stop operating? How does the neighborhood work? If the first floor fills up with water every three weeks, you want to know that before you sign the lease. Check out Chapter 6 for details on choosing the best location.

A common reason people sell a successful business is that the landlord intends to raise the rent. If you're buying the business, you may also be assuming the lease or be required to agree to this increase. Talk with the landlord and the business owner about future plans for the space.

✔ **Decide whether you're going to take over the business or just the location and equipment.** If you're buying the business, you probably want to keep the name the same. If you do change the name, you'll probably be hurting yourself, at least in the short term.

If you determine that the current business is working well, you may want to keep quiet about the fact that new ownership is in place. Your regulars will know, but for customers who come in only occasionally, why bother notifying them about the change? The idea of new ownership or management can affect people's perception of the place as they fall into the "back in the good old days" mentality. Suddenly, their old favorites don't taste the same, or the wait times are too long.

✔ **Work with a reputable contractor and inspector to thoroughly go through the restaurant from top to bottom before you finalize your deal.** You may incur lots of unforeseen costs when you take over an established restaurant, including repairs to older equipment and facilities. Check out Chapter 9 for tips on working with a contractor.

Partnering up with your current employer

If you're considering partnering up with your current boss, our advice is to look this gift horse in the mouth. When you buy into a restaurant, you buy into its profits and losses, its assets and liabilities.

If the restaurant is a profitable business that's well run, consider why someone is giving you a piece of it. Why is someone letting you buy into it? A number of legitimate and potentially profitable motivations exist:

✔ Reward for your hard work

✔ Part of an Employee Stock Ownership Plan (ESOP) that allows managers and employees to buy into the business over time through the fruits of their labor

✔ Selling off part of the business to generate capital required for expansion or remodeling

✔ An owner who wants to retire

However, other, less-positive motivations may be behind the offer:

✔ The operation is leaking money like a sieve. If someone wants you to put money in right away, be leery.

✔ The owner's attention is being diverted to another business, so by giving you a stake in this business, he's giving you an incentive not to rob him blind while he's distracted.

Anytime you consider entering into a partnership, you want to see the books before you hand over any money. Make sure that you get involved with a financially sound business that offers the potential for success.

When getting involved in any partnership, get definite answers about how much and what kind of say you're going to have in day-to-day operations and long-term planning. Clearly define on paper who gets what, including compensation, profit sharing, the best parking space, and Christmas Eve off. If something's important to you, write it down and make sure everyone signs it.

Starting from scratch

We can quickly sum up the pros and cons for this one: Starting from scratch is exciting and scary. This restaurant is your baby from the ground up. You may be taking over an existing space that's been abandoned for years, or you may decide to convert a shop or a house into a restaurant. (Take a look at Chapter 6 before you sign on the dotted line for any space.) Either way, you'll have limitations for what your space can do, but you can get very creative with the obstacles in terms of layout and flow. It's like putting together a puzzle — rebuilding the pieces to fit your concept.

Starting from scratch can involve a lot of work. Very few spaces are ready and waiting for you exactly as you want them. And implementing your idea isn't as easy as saying, "I want to make this bar 40 feet long and 4 feet high, mahogany with a marble top." You actually have to figure out how to build it and work out all the details. Work with a contractor to implement your vision. You'll face the fun of electricity, plumbing, heating, ventilation, air conditioning, placement of everything from ranges and coolers to the wait-staff stations . . . the list goes on. Check out Chapters 10 and 11 for info on laying out the front and back of the house. And get an inspector to come in and evaluate the space, just like when buying a home.

When you're starting from scratch, plan for the future. During the rebuilding after a fire, coauthor Mike left extra plumbing hookups under the floor in the middle of the lounge so he could add a sushi bar later if he wanted to. Always add more power outlets than you think you'll need, even in the office. Extra cable and wires for electricity are handy in case you have to move something around later.

Choosing the Right Type of Restaurant

Forty years ago, going out to dinner was an event. Now it's more routine, and the number and variety of restaurants that you can find illustrate the change in America's eating habits.

As a general rule, the atmosphere defines the type of restaurant more than the food does, but food and atmosphere usually go hand in hand. For example, out-of-this-world carnitas slathered in chili verde with fresh lime and cilantro could be served from a cart on the side of the road, at a casual Mexican eatery, or in a world-class fine dining establishment like Rick Bayless's Topolobampo in Chicago. Although some menu items may be similar, the atmosphere of each venue is very different.

In this section, we discuss fine dining, casual eateries, carry-out and delivery, fast food, bars, and catering services.

There's no magic formula or dollar amount that you need to start a restaurant. The cost varies based on the concept, size of your space, size of your menu, location of your space, number of employees you need to hire, cost of insurance in your area, and so on. Do your homework to figure out how much money you need to spend and why. Chapters 5 and 6 can help you with the details.

Just because you can open a restaurant doesn't mean you should. Many factors play into the decision of which type of restaurant to open, including competitive threats, the attractiveness of your concept to the local market, and the positioning of your concept. Understand these factors and remove any known barriers before you commit to a specific type of restaurant opportunity. We discuss these factors later in "Creating Your Concept."

Dining in style

Fine dining, dining with the highest quality food, service, and surroundings, usually includes the highest prices as well. If you choose to run a fine dining restaurant, your restaurant needs to cater to the guest's every need.

Soaking up the atmosphere

When your diners walk in your door, they should know they're in a fine dining establishment. If you choose to open a fine dining restaurant, include these atmospheric factors in your plans:

✔ **Ambience:** The tables should have starched linen tablecloths and top-notch dinnerware, glassware, and silverware. Choose lighting that's subtle, maybe even leaning toward the dark side. Select furniture and décor that reflect the mood you're trying to set. Decide whether you want to show the world a hip, trendy place or an austere, elegant old-world power room.

✔ **Service:** The servers should be almost clairvoyant without being smothering. Your guest's every need should be met before she even realizes she has a need. If a guest has to ask for a refill, a new napkin, or additional brioche to sop up the last of her lobster bisque, your servers aren't doing their job. You escort guests to the bathroom instead of directing them to it. Your servers place napkins in your diners' laps after they're seated. You must train your staff in every service detail imaginable, such as removing crumbs from the table properly and serving plates from the correct side of a diner.

✔ **Amenities:** You offer amenities such as valet parking service and a coat check. You must have a reservation system. Many fine dining establishments get creative while trying to outdo each other. For example, a restaurant may offer guests a choice of 10 or 15 high-quality pens to sign their bills with or specifically designed, ornate mini stools to rest their Hermés purses on. Are you ready for the challenge?

Focusing on food

If you're thinking about opening a fine dining place, spend some time thinking about what kind of food you want to serve. Go back to your positioning: How are your restaurant and your menu distinct? People have very high expectations about what they eat when they're in a fine dining restaurant. Here are a few things to keep in mind while you're mulling it over:

✔ **Food quality:** In your fine dining restaurant, the quality of food should be exceptional. It's characterized by top-notch ingredients, precise preparation styles, and intricate presentations, with a wine list to match.

✔ **Menu selection:** Your menu doesn't need to be extensive, but the items should be intricate. Sometimes, fine restaurants don't even offer a choice on their menus. Each guest is served the same food at a set price.

✔ **Wine and liquor:** Your liquor selection should be high-end with an extensive selection of aperitifs, cognacs, and brandies. The wine list is perfectly paired with the menu items and includes selections of superior quality. Some of these wines may be quite expensive, but a well-balanced list includes quality options in all price categories.

Kicking back casual

The term *casual dining* is a catchall for anything that isn't fast food or fine dining. You can get a broad range of food and service quality in casual dining, but the dress code is consistently casual in every casual restaurant. In general, *casual* refers to the ambience or atmosphere of the place and the style of the service rather than to the quality of the cuisine. You can have remarkable food in a very casual setting. Think about a bistro concept: You can get fresh, fabulous food while wearing your jeans and flip-flops.

Casual restaurants tend to be noisier than their fine dining counterparts with loud music, loud patrons, and maybe even loud service if servers, bartenders, and food runners are calling out orders back and forth. The food is generally reasonably priced, somewhere between $10 and $30 per entree. Guests tend to linger longer in casual restaurants than in fast food restaurants. They usually order from menus at the table rather than from a centralized menu at a cashier. Many chain restaurants run the gamut of casual restaurants, from family-friendly diners to lavish dinnerhouses with expansive menus. Examples include TGI Friday's, Olive Garden, Cheesecake Factory, P.F. Chang's, Outback Steakhouse, and Denny's.

In casual dining, sometimes the food matches the level of service, and sometimes it doesn't. The Oyster Bar in New York's Grand Central Station has an extensive seafood menu, with high-quality products and innovative dishes, but the service is friendly and efficient, not stuffy or smothering.

Many diners are opting for counter service these days, and casual dining is filling that need. If a diner is dining alone or in a hurry, the counter is a popular choice. Counter service is usually good for groups no larger than three or so. Typically diners can get the full menu at the counter, usually in a hurry. If you choose to set up counter service, make sure you set up an ordering system that prioritizes counter orders for this very reason.

Placing an order — to go!

You can view your takeout and delivery options as falling under one of two general categories:

✔ **Takeout/delivery-only operation:** This setup is most applicable if you're considering opening a pizza joint, Chinese (or other ethnic) restaurant, or sandwich shop. You may have one or two tables with chairs or just a couple of chairs where customers can wait for their orders.

✔ **Takeout or delivery as part of your larger operation:** Many restaurants successfully incorporate takeout and/or delivery options to varying degrees. Your options are numerous — you can offer a dedicated carry-out counter (with a separate entrance even), allow people to order take-out from the bartender, or simply permit eat-in guests to order food to go.

The menu for this option may be the same as your regular menu, or you may offer a modified menu. But takeout hours are often modified if it's part of a larger operation, usually with shorter hours for takeout and delivery. Takeout and delivery may stop one hour before close, and other takeout-only operations may be open 24 hours.

If you're not sure that your restaurant has a delivery market, consider looking into some kind of co-op delivery program. In some areas, a company contracts with restaurants to do delivery for them. Customers call the company and place orders with one of several different restaurants.

As with any restaurant, takeout and delivery business has high times and low times, and they usually coincide with mealtimes. Staff your delivery, kitchen, and ordering staff appropriately. See Chapter 16 for tips on scheduling.

Ordering

Make sure your customers can order in person at the restaurant or by phone, fax, or e-mail. Ordering online is also more and more common. Some diners order their meals, eat them in the restaurant, and then order more food to go (for a snack or for someone who couldn't join them for restaurant dining).

New third-party online ordering and delivery services are cropping up in markets across the country. Make sure the economics work for you. Some services charge as much as 15 percent and hold your money for 30 days, and others charge a flat per-order fee and pay you in a more timely manner. Consider the costs versus benefits to set up an account with a service in your area, and remember that part of service is marketing; it's not just about direct sales. If your competitors are on the site, should you be too? Also, if the service has a customer base that you might not otherwise reach, it may definitely be worth the fee. Don't forget, you can try a service and always cancel if it doesn't work for you and your business.

If you have some items on your menu that aren't available for takeout, make sure that they're clearly marked and that your order-taker knows which menu items aren't available for takeout. That employee also needs to be able to answer questions about menu options and ingredients.

If your takeout or delivery order system is integrated with your point-of-sale (POS) system, clearly designate the order as takeout in the system. Otherwise, takeout orders may get *plated* (placed on plates for service) as dining room orders instead of being packaged in to-go containers. You can distinguish between the two types of orders by creating different POS items (french fries versus TG-french fries), using modifiers (french fries with cheese versus french fries with cheese to go) or by simply noting where the order came from (for example, dining room Table 33 versus the to-go window).

Delivery

You want to deliver a quality product to your diner's door. Establish your delivery radius by determining how long your food holds in the containers you use and how long it takes to get to your customers. And consider that your delivery person needs to get back to your shop to deliver the other orders. Make your delivery area as large as you can reasonably serve. Do it well or don't bother doing it.

If you offer delivery, you need transportation, probably either a bike or a car. You'll likely need some kind of ID (for secure buildings or gated communities) and/or uniform that indicates that the delivery person works for you. A recognizable uniform also help keeps you in the loop on what he's doing outside the restaurant. If he's rude to people, litters, or rides on the sidewalk, you'll hear about it.

Overestimate the amount of time you need to get orders to your customer by at least 10 minutes. Things get dropped and lost, and you need some stub-your-toe room. Customers almost always react better when you call them to let them know a problem has occurred and give an estimate on how long fixing it will take instead of just showing up late.

Selecting self-service or fast-food

Many fast-food, self-service, or quick-service restaurants (QSR) are franchises, but you don't have to take that route for fast-food success. Pizza, Chinese food, coffeehouses, and ice cream shops are all great choices for fast-food non-chain restaurants. Even an independent sandwich or burger joint can be successful.

For quick-service restaurants, you really need to hone the points of difference between you and your competition (see Chapter 3 for details). Generally, you need to focus on the difference in your quality because you likely can't compete, at least initially, with the big boys in terms of price.

Fast casual is a relatively new trend in restaurant concept design. Fast casual takes the concept of a quick-service deli and blows it out into a range of cuisines, combining counter service, comfortable but basic furnishings, takeout, and occasionally delivery. The menu is usually small and focused on executing against a specific niche and doing it better, fresher, and with more style than the competition. If you aren't readily familiar with this emerging style of restaurants, look for names like Chipotle, Five Guys Burgers and Fries, and Panera Bread. They're part of a whole new genre of restaurants that are delivering a level of freshness with less overhead.

Running a bar — with or without food

If you're opening a bar, you probably need at least limited food service. Check out the laws in your area because your liquor license may require you to serve food during some of your business hours. Most bars offer some kind of food service even if the menu is very small and it's not available at all hours (the kitchen may close at 9 p.m., while the bar is open till 2 a.m.). The food may be something as simple as potato chips, popcorn, nuts, and pretzels. At a few places, when the kitchen closes, you can bring in food from other restaurants.

Lots of people eat at the bar not out of necessity but out of preference. More and more operations are incorporating food service in their bars as part of their regular business. With no-smoking laws in place in many bars and restaurants, the trend toward eating in the newly smoke-free bars will continue. If you're not serving food in your bar, take advantage of this trend by experimenting with a limited menu. See Chapter 11 for details on setting up and running a bar.

Providing catering and banquet services

In general, both catering and banquets serve large parties, anywhere from 15 to 50,000 people at a single time. *Banquets* usually take place at a designated banquet hall or facility, and *catering* takes place at a customer's location. More and more restaurants are getting into the catering business, and you may want to consider it as a component to your operations (or consider basing your operations only on catering).

Catering lends itself to highly controllable costs and consequently high profitability. In catering, you generally have the luxury of knowing, in advance, how many guests will attend, exactly what they'll eat and drink while they're there, and how many employees you need to staff the event. Therefore, in theory, you should know all the costs in advance: what it costs you to produce 150 servings of lasagne in terms of food, labor hours to produce that lasagne, and labor hours to serve that lasagne and clean up.

In catering, all direct expenses associated with the production of an event are transferable to the client. In other words, everything you spend for food, beverage, labor, disposables, transportation, rentals, flowers, and décor are billable to the client. You only need to factor in your administrative time, overhead, and profit margin to arrive at a price. Simple, right? Wrong.

The art of profitable catering lies in understanding how to work the numbers — that is, understanding how to prepare just the right amount of food, no more, no less.

Here's an example of how catering numbers work. If you have a party of 500 people outside in a tent, your prep list may look like Figure 2-1. Looking at Figure 2-1, you may say, "Hey! That doesn't add up! You have 408 pieces of cake (34 chocolate tortes × 12 pieces per torte) for 500 people." See, we know that in one hour, the average guest consumes four passed hors d'oeuvres. We know that on a buffet, only 80 percent of guests have salad, and those who do have an average of 1 to 1.25 ounces of greens. If you have two types of salad dressing and specify 60 percent of the guest count for each, you'll be fine. (Here's the math: 80 percent of 500 guests = 400 guests having salad. Then take 60 percent of 400 to decide how many 1-ounce servings of each dressing you need, and you get you 240 ounces = 3.75 gallons of each.) We know that a hotel pan of food feeds 25 average people (fewer if they're NFL linemen or more if they're ballerinas). And we know to always have vegetarian meals available for 5 percent of guests (in this case, 5 percent of 500 is 25), whether the customer orders them or not. These tricks of the trade can make the difference between having too much food and wasting profits and having just enough to cover the count and maximize your profitability.

Figuring out what to charge and where the opportunities are for increased sales is the trick. Do you sell food and beverage only, or do you become an event planner and coordinate the flowers, décor, china and linen rental, and the like? You need more info and experience to plan events effectively, but the profits are huge because you're simply the middleman for some of the services, coordinating them for a more-than-fair markup.

You can make big money feeding the masses. Many restaurants, such as Wolfgang Puck's Spago, have spawned hugely successful catering operations that have become as big as, if not bigger than, the restaurant. You get rid of the speculation of the restaurant, trying to decide how much food to prep, how many servers to schedule, and so on. Catering enables you to know there are going to be butts in the seats and about how many people will be present.

Your catering menu will be smaller than your regular dining room menu. Select items from your main menu that are easily produced in volume, don't require a lot of steps, and hold well. Your choices should embody your concept. People choose you to cater based in large part on your signature dishes. In most cases, you'll be fulfilling catering/banquet orders out of the same kitchen, so the items should fit the workflow you've established.

Catering Event Order Sheet

Client: National Association of Sleep-Deprived Restaurateurs
Attendees: 500   **Date:** December 15
Location: Tent (Grant Park)   **Time:** 6 p.m.

DINNER MENU	PREP QUANTITY
6:00 – Passed Hors d'Oeuvres (30 minutes)	
Bruschetta alla Caprese	300 each
Seared Tuna on Wonton Crisp	300 each
Maryland Crab Cakes with Spicy Aioli	300 each
6:30 – Client's Award Presentation (15 minutes)	
6:45 – Buffet Dinner	
Tossed Mixed Green Salad	30 lbs.
Balsamic Vinaigrette	3.75 gal.
Buttermilk Ranch Dressing	3.75 gal.
Seared Sterling Salmon with Herbed Potato Crust	60 lbs.
Carved Beef Tenderloin with Horseradish Cream	40 each
French Green Beans with Tarragon-Shallot Butter	16 pans
Roasted Garlic Potato Galette	20 pans
Flourless Chocolate Torte (12 pieces per cake)	34 each
(vegetarian dinners not on menu)	25 each
Beverages	
Merlot	15 cases
Sauvignon Blanc	8 cases
Bottled Water	15 cases

Figure 2-1:
Sample of
an order
sheet for
a catered
event.

The scope of your catering operation varies with your own desire. One caterer we know started out as a single banquet hall in Indianapolis. It grew steadily from those modest beginnings into a $50,000,000-plus catering enterprise. Start small and work your way up. Maybe you do small in-home parties for key guests at the restaurant. Maybe you provide off-site lunches to doctors' offices in the city. Whatever you choose, remember that transporting food must be done professionally, cleanly, and with food safety as a priority. We discuss food safety in Chapter 17.

Creating Your Concept

Your *concept* is the combination of your type of restaurant, your menu and prices, the ambience your offer (or how you present your menu), and the style of service you provide. One of the most common mistakes prospective restaurateurs make when starting a restaurant is to passionately focus more on *what* concept they want to open rather than *why* their concept will be successful. You need to take into account who your customers are, what they need and want, and why you're the one to give it to them.

Successful restaurants are well positioned in their market, make an emotional connection with their customers, have a clearly defined and unique selling proposition, and deliver on their promises to their customers over and over again. We discuss all these elements in this section.

Positioning your restaurant for success

Positioning your restaurant centers around developing, communicating, and leveraging the feature or benefit that is unique to your concept. We've heard it time and time again: young wannabe restaurateurs waxing on with wistful eyes about their quaint, 40-seat dream that will serve only a single prix-fixe menu of avant-garde dishes, employ only the finest culinary talent, offer only Riedel stemware and Limoges china, and clad their wait staff in Armani. These restaurateurs are convinced that because they're enamored by a particular style of cuisine, an immediate throng of savvy, likeminded guests will be beating down their door on opening night to sample their *Barolo-braised musk ox shortribs with Alba truffle polenta and roasted rutabaga foam.* They've made up their minds on what they want to do rather than why they should do it. They've failed to devote sufficient time to the most critical factor that determines their success or failure: how their restaurant is positioned in the marketplace.

To develop your concept's positioning, shift the focus from what you want to do to what there's a *need* for. Marketers are notorious for overusing fancy-sounding buzzwords like *consumer need states* and *appeal to the segmentation targets* when discussing how restaurant concepts or menu items will match the needs and desires of the marketplace. It all boils down to this: Does anyone want to buy what you're selling? If you were to open a clothing boutique that only offered tank tops, flip flops, and short skirts in International Falls, Minnesota, how well would your line of offerings meet the needs of your potential customers? If you've ever been to the coldest city in the lower 48 states, you'd quickly answer, "not very." You'd likely be much better off selling parkas, insulated boots, and snow pants. The same thinking applies to the restaurant sector.

Factors such as population, average median income, weather, commuter patterns, competing restaurants, local culinary traditions, and culture all play a role in deciding what type of restaurant will succeed and what type will fail. You must take into account these marketplace pressures when you're creating your concept. A feature is only a benefit if it's relevant and differentiating and meets an unmet need or desire of enough people in your marketplace. For example, opening a $300-per-person steakhouse in a flood plain in an impoverished Hindu community is probably not relevant to the indigenous population or intrinsically a sound business proposition.

Identifying the emotional connection

The best restaurants are more than just places to eat and drink; instead, they connect with their markets on an emotional level. In one case, an extremely large chain of sandwich shops has blurred the lines between being a restaurant and being a healthful and convenient provider of products that meet certain caloric goals — and their long-time spokesperson is walking, talking proof. In another case, the recent emergence of extremely high-end restaurants that combine cutting edge science with incredible culinary talent provides diners an opportunity to go on an adventure, pushing the boundaries of their senses. And a very popular West Coast burger chain has created an almost cult-like following with their "secret menu" that only regulars are aware of and thus able to benefit from.

Creating a unique selling proposition

Positioning is about understanding and then embodying the elements that make your restaurant different from the competition. But being different leads to success only if your differences are relevant to a sufficient number of potential guests in your market. How you begin to market and leverage those differences begins by understanding your USP. A *unique selling proposition* (USP) is a defined point of difference from your competitors. Discovering and defining your restaurant's USP within the marketplace is the first step toward ensuring your long-term success.

When we developed Urban Forge Pizza Bar, our imaginary pizza bar concept, we crafted a USP around a consumer desire for a new level of taste, service, and sociality within with pizza segment while still leveraging the near-universal appeal of pizza. We crafted an emotional connection with the pizza connoisseur looking for an authentic artisan pie that the competition just can't match with their mass-produced crusts, delivery warming bags, and cardboard boxes. We paired that with the social enjoyment of a warm and inviting pub atmosphere and with great drinks that pair with the menu, and we tied it all back to the authentic origins of Neapolitan-style pizza.

Using consumer insights to develop and test your concept

Big restaurant chains employ entire departments and spend millions of dollars researching the positioning of their concepts and menu items. They use *consumer insights,* or the opinions, feelings, and desires of their key clients, to guide their decisions.

How do they get these insights? Often they hire expansive (and expensive) firms that specialize in understanding and predicting consumer behavior. They conduct focus groups and test products, advertising, and ideas well before they hit the marketplace. These chains develop methods to have an ongoing conversation with their guests. In essence, the guest is shaping the decisions of the restaurant, not the other way around.

Most independent restaurateurs lack the financial means to emulate the big chains' rigorous consumer testing practices, but you can still get an idea of what your market needs and wants. How do you do that? You begin (and then continue) the conversation. Here are several ways to involve the consumer in your concept design:

✔ **Hold a meeting where you invite members of the chamber of commerce to review your business plan or restaurant concept and provide feedback.**

✔ **Select a representative sample of the local business community to try selected items from your menu and provide feedback.** (For details on conducting a focus group, check out Chapter 3.)

✔ **Conduct focus groups in which you ask respondents what types of restaurants they wish were in their marketplace and why.**

This focus group is a very simple version of what marketers call a *gap analysis,* a tool designed to discover — you guessed it — *gaps* between what consumers have and what they want or need.

✔ **When your restaurant is open, select a group of guests to act as an internal steering committee or test market.** Don't just select the people who will tell you what you want to hear; get a cross-section of savvy, articulate folks who will challenge you and provide honest feedback. Make sure to reward these guests, but change up the membership often enough so they don't soften their answers in search of their next free meal.

✔ **Leverage social media to open up the channel for a two-way conversation with your guests.** Create a fan site where guests can get early previews of upcoming promotions, provide feedback on potential concepts, and give insights into what they want from your restaurant.

We can't overstate the importance of understanding the overall positioning of your restaurant. Your unique points of difference, if relevant to your market, dictate whether your concept is packed with diners or "a nice, uncrowded place where we never have to wait for a table" — not a good thing. Every decision you make about your restaurant should flow out of the positioning. Your menu, décor, location, style of service, and marketing tactics are all based on reinforcing how your restaurant is distinct from the competition.

Developing your positioning statement

After you've crafted your concept on paper and have confirmed that there's a need in the marketplace for your restaurant, draft a positioning statement. A *positioning statement* clearly states what your restaurant is, why it exists, and who you want to serve with your restaurant. A well-crafted positioning statement becomes the litmus test of every decision you make regarding your restaurant.

To be useful, a positioning statement must be honest and must clearly state what makes your restaurant different from the competition. Here are the four key components of a positioning statement:

- ✔ **Your target audience:** Identify the specific group of diners that you want your restaurant to appeal to.

- ✔ **Your frame of reference:** Include the specific dining category in which your restaurant competes.

- ✔ **Your unique selling proposition:** Note the single most important benefit that your restaurant offers your target audience relative to the competition.

- ✔ **Your customers' reason to believe in you:** Write down the most convincing proof that your restaurant delivers what it promises.

After identifying each of these components, create your positioning statement by using this template:

> For (target audience), (your restaurant's name) is the (frame of reference) that delivers (unique selling proposition) because only (your restaurant's name) is (reason to believe).

You'll likely need a few extra words to smooth it all out, but you should have the nuts and bolts of your positioning statement together here. Your positioning should be easy to articulate.

Here's our positioning statement for Urban Forge Pizza Bar, our mock restaurant concept:

> For food-savvy gastronomic social explorers tired of warmed-over pizza in a box, Urban Forge Pizza Bar is the pizza and pasta bar that transcends the expected through elevated, inspired wood-fired pizzas and pastas with a Neapolitan heritage, paired with a specially selected menu of alcoholic and nonalcoholic beverage creations served in a hip social setting; Urban Forge encourages the mutual enjoyment of cuisine, conversation, and personal connections.

The positioning statement is a guidepost that you can use to shape decisions. For example, if one of the partners in Urban Forge Pizza Bar wants to menu hamburgers and french fries because other restaurants in our area seem to sell a lot of them, everyone could refer to the positioning statement and judge whether the decision to serve burgers and fries meets our core identity. The positioning statement would say, "That's a really dumb idea. Did you hit your head on the pizza oven when you came into work today?"

Putting It All Together

Make sure that your theme is consistent with your décor, cuisine, and style of service. For example, in the case of Urban Forge Pizza Bar, we focus the guests' attention on the beautiful artisan wood-fired pizza oven and the *pizzaioli* (pizza makers) making each guest's pizza by hand. This process helps to reinforce our positioning while exceeding our guests' preconceived notions of what a pizza restaurant can offer in terms of cuisine, style, and service.

Thinking about theme and concept

Just like in a movie or book, a *theme* is a common thread, idea, or image that runs throughout your restaurant. You can base a theme on many different things. Your *concept* is the whole package, including your food, menu, price points, design, décor, ambience, and how that package marries the theme. Here's the short list of what you can base your theme or concept on, but your only real limit is your imagination:

- **A style of cuisine:** For example, you may decide to base your concept on Brazilian *churrasco,* a cuisine that delivers various kinds of roasted meats sliced from the spit tableside. You're not offering the entire scope of Brazilian food; you're focusing on a single cuisine.

- **An individual dish:** A pizza place isn't necessarily Italian; it may have Sicilian, Hawaiian, and Californian cuisine all on the same menu, but it focuses on pizza. Some places specialize in desserts.

- **Ethnic influence:** Mexican, Italian, Thai, and so on are all well-known examples of ethnic foods.

- **Décor and ambience:** Maybe you want your guests to be surrounded by New Age music, soothing scents, sage green walls, and relaxing lighting. You then serve food that fits that environment.

- **A character from a book, movie, and the like:** Maybe you want to open the Sherlock Holmes Bookstore and Café.

- **Sporting events or hobbies:** Sports bars and Internet cafes are typical examples.

- ✔ **Games:** Some restaurants offer pizza for the parents and provide the kids with flashing lights, animatronic animals, and tokens for games. Others skip the kids' stuff and focus on video games, pool, and darts for adults.

- ✔ **Geography:** Maybe you're located in a train station. Continue the theme into your restaurant via your décor, menu titling, and uniforms. Or maybe you focus on cuisine related to your area of the country, like Cajun food in southern Louisiana or seafood on the coast of Maine.

If a restaurant's theme is very kitschy, it tends not to have fantastic food. Generally speaking, animatronic forest creatures or owls in orange shorts do not equal gastronomic ecstasy. This atmosphere is usually a result of focusing more time on the theme, décor, and look of the restaurant rather than the food. In these cases, a big part of their draw and of the product they're selling is the atmosphere. But for most diners, the food is always the most important thing. If the food is lackluster, they won't be back, so spend some time on your menu no matter how kitschy you decide to go.

Make sure that your theme and menu match. If you open Mike's Indian Bazaar, it's up to you whether it's a bazaar or just bizarre. Just be sure to do your research (and don't serve beef on the menu; the cow is a sacred animal and is rarely eaten in India). If you open an Indian-themed restaurant, you're trying to create an atmosphere that lets diners imagine they're in India. The smells, sounds, sights, and tastes you create can do just that.

Choosing a name

Your restaurant's name should be catchy, easy to remember, unique, and somewhat descriptive. Picking your name is fun, but don't get so caught up in it that you forget to take care of the necessary legalities (like making sure someone's not already using your favorite pick). Check out Chapter 7 for details on searching for trademarks. You may have picked out a name already, but consider these ideas before you inlay it in 24-karat gold on your signage:

- ✔ **Name of someone significant to you:** Consider your name, a relative's name, or the name of someone who inspired you. You may choose a figure in history who's been dead long enough not to have trademarked his or her own name. Examples are Rocco's, Crazy Horse Saloon, and Mama Carolla's Old Italian Restaurant.

- ✔ **Geography:** You can borrow your restaurant name from a natural formation, such as a river, lake, hill, crater, or mountain range. Or use your town's name, a street, a neighborhood, a bridge, a park, a sanctuary, or an area of town as inspiration. Blake Street Tavern, James River Grill, Breckenridge Brewery, and Everest are a few geography-based names.

✔ **Historic or traditional names and spaces:** Urban sprawl has incorporated many once-independent neighborhoods into larger cities and towns. Maybe you want to incorporate that tradition into your concept. In some areas, restaurants have taken over locations that used to be occupied by other businesses, such as banks. Those old names may be perfect for your new restaurant, especially if elements of the old business are part of your décor. At The Broker in Denver, you walk through a vault door to get to some tables. The Chicago Firehouse is located in a turn-of-the-century, fully restored firehouse.

✔ **Ethnic and cultural names:** Maybe you want your name to describe the influences of your concept. Comanche Curry Café, a Native American–Indian fusion restaurant, is an example.

✔ **Pop culture:** Hard Rock Cafe, Moe's Southwest Grill, Cheeseburger in Paradise, Bubba Gump Shrimp Co., and the like make their bread and butter by tapping into people's love of pop culture.

✔ **Weather:** Extreme weather (even weather that implies risk or danger) can influence your name. Think about the Fog City Diner in San Francisco, Typhoon! in Seattle, and the Hurricane Restaurant in St. Petersburg, Florida.

✔ **Your concept and theme:** You may include the term "Sports Bar and Grill" in your name. Or choose to call your restaurant Polynesia because you have poi on your menu and serve drinks out of coconuts. Tommy Gun's Garage is a 1920s speakeasy in Chicago.

✔ **Your preparation methods:** You may want a name that reveals how your food is cooked. Wok 'N' Roll is a Chinese concept, and Smashburger serves, yes, you guessed it — hand-pattied and pressed burgers. Il Fornaio means *oven* and serves lots of oven-baked Italian favorites.

✔ **Other business in the area:** Consider a name borrowed from a nearby business. Examples include The Bottom Line Bistro in a financial district, The Carnegie Deli near Carnegie Hall, The Green Room near the theater district, and The Bull and The Bear near Wall Street.

✔ **Humor and irony:** You may want to try a funny or ironic name, but be careful that the humor doesn't offend anyone. The Heart Attack Grill in Arizona serves an unabashedly high calorie menu, while Hot Doug's serves some of the best sausage and dogs in Chicago. Maybe a bar called The Hardware Store would do well in suburban neighborhoods. The Library may work as the name for a bar on campus.

Certain names alienate people. Avoid truly offensive terms at all cost. In your quest to appeal to your target market, you may ruffle some feathers — the extent to which you do so is a marketing decision you have to make.

We created our concept's name, *Urban Forge Pizza Bar*, using a mixture of many of these ideas.

- ✔ We chose the word *Urban* to help identify our clientele, reinforcing the idea they are a savvy, cosmopolitan group who appreciates a better pizza experience, values the more gastronomic elements of the menu, and has the disposable income to support more than a 10-dollar delivery pizza experience.
- ✔ *Forge* gives a nod to our predominant preparation method and menu item, wood-fired pizza.
- ✔ The addition of *Pizza Bar* reinforces the notion that we deliver a social experience and atmosphere.

We are not focused on food as fuel; instead, we've developed an ambiance and experience to contribute to our guests' appreciation of our inherently share-able food and beverage pairings, with an emphasis on social experience.

Creating a logo

A *logo* is the visual interpretation of your brand identity. A logo may be a simple graphic image (the Red Cross), stylized text (such as Coca-Cola or the New York Yankees), or even a combination of the two (think IBM).

Use your logo consistently, frequently, and often. Keep it at the forefront of your guests' minds, and they'll begin to automatically associate it with your restaurant. From signage to menus to business cards and advertising, continually and consistently reinforcing your logo is essential in promoting awareness of your brand.

Your logo should be memorable and meaningful. Differentiate your logo from those of your competition. If everyone in your segment, say pizza, is using a representation of pizza in their logo, create a logo that emphasizes your specific point of difference from the competition (remember that USP!). For Urban Forge Pizza Bar, we chose to focus on an image of a flame to reinforce our wood-fired, Neapolitan heritage.

Keep these key points in mind when working with a graphic designer to develop your logo:

- ✔ **Great logos are timeless.** Don't date your logo by including elements that may be obsolete in a few years as your restaurant evolves. One example of this is the use of real names. You and your founding partner may be best buddies now, but who's to say what the future holds? Having to change your logo due to a split in ownership can be costly, contentious, and detrimental to your brand's recognition.

- ✔ **Make the logo clear.** Make sure that your logo has enough differentiation in color that while it pops off the page in full color, it also looks great in black and white and in grayscale and is discernable by people who are colorblind.

- ✔ **Keep it simple.** The best, most iconic logos are uniformly simple, not busy or cluttered. Think about McDonald's, NIKE, Starbucks, and Apple. Their logos are each extremely simple, yet each one is instantly associated with the brand it represents.

- ✔ **Size matters.** Your logo must look as good and be as clear on a business card or web page graphic as it is on a restaurant sign or billboard. Use fonts that are easily legible at a variety of type sizes. You may love bold, daring fonts, but many are not generally favored for logos because they're difficult to read at smaller type sizes.

Don't design your logo by committee. Generally speaking, committees make lousy art. The smaller the group that's charged with finalizing a logo decision, the better the logo will be. And unless one of your partners is a trained graphic artist with a marketing degree, resist the urge to DIY. Remember, graphic design professionals have dedicated their entire careers to breaking through the clutter with succinct, memorable business identity graphics. Let them do their jobs so you can focus on what you do best.

Signing off on signage

Designing and placing signs for your restaurant follows many of the same rules as your logo (see the preceding section). In fact, your sign is one of the first places to deploy your logo. Professional sign companies are experts in creating and placing signs that are both memorable and meaningful, and for that we encourage you to resist the urge to go it alone when designing or placing your sign.

A sign must be simple and clear enough to instantly convey both the type of restaurant and your unique selling proposition (USP — see the earlier section "Creating a unique selling proposition"). Potential guests driving or walking by must be drawn to your sign, and they must be able to process what you're trying to tell them in only a few seconds. Your sign needs to be both compelling and visible to get your message out to the maximum number of potential patrons at any given point of the day. This is particularly important if your restaurant is located on a heavily traveled commuter route. For example, having your sign face the inbound traffic for the morning commute may be a great strategy if you're a breakfast house. But if you're a dinner house, your message will suffer. Place yourself in the potential guests' shoes. Think about how and where they need to see your sign, and your sign will work much harder for you.

Chapter 3

Researching the Marketplace

In This Chapter

▶ Getting your head in the game

▶ Finding customers

▶ Scoping out the competition

▶ Putting your plan in place and staying on top

*B*efore you read one more page or take another step toward realizing your dream of crowded dining rooms, ringing cash registers, and beach vacations, read the following definition of *competition* over and over and think about what it means in the restaurant business. Competition is

✔ A test of skill or ability; a contest

✔ The act of competing, as for profit or a prize; rivalry

✔ Rivalry between two or more businesses striving for the same customer or market

You're reading this book because you're making a decision to enter a *competition:* the restaurant business. And this is not some friendly game of Old Maid. You have a lot at stake: your business, your financial future, and your family's sense of security. That's why you have to analyze the competitive environment to make sure that you have a shot at success.

In this chapter, we show you how to investigate your competition. We give you tips on evaluating their strengths and weaknesses. If you're developing your concept, we help you use this information to shape your decisions about how to develop your concept and how to position it in your market. After you're up and running, you can use many of these same tools to continuously analyze the market and stay ahead of your competition.

Getting Your Mind Right: Profits Matter

To the casual outsider, the restaurant business is attractive for reasons that are byproducts of success (the fun, the glamour, the status). But success and all its trappings aren't guaranteed — a fact lost on many would-be restaurateurs. At its core, success requires you to look at the restaurant business *as a business,* a manufacturing enterprise whose products are only as good as they are salable.

The only way to measure success in any business is through profits. You can have the coolest space, the hippest crowd, and the trendiest cutting-edge food, but without net profitability, you might as well close the doors and save yourself a slow death.

You're a manufacturer, so accept that fact. We know that the title of *manufacturer* isn't as sexy as *chef de cuisine* or *restaurateur,* but it's the most accurate label. (If you still insist on a cool-sounding French term, you can use *fabricant,* the word for manufacturer.)

Creativity, vision, and equipment allow you to produce a product. That product is not just the type, quality, and presentation of your food or beverages. *Product* refers to the whole of your concept (restaurant), including the quality of the food, design of the space, appearance of the wait staff, and convenience of the location. All these factors affect the likelihood that a consumer will purchase your product over the competition's product. (Check out Chapter 2 for tips on choosing and developing your concept.)

Embrace the idea that your success is based on producing a salable product and turning a profit, just as it is with any business. If you create a product with no sale, you're only creating inventory, and in most cases, inventory in the restaurant business spoils, turning into a loss. Profits come only when you make the sale, and every restaurant in your market is competing for that sale. Your job is to continually win that sale over your competition.

Exploring the Consumer's Buying Decision: The Big Why

Why does one car sell and another doesn't? Why do you buy one brand of beer and not another? Why do you go to the restaurants you go to? If you think about your actions, you can begin to understand the criteria that others use in making buying decisions. How your product positively influences the buying decisions of customers determines your market share, your operational cash flow, and ultimately, your success.

Think about buying decisions with products you're already familiar with. Here's how:

1. **Pick five grocery stores and five automobiles.**

2. **Compare and contrast your feelings on each one.**

   Evaluate the stores and vehicles using criteria of your choosing. But definitely include price, value, design, practicality, and service. You can't have a good competitive analysis without them.

3. **Apply the same criteria to your restaurant concept in your market.**

As you go through this exercise, you gain an appreciation of all the factors that influence a buying decision. But you're only one person, so take the analysis a step further. You need to understand the potential consumers and what influences their buying decisions as they relate to your market.

Figure 3-1 illustrates the *competitive response cycle,* the process of research and action that you continually follow to ensure that your restaurant continually meets the needs of the consumers you're going after. You study the marketplace (including customers and competitors) and changes in the marketplace (including emerging trends) and then implement responses to your findings (marketing programs, menu changes, and so on) to develop your business. Then you analyze how well your efforts are working, which leads you back to square one.

In the rest of this chapter, we describe each part of the cycle in detail. The cycle never stops.

Identifying and Analyzing Potential Customers

Start by figuring out who you want your customers to be, and make sure they're likely to frequent your concept. Figure out which demographic group(s) you're likely to attract. The term *demographics* describes characteristics or traits shared by a group. A demographic group includes people who are within a specific age range or income level or who share other distinguishing traits, such as gender or marital status.

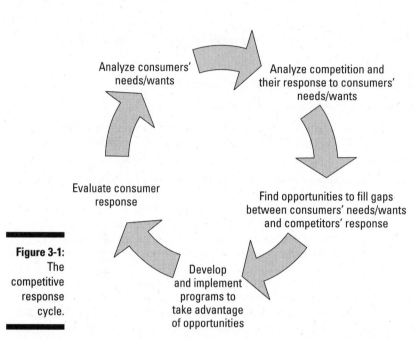

Figure 3-1:
The
competitive
response
cycle.

You're not excluding anyone from dining with you; you're simply trying to identify the clientele who's likely to visit your restaurant. These people are the same as the target audience you use in your positioning statement (see Chapter 2). You must make sure that your menu offerings, music (and its volume), entertainment choices, décor, and so on appeal to your proposed clientele.

Over time, build a profile of your desired diners and tweak your concept, as appropriate, to appeal to this group. Find out where they live. Figure out where they eat. Discover what motivates their buying decisions. Find out what else they do besides dine out. As soon as you have an understanding of your customers and their lives, you can begin to target your concept and your messaging directly to them. This process is often called *target marketing* or *niche marketing*.

Figuring out who your customers are: Target segmentation

A *niche* is a subset that's distinguishable from the larger group due to shared interests, lifestyles, and values. If you can discern and understand the various niches of the local population that frequent your restaurant, you can better target your menu, service, design, and marketing to address the needs of these specific groups instead of wasting time and money trying to meet the needs of everyone. *Target segmentation* is fancy marketing-speak for developing an understanding of who makes up your core group of diners so you can better meet their needs as a business.

To identify your potential customers, ask yourself the following:

- ✔ Are you looking for a male clientele, a female clientele, or both? If you're looking for both men and women, are you focusing on singles or couples?
- ✔ Is your concept geared toward families, or is it not kid-friendly?
- ✔ Are you targeting a particular ethnic or religious segment of your community?
- ✔ Do you want to attract people in suits, in hard hats, or in everything in between?
- ✔ Do you want to appeal to locals, or are you trying to draw out-of-towners, including business travelers and tourists?

Target segmentation really works a lot like high school (unless high school has changed a lot — it's been a while for us). In high school, you have a broad swath of kids from all the socioeconomic and cultural parts of the spectrum. However, kids with like interests and shared values generally find their way into smaller groups, or cliques. Think about the cliques in your high school — bring back any memories? Well, a clique is just another niche.

Restaurants that try to be all things to all people eventually fail because they have no unique selling proposition (USP). (See Chapter 2 if you need more information on creating a USP.) They can't compete with the niche players who are experts at what they do and draw a loyal following of fans who appreciate the craft of doing a few things extremely well rather than offering a wide variety of mediocre dishes.

Creating a profile of your Superfan, or brand hero

After you observe your restaurant's clientele and segment that clientele into groups, you have an opportunity to further discover that very special group of frequent users and lovers of your restaurant, your *Superfans*.

In many cases, restaurateurs are aware of their *regulars,* people who come in multiple times a month. These patrons develop a relationship with the staff, often order favorite dishes or drinks, and consistently make special requests for dishes, tables, or service staff to suit their desires. What restaurateurs often do not do is attempt to better understand the motivations behind their regulars' decisions to frequent their restaurant. Who are these regulars? Where do they live? What brings them here? What do they do when they aren't sitting at table 10 by the fireplace ordering their Grey Goose martini (dry, three olives) and having their shrimp cocktail (peeled, no tails, extra horseradish)? If you can consolidate that information about your regulars and describe the personality of your Superfans, you can better meet their needs and the needs of others like them.

A host management system like OpenTable can capture a lot of guest information for you and help you maintain profiles on your diners. Take a look at Chapter 16 for information on OpenTable.

By observing, involving, understanding, and embracing your Superfans, you can refine your concept and menu to better meet the needs of your most influential guests both now and in the future.

One great example of observing your restaurant's clientele, identifying a target market, and developing a strategy to meet the needs of the niche Superfan occurred recently when a large chain of 24-hour diners made a strategic decision to embrace and understand its young late-night patrons.

The chain, being a diner serving all-American breakfast, lunch, and dinner all day, every day, had a very broad appeal and served a huge, diverse cross-section of guests during the 24-hour day. From hungry construction workers to businessmen in suits to moms with kids, this was a place where you could come as you are . . . during daylight hours. When the sun went down, however, it became a different story.

In the wee hours of the morning, after the clubs let out and the concerts ended, the restaurants historically filled with groups of young adults looking to keep their evening, er, morning, going. However, over time, the corporation noticed that the late-night crowds were dwindling. Where had all the kids gone?

Well, instead of having a bunch of suits in the corporate office try to answer the question, the corporation decided to do something important: It asked the kids and developed a rich profile of these young patrons. It began to understand how these kids lived, what they valued, and what they needed from a restaurant before they chose to go there. Here are some of the key things the corporation discovered about this group:

- ✓ **These kids don't go where no one looks like them.** Young, hip, lavishly dressed kids with brightly colored hair don't go to a restaurant where the only other people there are 45 to 50 years older and look on them with disdain.

- ✓ **These kids don't eat alone.** They want to keep the party going, so they need big tables and big portions of sharable foods.

- ✓ **Music is very important.** These kids are coming from clubs or concerts playing the latest hits within their favorite genres. If your restaurant is playing big band show tunes, the kids ain't coming.

- ✓ **These kids are not coming in for salads.** They're looking for high fat, greasy, carb-and-protein wonderment. They've been out all night and need a certain type of grub and some strong coffee to cure what ails them.

This info provided the corporation with all the information it needed to change strategy, adopt new tactics, and create a place that, once again, was inviting to this important niche market. After the corporation understood first-hand what the late-night guests needed, the restaurants quickly lowered the lights, changed the music, hired specific staff from within the target demographic, and created a brand-new late night–only menu. It created this menu in partnership with some of the target guests' most influential bands and reversed the declining sales trends.

Focusing your research

Deciding what information you need is half the battle (the other half is actually doing the research and analyzing the information, but hey, you can't expect us to do everything for you). Here are our tips for focusing your research on what your diners want from you:

- **Location:** Determine how much importance your potential customers place on the convenience of the location and identify locations that fit. Maybe you're close to your customers' homes or workplaces, or maybe they drive past your place on their commute.

- **Hours of operation:** What hours are convenient to your potential customers?

- **Menu:** A big menu is a draw for some consumers; others prefer a short, simple format. Figure out what fits your desired clientele.

- **Food quality:** Given your concept, what do people expect?

- **Price/value:** The *price* is the amount of money that someone pays for a menu item. The *value* is how they perceive what they get (usually in terms of quality and quantity) compared to what they pay. Both need to be in line with the needs and wants of your consumer.

- **Service:** Determine the type, style, and efficiency of service that best fit your targeted customers' needs.

- **Applicable trends:** Determine how conscious your potential customers are of dining and lifestyle trends and how these trends are likely to impact their buying decisions. Do they largely ignore trends in favor of consistency, or are they largely trend-followers? Keep in mind that a trend doesn't have to be glitzy and hip to qualify. Past trends such as wraps, frozen yogurt, or low-carb dieting aren't real glitzy.

  Depending on your concept and the trends in question, think about how to take temporary advantage of them. Don't retool your concept to serve nothing but trends, but consider using them as a component of your concept. By watching for and interpreting trends correctly, you can either create the next trend or have a plan ready when the market is ready for the next big thing. Maybe you notice that people are digging Asian flavors. Even if you're not running a Chinese place, you can add a grilled chicken salad with cilantro lime dressing and shiitake mushrooms to your menu.

Gathering this intelligence is a key component to getting your restaurant up and running, but you must continue to do so on an ongoing basis. Truly successful businesses foresee, adopt, and maximize opportunities as consumer behavior changes. These businesses listen and then give customers what they want.

Keeping an Eye on the Enemy

Some restaurateurs think that they can peacefully coexist with the competition because plenty of market is available. This point of view is wrong on two fronts:

- ✔ **It doesn't account for new competition.** The next guy may just be better, faster, cheaper, and sexier than you are. The new kid on the block steals market share, at least temporarily. And if he lives up to the hype, you're really in trouble.

- ✔ **Peaceful coexistence doesn't actually exist.** Think about Ford and Mercedes. On the surface, these brands cater to two different markets. But Mercedes didn't build a $30,000 car by accident. It's looking to leverage a market it didn't have before. Mercedes made a cheaper car that's still sexy. It's targeted customers who, above all things, want a Mercedes because they get prestige they couldn't afford before.

In this section, we help you identify your competitors, examine how they approach customers, and scope out their restaurants.

Identifying your competitors

Your competitors are doing their own intelligence and implementing their own marketing strategies, just like you are. They're reaching out to the same group of potential customers. With your target customer in mind, you then have to figure out who your competitors are — both your *direct* and *indirect* competition. Here's how these competitors differ:

- ✔ **Direct competitors:** Direct competitors share similar prices, a similar ambiance, a similar style of service, and similar food. If your customers see your restaurant as similar to another restaurant, that restaurant is probably your direct competitor. If you have a burger restaurant, every other burger joint is your *direct competition.*

- ✔ **Indirect competitors:** When people go out, they don't just go out for burgers. They also go out for Mexican food, pizza, and sautéed foie gras. These other kinds of restaurants in are your *indirect competition.* Indirect competitors don't share the same food, but they share similar prices, similar geographic areas, similar styles of service, and/or a similar ambience.

Make a list of your potential competitors. Your research will confirm (or deny) that everyone on your preliminary list is indeed your competitor — the next few sections show you how to execute this research. And remember that to be successful, you must continue to do this type of research even after you open your doors. Old competitors die out and new ones are born on a regular basis. Some concepts that don't seem like competitors today may be tomorrow, depending on how you and they make changes to your businesses in the future.

Don't limit your attention to only direct competitors. Try to capture market share from indirect competitors as well. Chick-fil-A, a quick-service chicken concept, launched a campaign that featured cows holding up hand-painted (well, hoof-painted) signs that read "Eat Mor Chikin." Taco Bell uses the tag line "Think Outside the Bun," aimed directly at fast-food burger places. These companies have some of the most creative and calculating minds in the industry developing their marketing strategies for them, so learn from them.

You're competing not only against other restaurants; you're also competing against people eating at home. Think about the commercials for products like DiGiorno Pizza ("It's not delivery. It's DiGiorno") and frozen dinners. Swanson has developed two new lines of Hungry Man dinners, called Sports Grill and Steakhouse, aimed directly at restaurant diners.

Figuring out who they think their customers are

Study where your competitors place their messages, and you can find out a lot about your competition and their perceptions of the consumer. Every time people watch TV or read an airline magazine, a local community publication, or a grocery store periodical, these people are being influenced by your competition in varying degrees. You can then use that information on your competitors' perceptions to either make similar assumptions or try a different tack — whatever will break through the noise.

It's no secret that companies selling beer, pizza, cars, snack food, and burgers advertise during football games. Big companies spend millions of dollars to have someone tell them what may look obvious now: There's a gathering of their consumers at a certain time on a certain TV channel, so that's a good place to place propaganda — we mean ads. These same viewers are likely customers at your pizza restaurant. Maybe you can't afford Super Bowl advertising, but you can afford to advertise on the front page of the sports section of your local paper. Have your coupons delivered that Wednesday before the big game. People will see the ads, be hungry, and have the coupons. Who knows what could happen? Chapter 15 has more on advertising.

Reconnaissance: Mystery shopping till you drop

If you really want to know your competitors, spy on them. Be their customer, literally. Dine at their restaurants and experience their products. Take notes and share them with the other managers in your restaurant. Use them as a starting point for brainstorming sessions for new services and products. In the restaurant and retail industries, these activities are called *mystery shopping,* or more accurately, *mystery snooping.*

Don't get too caught up in the "my duck à l'orange can whip your duck à l'orange" type of thinking. Be objective enough to say, "They're beating my pants off with their salads, sandwiches, and hip interior décor."

Initially, you can shop your competition on your own. But hopefully, you'll reach a point where you won't be able to. You'll be so prominent in your restaurant community that the competition will pick you out like a rookie restaurant critic. You may need to hire a professional mystery shopping service.

Mystery shopping services aren't always the way to go. We've had mixed luck with their results and accuracy. You can also get friends and employees to go in and spy for you. But give them the specific criteria you're looking for and remember that people you know may have a hard time telling you what you don't want (or what they think you don't want) to hear.

Examine your competitors who do things right, but remember that looking at the failures is just as important. Spend some time thinking about why they failed. With few exceptions, they probably failed because they stopped being vigilant. They stopped being innovative. They ignored trends and failed to adapt to the ever-increasing savvy of the consumer.

We suggest using criteria, like those listed in Table 3-1, to begin to gather the facts about your direct competitors in the marketplace and to list your own. After you gather the info, you can take the next step, evaluating the information and making judgments about it. (See Table 3-2 for an example.)

Table 3-1	Comparing Your Concept to the Competition's		
Criteria	*Urban Forge Pizza Bar*	*Pizza Shack*	*Uncle Jonnie's Pizza*
Day parts	11 a.m.–11 a.m. (6 days/week)	11 a.m.–12 a.m. (7 days/week)	11 a.m.–1 a.m. (7 days/week)
Menu	Wood-fired Neapolitan pizzas and pastas; Italian-inspired plated appetizers, salads, and desserts; full bar featuring beverage selections paired to the food menu	Pan, hand-tossed, and thin-crust pizzas; bread-sticks, pastas, and wings; retail packaged soft drinks	Hand-tossed and thin-crust pizzas, breadsticks, and chicken tenders; retail packaged soft drinks
Price/value	Price based on positioning as a "better, more upscale" pizza experience with more varied and premium ingredient choices and table-service model	Value-priced and promotion driven; value is equated to the volume of food for the price	Value is driven by a barbell strategy offering deep-discounted promotions on one end and specialty pizzas occupying the premium end
Efficiency	Personal and attentive table service staff is knowledgeable about the concept and the menu offerings; appetizers and beverage offerings offset the extended wait time for the made-to-order wood-fired entrees	Built to leverage efficiency as all hot menu offerings must utilize the same cooking platform; mixture of delivery and dine-in business can incur long waits in dining room if delivery is slammed or vice versa	Focused on delivery, efficiency is streamlined through regimented training and product procedures

(continued)

Table 3-1 *(continued)*

Criteria	Urban Forge Pizza Bar	Pizza Shack	Uncle Jonnie's Pizza
Location	Affluent, urban locations targeting mixed-use destination featuring higher end shopping, entertainment, and plentiful secure parking	Suburban mass-market mall; outlot location or rural main thoroughfares	Strip mall in-line locations
Targeted demographic	Affluent, food-savvy social gatherers looking for an inspired pizza experience	Younger, moderate income households and young adults equating value with volume	Middle-class families of tween/teens who connect with the positioning as a better delivery pizza product
Type/style of service	Personal table service	Table, delivery, and some buffet service	Delivery
Novelty/other	The blending of upscale wood-fired pizza and related Italian specialties with a premium full-bar in a hip, design-driven space	Unique pizza constructions and deep-discount promotions	Focus on better-quality ingredients than competing mass-market delivery pizza chains

Developing and Implementing Your Battle Plan

How are you going to take your product, your information about your customers, and the scoop on what's going on with your competition and create a plan that brings people in your door, not to your competitor's? Your plan should take the following into account:

- Your strengths and weaknesses
- Your competitor's strengths and weaknesses
- Your local marketplace

If you need information on refining your definitions of who your clientele and your competition are, check out the sections earlier in this chapter.

Doing a competitive analysis

Start to brainstorm what you sell and what you're good at. Say that you sell innovative fresh Mexican food. Make a list of your strengths. Then figure out which strengths are yours alone. Decide whether your competition is better than you, equal to you, or deficient compared to you in this category. Unless you're the only person in town who does fresh Mexican cuisine, you don't own it. But if you're the only one who delivers, you own the delivery market for your type of cuisine. When you go through this exercise for your concept, you're trying to find the things that your competition doesn't have an answer for. Your point of difference is what you see as your strength. From your customer's point of view, that point of difference could be a strength or a weakness.

Suppose Señor Mike's Fresh Mex is a fictional yet already operational restaurant that's trying to stay competitive in a crowded marketplace. The business is having some success but needs to improve in some areas.

Your points of difference can become your greatest strengths. In Table 3-1, we focus on gathering the facts. In Table 3-2, you take the next step, evaluating the data and making judgments about the info. In the first column, we list everything that we want our restaurant to be known for. We want Señor Mike's Fresh Mex to be the market leader in each category. In this context, the *market leader* is the restaurant that's best known (usually measured in terms of sales dollars and reputation) in the category. In some cases, Señor Mike is the leader; in other cases, he needs to improve to be the leader (–); and in yet other cases, he may actually be better (+) but not yet known for being better.

Table 3-2   Refining Señor Mike's Fresh Mex Points of Difference

Desired Points of Difference	Market Leader	How Do You Compare?
Innovative Mexican	Poblano	–
American cuisine	Vera Cruz Fresh	+
Fresh (made from scratch)	Poblano and Señor Mike	Tied
Signature grilled flatbread tacos	Señor Mike	Leader
"Create your own" counter service	Señor Mike	Leader
Service time less than 5 minutes	Señor Mike	Leader

(continued)

Table 3-2 *(continued)*

Desired Points of Difference	Market Leader	How Do You Compare?
Broad selection of Mexican and domestic beers	Poblano Vera Cruz Fresh Don Victor's	– – –
Authentic Latin market soft drinks	Don Victor's	+
Broad kids' menu	Vera Cruz Fresh	–
Private-label salsas and sauces	Señor Mike	Leader
Location across from major mall and close to campus	Poblano	–
Low-carb menu	Señor Mike	Leader

The most effective point of difference that you can have is one your competition can't answer. If you have a location directly adjacent to a major destination (such as a stadium, cultural center, or mall), odds are your competition doesn't, and you can work this to your advantage. Big corporations make a tremendous effort to develop the next point of difference that competitors can't immediately duplicate or copy. The chicken nugget, the drive-through, and proprietary recipes or products are all historical examples of this type of temporary no-response point of difference. Eventually every fast food place developed its version of the chicken nugget, but for a time, a single restaurant enjoyed it as a point of difference. Whether your points of difference are long lasting or fleeting, maximize them while they exist. (For information on communicating those points of difference through advertising, see Chapter 15.)

However, most points of difference are subtler. These are the nuances that you *own*. In Table 3-2, for example, Señor Mike owns several clear points of difference (such as signature flatbread tacos and a service time less than five minutes) that he can leverage to his advantage. However, as in most competitions, his competitors also have their strengths (a broad selection of Mexican beer and proximity to campus). The process of analyzing competitive advantage requires objectively weighing your strengths against your competitors' strengths and developing plans to simultaneously improve your deficiencies while emphasizing your ownable strengths.

Having a strength isn't enough; you need to have a point of difference that will be a deciding factor in motivating a potential customer to select you over the place down the block. When weighing your strengths versus the strengths of your competition, put yourself in the shoes of your potential customers and determine which criteria matter most to them. You may own several minor advantages like a drive-through, cute kids' toys, and free refills, but if your competition owns the categories of fresh, better-tasting foods; better service; and lower item-specific prices, you're in trouble if that's what your consumers want.

Acting on your information

After you know who your most likely competitors and consumers are, you can use that information to develop your plan. Here are the high points to help focus your evaluation:

- ✔ Play up your strengths as long as you can make them matter to your audience.
- ✔ Analyze your competitors and determine and exploit their deficiencies.
- ✔ Continually strive to close the gaps on your own deficiencies, because these are weaknesses that your competitors will counterattack.
- ✔ Continually strive to create new points of difference. Your competitors aren't blind, so they'll develop new plans to counter your offensive. By creating new points of difference, you're always on the attack.
- ✔ Know your audience, how your points of difference matter to them, and how to reach your audience.

The strategy of evaluating and playing up points of difference helps smaller businesses exist in the face of competition from bigger ones. The simplest example of this strategy is "You may be bigger, but I'm better." This idea works in all markets. Take fashion, for example. Levi's is bigger than Armani, but both companies are able to exist because they leverage their distinct points of difference to generally separate consumers.

The lines blur when businesses go after the same potential consumer. Now, the difference is in the details. All you have are small points of difference, so focus on the importance of these points of difference to your potential customer. For example, maybe your direct competitor microwaves all his entrees, but you prepare yours over a wood-fired grill. You take this point of difference and convert it into a message on why your wood-fired cuisine is better, fresher, and less radioactive than your competition's.

Adjusting to a changing battlefield

You can't just launch your plan and assume victory. The minute after you launch your attack, you need to analyze your competitors' reaction and retaliation. You're threatening their market share, and they'll fight for it. Only by observing the successes and failures of your strategy can you implement a successful campaign and claim the market share.

Suppose that you built your strategy on your wood-fired grill products, attacking your competition on the use of a microwave. You played up your quality and your investment in equipment to ensure the quality. You're targeting a consumer who values freshness, made-from-scratch cuisine, and trendy cooking methods and is conditioned to assume that microwaved products are inferior. Your plan went well for a while, until a competitor launched a two-fold strategy that included getting his own wood-fired grills and attacking your location by playing up his proximity to campus.

Now it's time to change your strategy. You must leverage another point of difference. If you're out of points of difference, create a new one. By observing and evaluating the success and failure of your marketing strategy and noticing your competition's response, you can continually develop new marketing strategies based on your point of difference (existing or new) and continue to capture or threaten the market share of your competition.

The restaurant business is noted for its ever-changing array of new competitors, new advances in products and technology, and increasingly savvy diners. You can stay competitive only by analyzing, reinventing, and reevaluating your strengths and weaknesses and those of your competition.

Chapter 4

Writing a Business Plan

· ·

In This Chapter

▶ Discovering why a business plan matters

▶ Reviewing the components

▶ Getting your financials into shape

· ·

*I*f you're going somewhere you've never been, you need a map to get there. If you have to stop and ask directions from strangers, doing so will cost you time and maybe even money. And who knows whether you're going to get the right information? If you're running a restaurant, you need a similar kind of map to help you reach your destination. The *business plan* is your map to starting your business — and achieving success. It answers the questions before your investors, financiers, partners, or employees ask them. In this chapter, we help you write your plan.

Note: You need to do some things in a particular order when you're developing your business plan. Some steps are prerequisites for answering other questions. For example, if someone asks you about your advertising budget, you can't really answer until you know what your overhead is, what kind of food budget you're developing, what kind of sales you're forecasting, and so on. Feel free to skip around and read whatever interests you, but when you actually put pen to paper, remember that you need to follow some steps in order.

Don't Fly Blind: Understanding Why a Business Plan Matters

A *business plan* explains in a detailed way what you envision your business to be. You clearly explain your concept and why it's viable and outline your budget. You anticipate where you'll spend money (expenses), forecast how much you expect to take in (sales), and estimate when the money will be coming in and going out (cash flow). Your business plan helps you in several ways:

✔ It allows you to start analyzing your restaurant in a very detailed manner, which can help you avoid some problems altogether.

✔ It helps you answer questions that many people involved in your restaurant will ask.

✔ It helps you identify and define the goals of your business, the customers you're hoping to serve, and your ideas for getting there.

✔ It provides a tool for potential investors to evaluate your business, your philosophy, your operating savvy, and your market.

✔ It provides a mechanism for figuring out how much money you realistically need to get started and to keep going until the business can sustain itself.

✔ It creates a tool for you to use and update regularly in your daily operations to get you on track and keep you there.

✔ It helps you decide whether your proposed business is doomed to failure from the beginning.

Business plans vary from organization to organization. A business plan can be a relatively simple document, or it can be a book. Don't overwhelm yourself right out of the gate: Start with a simple one-page outline and flesh it out as you go. Not every business plan is an extremely detailed document, but we suggest you put in as much work as possible — to the point that creating the plan makes you think about even the smallest details, such as "How much does this teaspoon cost?" or "Should I go silver, stainless, or plastic?"

In the end, your business plan must contain these essential components:

✔ **Numbers:** Your financial projections are the core of your business plan. Include detailed sales and expense forecasts, cash flow estimates, and a balance sheet.

✔ **Funding:** Include details on how to meet your numbers. This part includes how much money you realistically need to start and maintain the business and how you intend to get it.

✔ **Action plan:** Note how you intend to realize the numbers. This is your plan of action. It includes your menu and marketing plan and anything having to do with running your day-to-day business.

✔ **Profit distribution strategy:** Indicate what you intend to do with the numbers. This strategy includes how you pay back investors, compensate yourself, and reinvest in your business.

The more detailed your plan is, the better off you are in the long run. Do as much planning as possible and save yourself some time and money. As a general rule, the more detailed your business plan gets, the more questions you find you don't have answers for. Including the details gives you great ideas for your to-do list and helps you realize the points you still need to ponder and research before you get your answers together.

Even with a business plan in hand, you're going to forget something. Pad your expense projections and be conservative in your sales forecast to account for this eventuality.

Laying Out a Business Plan

Before presenting your plan to anyone, we recommend you include a *confidentiality agreement* that the reader signs and returns before he receives your plan. Here are the basic pieces of most restaurant business plans:

✔ **Cover page and table of contents:** The cover page identifies your plan. Use it to differentiate your plan from those of other restaurants or companies that your potential investors may be looking at. The table of contents provides readers with a map for perusing your plan. You may also want to include an *executive summary,* a brief couple of paragraphs explaining what the plan's about.

✔ **Management team:** This section provides information about you, your management team, and any other key employees. Detail the experience, expertise, and strengths of your team in this section. Place this section up front in your plan if your team is a strong selling point; otherwise, it's usually better placed later in the document.

The management team section may not be available early in your planning process. In fact, until you have funding, you may not be able to pay a management team. Instead, you can give investors insight into your own experience or discuss the skill sets you're looking for to fill out this critical component of your plan.

✔ **Definition of your business concept:** Take a look at the later section "Articulating the concept and theme" for details in communicating your theme in your business plan. Chapter 2 goes into detail about choosing your concept and theme.

✔ **Your menu:** Include a copy of your menu. For details on developing, formatting, and figuring costs and prices for your menu, check out Chapter 8.

✔ **Market analysis and plan:** Here, you show the world how your business is different from other restaurants. You identify the market for your restaurant and discuss how you'll do it fresher, faster, cooler, or whatever and how that means "better" from your diner's point of view. Check out Chapter 3 for details on understanding your market and Chapter 15 for putting your marketing plan together.

✔ **Clientele demographics:** Discuss who your diners will be. Confirm that you have sufficient numbers to draw from in your market to make your business a success. Also detail why your concept and marketing plan will appeal to that audience. For info on winning and keeping your clientele, check out Chapters 15, 18, and 19.

✔ **Financials:** With this section, you try to communicate how much money you need, what you're going to spend it on, and how you're going to build upon it. Financial analysis is an important step, even if you're not looking to borrow money from anyone. You need to set up a realistic timeline for when money will go out and come in.

Depending on your plan, you may break up your financials into different categories, maybe *assumptions* (details about what you're basing your forecasts on) in one section and forecasts in another. You need to be the judge of what works for your business, but make sure you include a few basic elements:

- Forecasted sales

- Forecasted expenses

- Forecasted cash flow

- A break-even analysis

- An income statement

- A balance sheet

In this section, we provide you with the basics on writing a business plan in general, and we cover the restaurant-specific issues you need to account for. Later in this chapter, we cover financials. But people have written whole books on business plans, so if you want even more information, we suggest that you check out two — *Business Plans For Dummies* (by Paul Tiffany and Steven D. Peterson) and *Business Plans Kit For Dummies* (by Steven D. Peterson, Peter E. Jerat, and Barbara Findlay Schenck), both published by John Wiley & Sons, Inc.

Articulating the concept and theme

Most restaurants have a theme and a concept, which are really two sides of the same coin. The *theme* is the common thread, idea, or image that binds your restaurant together. The *concept* is the entire package, including your menu, price point, décor, and ambience. When someone tells you about a new restaurant in town, the person usually describes the establishment's theme and concept: the new *family-style seafood restaurant* or the new *Chinese buffet.* Definitely take a look at Chapter 2 for great tips on identifying and articulating your theme and concept.

The concept-and-theme section of your business plan is where you get to relate your vision of the business to the reader. It's the *qualitative,* or descriptive, component, as opposed to the *quantitative,* financial portion that lays out the numbers. Here, you describe what you're going to do, not how you're going to do it.

Consider your audience when you're developing the concept-and-theme section of your plan. Usually you write business plans for potential investors, a banker, and other financiers. But you may also use this section in other business documents down the road, such as your mission statement or employee manuals. The better you can communicate your vision of your restaurant to another person, the more likely you are to get the money you need to get started and to keep your focus on your goals so you can stay in business.

In the restaurant world, people sometimes use the word *concept* instead of the word *restaurant.* It's just sort of understood that you're talking about a restaurant, so you don't need to say it. For example, they may describe Papa John's as a delivery pizza concept or Applebee's as a casual dining concept. People use this convention most often when discussing chains of restaurants.

Creating your menu now

You need to develop your menu to match your concept, attract your desired clientele, and beat the competition. You can't do much in the way of predicting what you need to buy in terms of equipment, smallwares, table settings, and so on until you know your menu.

At this point, your menu is a work-in-progress. You'll likely modify your menu extensively during the development process, especially as you bring more people onto the team. Additionally, you'll make changes to the menu based on functionality in the actual physical restaurant.

You also need to figure out what your menu mix will be so you can figure out how many people you need to do what jobs. Your *menu mix,* or *product mix,* tells you how many of each dish you're likely to sell in a given time period, such as a shift, a week, or a month. If everything on your menu is fried, you may not need to budget for a grill cook. Figuring your menu mix also makes it much easier to figure out your forecasted *check average,* or the average amount an individual diner spends during a meal period, which you need to know in order to forecast your sales. For help on getting your menu together and forecasting your menu mix, check out Chapter 8.

You may also choose to include your projected menu mix in your business plan. We recommend that you do, because it shows potential investors that you've really done your homework. They can see that you're basing your numbers — such as check averages and revenue projections — on calculated assumptions rather than random guesses. Include your menu mix for a month so that readers can see what you're expecting to sell over a good chunk of time. Include your menu mix as supporting detail for your forecasted sales.

Analyzing your market

Your business plan must include a thorough market analysis. A *market analysis* identifies and describes both the market you want to compete in and your competitors in that market. Include specific information about your competitors that's relevant to your business plan, such as their proximity to your location, their hours of operation, and any special draws that you believe contribute to their success or lack thereof. If you're able to get any kind of sales information related to your competition, include that info as well.

Your competition doesn't have to be next door. It may be down the street, on the next block, or across town. Your *direct competitors* are those who are offering the same kind of food, the same style of service, and similar prices within an area that your common potential customers patronize. Your *indirect competitors* are those who don't have the same concept or theme you do but are vying for the same customers you are. For example, say that you want to open a Mexican restaurant right next door to a fish and chips place. If you're both going for a lunch crowd, you're competing with each other. A diner is probably going to eat lunch only once a day. Who is she going to choose? Check out Chapter 3 for details on researching the marketplace.

Identifying your target audience

As you develop your plan, you must decide who your diners are. Who are you trying to appeal to? Who do you want eating in your restaurant every shift? You must know this information before you can even identify your audience or your competition, and in Chapter 3, we provide you with suggestions and resources to accomplish this task.

When you're ready to compose your business plan, put together a few concise paragraphs that describe your clientele. Include information about their income levels, dining frequency, and where they currently dine. Make sure to include information highlighting why these people are likely to frequent your restaurant.

 You can contract with a demographic research company to put together reports for the geographic areas near your proposed restaurant, perhaps within a 1-mile, 2-mile, or 5-mile radius. Include copies of these reports in your business plan. Check out Chapter 3 for details on working with a demographics research company.

The Bottom Line: Focusing on Financials

Financial data helps you create a plan for making your business a reality, entices investors to take a chance on your venture, and can help you manage your business after you're up and running. You'll continually project sales and expenses throughout the life of your restaurant. Although you need to stay at least 6 months ahead in your planning, you can also devise long-term plans that cover 1 to 5 years. Plus, you'll use reports like the income statement, balance sheet, and cash flow analysis on a regular basis (with your real-life numbers, of course) to evaluate your business and its success.

We introduce these financial tools in this section and give you details about using them in the restaurant business. But to get a detailed picture on how to set them up and use them, check out the latest edition of *Accounting For Dummies* (by John A. Tracy; John Wiley & Sons, Inc.). If you choose to use a software program like QuickBooks, pick up a copy of *QuickBooks All-In-One Desk Reference For Dummies* (by Stephen L. Nelson; John Wiley & Sons, Inc.) to go with it.

Ultimately, your business plan comes down to the numbers. Your business plan must show that you can come up with the sales to fund the expenses you plan to incur. If you can't, you should rework your concept. If you're looking for investors in your business, they'll pay particular attention to this section of the business plan no matter who they are. Whether an investor is your uncle or a savvy real estate developer, he'll spend some time on your financials to decide whether your restaurant is a good place to invest his hard-earned cash. (For tips on getting financing, take a gander at Chapter 5.)

In the restaurant business, expect the worst and hope for the best to avoid at least some disappointments by anticipating and avoiding disasters. To be thorough, you want to show three sets of numbers for each *forecast* (prediction of what you'll spend or take in):

- ✔ A low-end, sort of worst-case scenario
- ✔ The best-case scenario that shows what happens if all the pieces of your puzzle fall exactly into place and the restaurant gods smile on you
- ✔ A mid-range set of numbers that show what happens if some things go your way and others don't

If you find you're unable to build this kind of data and develop forecasts, seek professional help from experienced restaurant consultants and/or accountants.

Take the calendar into account when you're forecasting your sales and expenses. February is the shortest month, with the fewest operating days. The months of January, March, May, July, August, October, and December each have 31 days. But if you're not open on Mondays, for example, look at the calendar for the years you're forecasting and make adjustments to your projections. (In the example used to create all the figures in this chapter, March had the most operating days in the 6-month period we were forecasting, so its sales and expenses are a little higher.)

Forecasting sales

Start your foray into the world of financial forecasting with sales. If you don't know how much you'll be taking in, you don't know how much you can spend. Forecast your sales before you forecast your expenses.

You have to develop some assumptions for estimating what your sales will be. Maybe you choose to estimate it based on your different *profit centers* (separate areas in the restaurant that take in money, such as the dining room, bar, takeout, and so on). Maybe you actually estimate how many guests you'll have at different time periods and estimate how much each guest will spend. Or you may use some combination of both methods. Eventually, you'll have to do all of the above, but maybe you only use part of it in your actual plan.

In Figure 4-1, we start with a simple example. We figure how many guests we'll have during a meal period, also known as the number of *covers,* and multiply that by the *check average,* or the average amount that each guest spends in the restaurant. ***Note:*** Don't let the term *check average* fool you; this standard industry term describes the per-person average spent in the restaurant, even though the term sounds like it should mean the average check size, no matter how many people are sitting at the table and paying on the same check.

We base all our numbers on Urban Forge Pizza Bar, the illustrative pizza bar concept we develop in Chapter 2. Our restaurant seats 100 in the dining room and another 20 in the bar. Urban Forge is closed Monday but open for lunch and dinner all other days of the week. We're planning to grow our sales 20 percent in Year Two and then an additional 10 percent in Year Three. Because we're aggressively targeting football-loving patrons, we expect big business during football season, especially October to January. Our rooftop dining will also give our summer a bump in business. Our forecasted numbers in the rest of the chapter reflect these changing business levels.

Here's one way to forecast your sales:

1. Figure out how many seats you have in your restaurant.

In the example we use in Figure 4-1, the restaurant has 120 seats split between the dining room and the bar area.

Cover Counts and Check Average

Food							
Lunch	Sunday	Tuesday	Wednesday	Thursday	Friday	Saturday	Averages
Covers	300	240	240	240	300	300	270
C/A	$15	$12	$12	$12	$15	$18 $	14.00
Dinner							
Covers	250	210	210	210	360	360	267
C/A	$15	$20	$20	$25	$35	$35	$25.00
Total:	**$8,250**	**$7,080**	**$7,080**	**$8,130**	**$17,100**	**$18,000**	**$10,940**

Beverage							
Lunch	Sunday	Tuesday	Wednesday	Thursday	Friday	Saturday	Averages
Covers	300	240	240	240	300	300	270
C/A	$5	$5	$5	$5	$8	$8	$6.00
Dinner							
Covers	250	210	210	210	360	360	267
C/A	$8	$8	$8	$8	$10	$12	$9
Total:	**$3,500**	**$2,880**	**$2,880**	**$2,880**	**$6,000**	**$6,720**	**$4,143**
TOTALS:	**$11,750**	**$9,960**	**$9,960**	**$11,010**	**$23,100**	**$24,720**	**$15,083**

Average daily food sales:	**$10,940**
Average daily beverages sales:	**$4,143**
Average daily sales:	**$15,083**
Total weekly food sales:	**$65,640**
Total weekly beverage sales:	**$24,860**
Total weekly sales:	**$90,500**
Annual food sales:	**$3,413,280**
Annual beverage sales:	**$1,292,720**
Annual sales:	**$4,706,000**

	Year One	Year Two	Year Three
Food sales:	**$3,413,280**	**$4,095,936.00**	**$4,505,529.6**
Beverage sales:	**$1,292,720**	**$1,551,264.00**	**$1,706,390.4**
Total Sales:	$4,706,000	$5,647,200	$6,211,920

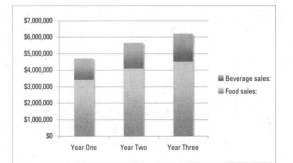

Figure 4-1:
A sales
forecast for
Urban Forge
Pizza Bar.

2. **Figure out how many guests will actually be in those seats for each meal period.**

   Depending on your business levels, every seat in the restaurant may be occupied multiple times. So take that fact into account when you decide how many covers you anticipate during each meal period.

3. **Estimate what each guest will spend during each meal period.**

   Your menu prices, your clientele, and your concept all affect this number. Diners usually spend more money at dinner because prices are higher (usually because portions are larger), they have more time to spend, and they're more likely to drink alcohol in the evening. Guests may have a bottle of wine at dinner instead of a glass of iced tea. They may choose an appetizer, a salad, and an entree at dinner, whereas they may order only an entree at lunch.

These steps offer a super basic representation of how you start the forecasting process. Before you include your forecast in your business plan, you need to do some additional estimating to account for how your income will ebb and flow over the months. If you're a resort-based business that's open only 4 months each year, you want your business plan to reflect that schedule. If you're attached to a shopping mall and hope to get most of your sales between Thanksgiving and New Year's Day, your business plan should show that goal.

Forecasting expenses

Even before you open the doors, your restaurant incurs expenses, monetarily and otherwise — like the cliché says, time is money. Even if you're not paying rent, you've bought the fridge, stove, pens, papers, computers, and so on. You invest money in your business before you realize a single dollar in *income* — notice we did not say *profit*. That's way down the line.

You already shelled out money when you bought this book. Save the receipt to claim it on your taxes. Consider buying at least two copies: one in your office to loan out and one at home as a backup.

In some ways, forecasting your expenses is very different from running your business. When you're forecasting, you anticipate every possible thing you'll need to spend money on; when you're running your business, you should be looking at every opportunity to control the costs.

Again, the more detailed you can be in preparing your forecasts, the better off you'll be in the long run. Figure 4-2 is a broad list for just about everything you could possibly need for your restaurant. Use it to start thinking about what expense categories you should forecast for your business. You may even find a few things that you hadn't thought about before.

Income Statement Accounts

3000	**SALES**		4500	**MARKETING**
3010	Food		4510	Selling & Promotion
3020	Liquor		4520	Advertising
3030	Beer		4530	Public Relations
3040	Wine		4540	Research
			4545	Complimentary Food & Beverages
4000	**COST OF SALES**		4550	Discounted Food & Beverages
4001	Food:			
4002	Meat		4600	**UTILITIES**
4003	Seafood		4610	Electrical
4004	Poultry		4620	Gas
4005	Produce		4630	Water
4006	Bakery		4640	Trash Removal
4007	Dairy			
4008	Grocery & Dry Goods		4700	**GENERAL & ADMINISTRATIVE**
4009	Non-alcoholic Beverages		4705	Office Supplies
4020	Liquor		4710	Postage & Delivery
4030	Bar Consumables		4715	Telephone / Communications
4040	Beer		4720	Payroll Processing
4050	Wine		4725	Insurance - General
4060	Paper (QSR)		4730	Dues & Subscriptions
			4735	Travel Expenses
4100	**SALARIES & WAGES**		4740	Credit Card Discounts
4110	Management		4745	Bad Debts
4120	Dining Room		4750	Cash (Over) / Short
4130	Bar		4755	Bank Deposit Services
4140	Kitchen		4760	Bank Charges
4150	Dishroom		4765	Accounting Services
4160	Office		4770	Legal & Professional
			4775	Security / Alarm
4200	**EMPLOYEE BENEFITS**		4780	Training
4210	Payroll Taxes		4785	Miscellaneous
4220	Worker's Compensation Insurance			
4230	Group Insurance		4800	**REPAIRS & MAINTENANCE**
4240	Management Meals		4810	Maintenance Contracts
4250	Employee Meals		4820	R&M - Equipment
4260	Awards & Prizes		4830	R&M - Building
4270	Employee Parties & Sports Activities		4840	Grounds Maintenance
4280	Medical Expenses		4850	Parking Lot
4300	**DIRECT OPERATING EXPENSES**		5000	**OCCUPANCY COSTS**
4305	Auto & Truck Expense		5010	Rent
4310	Uniforms		5020	Equipment Rental
4315	Laundry & Dry Cleaning		5030	Real Estate Taxes
4320	Linen		5040	Personal Property Taxes
4325	Tableware		5050	Insurance-Property & Casualty
4330	Silverware		5060	Other Municipal Taxes
4335	Kitchen Utensils			
4340	Paper Supplies		6000	**DEPRECIATION & AMORTIZATION**
4345	Bar Supplies		6010	Buildings
4350	Restaurant Supplies		6020	Furniture, Fixtures & Equipment
4355	Cleaning Supplies		6030	Amortization of Leasehold Improvements
4360	Contract Cleaning			
4365	Menu & Wine List		7000	**OTHER (INCOME) EXPENSE**
4370	Pest Control		7010	Vending Commissions
4375	Flowers & Decorations		7020	Telephone Commissions
4380	Licenses & Permits		7030	Waste Sales
4385	Banquet & Event Expenses		7040	Interest Expense
4390	Other Operating Expenses		7050	Officers Salaries & Expenses
			7060	Corporate Office Expenses
4400	**MUSIC & ENTERTAINMENT**			
4410	Musicians & Entertainers		8000	**INCOME TAXES**
4420	Cable TV/Wire Services		8010	Federal Income Tax
4430	Royalties to ASCAP, BMI		8020	State Income Tax

Figure 4-2:
Chart of
restaurant
income and
expense
accounts.

Figure 4-2 is actually the restaurant chart of accounts for an income statement (see the "Estimating profits" section later in this chapter). The numbers in the column to the left correspond to the account codes used in your *general ledger,* the master set of books that tracks all the financial transactions in your restaurant. Use whatever number system works for you, as long as you're consistent throughout your system. The National Restaurant Association (NRA) recommends the number codes shown in Figure 4-2, so if you're starting from scratch, you may as well start here.

When you forecast expenses, include *everything* — from produce to salaries to advertising expenses. We provide a scaled-back version in Figure 4-3. If we were to show you a full year of an expense forecast with every category, it'd take up way too much space in this book. Besides, you can really get a good picture of the process by using this snapshot. The next couple of sections give you the details on what we summarize in Figure 4-3.

Include at least a full-year forecast of expenses in your business plan, making sure you include three possible scenarios: best case, worst case, and most likely to make your plan complete.

Controllable expenses

Controllable expenses are expenses that you can change for the better by running your business well. At the same time, these expenses can quickly get out of hand. Here are the categories of controllable expenses:

- ✔ **Cost of sales:** This category includes your food and beverage costs. It represents your outlay for raw materials and reflects what you spend to buy the ingredients that go into your menu items. As the price of your ingredients fluctuates, your expense line does, too. If you're buying ice cream and dairy prices are high, your ice cream prices will be high.

    If you sell anything besides food and beverages, such as t-shirts or custom-labeled hot sauce, the expense you incur by purchasing them to sell to your customers goes in this expense line.

- ✔ **Payroll:** This summary category includes salaries and wages for both salaried and hourly employees. It also includes other costs associated with employees, such as benefits, taxes, and worker's comp insurance.

    The more sales you generate, the more hours your employees work, the more you pay them, and the more you pay in taxes and some benefits. Take those facts into account when you're forecasting your expenses.

    Salaries may not seem like a controllable expense because you pay a manager the same amount each period, whether she's at the restaurant 10 hours or 110 hours. But ultimately, if your sales can't support the expense of another manager, you can't hire one. Coauthor Mike took on an additional responsibility of running the wine program at his restaurant to save money on hiring a *sommelier,* or wine expert. Although his budget might support the extra salary now, he's found that he really doesn't need a sommelier, thus saving himself thousands of dollars each year in this category.

Figure 4-3: Sample 6-month expense forecast for Urban Forge Pizza Bar.

Q1 and Q2 Fiscal Year One	Jan $	Feb $	Mar $	Apr $	May $	June $	Total $	Total % of sales
CONTROLLABLE EXPENSES								
Cost of sales								
Food cost	78,221	66,488	70,399	74,310	78,221	82,132	449,771	25.00%
Beverage cost	26,070	22,159	23,463	24,766	26,070	27,373	149,901	22.00%
Total COGS	**$104,291**	**$88,647**	**$93,862**	**$99,076**	**$104,291**	**$109,505**	**$599,671**	
Payroll								
Salaries	43,138	36,668	38,824	40,981	43,138	45,295	248,045	10.00%
Hourly Wages	64,707	55,001	58,237	61,472	64,707	67,943	372,067	15.00%
Taxes & Benefits	43,138	36,668	38,824	40,981	43,138	45,295	248,045	10.00%
Contract labor	0	0	0	0	0	0	0	0.00%
Total Payroll	**$150,984**	**$128,336**	**$135,886**	**$143,435**	**$150,984**	**$158,533**	**$868,157**	**35.00%**
Other controllable expenses								
Direct operating expenses	10,785	9,167	9,706	10,245	10,785	11,324	62,011	2.50%
Music & entertaining	2,157	1,833	1,941	2,049	2,157	2,265	12,402	0.50%
Marketing	21,569	18,334	19,412	20,491	21,569	22,648	124,022	5.00%
Energy & utilities	8,628	7,334	7,765	8,196	8,628	9,059	49,609	2.00%
General & administrative	14,020	11,917	12,618	13,319	14,020	14,721	80,615	3.25%
Repairs & maintenance	4,314	3,667	3,882	4,098	4,314	4,530	24,804	1.00%
TOTAL OTHER CONTROLLABLE EXPENSES	**$61,472**	**$52,251**	**$55,325**	**$58,398**	**$61,472**	**$64,546**	**$353,464**	**14.25%**
NONCONTROLLABLE EXPENSES								
Rent	30000	30000	30000	30000	30000	30000	180,000	
Real estate Taxes	6,667	6,667	6,667	6,667	6,667	6,667	40,002	
Lease expenses	1,200	1,200	1,200	1,200	1,200	1,200	7,200	
FF&E reserve	8,300	8,300	8,300	8,300	8,300	8,300	49,800	
Insurance	8,300	8,300	8,300	8,300	8,300	8,300	49,800	
TOTAL OTHER EXPENSES	**$54,467**	**$54,467**	**$54,467**	**$54,467**	**$54,467**	**$54,467**	**$326,802**	
DEPRECIATION	5,200	5,200	5,200	5,200	5,200	5,200	31,200	
INTEREST	4,300	4,300	4,300	4,300	4,300	4,300	25,800	
TOTAL INTEREST AND DEPRECIATION	**$9,500**	**$9,500**	**$9,500**	**$9,500**	**$9,500**	**$9,500**	**$57,000**	

✔ **Other controllable expenses:** This category includes the following:

- **Direct operating expenses:** Here's where you account for incidental expenses, such as uniforms, linens, tableware, paper supply, cleaning supplies, and so on, that you must incur for your business. They're the result of your processes and are required to some extent for every business.

- **Music and entertainment:** Include the costs for a live musician, satellite TV, or your sound system.

- **Marketing expenses:** You can control how much you spend, but most restaurants should spend something on ad campaigns, public relations, and research (trends, competitive analysis, and industry knowledge).

- **Energy and utilities:** Everyone can turn off lights that aren't needed and fix leaky faucets. We discuss cutting utility costs and reducing waste in Chapter 13.

- **General and administrative:** This category includes office supplies, postage, phones, dues, and subscriptions. Account for professional fees, such as attorney's fees, here. Credit card fees that you pay as a business owner and banking fees also go here.

- **Repairs and maintenance:** This category includes upkeep of your facility and your equipment.

Noncontrollable expenses

Some noncontrollable expenses are *fixed expenses,* or expenses whose amounts don't change. Some may be *variable expenses,* or expenses whose amounts do change. The items in this list can get confusing, especially when you're just starting out. (Get a copy of *Accounting For Dummies*, by John A. Tracy [John Wiley & Sons, Inc.], and keep it handy as you work through the first few months of your real restaurant reporting.) Here are the details of the noncontrollable expenses (see Figure 4-3):

✔ **Occupancy costs:** This expense includes your rent (or mortgage), equipment rental, real estate taxes, insurance on the building and its contents, and personal property taxes. This number may be a constant flat rate, as in the case of your rent payment, or it may fluctuate depending on your sales. Also think about any assessment for grounds maintenance or common area maintenance (CAM) when you're filling out this section. CAM includes the upkeep of things like the landscaping and snow removal. CAM also applies to tenants in malls or multi-tenant buildings for the upkeep of the lobby, public restrooms, and shoveling and sweeping the front sidewalk.

✔ **Depreciation:** Depreciation is basically the accounting process of booking the expense of a capital purchase over a period of time known as its *useful life.* Accountants usually take care of depreciation, so seek help from your accountant in figuring out your depreciation schedules.

✔ **Interest expenses:** Include any charges you'll sustain for long-term debts or notes that you plan to take out. If you make payments to investors, they can show up here. These costs can be variable or constant, depending on what you set up with your investors. For example, some investors may want to be paid back in equal payments over 5 years, whereas some want a percentage back each year, with a *balloon payment,* a payment that includes the remainder of the principal in one lump sum, on the fifth year. See Chapter 5 for tips on finding financing and working out payment arrangements.

Figure 4-3 contains an FF&E Reserve line. FF&E stands for *furniture, fixtures, and equipment.* You can put money aside in an FF&E account in preparation for replacing these items. Your FF&E reserve account isn't a separate bank account; it's part of your operating bank account, but from an accounting perspective, this money is separate.

Breaking even

After you forecast all your expenses, run a break-even analysis, like the one in Figure 4-4. A *break-even point* is the point where your revenues equal your expenses. The break-even analysis helps you determine that point, or how much you need to sell to cover your expenses before you make even $1 in profit. This step is critical. If you can't get the revenue to support your projected expenses, you must adjust your expenses.

In Figure 4-4, we add most of our projected monthly expenses from Figure 4-1 to create the Monthly Expenses line. We pull out the cost we pay for food and beverages (lumped together as *cost of goods sold,* or COGS) and show it on our graph as Monthly COGS. We add them together to get our Monthly Expenses + COGS so we can see what our minimum revenue must be to cover our costs.

Split your expenses into Monthly Expenses and Monthly COGS so you can see how and where your cost control measures are helping you. So if you negotiate a better lease, it'll show a dramatic improvement in your Monthly Expenses line but will have less of an impact overall. If you negotiate a volume purchasing agreement for your food, you'll see a dramatic improvement in your Monthly COGS line but less of a change in the overall numbers. Having this information cut into smaller pieces helps you manage your businesses more effectively.

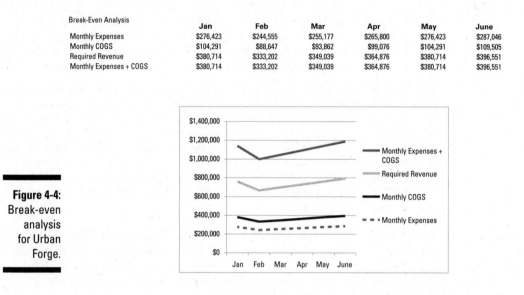

Break-Even Analysis	Jan	Feb	Mar	Apr	May	June
Monthly Expenses	$276,423	$244,555	$255,177	$265,800	$276,423	$287,046
Monthly COGS	$104,291	$88,647	$93,862	$99,076	$104,291	$109,505
Required Revenue	$380,714	$333,202	$349,039	$364,876	$380,714	$396,551
Monthly Expenses + COGS	$380,714	$333,202	$349,039	$364,876	$380,714	$396,551

Figure 4-4:
Break-even
analysis
for Urban
Forge.

Ultimately, if you want to just provide the combined total of your monthly expenses and COGS to show your ultimate break-even point, you can do that. Use whatever method works for you. The important thing is to know how much revenue you need to cover your costs.

Estimating profits

In a nutshell, you estimate your profit by taking your sales and subtracting your expenses. The remainder is your profit. In the real world, the situation isn't quite that simple, but it follows the same principle. Figure 4-5 shows you a sample income statement. We use the same summary categories that we've worked with throughout the chapter, so if you need additional explanation on what detailed accounts are included in the summary categories, check out the preceding sections and look at Figures 4-1 and 4-3.

Basically, we take our forecasted sales, or revenue, and subtract all our expenses (controllable, noncontrollable, and depreciation and interest) to come up with our *final net profit/loss figure*. This figure is a key indicator for many investors. Many consider the net profit/loss figure the bottom line. Of course, you must prove all your other assumptions are correct, but many people start with this number.

Q1 AND Q2 YEAR ONE

	Jan	Feb	Mar	Apr	May	June	Total
	$	$	$	$	$	$	$
CASH RECEIPTS							
Food Sales	312,884	255,996	270,218	284,440	312,884	327,106	1,763,528
Beverage Sales	118,499	96,953	102,340	107,726	118,499	123,885	667,901
Sales Receivables	0	0	0	0	0	0	0
TOTAL REVENUE	**$431,383**	**$352,949**	**$372,558**	**$392,166**	**$431,383**	**$450,991**	**$2,431,429**
CASH DISBURSEMENTS							
Food cost	78,221	66,488	70,399	74,310	78,221	82,132	449,771
Beverage cost	26,070	22,159	23,463	24,766	26,070	27,373	149,901
TOTAL COST OF SALES	**$104,291**	**$88,647**	**$93,862**	**$99,076**	**$104,291**	**$109,505**	**$599,671**
Payroll							
Salaries	43,138	36,668	38,824	40,981	43,138	45,295	248,045
Hourly Wages	64,707	55,001	58,237	61,472	64,707	67,943	372,067
Taxes & Benefits	43,138	36,668	38,824	40,981	43,138	45,295	248,045
Contract labor	0	0	0	0	0	0	0
TOTAL PAYROLL	**$150,984**	**$128,336**	**$135,886**	**$143,435**	**$150,984**	**$158,533**	**$868,157**
Operating expenses							
Direct operating expenses	10,785	9,167	9,706	10,245	10,785	11,324	62,011
Music & entertaining	2,157	1,833	1,941	2,049	2,157	2,265	12,402
Marketing	21,569	18,334	19,412	20,491	21,569	22,648	124,022
Energy & utilities	8,628	7,334	7,765	8,196	8,628	9,059	49,609
General & administrative	14,020	11,917	12,618	13,319	14,020	14,721	80,615
Repairs & maintenance	4,314	3,667	3,882	4,098	4,314	4,530	24,804
TOTAL OPERATING EXPENSES	**$61,472**	**$52,251**	**$55,325**	**$58,398**	**$61,472**	**$64,546**	**$353,464**
OTHER EXPENSES							
Rent	30000	30000	30000	30000	30000	30000	180,000
Real estate Taxes	6,667	6,667	6,667	6,667	6,667	6,667	40,002
Lease expenses	1,200	1,200	1,200	1,200	1,200	1,200	7,200
FF&E reserve	8,300	8,300	8,300	8,300	8,300	8,300	49,800
Insurance	8,300	8,300	8,300	8,300	8,300	8,300	49,800
TOTAL OTHER EXPENSES	**$54,467**	**$54,467**	**$54,467**	**$54,467**	**$54,467**	**$54,467**	**$326,802**
DEPRECIATION	5,200	5,200	5,200	5,200	5,200	5,200	31,200
INTEREST	4,300	4,300	4,300	4,300	4,300	4,300	25,800
TOTAL CASH DISBURSEMENTS	**$380,714**	**$333,202**	**$349,039**	**$364,876**	**$380,714**	**$396,551**	**$2,205,095**
CASH FLOW FROM OPERATIONS							
Cash Receipts	$431,383	$352,949	$372,558	$392,166	$431,383	$450,991	$2,431,429
LESS: Cash disbursements	$380,714	$333,202	$349,039	$364,876	$380,714	$396,551	$2,205,095
NET FROM OPERATIONS	**$50,669**	**$19,748**	**$23,519**	**$27,290**	**$50,669**	**$54,440**	**$226,334**
CASH ON HAND							
OPENING BALANCE	0	$50,669	$70,417	$93,935	$121,225	$171,894	
PLUS: New loan (debt)	0	0	0	0	0	0	
PLUS: New investment	0	0	0	0	0	0	
PLUS: Sale of fixed assets	0	0	0	0	0	0	
PLUS: Net from operations	$50,669	$19,748	$23,519	$27,290	$50,669	$54,440	
TOTAL CASH AVAILABLE	**$50,669**	**$70,417**	**$93,935**	**$121,225**	**$171,894**	**$226,334**	
LESS: Debt reduction	5067	7042	9394	12122	17189	22633	
LESS: New fixed assets	0	0	0	0	0	0	
LESS: Accrual: Profit distributions	0	1975	2352	2729	5067	5440	
TOTAL CASH PAID OUT	**$5,067**	**$9,017**	**$11,746**	**$14,851**	**$22,256**	**$28,073**	
ENDING CASH POSITION	**$45,602**	**$61,400**	**$82,189**	**$106,374**	**$149,638**	**$198,261**	

Figure 4-5:
Urban
Forge's
income
statement.

Notice in Figure 4-5 we list both Debt reduction and Profit distributions as line items. We're assuming that we're paying down short-term debt at a rate of 10 percent of available cash each month. We're also accruing for a profit-sharing scenario of 10 percent per month for our investors. In reality, you as a business owner may want to reduce debt first and keep cash in reserve in Year One and wait to pay back investors until Year Two. In the long run, your restaurant is more profitable if you reduce the amount of interest paid; thus, your investors ultimately make more money but have to wait longer to get it.

Projecting cash flow

Your *cash flow projection* maps out when your sales are coming in and when your payments are going out. It shows you how, over time, your business should be able to keep itself afloat. Take a look at Figure 4-6 for an example.

Figure 4-6: Sample of cash flow projections for 6 months.

Q1 AND Q2 YEAR ONE

	Jan	Feb	Mar	Apr	May	June	Total	Total % of sales
REVENUES								
Food Sales	312,884	255,996	270,218	284,440	312,884	327,106	1,763,528	72.53%
Beverage Sales	118,499	96,953	102,340	107,726	118,499	123,885	667,901	27.47%
Other Income	0							
TOTAL REVENUE	$431,383	$352,949	$372,558	$392,166	$431,383	$450,991	$2,431,429	100.00%
EXPENSES								
Food cost	$78,221	$66,488	$70,399	$74,310	$78,221	$82,132	$449,771	25.00%
Beverage cost	26,070	22,159	23,463	24,766	26,070	27,373	149,901	22.00%
Total COGS	$104,291	$88,647	$93,862	$99,076	$104,291	$109,505	$599,671	24.66%
Payroll								
Salaries	43,138	36,668	38,824	40,981	43,138	45,295	248,045	10.00%
Hourly Wages	64,707	55,001	58,237	61,472	64,707	67,943	372,067	15.00%
Taxes & Benefits	43,138	36,668	38,824	40,981	43,138	45,295	248,045	10.00%
Contract labor	0	0	0	0	0	0	0	0.00%
Total Payroll	$150,984	$128,336	$135,886	$143,435	$150,984	$158,533	$868,157	35.00%
Operating expenses								
Direct operating expenses	10,785	9,167	9,706	10,245	10,785	11,324	62,011	2.50%
Music & entertaining	2,157	1,833	1,941	2,049	2,157	2,265	12,402	0.50%
Marketing	21,569	18,334	19,412	20,491	21,569	22,648	124,022	5.00%
Energy & utilities	8,628	7,334	7,765	8,196	8,628	9,059	49,609	2.00%
General & administrative	14,020	11,917	12,618	13,319	14,020	14,721	80,615	3.25%
Repairs & maintenance	4,314	3,667	3,882	4,098	4,314	4,530	24,804	1.00%
TOTAL OPERATING EXPENSES	$61,472	$52,251	$55,325	$58,398	$61,472	$64,546	$353,464	14.25%
GROSS OPERATING PROFIT	$114,636	$83,715	$87,486	$91,257	$114,636	$118,407	$610,136	
OTHER EXPENSES								
Rent	30000	30000	30000	30000	30000	30000	180,000	
Real estate Taxes	6,667	6,667	6,667	6,667	6,667	6,667	40,002	
Lease expenses	1,200	1,200	1,200	1,200	1,200	1,200	7,200	
FF&E reserve	8,300	8,300	8,300	8,300	8,300	8,300	49,800	
Insurance	8,300	8,300	8,300	8,300	8,300	8,300	49,800	
TOTAL OTHER EXPENSES	$54,467	$54,467	$54,467	$54,467	$54,467	$54,467	$326,802	
ADJUSTED PROFIT	$60,169	$29,248	$33,019	$36,790	$60,169	$63,940	$283,334	
DEPRECIATION	5,200	5,200	5,200	5,200	5,200	5,200	31,200	
INTEREST	4,300	4,300	4,300	4,300	4,300	4,300	25,800	
TOTAL INTEREST AND DEPRECIATION	$9,500	$9,500	$9,500	$9,500	$9,500	$9,500	$57,000	
NET PROFIT/LOSS	$50,669	$19,748	$23,519	$27,290	$50,669	$54,440	$226,334	9.31%

Buying in bulk can hurt your short-term cash flow but help you in the long run. But don't sit on the inventory too long, or you miss the opportunity to use the cash on another money-making opportunity. Check out Chapter 19 for details on managing your cash flow.

Keep the flexibility to cover some unforeseen expenses. Managing your cash flow is managing your sales and expense projections in a timeline. For example, why are you getting a lobster order on Monday when you know you're not going to sell them until Thursday, Friday, and Saturday? Your money is sitting in the tank for days waiting to be recouped.

Creating a balance sheet

A *balance sheet* is a summary or snapshot of your business on a given date, usually at the end of an accounting period. It summarizes the money you have *(assets)* compared to the money you owe *(liabilities)*. Basically, balance sheets are designed to show that your assets (cash on hand, receivables, and inventory) balance out your liabilities (your upcoming payments and debts) and *owners' equity* (which includes the amount you initially invested and anything you've earned and then reinvested in the business).

You can evaluate the efficiency of your restaurant by measuring the number of turns on inventory for the accounting period. The inventory dollar amount for the period is stated on the balance sheet in assets. Divide this figure by revenues to arrive at a ratio that tells you how efficiently you use your money. In the restaurant business, you want to get around four turns a month. Otherwise, you're tying up more cash than you need.

Selling Your Plan: The Unwritten Part of Your Business Plan

We describe your plan for selling to investors as the *unwritten* part of your plan, but that doesn't mean it's not important. In fact, *for internal use only* may be a better description. You likely do want to create a written presentation plan (unless you have a great memory!) to sell your business plan if you expect to find capital to make the project happen. It's time to put on your salesman's hat. (If you haven't ever been in sales or feel like you need help creating your presentation, get a copy of *Selling For Dummies,* by Tom Hopkins [John Wiley & Sons, Inc.]).

Know your audience and what they need to hear from you. Just like any successful salesperson with ethics, you want to pitch to any particular investor by presenting your opportunity in a format they can relate to. *Who* your potential investor is shouldn't change your plan as much as it may change how you present it. A bank isn't as interested in the color of your drapery as it is in hard numbers, but the bank may check whether you've thought about your plan in enough detail to include the color of your drapery. No matter who you're pitching your plan to, the plan must be sound and comprehensive.

Rejection is part of the process. You may hear "no" many times before you hear that "yes." So you may need to revise this presentation plan — several times — if you don't consummate a deal with the person (people) you originally thought may be your investor(s).

You may not want to include every controversial detail in your *business plan,* but be prepared to answer any questions that may arise. Even if you haven't included specific addresses of properties you'd like to consider, you may get questions about the neighborhoods you're looking at. Be prepared to discuss them.

Part II
Putting Your Plan in Motion

The 5th Wave   By Rich Tennant

"I appreciate you sharing your dreams and wishes for starting your own French restaurant, but maybe I should explain more fully what we at the Make-A-Wish Foundation are all about."

In this part . . .

*I*t's time to move from idea to action. We help you pound the pavement to round up financing in this part. We also show you how to scout out the best location and make the best choice for your concept. Finally, we cover permits, licenses, laws, insurance, and a host of other legal issues — including how and when to call in some professional help for these matters.

Chapter 5

Show Me the Money! Finding Financing

Finding the money to start a restaurant is one of the toughest hurdles for any budding restaurateur. You can have dreams of a popular restaurant, featuring great food and bustling with happy diners, but you need money to make it a reality. How much you need varies with how large your dreams are, the size of your own savings, and how many investors you can sway with your business plan (see Chapter 4 for the details on creating a business plan). In this chapter, we help you figure out how much money you need and how much money you already *have,* and we give you tips on getting more. Finally, we give you some suggestions on clever ways to free up some cash at start-up.

Knowing How Much Money You Need

Most people, including the experts, find it challenging to start figuring out how much money they need to run a restaurant. Every restaurant concept is unique. Your costs vary with your location, your construction costs, the china you pick out, and a thousand other factors. Use Figure 5-1 and the expense worksheets in Chapter 4 to help you figure out how much money you need. In this section, we discuss start-up costs and operating reserve.

Calculating start-up costs

Many of the things that you need for your business are one-time-only purchases. Items such as tables for your dining room, racks for your glasses, and shelves for dry storage usually fall under this category. Unfortunately, you have to buy these things before the cash starts rolling in, so you need to plan for these expenses when you're finding your financing.

Figure 5-1 can help you get started. Make lists of all the items you need and then consolidate your list on this worksheet. So for the furniture category, include things such as the cost of your tables, chairs, barstools, seating for the lobby, your host podium, benches for the bathrooms, artwork, vases on your tables, a fish tank (if you have one), and your office desk.

Start-Up Costs		
	Range of Costs	Final Projection
Deposits including utilities and landlord		
Construction, remodeling, and design costs (Chapters 9 and 10)		
Furniture and decor (Chapter 9)		
Signage (Chapter 9)		
Fixtures and equipment (Chapter 10)		
Licenses and permits (Chapter 7)		
Professional, legal, and consulting fees (Chapter 7)		
Initial advertising and PR (Chapter 15)		
Starting inventory of goods and supplies (Chapters 13 and 14)		
Operating reserve (this chapter)		
Other		
Total One-Time Start-up Costs		

Figure 5-1: One-time start-up costs worksheet.

The figure includes chapter references to tell you where to find information about each category of start-up expense. But remember, all these costs are directly related to your particular concept, including location, schedule, and how soon you hire the first manager and dishwasher, so the advice we give isn't specific to how much you will (or even should) spend. You have to research costs for your particular needs.

Opening with operating reserve

You don't stop needing money the day you open your doors. When you're planning for the amount of money you need to get started, include at least three months' worth of operating expenses. This cushion allows you to stay open until your business level picks up. You'll have some sales early on, but you can't expect to hit your stride until a few months into the process.

Take a look at the figures showing expense forecast and cash flow projections in Chapter 4 to help determine what your monthly operating expenses will be. Chapter 4 also gives advice on forecasting your expenses and sales.

Looking at How You Can Contribute

As scary as it may sound, you have to contribute a significant amount of your own money to your new venture. If you don't believe in your restaurant (and put your money where your mouth is), no one else will.

Using your own money does have benefits, such as allowing you to keep complete control of your business. You don't have to share control with investors (see the section "Working with Investors" later in this chapter). You can also skip the paperwork involved in getting a loan (see "Getting a Loan"). And ultimately, most investors want to see that you have some skin in the game.

Using your own money to finance your restaurant does have a downside: You have no guarantee of success, so you could lose all the money you invest, your credit rating (if you get behind on payments), and any collateral (including your home if you've borrowed against it). You want to be able to feed yourself even if your restaurant doesn't succeed, so make sure that you don't compromise your future — or your family's future. Make sure that anyone who depends on you financially (such as your spouse, significant other, or children) understands the risks involved if you decide to sink your life savings into this kind of a venture.

Here are several common ways in which people financially contribute to their own restaurants:

- ✔ **Use savings.** To get money for their restaurants, people may use their general savings, retirement savings, and kids' college funds. They cash in savings bonds. They also pilfer their Christmas-club funds, tap into their securities accounts, and sell other investments.

- ✔ **Have a great credit rating.** Your credit rating directly affects the interest rate at which you can borrow money. You can contribute significantly to the cause simply by having a great credit rating that allows you to borrow money at a relatively low rate. On the other hand, if your credit rating is poor, your interest rates will be higher or, worse, the banks and investors won't even be willing to take the risk.

- ✔ **Get a home equity loan or line of credit.** Okay, technically speaking, this isn't the aspiring restaurant-owner's money; it's a bank's money. But should the restaurant go belly up, the loan-taker is still *personally* responsible for paying back 100 percent of this loan.

- ✔ **Use credit cards.** Credit cards can be good for short-term financing options because the funds are ready when you need them. They can even help you order supplies, décor, and other items online. Plus if you shop for competitive perks, you can find low rates (usually only in the short term), get cash back on your purchases, earn reward miles, and get consolidated billing.

Instead of using credit cards to cover a liquor order or pay for COD (collect on delivery) transactions, save credit cards for true emergencies. One winter, an ice storm contributed to a broken water main that flooded the basements of several restaurants. The restaurants had to pay for the cost of pumping out the water, and they also suffered further financial losses resulting from flood damage to the heating units and the subsequent freezing from loss of heat. Settling claims with your insurance company for these types of losses often takes several weeks. You'll likely need to pay for the plumbers and other service technicians you need and then get reimbursed later. Make sure you keep enough credit available on your cards to handle these emergencies.

Don't bite off more than you can chew on your credit cards. Pay the balance off as soon as possible to avoid paying high interest rates or worse.

Even if you don't borrow dime one from anyone else, we highly recommend that you write a business plan. Not only is a business plan essential when searching for investors, but it's also a great tool. Your business plan can save you a lot of your own money, help your restaurant make money faster, and hopefully spare you a few headaches. See Chapter 4 for details.

Working with Investors

Most prospective owners can't completely fund their own restaurants initially, so they need to look for outside sources of financing, including investors. Investors can include partners (both silent and not-so-silent), people looking for a new investment, your friends and family, or a combination of all these people. We cover these scenarios in the following sections. (And check out Chapter 7 for the legal details on setting up your business as a partnership or corporation.)

Looking at types of investors

Investors can come from almost anywhere, but locating them isn't a simple process. You improve your chances of finding investors by constantly networking and having a great reputation and a strong business plan.

Partnering up

A *partner* is someone who is actively involved in the running of the restaurant or who lends expertise to enhance the business but is not necessarily connected to day-to-day operations. Usually, a full partner is more involved in the business than a typical investor, also called a *silent* or *limited partner*.

Identifying reasons to bring in partners

Some partners don't actually invest cash. Instead, they invest their expertise. Normally, you select your partners because they bring something to the team that you're lacking. It could be money, bookkeeping abilities, or culinary prowess. Whatever the situation, each partner should bring something valuable to the party, or that person shouldn't get a seat at your table.

Bringing in a partner is always a strategic move. Here's a list of good reasons to bring in a partner or two:

- ✔ **They bring capital.** This is the most common reason to bring in a partner: You need the money.

  - **They bring other services.** Sometimes you can barter a percentage of your business for other services that you need, such as accounting tasks, marketing expertise, contractor or trades services, or rent. Get creative, but don't give too much away. For example, you probably don't want to give free meals for life to the accountant who prepares your tax return once a year.

✔ **They bring a particular restaurant expertise.** Maybe your potential partners have spent time in the business doing something that you have zero experience with. Teaming up can go a long way to ensuring your success. Look for the following skills in a potential partner:

- Culinary abilities

- Hospitality or service expertise

- Restaurant operations skills

✔ **They bring reputation or name recognition.** Maybe your partner doesn't lend cash or involvement in the day-to-day operations of the business, but he brings a reputation and is available to consult as needed. For example, you may decide to bring in a big-name chef to consult on your menu and advise you on various aspects of your back-of-the-house operations (see Chapter 12 for information on hiring a chef and other employees). Or perhaps you team up with a local wine expert who comes in to oversee changes in your wine program.

Making the relationship work

You may have heard the adage "too many chefs spoil the soup." The more partners you have, the more different ideas you'll have about where the restaurant should be going and how it should get there. Additionally, you'll be carving up the profits into smaller pieces.

You must clearly define the roles of each partner in the beginning. This critical step helps you avoid trouble later. Someone should have the final say in your restaurant. In the best-case scenario, one person makes the calls. If you need to have a committee meeting to take care of minor decisions, such as which brand of olives to serve in the martinis, you'll end up wasting a lot of time. Don't think, "We'll just come to a decision. We're united. No big deal." It usually doesn't work that way. One person doesn't have to make every minor decision; in fact, different people can take charge of different areas in the restaurant. But you must have a clear hierarchy, and the ability to make a final decision should rest with a single person.

Seeking other outside investors

If you're considering going to outside investors, or silent partners, complete your business plan (see Chapter 4) and figure in the one-time-only start-up costs we outline in Figure 5-1. Before you have the first conversation with the first potential investor, you want to know how much you're going to need from your investors and be able to tell them how soon they'll get a return on their investment and how much it will be.

Investors may say that they don't want to get involved in the restaurant operations . . . until things don't go as well as quickly as you hope. Even silent partners can become not-so-silent if they spend time in the restaurant ("Why did you get those curtains? They don't go with the spaghetti sauce"). Don't give investors a valid reason to comment. Run your business right from the beginning.

Some investors expect to eat in the restaurant for free as one of the perks of "ownership." Consider offering your investors discounted meals if you think they're appropriate for your business. Make sure to write down the full terms of repaying your investors, including any perks such as free or discounted meals, so that everyone knows what to expect. (See the upcoming section "Compensating your investors" for details.)

Hopefully, your investors will encourage their friends to come to the restaurant. If your investors are paying for their own meals, that's even better.

Asking family and friends to chip in

You've probably heard all the warnings about being careful about borrowing money from friends. Borrowing from friends puts both the borrower and the lender in tough situations. You don't want to lose your life savings or your relationships with friends and family. Instead, rely on friends and family for emotional support and encouragement.

If you do decide to borrow from friends and family, treat them with the same terms you'd treat your other investors, including a signed contract with deadlines for repaying the loan.

Compensating your investors

No one buys into the risky proposition of starting a restaurant without significant opportunity for a return on that investment. How you structure your compensation deals is important to the long-term success of your operation and the short-term success of your drive to raise money. You have to strike a balance of compensating investors fairly without burdening the business with high salaries, free meals, and unrealistic payment plans. The following sections explain a few typical compensation plans.

There's no right or wrong way to structure a compensation plan. Some investors don't want an open-ended deal; they're looking for a short-term investment. Others may want to stay involved in the business so they can say that they have a restaurant. No matter how you set up the plan, work with your attorney to draft the document that stipulates the terms of each agreement. Make sure that the attorney who draws up the agreement isn't also an investor in your business — that's a conflict of interest.

The sooner you pay back your investors, the faster you can reap the benefits of your hard work.

Earning your percentage

Even if you don't have cash to contribute, you can still be a viable partner and earn your stake in the business. Suppose you have a partner who brings money to the operation; you, on the other hand, bring a little money but a lot of experience. In fact, you're the one who runs the restaurant day in and day out, and you draw a salary from the business. Assuming that the business goes well, your partner will get a return on his investment.

Here are a couple of ways you can structure the partnership agreement:

- **Growing equity:** You can gradually gain a larger equity stake in the business over time (meaning you earn a bigger share of the business), which, you hope, will eventually pay you a larger return on your share of the investment.

- **Profit sharing:** You can forgo the growing equity and get a return on your hard work through profit sharing. In this scenario, you won't build a larger share of the business unless you invest more cash, but you do get a chance to share in the profits of the business as soon as there are any.

Paying an investor back with interest

In this scenario, an investor provides you with an initial investment amount, with the assumption that you'll eventually return the stake plus interest. The timing for each — repayment of initial stake and interest payments — varies. You can find as many repayment scenarios as you can find investors. Each investor probably has certain things that appeal to him more than others.

Suppose that you borrow $10,000 from an investor. In one scenario, you can pay him 10 percent annually ($1,000 each year) for each of four years and return the principal (the $10,000 you borrowed) on the fourth year, for a total of $14,000 over four years. Or you can pay him back another way, say, over three years. Maybe you pay him $4,000 the first year, $4,000 the second year, and finally $5,000 the third year, for a total of $13,000 over three years.

Revving up performance-based percentages

If you pay someone back based on how the restaurant performs, this person is considered more of a limited partner. She's hoping for you to do well, so you pay her more money as a return, while she maintains a percentage of your business. Suppose that she invests $10,000 in your company, and that's 10 percent of the value of your business. For every $10,000 of profit you make, she gets $1,000. You could add a buyout clause to her compensation plan, so in addition to getting her principal back, she gets a lump sum cash bonus. You continue to pay her dividends until you buy her out.

Getting a Loan

Because the restaurant business is so risky, many banks won't loan money to a restaurant that's just starting out. If they do, they usually require the owner to personally guarantee the note, meaning that the owner is personally responsible for repaying the note, no matter how the restaurant does financially. In this section, we give you some tips on how to make yourself look like the best possible financial risk for a bank, and then we give you some tips on getting some help from Old Uncle Sam if you qualify.

Visiting your local bank

For most start-up restaurants, getting a bank loan is probably not an option. Even if you have a great reputation and working relationship with your bank, most banks look strictly at the numbers. You're better off looking for individual investors.

On the other hand, if you can show that you have collateral and a proven track record for success and are looking to expand an already-successful business, you may qualify for a loan. For example, you may have a shot at getting a loan if you have a bakery and want to expand your business to include a café. The bank may require a cosigner or ask you for collateral, such as your other business, your house, or anything that minimizes the bank's risk of losing its money.

Either way, the bank looks at some of your financial and business records to decide whether you get a loan. Banks usually ask for the following info:

✔ **Proof of your ability to repay the loan:** Use your business plan to get this point across. For details on creating your own business plan, check out Chapter 4.

✔ **Your personal credit history:** The bank runs your personal credit report and assigns you a credit rating.

Making multiple loan applications can adversely affect your credit rating. Shopping around for a loan through repeated applications to different banks can hurt your chances. Do some research on the terms that different banks offer before putting in your application.

✔ **Equity:** Equity usually takes the form of your investment in the company. It's sort of like a down payment on a house.

✔ **Collateral:** This is any asset that you can use as security, such as your house, your car, and certain kinds of investments (such as certificates of deposit), if you default on your loan.

✔ **Experience:** Here's where your industry-specific experience pays off. To leave the best impression, make sure that your business plan includes details of your experience working and managing in the restaurant.

For more info, check out *Small Business For Dummies,* 3rd Edition, by Eric Tyson and Jim Schell (John Wiley & Sons, Inc).

Finding government assistance

Most start-up restaurants are eligible for help from the Small Business Administration (SBA). In all likelihood, you'll work either directly with your bank or with an SBA *intermediary,* someone who helps you get your business plan together, helps you complete the required SBA paperwork, and gets you prequalified for an SBA loan.

After you're prequalified and your paperwork is complete, you then work with the bank to qualify for the loan. If you qualify, the SBA will guarantee the loan or part of the loan, reducing the bank's risk. So if you default on the loan, the SBA will pay the bank back.

This guarantee doesn't eliminate your responsibility to repay the loan. It only reduces the bank's risk, making it easier for it to lend you money.

As with any loan, the SBA evaluates your application, using the same standard criteria that we go over in the "Visiting your local bank" section, earlier in this chapter.

Some SBA services are free of charge, but others are provided by contractors who may charge you a fee, so make sure that you know what charges you may incur.

Chapter 6

Choosing a Location

In This Chapter

▶ Checking out the real estate market

▶ Diving into location details

▶ Identifying cost considerations

*Y*ou've heard it countless times before: The cardinal rule in real estate is *location, location, location.* But finding the perfect location for your restaurant is much easier said than done. Part of the reason is that what works for some concepts definitely doesn't work for others.

The key in choosing a location is finding a spot that makes it easy for *your* targeted or desired clientele to reach your restaurant on a regular basis. Your restaurant may be a freestanding restaurant in a busy shopping district. It may be by a kiosk in a mall. It may be a lunch truck in a parking lot. No one right answer fits every concept or area. Use the suggestions in this chapter to figure out the best spot for your restaurant.

Looking at the Local Real Estate Market

Everything starts with the local real estate market. Here are a few ways to find potential locations for your restaurant:

✔ **Work with a commercial real estate broker.** Your best bet is to find one who knows the restaurant market.

✔ **Comb neighborhoods you think match your concept and desired traffic.** Look for locations that interest you even if it's not obvious that they're up for sale or lease. And check out the "Paying attention to traffic" section later in this chapter.

✔ **Investigate potential locations on the Internet.** Often you can see interior and exterior pictures online, get detailed dimensions, and take note of amenities. Take a look at the National Association of Realtors website (`commercial.realtor.com`) to get started. If you're interested in purchasing an existing space, take a look at Restaurants For Sale Online (`www.restaurants-for-sale.com/`).

✔ **Check in with your local chamber of commerce.** It's a good source of information.

✔ **Get info from your local governing bodies.** Consult town councils, zoning boards, and any other agency or board that doles out licenses and is likely to know of new development and rezoning opportunities.

Some people start a restaurant in an already established area and hope to make some profit. Locations where people are often mingling provide a built-in customer base, but these places come at a price: a hefty amount of money to get the space. (See the section "Looking at other businesses in the area" later in the chapter for related info.)

Other folks choose to be prospectors and hit an area before it becomes a great restaurant neighborhood. Choosing to be one of the developers of the neighborhood means paying less in rent than in established neighborhoods. But it also means not having the built-in customer base of lots of traffic nearby (which can translate into increased marketing costs). Just keep in mind that the greatest potential for profit may come with the greatest possibility of failure. Your real estate agent should be able to help you find up-and-coming locations.

If you choose to establish your restaurant in an area before it becomes hot, you may not realize your business potential for a couple years. Note, too, that business patterns change over time as a neighborhood evolves. Make sure that you have enough cash to last through the wait — few people have unending money supplies. Your overhead will be heavier while you wait for business levels to improve and sustain you.

Examining Location Specifics

No two locations are identical. What works for some restaurants definitely doesn't work for others. In this section, we cover some key concerns, including visibility, traffic, security, and more.

Research the history of your proposed space, building, and neighborhood. Find out what was there before and what has succeeded and failed. Try to figure out why businesses in the area either made it or didn't survive. Here are a few ways to get started on your research:

✓ **Ask landlords for info.** Even if landlords can get you only the names of the previous tenants, you at least have a starting point for your research.

✓ **Check it out on the Internet.** Often you can get quite a bit of information from some unexpected places. You may find old customer reviews of past businesses in the space. Or you may see pictures of how the space was previously configured. Run a search on the physical address of the space and see what pops up. If you know the name of the previous businesses, search those, too.

✓ **Talk to past leasers.** If you can talk with the past leasers, you can get invaluable information on their problems and solutions for the space, saving yourself some trial and error down the road.

✓ **Talk to your local building department.** Try to get information on renovations that have been made, when they were made, and so on. All renovations, additions, and many minor construction projects require permits that must be granted by the building department. The department keeps a copy of each plan and permit on file.

✓ **Chat with the neighbors.** They're always a source of information, but take whatever info you get with a grain of salt. They may have accurate observations but off-base conclusions.

✓ **Contact your local restaurant association.** If the space you're considering used to be a restaurant, the association may have insights to share about why it's no longer used for that purpose.

Considering access and visibility

You may not be in the market for a unique location, but here's a list of things to look for that benefit most restaurants:

✓ **Easy access:** Think about your restaurant from the guests' perspective. If they have to drive past your restaurant, turn left at the next light, and then backtrack to get to you, they may not bother. Having a traffic light with a protected left-turn arrow close to your location is a great plus. Often when people eat out, their first consideration is convenience. Make getting to you as convenient as possible.

✓ **A high-profile location:** Corners are desirable because people can see you from two streets instead of one. You get more exposure instead of being buried in the middle of the block. Or say that your restaurant is close to the mall. If possible, you want to be out in front of rather than behind the mall, because the most exposure is in front. If you can get the front corner of a large parking lot (known as an *outlot*), right on the street, all the better.

✔ **Availability of parking:** Unless you're in an urban area that benefits primarily from foot traffic or public transportation, abundant, well-lit parking is a must. If you have to hire a valet, it will cost you some cash, so budget for it.

Paying attention to traffic

Traffic doesn't just mean cars. It means potential customers passing by your restaurant. Traffic includes walking people, biking people, people in cabs, people on public transportation, people driving by — any means people use to travel near your business.

Visit your proposed location many different times, at different times of day and on different days of the week, to get a feel for the traffic flow. Look for patterns to help you evaluate the location. Make notes about the volume and type of traffic you see. Here are some thoughts to ponder to get you started:

✔ Where are these people going? Are they going to or from work, shopping, visiting a nearby museum or theater, going to school? Are these the folks you're targeting? Are they likely to stop in?

Sometimes, putting a sign in a proposed location works better than placing a restaurant there. For example, being located along a busy commuting thoroughfare isn't a guarantee of success. People may see you but not want to give up their spot in traffic or return later to your restaurant if they'll have to fight the same traffic again.

✔ How well do the people fit the profile of your proposed clientele? If you have a concept nailed down and a great flow of traffic but the traffic isn't your desired clientele, you'll have a tough time succeeding. For example, most truckers want a good, hearty meal that's a good value. If you're trying to sell them small, expensive portions, forget it. See Chapter 3 for info on targeting the right customers.

✔ Do your proposed operating hours match the traffic flow? If you open at 5 p.m. in a business district, you may have already missed the traffic flow that existed from 9 a.m. to 5 p.m. But in a suburb, opening at 5 p.m. may be ideal — people start returning from work around that time.

Make sure your location is on the *right side of the street,* by which we mean the side of the street that your core customers can easily access at the right time of the day. Often, traffic tends to flow one way in the morning and the opposite way in the evening. So, for example, if your restaurant depends heavily on breakfast traffic, you want to be easily accessible from the morning traffic flow, either foot traffic or vehicular traffic. You're asking for trouble if you set up your coffee concept against the flow of morning commuters.

Commercial sources, such as Claritas (www.claritas.com) or ScanUS (www.scanus.com), can help you identify demographics, average car traffic, and so on. Start with your local chamber of commerce, but then look for companies that specialize in segmenting the population into different demographic groups.

Knowing which locations to avoid

WARNING!

In a perfect world, people come to your restaurant for your restaurant's sake. If it's good, they come back; if it's not, they don't come back. But in the real world, outside factors affect your business more than you may guess. Spend some extended quality time getting to know your potential location at all hours of the day and night. Coauthors Andy and Heather recall just sitting down to a nice al fresco meal at a new bistro in a Western town north of Denver. All was well with the location until the winds shifted and with renewed force brought over the ripe smells of a neighboring cattle processing operation.

Your best bet is to pinpoint and avoid things that may keep customers away from your restaurant. For starters, avoid locations that feature the following:

✔ **Businesses that your customers may find unsavory:** Your customers may feel uncomfortable and may stop coming altogether.

✔ **Permanent construction zones:** You don't want heavy machinery and trucks going through during dining hours. Also, guests may have trouble getting to you through the construction mess. If the construction is short-term or pervasive throughout your area, you may not be able to avoid it.

✔ **Remote or hard-to-find addresses:** Don't locate your restaurant in a remote or hard-to-get-to location. In a very few cases, remoteness can be a draw, such as in ultrafine dining, where you're going after exclusivity. In most cases, though, people want convenience. They consider the efficiency of their time when making dining and drinking choices. Another consideration is that people are unlikely to venture far from home when drinking.

✔ **Mismatched clientele:** For example, if you're targeting a business clientele, don't locate your restaurant near a high school where kids go out for lunch. They may discourage other patrons from coming in. Depending on your concept, however, teens may be your ideal audience — they do have considerable disposable income these days.

Ultimately, let your conscience be your guide when it comes to avoiding certain situations and neighbors. Remember who you want to attract to your business and how they see the world and your restaurant.

Looking at other businesses in the area

Your neighbors affect your business and vice versa. Businesses such as theaters, entertainment, and shopping go hand in hand with restaurants. Attractions such as a scenic river walk in a downtown area, an ocean view, mountain peaks, and wildlife are great restaurant hooks.

Look for businesses that feed restaurants. Think about the relationship between the remora and the shark: The shark attacks and claims its prey. The remora, swimming close to the shark, sustains its life off the successes of the shark. Restaurants and their neighbors are similar to the remora and the shark. Think about the number of chain restaurants located close to malls, tourist attractions, and so on. Many restaurants, chains and independents alike, locate themselves near a busy office building, office park, or business district, hoping to capture a booming breakfast, lunch, and even takeout dinner business. Putting a restaurant in such a location is a completely calculated move, designed to capitalize on already-present traffic.

Also consider how your particular restaurant fits in with the current restaurant mix. If you want to bring in a Mexican café but two other Mexican concepts are established within the open block, do you want to be the third? You may be successful if the other two are both highly commercialized versions of Mexican cuisine and yours is truly authentic *and* your clientele can appreciate the difference. But if you're offering more of the same, choose a different location. There is a big exception, though: In larger metro areas, common cuisines can make up large city blocks that become areas known for different cuisines, such as Little Tokyo or Greektown.

Considering security

Security is a key concern for any business owner. Some restaurants have been under fire in highly publicized lawsuits for inadequately ensuring the safety of their patrons. Whether or not these suits were just, people know that restaurants regularly have a decent amount of cash on hand, and they can make tough-to-resist targets for thieves. Therefore, you must evaluate a potential location for security. Keep the following advice in mind:

- ✔ Avoid blind interior and exterior corners. Blind corners, like blind driveways, are corners that can't be seen from the normal flow of traffic.

- ✔ Stay away from buildings with poorly lit stairwells and hallways.

✔ Consider potential terrorist targets in your location selection. If you're planning to be located near a courthouse, a power plant, or a federal building, consider the possibility that you may have to temporarily close your doors during erroneous bomb threats, evacuations, and the like. These locations can still be lucrative; just make sure you have an adequate cash reserve and an emergency plan (for a variety of scenarios) in place.

✔ Avoid natural disaster areas (including flood plains) when possible. If you're in an area where natural disasters are prevalent, simply try to find the safest area possible in this regard.

Factoring In Cost Considerations

The primary cost of your location is your rent (or mortgage). For the most part, the restaurant owner isn't also the building owner. Purchasing the building is typically too expensive for a new restaurateur, so unless you're very established and successful, you'll likely have a landlord. Ultimately, a building's landlord doesn't want to keep the space vacant. He makes money only when the space is leased. Unless his is a highly sought-after locale, he should be motivated to help you get up and running. Check out Chapter 5 for information on negotiating with your landlord.

Here's a quick list of questions that affect your decision to lease a particular space:

✔ **Is your landlord pro-business?** Is he making it easy for you to make money? Your success increases the value of his property. You want to sign with someone who is looking for you to be there in the years beyond your initial lease.

✔ **Is your landlord willing to adjust your rent on a short-term basis?** Look for a landlord who's willing to give you some months of free rent — known as *rent abatement* — especially while you're setting up. It's not uncommon to ask for and get a 90-day abatement so that you can keep expenses down during your pre-opening period. Other tenants may depend on your being open because a closed space is an eyesore. If the rent is based on sales, the landlord wants to get you up and running as soon as possible. But keep in mind that it's also not uncommon for your landlord to give you nada, nothing, zip.

> ✔ **Is your landlord willing to foot some of the bill for construction costs?** This situation is less common, but you can still ask. Landlords are more likely to give you free rent than money out of their pockets. In some cases, you can get landlords to give you *x* amount of dollars per square foot toward the tenant improvements (known as TIs). One key factor in getting contributions is the state of the local commercial leasing market. If the market is soft and space is sitting vacant for extended periods, you can be more aggressive in negotiating.

> ✔ **Is your landlord willing to help pay for required upgrades to the HVAC (heating, ventilation, and air conditioning system) and/or electrical systems as needed?** Sometimes when you get into a space, unforeseen complications occur that have more to do with the landlord's building than with your restaurant. Find out what the landlord's policy is on these kinds of upgrades before they happen.

If you're looking at a space that wasn't previously a restaurant, retrofitting it to accommodate the kitchen, dining room, and so on is very expensive. Have an experienced restaurant contractor look at the space and help you understand all the ramifications of construction before you sign the lease. Ducts and plumbing don't just appear; they require hard work and money.

Depending on the age and configuration of the space you're considering, you may not be able to make the modifications necessary for a restaurant. Maybe the infrastructure of the building can't support the configuration, or perhaps the building's a historic landmark and the modifications necessary aren't within the charter. You don't want to get locked into a lease and then discover that you can't install a range hood in your kitchen. You still owe five years' rent. Don't go bankrupt before you make a dollar.

If you decide to lease a space, consider talking with the other tenants about their experiences with the landlord. You'll get info that's not in the public record about the history of the space, and you can probably find details on why the previous tenant left. You're guaranteed to get a different perspective than what the landlord gave you.

In addition, get the true story regarding the zoning situation of your space from the appropriate agency in your area. Make sure that you have the exact address of your proposed space because zoning ordinances can vary from block to block. Maybe ordinances don't allow for an outdoor café but your business plan and concept demand one. On the other hand, the governing agency may try to promote outdoor eating in specific areas and provide financial incentives to develop restaurants that offer it.

Chapter 7

Paying Attention to the Legalities

· ·

In This Chapter

▶ Figuring out who can help you with legal affairs

▶ Choosing the best legal setup for your restaurant

▶ Obtaining permits and licenses

▶ Putting together your insurance plan

· ·

More than any other topic in this book, legal issues vary from state to state and concept to concept. You need to know about the specific laws in your area so you stay out of legal trouble that may result in fines, loss of your licenses, or jail time. Laws dictate some details of your business that may surprise you. For example, laws tell you the number of alcoholic beverages that can be sitting in front of a single patron at one time, the hours your business can be open, whether you can serve diners on your patio, and how many people can be seated in your dining room at the same time.

To help sort through these complex issues, just about every restaurant needs the assistance of outside professionals, including a good attorney, a thorough accountant, and a reputable insurance agent. These business-savvy pros can help you navigate the legal necessities that are part of every small business and those that are unique to the wonderful world of the restaurant business.

In this chapter, we get you thinking about the legal realities of the business. We tell you exactly who you need to help you. Then we go over details concerning how to set up your business, what you need to know about local laws and licenses, and the types of insurance you need to be thinking about.

Identifying the Help You Need

Professionals you turn to for assistance should have experience in the business. If you get a "deal" from someone without restaurant experience, you may actually lose money in the not-so-long run. If your attorney doesn't know how to get a liquor license, you may get a license that won't work for your business. Then you're out the money you paid and you have no liquor license. And if your accountant doesn't depreciate your furniture correctly, you may not have the money to buy the new stuff when the old has got to go.

In the following sections, we talk about what kinds of legal experts you want on board and how to find good people for the job.

Looking at the roles to fill

Our advice is to contact experts with experience in the industry for specific advice in

- How to set up your business
- How to get the right insurance for your business
- How to get the necessary permits and licenses to do the business you want to do

In the following sections, we discuss your legal crew: lawyers, accountants, and insurance agents.

Cross-examining attorneys

Lawyers can expedite your paperwork through the maze of bureaucracy and advise you as to what's necessary to do things the right way. Attorneys can be very helpful to the new restaurateur, especially when you're setting up your business. They can do the following:

- Recommend and file the appropriate paperwork to set up your business as a corporation, partnership, or sole proprietorship.
- Draw up partnership agreements and any other agreements.
- Review contracts, such as your lease and your vendor agreements.
- Do the hard work of filing proper paperwork for permits and other licenses. In some states, you need an attorney to complete paperwork for your liquor license. Check with your local governing agency. For more help, see the section "Acquiring a liquor license," later in this chapter.

Depending on the size of your operation, you also may eventually need a few different attorneys, such as a labor lawyer, an intellectual property lawyer, a tax attorney, and a divorce lawyer . . . er, we mean, a general business attorney.

Your attorney may also have contacts, clients, or colleagues looking for a good investment. She may be willing to pass along your name to interested parties. Ask her.

Auditing accountants

If you're brand-new to running a restaurant, an accountant should be one of the first people you speak with. In the early stages, before you even open your doors, an accountant can walk you through the financial planning aspects of creating your business plan. He can explain complex financial stuff like depreciation, amortization, and capitalization. He can work with your attorney to show you the tax advantages of setting up your business in one way or another. Using a qualified accountant to guide you can help you avoid paying for an attorney to get you out of trouble later. After you're up and running, an accountant can help with preparing the monthly books and reports, preparing taxes, and conducting internal audits and reviews.

If your landlord bases your rent on the sales that you generate, you probably need to hire an accountant to review your books and make a statement to your landlord. See info about negotiating your lease in Chapters 5 and 6.

Ensuring you have a good insurance agent

Insurance coverage is important in any business. You need liability insurance, property insurance, and workers' compensation. Your insurance agent should be able to walk you through the basics of balancing deductible amounts, giving you the appropriate amount of coverage with reasonable payments that protect your business without putting you in the poorhouse. See the later section "Buying the Insurance You Need" for details.

Setting Up Shop on Legal Grounds

Your attorney and your accountant can help you decide how to set up your business. You have a number of options, from going it alone to setting up a partnership to incorporating your business. Your decision determines how your company is taxed, how you earn an income from the business, what your obligations are if your business fails, and many other expensive decisions. In the following sections, we discuss some of the most common options.

Even if you're the only investor or are involved in a partnership, you still may want to incorporate. Without the legal protection of incorporating your business, your creditors can come after you if your business goes under. They can lay claim to your home, cars, savings, and anything else of value.

Going it alone: Sole proprietorships

A *sole proprietorship* is owned by one single person — in this case, you. Your attorney registers your business as a proprietorship by completing a simple form. You keep everything that you make, and you personally owe everything that you spend.

Teaming up: Partnerships

A *partnership* is similar to a sole proprietorship, but you're adding extra people to the mix. You share all the profits and all the risk. No two partnerships are the same, but the partners should spell out the details in writing, with an attorney, before they begin. Each partner should consider hiring separate counsel to make sure that the agreement is on the up and up. (Check out Chapter 5 for info on finding financing through partners.)

Almost teaming up: Limited partnerships

Limited partners are more like investors in the business than actual partners. They limit their liability legally because they aren't involved in the operation. Say that your friend Joe Blow wants to invest in your restaurant. He doesn't want to be involved in the day-to-day, but he thinks you're a savvy businessperson and wants a piece of the action. He gives you $25,000, and he owns a corresponding percentage of your business. You draw up an agreement that specifies what he gets as a *return on investment* (or ROI) and when he gets it. Maybe he gets a percentage of profits paid quarterly or annually. Fast-forward five years: Things have been going well for several years, but the worst-case scenario occurs and your business folds. Joe Blow doesn't get his money back, but he also doesn't incur any debts as a result of your business folding. Creditors may take your house, but Joe's is safe and sound. That security for the investor is the beauty of limited partnerships.

As with any partnership agreement, have your attorney draw up a document with the specific language detailing the terms of your agreement with any limited partners.

Playing it safe: The corporate entity

Incorporating, or creating a corporate entity that owns your restaurant, offers you some protection if your restaurant goes under. Your attorney can set up your corporation for you, and you can be the only shareholder in your corporation and still own it completely. But incorporating also has some significant tax implications. *Double taxation* can be an issue: The government taxes the profits of the corporation and then taxes you on them again, as income. Depending on how you set up your corporation (different types of corporations exist), you may be able to lessen the tax burden. Definitely discuss your incorporation options with your attorney and accountant for the pros and cons of the type of corporation you're considering and for the details and nuances of your specific situation.

WARNING!

Creating a corporate entity doesn't remove all your responsibility in the event that your business fails. As a new restaurant owner, many lenders require you to personally guarantee loans, which means that even if your business fails, you're still responsible for the debt. Guaranteeing a loan personally is kind of like cosigning a loan for your corporation. Weigh the options. We know of many people who lost both their businesses and their personal credit ratings when their businesses fell apart. And don't plan to use your corporation as a shield if you have less-than-honorable intentions. If you run out on your rent or creditors, you develop a negative reputation that will follow you throughout your career.

Blend of three: The LLC

A limited liability company (not corporation), better known as an *LLC,* blends elements of a sole proprietorship, partnership, and corporation. Although unincorporated, it offers the owner(s) of the company limited liability and pass-through income taxation. For information on LLCs, check out *Limited Liability Companies For Dummies,* 2nd Edition, by Jennifer Reuting (John Wiley & Sons, Inc).

Knowing Your Local Laws

Laws govern just about everything about any business. The restaurant business is no different. Most laws related to this industry are governed and enforced by local and state agencies. Your local health department determines the many specific health codes you must follow to continue to serve diners in your area. Your local building department determines which steps you must take to make your facility safe to be occupied by people. And who knows who handles liquor licenses in your area? (Well, actually, we show you how to find out who handles them in your area, so don't worry.) Your local or state government probably has laws and ordinances governing the following:

- ✔ When you must close and when you can open
- ✔ How big you can make your signage and where you can post it
- ✔ The process for applying for required permits
- ✔ Where you can have your outdoor seating
- ✔ Details about building codes that you must follow
- ✔ How you can sell liquor

Most areas have very specific liquor laws. The government specifies when, where, in what container, in what quantity, and sometimes even at what price restaurants, bars, or clubs can serve alcohol.

Getting Permits and Licenses

A *license* is a legal document issued by a government agency giving you permission to do a very specific thing. For example, in the case of the restaurant business, you need a license to serve liquor. If you serve liquor without one, you can be shut down, fined, and even go to jail.

The words *permit* and *license* mean the same thing. Some agencies choose to use one word rather than another, but we don't really know why. Just call it whatever the agency calls it and don't worry about it.

In most cases, getting licensed is not a one-time thing; you usually need to update your licenses and permits annually. Work with your attorney, bookkeeper, or other support personnel to create a system for alerting you when you need to renew licenses and permits and for processing any applications and fees required to get and stay current.

Make permits and licenses a priority. By doing so, you're not just trying to keep yourself out of trouble; you're truly making sure that everybody's going to be safe in your restaurant. Go above and beyond to ensure that your customers and employees are safe and sound.

Acquiring a liquor license

Every restaurant that serves liquor must have a license to do so. Depending on the state, different agencies regulate and administer liquor licenses — the Department of Public Safety, the State Liquor Authority, and the Department of Alcoholic Beverage Control, to name a few. Start the process of getting your license in the early stages of starting your restaurant. Depending on the system in your area, getting this license can take a year or more.

Most licenses are valid for a year and require an initial license fee. If you maintain good standing with your local agency, you can probably get an automatic renewal for a smaller annual renewal fee. But if someone files complaints against you for overserving patrons alcoholic beverages, serving minors, or violating other terms of the license, your license may be revoked.

The cost of a liquor license varies greatly. If the government issues licenses directly, the price may be as low as $500. But if your area has no licenses available because it has met its quota and you need to buy one from an existing establishment or a third-party broker, the laws of supply and demand apply. In a really hot area, they may go for hundreds of thousands of dollars.

A *quota* is the fixed number of liquor licenses in a given area. Some states base quotas on the population living in an area. Utah, for example, allows one liquor license to be issued for every 5,000 people in the state. Other states set them based on population density or other criteria. So, for example, in some cities, you may find two to three licenses per city block.

The easiest way to get started: Get online and type something specific, such as **restaurant liquor license [with your state],** into your search engine.

Your local agency offers liquor licenses in different *classes.* The kind of establishment you have determines which kind of license you need and how much you pay for it. The class of license you require depends on your concept. Here's a list of the broad, common classes of licenses. Similar licenses in your area may have different names, and licenses with similar names to these may have different provisions.

- ✔ **Beer and wine:** This license allows you to serve only beer and wine. Licensees can't sell liquor or distilled spirits. In some areas, smaller restaurants (40 to 100 seats) can get only this type of license.

- ✔ **Hotel and restaurant:** This license allows you to serve liquor, beer and wine. This license may be called a *resort-and-restaurant license* in your area. You may also be eligible for a *bed and breakfast license* (which you can find later in this list) at a reduced rate. Check with your local agency.

- ✔ **Restaurant:** This license usually requires that no more than a certain percentage of your sales come from alcohol. States have varying percentages, but most requirements fall somewhere around 40 percent. Some states require you to have a minimum number of seats to qualify for this license. A restaurant license usually allows you to serve beer, wine, and liquor. Some people call it an *all-liquor license* for that reason.

- ✔ **Eating place:** This license is usually reserved for carryout places, like delis, that may offer a small amount of carryout beer.

- ✔ **Retail:** A retail license applies to grocery stores, drug stores, liquor stores, or any other retail establishments where the average consumer can walk in and buy liquor. It doesn't apply to restaurants, so don't buy this type of license.

✔ **Bed and breakfast:** In some states, this form of establishment is lumped in with the hotel and restaurant license. Some states have created two separate licenses to account for the size and sales of smaller establishments. This license may be cheaper in your area than the hotel and restaurant license. You're required to have a certain number of bedrooms, a separate kitchen, and so on to qualify for this license.

✔ **Tavern:** Some states require taverns to offer a food menu, but others don't. If you consider yourself a restaurant but half of your sales are alcohol, your state government may require you to apply for a tavern license. In some states, no such separate license exists.

✔ **Club:** Private clubs, such as country clubs and golf clubhouses, are eligible for a separate license allowing them to serve alcohol to their members. Some states allow only beer and wine in clubs, but others allow for all liquor.

✔ **Brewpub:** Many places brew their own beers, and in some states, you need a separate license to serve it to the public. Check your local agency.

Some states issue an *alternating premises* (AP) liquor license for places like wineries and breweries that allows these establishments to brew and ferment alcohol at certain times and serve patrons at other times.

✔ **Arts:** Some places, such as theaters, may get a special license that allows them to serve alcohol in connection with certain kinds of cultural events. This license is for a niche market of restaurateur, but it's good to know about if you fall into that niche.

✔ **Wholesale or distributor:** Some states require different licenses for importing liquor versus selling domestic liquor. If you're selling liquor to restaurants, retail establishments, hotels, and so on, you need this class of license. And on the other side of the equation, you need a restaurant (or retail establishment, hotel, and so on) license to buy from a wholesaler.

Here are the general steps to follow when you're getting your liquor license:

1. **Figure out which government agency issues licenses in your area.**

   Conduct an Internet search or check with other restaurants.

2. **Research the classes of licenses in your area.**

   Request a list from your local agency. Many agencies post descriptions on their websites.

3. **Figure out which class of license works for your business.**

   Based on what you find out, look at your business, your projected food-to-beverage sales mix, and so on to determine which license you'll likely need. Do your homework and work with your attorney.

4. **Contact the local agency to find out the availability of licenses, the costs, the application process, and a timeline for completing the process.**

   Your attorney may be able to handle this, but make sure it gets done.

5. **Update your business plan with the information on the costs and timeline.**

   Budget both the time and money to get your license before you open. This step is essential, whether you're using your own money or have partners, because you can't sell liquor without a license. Revise your plan anytime you run into a new schedule or budget factor.

6. **Apply for the new license or for the transfer of the soon-to-be purchased license.**

Consulting companies have sprung up because this licensing process can be so expensive and complicated. These companies can help you streamline your applications. They file your paperwork and the like — for a fee, of course.

Before you agree to work with any third party to secure a license, check with the state agency that issues licenses and with your attorney. You may be able to avoid additional fees and charges just by making a couple of phone calls. Your local agency may have a list of recommended brokers that handle the buying or selling of existing licenses.

Heeding health codes

Every restaurant needs a permit from the health department to do business. The permit process requires you to complete an application and pay a nominal fee (usually under $500). In larger metro areas, the cost may be closer to a few thousand dollars per year. As with most legal issues in this business, the requirements vary from state to state, so check with your local health department for details. In some states, requirements and ordinances vary county by county or municipality by municipality.

In addition to the restaurant's permit, some states require employees to be licensed by the health department. The names for the licenses vary, but these licenses are sometimes known as *certificates of qualification, food handler's permits,* or *food protection certificates.* Some municipalities issue identification cards instead of certificates so that individuals can carry them at all times. This format is especially valuable if an individual works in more than one location. Typically, at least one certificate holder must be on the premises during all business hours or during any food production times. In addition to taking a test that ensures knowledge of proper food-handling techniques, employees may be required to submit to a health check for highly communicable diseases such as tuberculosis and hepatitis.

Check out Chapter 17 for an overview of food safety concerns and details on creating a successful sanitation program in your restaurant to keep your customers safe and pass your health inspections with flying colors.

Paying attention to building codes

Before you can begin construction or remodeling of your new space, you need to get the appropriate building permits. Check with your contractor and attorney to make sure you have the appropriate paperwork in hand before starting construction.

After you finish construction, your local building department must issue your certificate of occupancy (CO) in order for you to open your doors. After you file your application for the certificate, an inspector from the building department visits your facility and makes sure the plans you filed correspond to the reality of the premises. If you pass, he issues your CO; if you don't, you'll be reinspected later to see whether you pass before the department issues your CO.

Be nice to your inspectors, but don't be too nice. It's absolutely no use, not a good idea, and, in fact, detrimental to your business to attempt to bribe or influence any inspectors. Be friendly and agreeable but always professional.

The certificate of occupancy shows the following:

- ✔ That you're in compliance with all building codes, which include things like having the right electrical systems and wiring and having ADA-compliant restrooms and entries
- ✔ That your facility conforms to current safety requirements, including having exit signs in the appropriate locations and not having any asbestos or lead paint on the premises
- ✔ That any modifications that you've made to your space are sufficient and appropriate for your new use of the space; typically, you must submit copies of your plans with your application for the inspector to review

Depending on the laws in your community, you may need another permit from the building department that stipulates that your building allows smoking. Discuss the details of your business with your attorney so that she can advise you on what paperwork you need for your business.

Considering fire codes and capacity

Before you open, you must also get a permit from the fire department. The fire marshal inspects your facility during and after construction to ensure that you have appropriate emergency exits, to determine maximum capacity, and to check all fire suppression systems.

Expect annual fire inspections, but you may need more frequent inspections. Coauthor Heather inadvertently set off a fire suppression system during training for her first management position. The system had to be reset, and the fire department had to fully inspect the system to ensure it was again in full working order before the restaurant could reopen. Your fire inspector verifies that all your fire extinguishers are in working order, too. Make sure that you locate them in handy places with their current inspection tags attached.

Some governmental agencies have overlapping oversight responsibilities. For example, your local building and fire departments likely both oversee structural and systemic building issues.

Checking out other permits

Depending on your local laws, you may need to get these official permits:

- ✔ **Employer tax ID:** This permit identifies you when you're paying employee taxes and other required fees.

- ✔ **Business license:** Every business owner has to have these permits in some communities.

- ✔ **Permit to collect state and/or local sales tax:** This permit has many names in various states, but don't forget to secure one for yourself.

- ✔ **Elevator:** You need to get annual inspections done if you have an elevator in your establishment.

  A *dumbwaiter* is considered an elevator. If you have one, make sure it gets inspected! But a dumb waiter has his ups and downs, too.

Depending on your business and concept, you may also have to get separate permits to operate specific parts of your business. Here are a few examples:

- ✔ A special license to sell specific food products, such as oysters

- ✔ An outdoor seating permit, which some areas require for outdoor dining

- ✔ A retail tobacco license if you sell cigars

- ✔ Permits for catered events outside of your premises

Taking up trademarks

As you build your business, you build your reputation. Customers come to understand your style of service, menu, and quality standards, and they have expectations when they step in the door. If you're successful, they associate all the terrific things about your restaurant with its name and its atmosphere.

The last thing you want someone to do is to sabotage your hard work by stealing your name and using it to open a restaurant.

Plan ahead and trademark your name, logo, tag lines, and so on. Get the proper paperwork to protect your intellectual property in your state and in the entire country.

An attorney can help you navigate through this confusing landscape. But to get started, incorporate your restaurant to make it a legal entity (we discuss incorporating earlier in the section "Playing it safe: The corporate entity"). Then check with the county or state governmental office that deals with trademarks to determine the protection you can obtain for your name, logo, and so on at the local level. Finally, check out the United States Patent and Trademark Office (USPTO) website at www.uspto.gov for info on establishing trademarks and to search the database of registered trademarks to see whether someone is already using your proposed name or logo.

Don't assume that because your future mark isn't listed that someone hasn't applied for it. The only way to be completely sure is to file your own application and get it approved.

After you're registered, you must protect your marks or risk abandoning them. Get your attorney to help you establish a strategy for maintaining your rights. You can also check out *Patents, Copyrights & Trademarks For Dummies,* 2nd Edition, by Henri J.A. Charmasson and John Buchaca (John Wiley & Sons, Inc).

Buying the Insurance You Need

The law requires you to obtain certain insurance, but other forms of insurance are optional. The amount of coverage you carry and the *deductible* (the amount you're required to pay before your insurance kicks in) you choose affects your *premiums* (the amount you pay for your insurance).

Talk with your insurance agent to find the best, most appropriate coverage for your business. Here's a list of common business insurance coverage:

- ✓ **Property:** Property insurance protects your property in the event of damage. Many policies cover only specific damages. You may want to consider other coverage, such as earthquake, flood, wind, and hail insurance, if those natural disasters are likely in your area.

- ✓ **General liability:** Liability insurance protects you in case someone sues you for something. For example, someone may file a lawsuit if he falls on the sidewalk outside your restaurant or claims that he got sick after eating in your restaurant.

You need to contact your insurance carrier for special events outside of your premises for appropriate coverage (even when participating in charity events). Check your lease for any required minimums for liability insurance and who is required to be covered. Your agent may have additional recommendations for how much liability insurance you should carry, based on the assets of your business.

✔ **Liquor liability:** When you get your liquor license, check with your local agency to see how much liquor liability insurance you need.

✔ **Automobile liability:** Automobile liability insurance covers any lawsuits that arise from an employee, including you, driving a company vehicle. Automobile liability may be covered in your general policy, but you may have to get a separate *rider,* or additional coverage, added to a larger policy.

✔ **Workers' compensation:** This insurance takes care of medical bills for employees injured on the job.

✔ **Unemployment insurance:** This insurance pays your out-of-work, ex-employees until they find another job.

The federal government requires you to have workers' compensation and unemployment insurance. Having the other forms of insurance on our list simply makes good business sense. Protect what you have with the right insurance. See your agent for the best coverage for you.

Consider protecting yourself with life insurance and long-term disability insurance as well. You or your heirs may need to pay someone to run your business if you're injured or killed in an accident. Having this kind of insurance can mitigate the extra expenses.

Also consider the following riders to your policy. Some types of coverage are available only in certain states or are available only for established restaurants, so check in your area to see whether these policies apply to you:

✔ **Employment practices liability:** This addition protects you against wrongful termination cases, sexual harassment suits, and so on.

✔ **Loss of business income:** This insurance enables you to recoup income if you lose sales through one of the covered causes.

✔ **Food contamination and spoilage:** This policy covers your losses if something like a lightning storm knocks out the electricity that powers your coolers and results in large-scale food spoilage or contamination.

✔ **Specific peril:** This policy addition covers flood, earthquake, or other weather-related perils.

Additional policies may seem attractive, but the premiums required are often much more expensive than standard insurance. Think of it like insuring your jewelry: You can add the jewelry rider to your homeowner's policy, but the cost of the insurance can be close to the cost of replacing that jewelry. Consider what you're saving and gaining by adding the coverage. Your insurance agent can help you weigh the pros and cons of additional coverage.

Part III

Preparing to Open the Doors

The 5th Wave   By Rich Tennant

©RICHTENNANT

JUST CAKES AND PIES AND ICE CREAM AND BURGERS & Deli Wraps

JUST CAKES

Coming Soon! SALAD BAR

In this part . . .

We cover all the tasks you need to take care of to make your idea a reality. In this part, you can find information, tips, and tricks on planning your menu; setting up your beverage program; designing your exterior, dining room, bar, and kitchen; negotiating with suppliers; setting up your office (including all the electronics); and implementing a marketing campaign, including information on using social media to build your customer base.

Chapter 8

Creating the All-Important Menu

The menu is the epicenter of your restaurant. *Everything* revolves around it: the ingredients you order every day, how you design your kitchen, which equipment you purchase, how you organize and train your staff, who your chef is or whether you have a chef at all, what selections are on your wine list, even the name of the restaurant. If the idea behind the menu wasn't the inspiration for your restaurant in the first place, you must focus on it now. Creating your menu should be fun.

As important as the menu is, flexibility should be a consideration in almost every choice made for it. Ultimately — and very important to know and accept —your diners, not you, will make the final decisions about what's on your menu based on their consistent purchases of some items and avoidance of others. In this chapter, we go over what you need to know to plan your restaurant's menu, from deciding on core items to determining its layout to deciding how often to change it.

Making Some Initial Decisions

Your menu should match your restaurant's *concept* (or theme) and atmosphere, your guest's expectations, and your kitchen's capacity to pull it all off. Toss out any items that don't. After you have a general idea of what you want to put on the menu, you must decide what makes the final cut. In this section, we get you started with your menu planning by tailoring your menu to your restaurant, your clientele, and your kitchen.

The basic premise "quantity doesn't necessarily equal quality" applies. Some of the most acclaimed restaurants in the world have modest-sized menus. Other concepts are based upon the diversity of their menus. Success or failure doesn't depend upon the size of a menu in general. How well the size of your menu works within your overall operation and connects with your guests determines your level of success.

The first thing you need to do is get together a core group of menu items that you think you want to serve based on your understanding of your concept and target guest (for info on this, see Chapters 2 and 3). The number of menu items you begin with depends on the approximate number you envision ending up with. As a general rule, start with three times as many items as you need. You can get a good core menu from this group, plus have some backup items ready when you need to revise.

Matching your menu to your concept

Do all your menu choices match the feel of the restaurant? Veal parmigiana may be your favorite dish, but having it on your Cuban restaurant menu doesn't make sense. Okay, maybe that example is too obvious, but you want guests to have a consistent experience the entire time they're in your restaurant. If your menu is inconsistent, now's the time to figure that out. Here are a few questions to get you thinking along a matching line:

- ✔ **Is your restaurant an ethnic restaurant?** If so, do all the dishes on the menu come from the culture or country that you're showcasing?

- ✔ **Is your restaurant themed?** For example, if you want to become known as the old-school Italian joint in your neighborhood, you may have decorated accordingly. Does your proposed menu match that theme, with spaghetti bolognese, lasagne, linguine with clams, and the like?

- ✔ **What's the atmosphere like?** Are you located just off the local walking trail? You may consider having a menu conducive to the activities going on around you. For instance, consider beefing up your takeout menu so people can grab snacks and bottled water and get back on the trail. But if you have white tablecloths and candles, you may want to skip the bottled-water display and offer a wine list to diners as they're seated.

- ✔ **What cycle of service are you planning to follow?** If you plan on finishing all dinners with a traditional Tuscan salad, you probably want to make that plain on the menu and consider adjusting your salad section accordingly. If you're strictly a dessert joint, you may want coffee drinks to play a starring role.

✔ **What are your hours of operation?** If you're open at 9 a.m., people will likely expect some breakfast items. But they'll be surprised to see a ham-and-cheese omelet on the menu of your martini bar.

✔ **Are you a drinking place that serves food or a food place that serves drinks?** That particular question doesn't have a right or wrong answer, but it's one that you should answer. And when we say *drinks,* we don't mean only those that contain alcohol; drinks can be smoothies, coffee, and/or anything else. If you're a bar and your goal is to sell drinks, you'll likely have a limited menu, with some munchies and some salty things, which make people — you guessed it — thirsty. You get the idea.

Considering customers: Feeding the need with an insights-driven menu

It isn't about you. Think about your restaurant from the diners' point of view. What would they expect and demand? How can you delight and surprise them? How can you keep them coming back for more? Map your menu to your clientele and their needs. See Chapter 3 for info on figuring out your customers, and take a look at a few questions to get you started:

✔ **Are you looking to lure in the lunch crowd?** Because lunch diners often take a break from their workdays to visit restaurants, they have less time to linger. Be sensitive to their need for speed and efficiency. If you want to be a big lunch stop, offer items that can get them in and out in 30 to 40 minutes. They'll appreciate the consideration and may make you a regular stop on their lunch hour.

✔ **Do you want to focus on takeout?** Takeout customers want convenience: easy menus, easy ordering, easy pickup. Consider *combo-ing* — creating a single menu item that actually includes several menu items. For example, maybe your roast-beef-sandwich combo includes a small salad and a drink. That way, they can order a whole meal with a single item. If you're planning on doing a lot of takeout business, have food that is portable and *holds* (stays fresh after it's cooked).

✔ **Are you meeting a specific health need?** Health-related food trends are on the rise. Whether it's born from an ethical cause (like vegetarianism) or a medical necessity (such as an allergy to gluten), many diners are looking for restaurants that meet their specific dietary needs.

✔ **Are you starting a family-style business?** Busy families turn to restaurants to give parents a cooking break. They want familiar, easy-to-eat items for their finicky pint-sized sidekicks. If you're targeting families, offer a few kid-friendly items or maybe a separate menu.

✔ **Do you want to be a destination?** People love to feel special, especially during a celebration in their honor. If you pride yourself on being a celebration or destination restaurant, make sure the customer-service touches complement your fantastic menu. Offer personalized menus for the guest of honor. Create a special dessert for celebrations. Give the party a behind-the-scenes tour of the restaurant. Do a follow-up call with them afterward. Find whatever works for your restaurant.

✔ **Is your food familiar to guests?** Consider how familiar the food is when determining the final menu. If you're going for eclectic (taking influences from many different sources or styles of cuisine) or haute (by which we mean *fancy* — haute is French for high cuisine), you probably want fewer items on the menu than you would if you were starting a diner or family restaurant. People will likely take longer with a menu full of items they're not familiar with.

Matching your menu to your kitchen

The size of your kitchen, its layout, the size of your coolers, and your dry-storage capacity all affect your menu. If you want to serve only from-scratch items, you need lots of refrigerated cooler space to store it. If you need to have 15 different kinds of ovens to produce the items on your menu, you have to determine whether you have the space (or budget) to accommodate them. Answer these questions early in your menu development process and save yourself hassle later on:

✔ **How big will your dining room be?** The size of your dining room dictates the amount of room for the kitchen and related storage space. Too much area dedicated to the dining room may severely limit what the kitchen can produce. You have to consider space for fixtures, equipment, storage, and maneuverability, but keep in mind that too much space in the kitchen can steal seating from the dining room and curtail revenue potential.

In general, restaurants use between 15 and 25 percent of their total space for kitchen space. The perfect balance depends upon what you do with the space in each. Take a look at Chapters 9 and 10 for dining room and kitchen layout and design tips.

✔ **Does your menu have a diversity of preparation techniques?** Assuming that you have several different *stations* (areas to prepare food, such as the grill and the fryer) in your kitchen, you want to have dishes with a diversity of prep techniques so that you maintain a balance of the number of dishes coming out of one station at a single time.

Finding a 57-burner range or managing that many sauté cooks in the kitchen at one time is difficult, so give the grill cook something to do. As they say, too many chefs spoil the sauté, er, soup. (For info on the different stations in a restaurant kitchen, take a peek at Chapter 10.) Of course, if your concept centers on a particular preparation technique, don't feel like you *must* diversify. A well-known restaurant concept fries chicken all day and all night. You can't argue with success!

✔ **Do your menu items have a consistent preparation time?** You want most items to be prepared in about the same amount of time. That way, all items are *fired,* or ordered to be cooked, at about the same time and come out at about the same time. Or if you have inconsistent preparation times, you can find ways to *par-cook* (partially cook) items so that some of the work is done early, and the dish is finished when it's fired.

✔ **Does your menu reflect a synergy of inventory?** Or more simply, do the items on your menu work well together and represent a modest, high-velocity inventory? For example, unless you're known for the variety of seafood you have available, you may want to just keep one variety of clams on the menu and use them for linguini and clam sauce as well as seafood stew. For tips on managing inventory, check out Chapter 13.

Cutting your chef (if you have one) in on the action

If you're opening a restaurant that requires a chef, you may choose to hire her before designing the menu. Or you may opt to hire a chef later and determine the appropriate candidate based upon her expertise in light of the menu. If you're the chef, even better. Either way, the chef will run the show and must be completely synchronized with how you want the menu to be executed. Take every step to ensure this eventuality. (For information on deciding whether you need a chef, check out Chapter 12.)

Test runs of all recipes with the chef are essential. You can do this in a test kitchen, in your home, or in the restaurant if you already have possession and the fixtures are in place. These very important sessions should occur as early in the process as possible. During testing, you'll likely decide to tweak some recipes or scrap ideas. You may even make an accidental discovery of a great menu item.

Test runs are an excellent time to get a good sense of how you and the chef will work together. They're not real-time scenarios because you don't have the stress involved with guests waiting in the dining room. But you do get a good idea of your chef's food philosophy, creativity, cleanliness, management style, and efficient work processes (or lack thereof). And you get a sense of how a chef deals with feedback, both positive and negative. These important attributes don't show up on a resume, so pay attention.

Figuring Out How Much to Charge

You can follow several different strategies when pricing a menu. No matter where you start, you'll end up with the old-fashioned, tried-and-true process of trial and error. Books such as this one can give you basic strategies, but ultimately, if your customers won't pay what you charge, you have a problem. Conversely, if they'll pay more than what you charge, you're missing an opportunity.

Several components determine menu price points, including consumer demographics, competition, and accepted standards. In the following sections, we help you fix your price points and get a handle on food costs and how they affect your menu prices. We even show you how to keep your menu priced to compete even when some of your costs don't cooperate.

Determining your menu price points

Price points are ranges of prices for types of menu items. For example, on your lunch menu, your sandwich price points may be between $4.95 and $7.95, and your salad price points may fall between $7.95 and $10.95. Using price points to determine your menu pricing is particularly useful (and darn near necessary) if you're entering a highly competitive market. For example, if you're opening a steakhouse in an area with several successful steakhouses, you have to pay diligent attention to the prices your competitors charge for what diners perceive to be similar products. If you're charging more for your product, you must establish a point of difference (in quality, atmosphere, service, and so on) to justify the price.

A consumer will pay more for quality food, but exactly how much more is a question that only the consumer can answer.

Determining your price points isn't an exact science, but asking yourself a few key questions may help you get started:

- ✓ **What type of clientele are you trying to attract?** Suppose that you want to be a family restaurant that serves lunch and dinner six to seven days a week. Create an atmosphere through your pricing that encourages people to eat there on a weeknight and bring the family for sustenance. If you've done your research and determined that you can't sell an entree that costs more than $12.95, stick with that plan even if it means you can't serve your personal favorite, filet mignon.

- ✓ **What are your competitors' price points?** Think about the $1 menu war waged by fast-food restaurants. Most have a $1 or 99¢ menu, but each restaurant varies the items on the list based on what it can sell at that price without losing money.

 ✔ **What price points are consistent with your atmosphere?** If you're open-ing a diner with counter service, you'll be hard-pressed to have many $20 items. When people pay $20 for an entree, they usually expect to sit down at a table with a tablecloth. They may also expect to be able to order a drink from the bar or a glass of wine. If your restaurant offers neither, you probably want to lower your price points.

 ✔ **What ingredient solutions can you find to help you serve the food you want and hit your price points?** Can you use less-expensive cuts of meat to produce wonderful flavors through braising? Can you menu a fantastic pot roast for $12.95? Because pot roast has a much lower food cost than your favorite filet, you have a much higher profit margin. You make more money and have a great beef dish on the menu.

Using food cost percentage to set prices

Your *food cost percentage* is the cost of all the ingredients used to make a dish (your *food cost* for that dish) divided by the menu price. It's a bench-mark you use to help control costs and gauge profitability.

Restaurants take in money when diners choose items from the menu and pay for them. This stream is your *only* source of revenue. Therefore, your menu prices have to cover the cost of the food you're serving, the wages of your employees, your rent and utilities, and most importantly, your profit. So when you're running a restaurant, you set a target food cost percentage to cover all your costs of doing business.

Most restaurants target food cost percentage somewhere between 20 and 40 percent, but your choice depends on a number of factors, including your overhead costs (like rent and utilities) and accepted pricing standards for your type of restaurant. To figure out your menu price of a particular item by using your food cost percentage, follow these steps (and see "Creating dishes and recipes and then costing them," later in the chapter, for more details):

1. **Find the food cost of the item.**

   Factor in all the raw ingredients costs associated with creating a dish, including any freebies like bread and salad (if these are complimentary in your establishment), to create your food cost.

2. **Divide the cost by your food cost percentage goal.**

   If you want to run a 30-percent food cost, a dish that costs you $3.75 in ingredients costs the customer $12.50: $3.75 ÷ 0.30 = $12.50.

At various food cost percentages, your prices would look like this:

Percentage	Food Cost	Menu Price
20	$3.75	$18.75
25	$3.75	$15.00
30	$3.75	$12.50
35	$3.75	$10.75
40	$3.75	$9.50
45	$3.75	$8.50
50	$3.75	$7.50

If you get your calculator out to check our math, you may notice that some of these percentages aren't exact. For example, a 40 percent food cost is actually $9.38, but that price would be, well, just weird to see on a menu.

Round up and end in 25¢ increments (like $12.50, $10.75, $15.00 and so on) or just shy of full-dollar increments (like $12.95). That way, guests can roughly add the prices in their heads.

At first glance, you may seem to be making a bundle on each dish. In our 30-percent food cost example, you net $8.75 for each person ordering the dish. But before you book your next Caribbean vacation, don't forget all the overhead required to run the restaurant. You have wages to pay — including the wages of the greeter (hostess or host), the server (yes, the guests tip them, usually, but you still pay them some wages), the dishwasher, the prep cooks, the bussers, the line cooks, the chef, your bar manager, the delivery guy . . . the list is almost endless. And that doesn't even begin to cover the utilities, rent, linen service, plant service, décor, cleaning service, and so on. And what happens when the guest doesn't get the dish he ordered or a waiter drops a plate full of food? Guess who eats that food cost? You do.

Food cost is only one part of the equation. Ultimately, the lower the food cost you can run, the better off you are. That way, you'll have more left over for the other percentages, like labor, overhead, and the like. But don't take the "lower the better" guideline as an absolute rule. The kind of food you serve and your atmosphere affect your food cost percentage, because they're key indicators of what prices your clientele expects to pay. If they expect shaved truffles in their risotto, the darn things are expensive enough (at $150 per pound) that you probably won't make a huge percentage off them, but you will make a decent dollar figure. Stay flexible!

In your drive to maintain low food costs, don't sacrifice your quality. Doing so will backfire on you eventually. As people see your quality deteriorate, they'll stop coming. Stay true to your concept and standards, but run an efficient business.

Creating dishes and recipes and then costing them

Go through each recipe and determine its food cost and food cost percentage (see the preceding sections). Determine whether those numbers meet your goals for the restaurant. If they do, keep them. If they don't, toss them. If you still want to keep them, see whether you can adjust portion sizes and ingredients to bring the costs in line with your goals for the restaurant.

In this first scenario, you pick some recipes, test them (check out "Cutting your chef (if you have one) in on the action" earlier in this chapter), create standardized recipes, and then cost your menu. Follow these steps:

1. **Add the costs of the components that go into a single serving of your dish.**

   So if you're serving pasta with marinara sauce, maybe an 8-ounce portion of pasta for each serving costs you approximately $0.50.

   A single serving of made-from-scratch marinara sauce costs you approximately $0.85, so you're up to $1.35 per serving.

   And if you use ½ ounce of Parmesan cheese on each serving, add $0.25. Now you're looking at $1.60 per serving.

2. **Include garnishes in the food cost.**

   A little sprinkle of parsley costs around $0.10, so your current total is $1.70 for this dish.

3. **Add in the costs of any complimentary items that each customer enjoys to the food cost for each entree.**

   If you serve bread and butter to each guest, add $0.50 to the food cost. Also, add an additional 5 to 10 percent of your current total ($2.20) to cover things like foil, plastic wrap, beverage napkins, stir sticks, and sugar packets, bringing your grand total for the food cost of this dish to $2.42.

This process is for costing one recipe. It tells you how much money you spend for the raw materials to put a dish on a plate and serve it to a guest. Determining the complete food cost percentage picture for your restaurant overall requires you to look further at your inventory to determine the extent of wasted food (which occurs when food spoils, is dropped, or is overportioned, meaning, for example, cutting a 10-ounce filet instead of the 8-ounce portion specified on the menu). You also need to consider factors such as miscooked food that must be cooked again or losses from theft. For details on gauging your restaurant's food cost percentage, check out Chapter 19.

Dealing with price fluctuations

There are no guarantees in the restaurant business, and the price you pay for your products is no exception. Even if you negotiated the best possible pricing with your *purveyors* (suppliers), some products vary in price almost every time you order them. This variation can wreak havoc with your precisely laid-out food cost percentages and menu pricing. But never fear, because we have some strategies for dealing with these situations on your menu:

- ✔ **Use a "market price" designation in place of an actual price on the menu.** This strategy is acceptable for items such as seafood, imported items (like truffles), or seasonal or specialty produce (like broccoli rabe or wild leeks with very limited availability) that can have very large price swings (multiple dollars per pound). Normally, you communicate the daily market price to your staff, and your staff passes it along to your diners.

- ✔ **Create a cost factor based on the worst-case scenario and price accordingly.** If you know that tenderloin is $9 per pound during the holiday season but $7.50 per pound the rest of the year, cost your menu as if tenderloin costs $9 per pound year-round and price your item to fall within your margins. When tenderloin is cheaper, you make more, but you can still keep it available year-round.

   Items that experience massive price swings, such as lobster, aren't good choices for this strategy. You could be cheating yourself out of revenue (and profits) because the highs are too high for your clientele but the lows are just right.

- ✔ **Print your menu daily.** This is a great choice if you have the capability to do it on site and you have many items with prices that fluctuate. Printing your menu daily is much easier than having a hostess or server rattle off the prices of 15 fish entrees to each table.

- ✔ **Deal with it.** Maybe the most common strategy for handling price changes is just dealing with it. This strategy is particularly effective when the price increase is only temporary (expected to last only a couple of weeks) or it affects smaller components of your menu. For example, maybe a light freeze occurred in the citrus-growing states, and the immediate crop of lemons was damaged. As a result, for a week or two, your lemon costs double. You probably don't want to change your menu prices to account for the difference; the costs will return to normal soon.

Mixing your menu to meet an overall percentage goal

Not all dishes will come out to a perfect food cost percentage; some will have a higher percentage, and others will be lower. Make sure that you sell the right amount of each, called a *menu mix,* to maintain your overall food cost percentage goals.

Check out Table 8-1 to see how this works. You may set the restaurant's food cost percentage goal at 27 percent and achieve it with an overall food cost percentage of 26.8 percent. But notice that you don't set the price for each and every entree at an exact 27 percent food cost. Instead, you *weight* your prices (price some a little higher and some a little lower) to achieve your overall goal. If you sell 20 steaks for $20 each at a 35 percent food cost, 40 orders of pasta with marinara for $16 at 25 percent food cost, and so on, you'll end up with a food cost well under your goal.

To figure your overall food cost, take your total cost from all items sold and divide it by the total revenue from the items sold. For details on creating a detailed menu mix analysis, see Chapter 20.

Table 8-1				Sample Menu Mix Analysis		
Item	**Number Sold**	**Menu Price**	**Food Cost**	**Total Revenue (Number Sold × Price)**	**Total Cost (Number Sold × Food Cost)**	**Food Cost %**
New York Strip	20	$20	$7	$400	$140	35%
Pasta	40	$16	$4	$640	$160	25%
Salmon	15	$18	$4	$270	$60	22%
Chicken	30	$16	$4	$480	$120	25%
Total				**$1,790**	**$480**	**26.8%**

Don't be afraid to include some dishes that are trendy, local, or just cool and that don't fit the food cost percentage mold. Experimenting is a good thing. But remember: Your overall menu should be priced so that the overall cost of the items you actually sell balances out to achieve desired food cost percentage. So the 25 percenters and the 40 percenters should balance out.

Deciding When to Change Your Menu

Even franchises change their menus, in large part because of an increasingly savvy dining public. With more people going out to dinner more often, the question isn't *whether* you're going to change your menu but *when*. In this section, we discuss various times to change your menu and ways to let your customers know what's new.

Staying flexible when you first open

Give your menu a chance to work. After a change or new opening, allow at least a couple of weeks or maybe a month to let people get familiar with your offerings, try out several different things, and establish favorites. Watch for trends at different times of the day and different meal periods. If your appetizers are selling better at lunch than at dinner, try to figure out why.

Don't get locked into a *tiered menu pricing system* (requires all appetizers to be x, all entrees to be y, and so on) with no room for change. If your appetizer list is really working well but no one is interested in ordering the crab-stuffed mushrooms, consider dropping the price by a buck or so. Be open to that possibility. Ultimately, diners determine what works and what doesn't based on their willingness to buy menu items.

Revisiting your menu later on

When you change your menu, you're trying to capture that new prospective diner and keep him coming to your restaurant while keeping your signature dishes that made you successful to begin with. Here are a few reasons you may want to change your menu:

✔ **Keep up with rising (or falling) trends and competition in dining:**
Being at the forefront of the wraps trend was great, but if you're still tied to it, that's not so good. If the steakhouse down the street is packing them in and your steakhouse is empty, figure out why. Look at your competitor's menu and analyze what it's doing right and wrong. You can capitalize on its mistakes and improve on its successes.

✔ **Adjust for seasonality:** You may want to take advantage of the seasonal produce and other items. Or if you live in an area that sees dramatic climate changes, consider embracing the way dining habits change with the seasons. So in July, you may include a gazpacho (a light, fresh, cold veggie soup) on your menu but replace it with beef stew in October. Seasonality dramatically affects top-end restaurants, but it's less important if you don't promise fresh items to your diners.

✔ **Generate new excitement within your concept:** You always want to "dance with the one that brung ya." But you can still try new items. If the name of your restaurant is Andy's Big Taco Shack, don't put lasagne on the menu just because you read an Italian cookbook this week. Instead, consider adding a taco bowl or a shredded beef option to your taco menu. You can also make these changes to showcase trendy, new, popular ingredients; celebrate holidays; or commemorate local activities.

Very seldom do you ever want to change the entire menu. In fact, we can't think of a single time when you'd change it all at once. Changing an entire menu isn't effective. Your regular patrons walked in your door for a reason. They probably developed favorites and may not come back if they can't get them. Plus, changing an entire menu isn't efficient; many hidden costs are associated with changing your menu, including testing and tasting new recipes, reprinting the menu, retraining your staff (both kitchen and floor), retooling your processes, and reprogramming your ordering system. Although how much you change at once ultimately depends on factors such as your appetite for retraining the entire staff, we recommend changing only three to five items at a time.

Offering specials

Restaurants run *specials* (items with temporary availability or pricing) for three big reasons:

✔ **To showcase limited availability and truly special things:** Maybe you can order Copper River salmon (wild Alaskan salmon available only a few months each year) and want to offer it to your customers.

✔ **To create efficiency within your inventory by reducing waste from perishables that go bad before they're sold:** Specials can repurpose these ingredients at a discounted price to sell them before they perish.

Never use specials as the last stop before the trash. If you're concerned that a perishable may have already perished, toss it. Don't risk making someone sick and ruining your reputation just to save a few bucks. When in doubt, throw it out!

> ✔ **To promote your favorite, high-margin items:** You can offer items at a discount, hoping to increase customer counts and increase profits. You can even create a regular weekly schedule for specials (Thursday is chimichanga day, for example) so diners know what to expect and put you on their calendar.

One added benefit of changing the menu is that the change gets your staff excited. Consider giving your cooks or culinary team an opportunity to create items when you plan on offering specials or doing a menu revision. They get a chance to be creative, which usually increases morale. (For more on motivating employees, check out Chapter 16.)

Highlighting new news

Having a forum to regularly introduce new menu items, new promotions, or new services to your guests is vital. This provides a mechanism for your concept to evolve and improve your connection to the guest. Additionally, it provides guests with a reason to come back.

Communicate news by using a variety of integrated marketing tactics, including website, direct-mail, social media, point-of-purchase (including server recommendations), and yes, the good old menu to showcase your new introductions and reach the maximum amount of potential guests regardless of where they receive their information from. Take a peek at the later section "Validating Your Menu before You Go Primetime" for tips on using in-restaurant interviews to test new menu ideas.

Choosing Your Menu Format

Designing the menu on paper can be fun and challenging. You must balance artistic creativity with informational considerations in the design. Today, with simple software available, you can create new and attractive menus quite easily, every day or even every meal. But be careful. You don't want to change the menu *style* day to day. Your customers will note the change, which takes away from the familiarity you hope they develop.

If you don't want to invest in software specifically for menu development, consider using a program such as Microsoft Word or Microsoft Publisher. Both have a decent selection of templates, fonts, and graphics that add a professional touch to your printed menus without costing much, and both are fairly easy to use. If you need help getting started, check out the latest version of *Word 2010 For Dummies,* by Dan Gookin, or *Microsoft Office 2010 For Dummies,* by Wallace Wang (both published by John Wiley & Sons, Inc).

After you know what to put on the menu, you must put pen to paper (or fingers to keyboard). Whenever possible, keep your menu-printing options open. If you have the means and expertise on staff to print your menus yourself, do it. You'll likely save money, be able to fix errors and price fluctuations immediately, and make changes on *your* schedule, not the printer's.

If you're new to the business or you don't consider yourself a desktop publishing whiz, consider hiring a firm to design your menu for you. If you had an outside firm design a company logo or signage, ask whether it provides menu services as well. The firm may be able to help you with layout and set up a template so you can still maintain some independence to print your menu daily. Also check with other restaurant owners for suggestions for menu design firms.

Whether you design the menu yourself or hire someone else to do it, use the information in the following sections to get started and make decisions on the design.

Counting your main menu options

Most restaurants use a main menu and a supporting cast (like table tents, beer lists, wine lists, and takeout menus). As you develop your menu, consider which format best serves your diners' needs, matches the feel of your restaurant, and adequately showcases the items on your menu. An outdoor café, for example, may choose a one-pager, because the café offers a few simple items that diners are familiar with. A family-style diner may pick the multipage menu to show that it has something for everyone. And a Chinese takeout place may opt for the centralized menu to quickly move diners through the ordering process.

One-page menus

A one-page menu (or *one-pager*), which can be one- or two-sided, is commonplace in restaurants of every size, shape, and service level. These menus contain all the restaurant's offerings, from appetizers and salads to entrées, desserts, and beverages. They offer several advantages:

- ✔ **Flexibility:** You can easily revise or update one-pagers without generating huge amounts of paper or going to a professional printer.

- ✔ **Simplicity:** They provide the guest with a simple and quick tool to guide her through the meal. Diners appreciate uncluttered menus that are straightforward and make the selection process smooth.

- ✔ **Quicker orders:** A menu that's easy and quick for the customer to read cuts down on her perusal time, which means you may be able to turn over the table more quickly. If you can seat more customers during a given dinner shift, you can make more money in the same amount of time for about the same overhead.

Quick turnovers are ideal (even essential) for just about any restaurant, with two notable exceptions: high-end-casual and fine-dining restaurants. If you don't encourage multiple courses or offer an extensive wine list, you make your money on the number of people you bring through the door each and every meal period. Turn 'em and burn 'em.

If you want to make sure a guest *doesn't* come back, make him feel rushed, like he's not welcome to linger as long as he wants. Making diners feel rushed or hurried is usually not a good idea. Your goal is to make it easy for them to get in and get out, without making them feel like you *want* them to get in and get out. A well-designed menu can help you strike this delicate balance. (For more on building a clientele, check out Chapter 18.)

Consider the complexity of your food when you choose your menu format. Although a one-page menu can prove advantageous for many restaurants, it does have a few downsides:

- ✔ **Space:** It reduces the space that you may use to explain a particular dish to your customer. We've had customers say, "I had no idea that the Cajun Grilled Catfish with Creole Rémoulade would be spicy."

- ✔ **Lack of variety:** A limited number of offerings may turn off some diners who choose restaurants because of the variety they offer. If you limit yourself to one page, you probably won't draw in those diners.

Multipage menus

A multipage menu consists of — you guessed it — more than one page. For example, it may include a page for appetizers, soups, and salads; another page for house specialties and entrees; and a third for desserts. This format offers the following advantages:

- ✔ **Details:** A longer format or multipage menu offers your guest a more detailed look inside your menu. You can list key ingredients and cooking methods if they aren't apparent in the name of the dish itself.

- ✔ **Busy work:** Multipagers can also provide a conversational icebreaker at a table or just enough literary substance for an on-time diner waiting for a tardy guest.

But every yin has its yang, and multipage menus have some drawbacks:

- ✔ **Intimidation factor:** Some patrons complain of the intimidation factor of a big menu. "There are just too many choices. I can't decide!"

- ✔ **Production issues:** Although you can print multipagers yourself, doing so is also multi-difficult. You must take special care to ensure all the old pages are replaced by all the new pages. Embarrassing customer moment #343: "Why is the dessert page between appetizers and entrees?" Also, the difficulty in producing and maintaining these menus will likely decrease your flexibility and increase costs in revising the menu.

Centralized menu

You may recognize the centralized menu from your favorite fast-food restaurant or coffee shop. Any establishment that has a single menu posted in a central location has a centralized menu. Usually, the order taker is also the cashier. Your diners order, pay for their meals, and then receive their meals.

This style of menu may be the way to go, thanks to the following advantages:

- ✔ **Ease of setup and maintenance:** You set the menu up once. When you change it, you change it once. No printing, no wiping down food spills.

- ✔ **Quick ordering:** People peruse the menu while they stand in line to order and then make quick selections when their turn comes up.

But the centralized menu doesn't work for everyone; here's why:

- ✔ **Limited space to explain menu items:** Because you're likely just starting out, your customers may need a little more guidance and explanation of menu items.

- ✔ **Doesn't match the atmosphere:** Unless you're running a quick-service restaurant of some kind, this style of menu may be off-putting to diners. As with just about everything we mention in this book, make sure that your menu decisions are consistent with the feel of your restaurant.

Although many very successful chains and franchises have adopted a centralized menu, don't take your imitation of it too far. Other restaurants may be able to get away with centralized menus, sometimes showcasing just new items, but you probably won't. They rely on brand identity, the diners' familiarity with their menu offerings, and longevity of their product lines to lead diners to their menu selection.

Considering additional presentations

Most restaurants don't rely on a single kind of menu to address the needs of every diner. They often supplement the dining experience with other formats. Take a look at the following sections and decide whether your establishment could benefit from these hard workers of the restaurant world.

Table tents and special boards

Table tents and special boards serve the same purpose with slightly different formats. A *table tent* becomes part of the table decor and is typically multi-sided, offering everything from an advertisement of special events to drink specials to chef's specials to, in rare cases, the entire menu. You may even consider it a one-pager in its crudest form.

Special boards are large chalk, marker, or electronic boards used to display specials. They sometimes morph into encompassing the entire menu. Place them in a prominent spot where customers can view them with ease. You may want the waiters to bring the board to the table and explain it there (or just leave it!).

Special boards are handy because they're easy to change, but as a rule, the simpler, the better. Make the information large and clear enough that people can easily read it with just a few items.

Takeout/delivery menus

Takeout menus are particularly handy because guests can take them out, you can give them out, and so on. Many people collect them, so they have the menus on hand when making decisions on where to dine or order takeout. Takeout menus are great marketing items. Always have your address, phone number, and fax number on them. If diners can place orders at your website, include that address as well.

If you have items on your regular menu that aren't available for takeout, do not, we repeat, do *not* put them on your takeout menu. Most people assume that they can call in an order and come in to pick it up, or have it delivered, when they see the item on a takeout menu. If they choose a selection from your menu that can't be carried out, they get grumpy. You've now taken a prime opportunity to make a sale and blown it by frustrating your diner.

Navigating legal nutritional information requirements

In 2010, the U.S. federal government signed into law the Federal Patient Protection and Affordable Care Act. This law includes a nutrition disclosure provision (in Section 4205) that amends the federal Food, Drug and Cosmetic Act and requires restaurants, retail food establishments, and vending machines with 20 or more locations to provide specific nutrition labeling information.

Though this legislation was largely targeted at chain restaurants, all restaurateurs need to remain informed about the specific regulations that affect their operations on a state, county, or local level. Regulating and legislating menu and other controls on restaurants are political hot-buttons and likely will be in the foreseeable future. Be intimately aware of how nutritional labeling legislation affects your operation right now, in your county, in your state, and in your town.

If you want to keep your finger on the pulse of the debate, we suggest you visit `www.restaurant.org/advocacy` or `www.cspinet.org` for perspectives on both sides of the issues affecting the restaurant industry.

Selling the Sizzle: Setting Up a Menu with Sales in Mind

You can have the best food on the block, the most knowledgeable staff, and the best beer, but if diners don't order the high-margin items on your menu, you're missing a huge revenue opportunity. In this section, we show you how to lay out your menu and describe the items on it the most effective way.

Directing eyes with menu engineering

Menu engineering is the strategy of laying out your menu to encourage diners to order the food you want them to buy, usually your highest-margin items. The location of an item on the menu, highlighting, graphics, and formatting all have an effect on your customers and the choices they make.

Think about going to a grocery store. Grocery stores put the things they want to sell you in the most accessible, most visible locations, usually at the ends of aisles or at eye level on the shelves. On menus, the first place the diner looks is the middle of the upper half of the menu (see Figure 8-1).

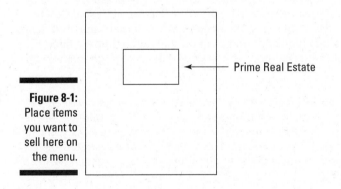

← Prime Real Estate

Figure 8-1:
Place items
you want to
sell here on
the menu.

One emerging technology that's beginning to impact restaurant menu engineering is the science of *eye-tracking*, the study of where people look first when confronted with new stimuli. This technology has been used for several years to guide website developers and software engineers, automotive designers, and advertising creatives in the placement of information. In the restaurant business, several large chains use eye-tracking to study the most impactful place on the menu to locate their most appealing, high-margin items. And the results indicate that diners first gaze at the center of the menu first. So when you're laying out your menu or your wine list, place your best, most craveable, most profitable selections right in the bulls-eye.

Understand the "power of three." If you have something you want people to buy, put two similar items on either side of it. Price one higher and one lower. They'll go for the middle-priced one all night long. For example, if you have three sizes of the same cut of steak, your menu may look like this:

Petite-Cut Rib-eye (8 ounces)	$9.95
House Rib-eye (10 ounces)	$10.95
Grande Rib-eye (12 ounces)	$12.95

You're practically guaranteed to sell more House Rib-eyes than either the Petite or Grande.

Getting people salivating: Considering visual representation on the menu

Some segments of the industry use pictures extensively to boost the sales of certain products. Family Dining (Denny's, IHOP, Perkins) and Casual Dining (Applebee's, TGI Fridays, Chili's) are segments that use large, laminated main menus and other special menus offering promotional items that are filled with professionally shot (and often highly stylized) images of the menu items they want you to buy.

In one chain we worked with extensively, the difference in sales between pictured and nonpictured items was tenfold. Yep, pictured items sold *ten times* more often than nonpictured options in the same menu category. As you can imagine, we included pictures of new signature dishes that *we* wanted the guests to try or pictures of our highest-margin items that our *accountants* wanted the guests to try.

Other industry segments like quick-service-restaurants (fast food) use pictures of their menus on large, backlit reader boards (called *translights*) in the restaurant or on in-store point-of-purchase materials and signs. The more upscale you go, the less likely you are to see photos. Photos are in the wheelhouse of concepts that have fairly fixed menus, drive-throughs with limited time to order, and/or a clientele more comfortable with pictures than fancy food speak.

Menu photography is not a DIY opportunity for you and your pocket digital camera. We've seen it done, and in each case, the operator would've been better off leaving the pictures out. Blurry, poorly lit, photos make any food appear uninviting. Skilled women and men out there have dedicated their entire education and professional careers to the art and science of styling, lighting, and photographing food, so use them.

Money for ink: Using lingo that sells

A few choice words can improve the perceived value of your menu items, which means you can charge more money and have more money in your pocket. When coming up with your own menu descriptions, think about these questions:

- ✔ **What's in the dish?** Great ingredients make for great descriptions. Are there any standouts or hard-to-find items? Does a dish contain seasonal items that you should highlight?

- ✔ **How is it prepared?** Many great menu items start with the preparation method. Words like *braised, seared, pan-fried, oven-roasted, wood-fired,* and *poached* lend another level of prestige to a dish that increases a diner's perception of the value of it.

- ✔ **Why is it unique?** Is your beef *aged to perfection?* Are your eggs *farm fresh?* Is your bread *baked in-house each morning?* Is your produce *locally grown* or *organic?*

- ✔ **Where do the ingredients come from?** *Kansas City* beef and *New Zealand* rack of lamb mean something to people.

- ✔ **Do all the foods in a dish share a theme?** Maybe you include an autumn root vegetable soup, an Asian chicken salad, or New England clambake on your menu. Use commonalities (seasonal, ethnic, geographic, and so on) to describe and name menu items.

- ✔ **Can you be more specific?** Sure you're serving *pasta,* but what kind of pasta? Say whether it's *fettuccine, linguine, capellini,* or *radiatore.* And that *sauce* you're serving tonight is probably great, but be more descriptive — *ragout, coulis, demi-glace,* or *reduction,* for example. Getting down to specifics has the dual advantage of providing more information and enhancing the diner's perception of the dish.

Never, ever mistake creative menu writing for misleading the diner or outright lying. If you're cooking pizzas on a standard conveyer oven, don't menu them as *wood-fired pizzas.* Or if you deep-fry your shrimp, don't say they're sautéed.

Diners will know the difference and feel cheated. Not only will you lose customers, but you could also be subject to legal action, including heavy fines for misrepresentation or fraud.

Validating Your Menu before You Go Primetime

With advancements in technology have come amazing new ways to validate your restaurant's menu before it even goes to print. Here's how to test your menu before you roll it out:

- ✔ **Online concept testing:** Type "online concept testing restaurant" into a search engine, and you quickly find a number of firms that specialize in retail product testing and validation, including restaurant menu items. Formal testing through a service involves posting pictures and menu descriptions of prospective dishes for review by a set of carefully screened respondents who provide feedback on the dishes.

- ✔ **In-restaurant intercepts (interviews):** In an *intercept* testing format, an interviewer somewhere in your restaurant directly engages (or *intercepts*) your diners, usually before or after they eat. Again, you can have a firm that specializes in this type of first-person research conduct the test and prepare the results, or you can conduct it yourself with relative ease.

- ✔ **Focus groups:** Whether you spend $60,000 or $600 dollars on the research, well-planned focus groups are the best way to gain actionable first-hand knowledge to predict the success or failure of potential menu items. No major restaurant chain makes a menu move without them. Tons of firms specialize in conducting focus groups, and many individuals have specific training in how to moderate these encounters between operator and guest. The problem for the average restaurant operation is that formal, professional focus groups are very expensive.

Chapter 9

Setting Up the Front of the House

The *front of the house* (or FOH) is restaurant lingo for any place a guest has access. The FOH includes the dining room, bar, restroom, banquet room, lobby, and exterior. These areas set the mood, set your guests' expectations, and set you apart from your competition. Spend some quality time developing the environment and atmosphere that you want your diners to experience. The front of the house is your face to the world. Show them your best.

In this chapter, we help you figure out what you want from your restaurant design and decide whether you need help. Then we take you through a tour of the inside and outside of your restaurant to help you decide what needs work. Finally, we go over two things you may not think of as part of the FOH but which are essential to creating a good impression on your clients: your wait stations and your reservations systems (if you choose to have one).

If you're planning on incorporating a bar into your concept or opening a bar without a restaurant, take a look at Chapter 11. Because the bar is a key part of some restaurants and nonexistent in others, we separate the details about bars and put them all together there.

Digging into Design

Design and décor often impact the success of a restaurant. They provide a basis for diners to form initial expectations about your concept and the experience it'll provide. You have two missions: Provide a design and décor that accurately convey what you want your concept to be, and then live up to the expectations they set. If you have stylish décor, your customers may not be surprised to find $40 entrees on your menu.

Remember, throwing money at the design doesn't make it good. Anything you do must fit your concept. When thinking about design, make sure it's

- **Flexible:** Make sure that the design is flexible and can be updated. If you're adding a wall to separate a dining room, consider making it a movable (or *re*movable) wall to keep your options open.

- **Comprehensive:** Be sure that your design covers all the bases, including furniture, floor tile, the ceiling, and ceramics. Small touches can make a huge impact.

Address all five senses: smell, taste, sight, hearing, and touch. The menu covers taste and smell, and sight is usually the focal point of interior design and appropriate lighting, but don't forget about sound and feel to complete the experience. How many times have you heard that music sets the tone? Music should be conceptually and time-of-day appropriate. Remember to adjust the volume as needed.

The sense of feel speaks to comfort. If you don't have enough capacity to cool your guests on a hot summer's day, they'll find a place that does. Likewise, make sure you choose suitably comfortable furniture. People won't stick around if your chairs are uncomfortable, but you don't want them falling asleep in their soup, either.

- **Coherent:** Confirm that the design will fit in with dinnerware, glassware, silverware, and your menu. For example, if you're serving Chinese food, you don't want a Moroccan motif. Also, make sure your chosen design works both inside and out. We discuss the exterior later in "Thinking outside the Box: The Exterior."

- **Practical:** Make sure the designer considers all the front of the house spaces and the flow between them before implementing the design.

Also, only select dinnerware, glassware, silverware and linens that can stand up to the rigors of a commercial restaurant setting. We've seen numerous newbie restaurateurs select the latest, avant-garde china from retail boutiques only to have it chip, break, or fade after only a few shifts in the restaurant. Remember, just because it looked really cool at your sister's Oscar party doesn't mean that plate can withstand being handled hundreds of times and endure a harsh environment of bus pans, plate warmers, and commercial dish machines. An experienced restaurant supply company or designer can offer suggestions and help you weigh the pros and cons of almost any purchase. Take this advice to heart before choosing your stuff.

In the following sections, we discuss types of design professionals you may want to hire and how to find good candidates.

Weighing going green with making green

Consider how an eco-friendly design works for your concept. These days, designers can utilize elements that lower electricity and water use, HVAC costs, trash expenses, and so on. Some restaurants make their reputations by attracting customers based on sustainability measures. Many large chain restaurants, including Wendy's, McDonald's, and Darden restaurants (Olive Garden, Red Lobster, Longhorn Steakhouse), released press releases on opening LEED-certified (Leadership in Energy and Environmental Design) stores.

But make sure that before you deploy these elements, you've considered all the costs involved. You have to balance the costs of using eco-friendly disposables and design with the financial return on investment. Absorbing these costs is very tough in a highly competitive marketplace because you often can't pass them on to the guest.

Not everyone needs to worry about design. If your margins are low to begin with and your concept doesn't require a particular ambience, don't spend a lot on your restaurant's design. For example, if you specialize in takeout, focus on speed and efficiency in your kitchen and in the front of the house. Maybe your FOH just consists of a few chairs with or without tables so people can sit while waiting on you to finish their orders.

If you're taking over an existing successful restaurant, consider whether you want to change the look at all. If the design is working, consider how the décor benefits the atmosphere and decide whether your changes are improvements or may negatively impact your diners' expectations.

Identifying pros who can help

If you're interested in creating a particular atmosphere or maintaining a theme throughout, a good interior designer, architect, and/or contractor can help you accomplish your goals. We say *can* because, depending on the state of the existing space, your budget, and your concept, you may want to perform many of the functions these pros provide on your own (or skip them entirely). But whether your restaurant is upscale, fine dining, casual, or quick service, these professionals can help you make choices to deliver a consistent experience throughout your establishment.

We discuss designers, architects, and contractors in the following sections. Be prepared to be the mediator if you're working with more than one of these folks. They may all have different priorities, but you have the final say.

Drawing out the designers

Look for an interior designer who can implement your vision — someone who can hear your thoughts and turn them into the restaurant of your dreams. Walk through your space with the designer. Give the designer a budget and your vision and see what she can come up with. Or have several designers compete with each other by asking them to present sketches and bid on the job before you make a selection.

Your design must convey the concept, but it must balance with functionality. Walk through the theoretical design as the guests will walk through it to picture their experience. You don't necessarily need a designer that exclusively designs for restaurants, but if you don't have a lot of restaurant experience, such a designer can help, particularly in mapping out functionality — the path guests will take, how deliveries will come in, the flow of staff members, which soft surfaces can absorb sound, and what furniture looks great but can take the wear and tear your guests will give it.

Make sure that the designer coordinates her work with any architects and contractors; the last thing you want is the beautiful fireplace to bellow smoke into the dining room because the new flue didn't make it to the contractor's to-do list.

A new trend in restaurants is for kitchens to be partially or fully open to public view. As a result, interior designers may be involved with restaurant kitchen design. But in most cases, their decisions are secondary to those of the kitchen designer, who's charged with creating an efficient, workable kitchen. A kitchen, no matter how open, isn't technically part of the front of the house, but the design matters here more than ever.

Accessing architects

An architect is like the interior designer, but he deals in the structure of your space rather than the accessories. Many design firms have architects on staff and vice versa. Usually, you select a single firm, and it provides both types of resources as you need them.

Architects are essential if you're putting a restaurant or other commercial space in what used to be a house or other nontraditional space. They can help you reinforce the floors to hold commercial equipment, widen stairs if necessary (for traffic flow and safety reasons), and make sure your restrooms are up to code as well as aesthetically pleasing. Additionally, if you need any structural changes, you must have an architect to sign off on them.

If you're located in a historic area, an architect familiar with your neighborhood can help ensure that your design is consistent with the integrity of the neighborhood. Preemptively plan your design with the neighborhood in mind. If you don't, you may get tied up in bureaucratic meetings and other red tape and end up where you should have started: with a harmonious design.

Coming up with contractors

Basically, a *general contractor (GC)* supervises construction work at your site. A good general contractor can spot practical flaws in the design and suggest workarounds. He's charged with keeping *subcontractors* (such as carpenters, electricians, and plumbers) on schedule and monitoring their workmanship.

If your contractor has restaurant experience, he'll be a huge asset to the process. Contractors should be familiar with all building and fire codes and maybe even health codes related to building issues, such as electrical requirements to maintain cooler temperatures required to hold foods at the proper temperatures while opening and closing walk-in doors all day. Don't attempt to be the general contractor unless you have the required experience.

Getting the scoop on potential pros

Your design professionals are only as good as the projects they complete on time, on budget, and to the agreed-upon specifications. Check references, look at completed projects, and talk with satisfied clients. Here are a few ways to find good professionals:

- ✔ If you go into a restaurant and love the ambience, ask the manager or owner whether he'd recommend the designer. If the design is great but you find out that the designer is habitually late or a bit flaky, you may want to keep looking. But take this advice with a grain of salt. You don't want to be too cynical, but consider the manager's motivation for helping you if you're going to be a competitor.

- ✔ The Internet can help you make your first steps toward finding an architect, designer, or a contractor. Websites may be more helpful in ruling out certain businesses than in actually choosing a designer. Use websites to compile a list of a few firms you'd like to interview and collect bids from. Look at websites of restaurants similar to your concept. If a site has pictures of the interior and exterior of a restaurant, use those pictures to virtually visit that restaurant. If you like what you see, ask who the designer is.

Never base your decision entirely on what you see on the Internet. Anyone can design a site with flashy graphics and a fake client list. Check the references and confirm with clients who had projects similar to yours.

✔ Contact the American Society of Interior Designers (www.asid.org) for members in your area.

✔ Check your potential contract employees out with the Better Business Bureau. Doing so seems like a small thing, but it can make a huge difference. If you find out that they left the last three clients high and dry with no completed design, think twice before signing on the dotted line.

✔ If a contractor claims to be a member of a particular organization, check it out. Professional trade organizations often license their members.

Anytime you deal with consultants or other contract workers, get the detailed terms of your agreement in writing. Always have a timeline for finishing work, with a financial penalty if the work isn't completed on time. Every day their schedules lag is a day that you're not open, not bringing in revenue, and not turning a profit. Be fair with these workers, but don't let them run the show. You're the customer, and your business is affected by how well they run theirs.

Thinking outside the Box: The Exterior

The exterior sets the tone for the interior and atmosphere. The exterior of your restaurant is your first impression to the public. Depending on what the exterior looks like, potential diners may never make it through the front doors. Take your exterior seriously, or you risk failure before you start.

Here are a few points to ponder regarding your exterior:

✔ **Announce the concept with appropriate logos and signage.** Think about what works for your concept. Do you need signs that people can see (and read) from miles away? Are you located in an urban area with lots of foot traffic and in need of eye-level signage?

One of our (Heather's and Andy's) favorite local Mexican joints announces its presence to the world with a huge neon red pepper on the roof. (As a toddler, our daughter couldn't pronounce its name, and the whole family still calls it the Pepper restaurant in her honor.) A national chain of seafood restaurants publicizes each and every location with a glowing red lobster, even in Times Square in New York. Both restaurants want to draw in the masses with signs, specials, and a festive atmosphere.

On the other extreme, a world-class fine-dining restaurant in Chicago has minimal signage — only the chef's signature T on a plaque outside the door. If you don't know what you're looking for, you'll miss it completely. This signage matches the owner's goals, the restaurant's atmosphere, and the diners' expectations. It contributes to the exclusivity and understated elegance that the restaurant consistently achieves.

✔ **Fit in.** When designing the exterior of the restaurant, be sensitive to the neighborhood. If the neighborhood is full of restored Victorians and remodeled stone and brick row houses, don't panel your exterior with galvanized tin, wagon wheels, and a life-sized sculpture of an Angus steer just because you're using a Texas barbecue concept.

✔ **Consider how guests will enter and exit your restaurant.** If you have tables near your entrances and exits, make sure that diners sitting there are comfortable. If you operate in a seasonally cold climate for even part of the year, consider installing a second set of doors at the main entrance to keep the wind chill to a minimum. Set out floor mats to prevent slips and falls during rainy or snowy weather.

✔ **Decide how much of the outdoors you want indoors, and vice versa.** Outside noise from traffic and weather affects your atmosphere. Do you want to be able to open windows (or even move walls) on sunny spring days? If you have outdoor seating, is it an extension of the inside or a completely different space? Maybe your outside dining is more casual, with all-weather furniture, awnings, and logoed umbrellas. Do you have the option for a rooftop bar?

If you're planning outdoor seating, check to see whether you need a permit or any special or separate licenses. Permits are required in many areas. You may need a separate liquor license for an outdoor service bar. (Check out Chapter 7 for info on permits and licenses.)

✔ **Keep it clean.** As smoking in public places decreases in popularity (and legality), more diners smoke outdoors, usually right outside a restaurant. If you keep ashtrays handy, make sure you maintain them as needed. Pick up any trash in your parking area or landscaping. Find out whether ordinances in your area require a certain cleaning schedule. In some urban areas with lots of foot traffic, owners must wash the sidewalk in front of their stores at least once each day.

✔ **Decide how delivery and service people will enter the restaurant.** Do you have a separate service entrance, or are deliveries coming through the front door? If it's separate, is it a secured entrance with a bell or maybe a video camera? Who has the key? Make sure you control this entrance for security purposes.

If you share any common areas with your neighbors, make sure they also maintain their responsibilities. Even if it's not your property, it's close to you and reflects on you and the neighborhood. Hopefully, you can keep neighbors on the ball just by contacting them, but if they're violating an ordinance or law, you may be able to exert pressure through your landlord, the Better Business Bureau, fellow neighbors, and so on. Choose your neighbors wisely. For info on choosing the right spot for your restaurant, check out Chapter 6.

Laying Out the Interior

Your diners spend more time in the interior than anywhere else in your establishment. They relax in your bar. They wait for a table in your lobby. They read a menu and enjoy a meal in your dining room. They freshen up in your restrooms. Each area performs a different function, but they all must work together to deliver a consistent experience.

For example, how will your bar and restaurant affect each other? Will your bar be a service for your restaurant diners, or do you plan on doing independent bar business? The clientele can be very different for each, so consider creating a barrier, either a fixed barrier (like a wall) or a movable barrier (planters or a fish tank), if you want to keep them separate.

In the following sections, we discuss room flow, floor plans, and waiting spaces for your guests.

Allowing space for the flow

The flow of service in your establishment has a lot to do with the design and layout. The term *flow of service* means keeping service going at the pace and schedule that you've determined fits your concept. It's keeping guests flowing in and out of the restaurant at the right pace and continually producing food to flow out to the dining room quickly and harmoniously to and from the kitchen. Consider these points:

✔ Think about how your food flows into the dining room and how the dirty dishes flow out. Sometimes a side avenue for the dirty stuff lends itself to a better atmosphere for diners.

✔ Determine the paths diners will take to get to their seats, your bar, the restrooms, the salad bar, and so on. Make sure the paths are clear and easy to navigate. Minimize tight areas that would cause a guest to squeeze through or require them to move chairs or other furniture to move freely around the restaurant.

✔ If you offer food that servers prepare or finish beside diners' tables (like mashing avocado with spices for the perfect guacamole or wrapping Chinese pancakes around moo shu pork), leave adequate floor space for it in your layout and logistical planning. If you need to move a cart around the dining room to prepare a Caesar salad at the table, you need plenty of aisle space to maneuver your cart, plus space to stand next to it and prepare the dish. And if you have low ceilings, you may want to rethink your idea about serving flaming dishes like bananas Foster. Safety first!

Building your floor plan

Check out Figures 9-1 and 9-2 for examples of good and bad layouts. In both examples, the dining rooms, kitchen, and restrooms are equally sized, but the key differences can improve traffic flow and layout:

- **Entrance and host desk:** Tough-to-seat tables are usually located near doors or heavily trafficked paths. We've marked these tables with an X in Figures 9-1 and 9-2. In Figure 9-1, the placement of the front door and the host desk in one corner, rather than in the middle of the front wall, cuts down on the number of "bad" tables around the host desk. This layout helps cut down on traffic moving from the front door through the dining room to tables.

- **Bar:** Positioning the bar along a wall rather than in the middle of the restaurant cuts down on traffic around the bar. Check out the partition between the bar and the dining room in Figure 9-1 for extra traffic-flow control.

Most local and state governments no longer permit smoking in public spaces, so a smoky bar typically won't affect the rest of the restaurant. But if you do live in an area that allows smoking, consider getting *smoke eaters,* a commercial air filtering system that "cleans" smoke, allergens, and odors from the air. Installing these devices is a much better choice than relying on open doors or windows — you can avoid letting in nasty vermin with the fresh air, and you can maintain a more stable, comfortable air temperature.

- **Service entrance:** Locate the service entrance in the kitchen rather than in the dining room. At some point, you'll get an untimely delivery during the middle of the lunch rush. Running it through the dining room isn't an option. Plus, you can save some wear and tear to your dining room carpets if you accept all deliveries through a back entrance.

- **Restrooms:** Place restrooms in a corner so you don't lose space on both sides of them. And avoid placing tables near them when possible. Seating people in these tables is tough because people line up outside the restrooms, making the guests seated nearby uncomfortable. Also, whenever possible, make more space in the women's room than in the men's room. You won't be sorry.

Arrange your tables so that you can easily create and take apart larger tables. Booths are nice, but you can't really move them around. For flexibility's sake, use mostly tables rather than booths.

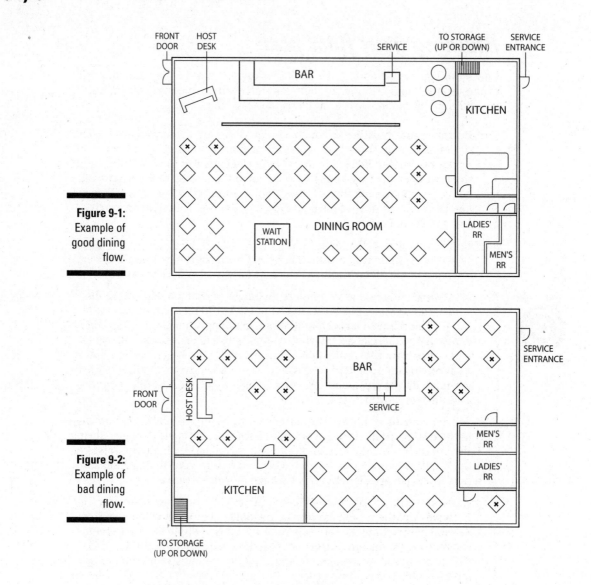

Figure 9-1:
Example of good dining flow.

Figure 9-2:
Example of bad dining flow.

Creating space to wait

Hopefully, your restaurant will be so successful that you'll have more diners than tables at some time each day. Consider these ideas when you're deciding how much space to create for waiting:

✔ Where are people going to wait to be seated? Decide how much space you're going to allot to a waiting area, lobby, and bar. Decide what you want them to do while they're waiting. Should they admire your décor (or other interesting stuff to look at) or get a drink or appetizer? Should they have menus and wine lists to read? Will you offer cocktail service (service by a server at tables next to the bar), or will patrons get their own drinks from the bar? If video games fit your concept, do you offer them as a way to pass the time? How do you ensure that people are comfortable and that the thermostat is set at the right temperature?

✔ Where do people store their stuff? Are you located near or in a transportation hub (like an airport, train station, and so on) with traveling clientele who may have luggage? Are you located in a geographic area that experiences cold, rainy, or snowy weather at least part of the year? People need to hang coats and weather gear close by. Are you going to devote space to a coat room?

✔ Do you want guests hanging around? Are you planning on being a take-out place, or do you want a restaurant where people want to come early, relax, and take in the ambience?

✔ Who will seat your diners? If you need a host stand, leave space for it and all the equipment involved, including menus, telephones, pagers, a computer, a reservation book, pencils, breath mints, toothpicks, and whatever else is essential for your operation. See the section "Setting Up a Reservation System," later in this chapter, for tips on getting all the necessities together.

If you don't have a host stand, diners usually take this as a sign that they have to seat themselves. A centralized menu (see Chapter 8 for details) and a cashier may be other clues. Some restaurants allow the wait staff to seat patrons and then serve them as well. Many restaurants simply have a sign that says, "Please wait to be seated," so diners don't have to guess about what to do.

Nothing says *uncomfortable* from a customer's perspective like walking in the door to a restaurant and not knowing what to do. Make sure the host stand is visible to all guests entering, even when the restaurant is very busy. That way, you keep your guests moving and the cash register ringing. Whatever your decision, make sure that it's obvious what the customers should do, either wait to be seated or seat themselves.

Keeping Service Support Close

Staff support is basically anything staff members need to do their job and to provide the best possible guest service. Depending on your concept, you'll likely need at least one wait station and a few POS (or *point of sale,* meaning computers to order food and drinks) stations in your restaurant. The secret to good use of space in this area of the restaurant is efficiency. Keep everything you need to complete a task close at hand. Keep coffee cups and teaspoons near the coffee pot, glasses near the ice well, and so on.

For the following reasons, don't be tempted to combine your POS and your wait station:

- ✔ Your POS is electrical, and you want to avoid spilling ice water, tea, sticky sodas, and so on, on its components and backup supplies, such as printer ribbons and paper refills.

- ✔ You don't want servers waiting to ring up orders in the way of servers trying to get drinks to tables.

- ✔ You run the risk of having waiters congregating, hanging around, talking, and holding up walls for you.

You want to keep service, and bodies, moving and flowing, not getting in each other's way. If you have to combine POS and wait stations, make sure that some sort of physical barrier, such as a partition, divides the space and minimizes congestion.

Wait stations

The wait station is the supply area for the FOH staff. They make and pour their nonalcoholic drinks here and may clean and restock the dining room tables from here. The wait station should contain anything servers need to do their job. Here's the short list of things to include in your wait station:

- ✔ Coffee station, including the machine, pots, warmers, coffee, filters, teaspoons, and cups

- ✔ Reach-in cooler, stocked with milk, cream, half-and-half, and butter

- ✔ Soda station, including glassware, ice well with cover and scoop, and straws

- ✔ Iced tea station, including tea machine, lemons, ice, glassware, and spoons

- ✔ Hot tea supply, including tea bags, lemons, teaspoons, cups, and saucers

- ✔ Wine buckets

- ✔ Bread baskets

✔ Extra linens, including napkins, tablecloths, and a few bar towels

✔ Sanitizer bucket, to clean and disinfect spills

✔ Clean china, silverware, and glassware (usually not barware)

✔ Carryout containers

✔ Ashtrays and matches, if your restaurant allows smoking

✔ Trash can

✔ Oil and vinegar cruets, a pepper mill, and any other condiments that *float* (meaning items that aren't on the tables but a guest may need on occasion)

Depending on the size and layout of your restaurant, you may need additional, or *satellite,* wait stations. A satellite wait station is usually smaller than the main station and contains less stuff. For example, your main wait station may have the coffee machine, while a satellite station may have only a warmer to keep already-brewed coffee warm. The satellite station also probably won't have a reach-in cooler or plumbing. Satellites are designed to keep a few essentials at the ready but not take the place of the main station.

No restaurant rule says that you can have only one wait station. If you have the space, budget, and a logistical challenge, a second (or third) full wait station may help you solve it. If your staff has to use stairs to get from your kitchen to your diners, an extra station on the dining floor may really help. Or if you do an equal amount of indoor and outdoor dining, you may consider a second station close to your patio or even a rolling portable station that you can bring inside when you close your patio.

Point of sale (POS) stations

Your POS (point of sale) system is the computerized system for ordering food and drinks. The system may consist of individual computers, or you may have dummy terminals connected together to a single computer in the office. At a minimum, each terminal allows a server to enter food orders, which are automatically sent and printed at the stations that prepare the items and to the *expediter* (the person in charge of the kitchen on a given night — check out Chapter 10 for details). Drink orders are automatically sent to the bar. Servers also prepare and finalize checks to present to diners in these stations.

If your budget allows it, we recommend having one POS terminal for every three servers on the floor per shift.

Your POS supply list may be a little longer than you'd think:

✔ **POS terminal:** This is the actual screen that servers use to process orders.

✔ **Printers:** A printer is attached to the system to print credit card receipts and copies of checks to present to diners.

✔ **Operation manuals for the POS and the printer:** Manuals are extremely helpful for new employees and veterans alike.

✔ **Backup ink cartridges and extra paper:** Keep at least one ink cartridge in the POS station, and store extra rolls of paper nearby for mid-shift changes.

✔ **Check folders:** A check folder is the plastic or pleather holder that you present a guest's check in. You can usually get these folders from your credit card companies. Make sure you have enough extras for servers to keep their working tickets in. The folders really help them stay organized.

✔ **Manual backup checks:** Computers are great — when they work. Don't get caught with your apron down; keep a supply of manual checks (with multiple carbons) on hand for emergencies. Match up the carbons at the end of the night to account for any tickets that may have gotten "lost" without being paid for.

✔ **Credit card machine:** Often this is just a swipe pad connected to the terminal. But if your system requires a separate machine, make sure to allot space for it.

✔ **Credit card imprinter:** Computerized credit card systems occasionally die, so it's good to keep these dinosaurs (and their corresponding paperwork) on hand for emergencies. Keep a list of the credit card companies handy as well so you can call for a verification of charges. Servers can get an authorization code from the credit card companies and manually write it on the paperwork in case of a dispute later on.

Check with your credit card companies and make sure that using these credit card imprinters is in keeping with current federal local and state laws. Because using the imprinters creates a permanent visual record of your diners' credit card numbers, some consumer advocates are working to outlaw this backup system.

If your staff hand-writes orders and doesn't use a computerized system for ordering, you can disregard this supply list. Instead, you need only check holders, checks, and a central cashier. Make sure you set up some kind of inventory and accounting of your check numbers so that guest checks don't "disappear." This loophole can be a slow leak of revenue that adds up quickly.

Computers are great tools for keeping track of these kinds of things, checks, money, and so on. If you're intimidated by the thought of it, check with other restaurant owners in your area to find a reputable hospitality software salesperson. She can demonstrate how a computerized system can benefit even small operations. (And check out Chapter 15 for the technical details of POS systems.)

Tabletop settings

Think of the tabletop settings as little self-service mini wait stations. They're made up of all the stuff your diners need to comfortably make it through a meal. As with most things in this business, what shows up at your tables is based on your concept. There's no right or wrong answer. We've seen it all, ranging from a single linen napkin on the simple side of the spectrum to a pound o' individual butter containers, a roll of paper towels, and a galvanized bucket full of silverware on the other. You want to provide guests with the tools and condiments they need without encroaching too much on the eating area.

The tabletop is an extension of your concept. If you're a fine-dining establishment (with prices to match), your diners expect good linens, heavy silverware, and great glassware waiting when they arrive. If you're a family restaurant, they expect to find the familiar sweetening selection (the blue, the pink, and the white) and probably ketchup, salt, and pepper. Latin-themed and Japanese places often include their preferred pepper sauce and soy sauce selections, respectively, on the table.

Setting Up a Reservation System

Often, a diner's first direct communication with a member of your staff is via telephone. The diner may be calling about menu offerings or business hours and will likely ask about reservations. Make the most of this opportunity by training anyone who answers the phone in basic phone etiquette and spend some time educating them on your reservation policy.

You can't stress enough that anyone answering the phone must be friendly, informative, and helpful. People do not appreciate being treated with any kind of negative attitude, a harried voice, or lack of respect. One restaurateur in New York has a centralized phone line for all his restaurants, and two or three people do nothing but answer the phones, answer questions, and take reservations. Spending this kind of time on customers pays off.

Decide whether you want to take reservations. More than just about anything else we cover in this book, this is a personal choice. Many places take only customers with reservations (sometimes months in advance), and others don't take any reservations at all — ever. If you take reservations and people stand you up, you lose revenue. At many exclusive restaurants, diners provide a deposit via a credit card to reserve the table. If the diners don't show up, their credit card is charged a standard amount.

If you decide to take reservations, you must do it well. You probably won't get a second chance with customers if you disappoint them. People expect their table to be waiting when they get there if they've made a reservation.

Here's a quick list of the basic supplies you need to get your reservation system started:

- ✔ Podium
- ✔ Clipboard and wait list
- ✔ Reservation book
- ✔ Pens and pencils
- ✔ Phones

You can add convenience to your system with a few technological advances:

- ✔ **Computer:** Keep track of reservations and estimate wait times. People may argue with your host, but they won't argue with a computer. Many computerized reservation systems are available. Some online services lease you a computer terminal to track all your reservations, online and traditional.

- ✔ **Online reservation system:** Some third-party systems, such as OpenTable (www.opentable.com), process reservations for you and integrate their system with yours. You usually pay a fee for this service, so read the fine print. Take a look at the later section "Accepting online reservations" for details on how this works.

- ✔ **Pagers:** These personal, hand-held devices alert customers (usually with vibrations and lights) when their tables are ready.

If you don't take reservations, have the overflow space to keep customers there while they're waiting. If not, people probably won't stick around, at least not until you've established yourself. Check out the earlier section "Creating space to wait" for tips on allocating this space.

Taking traditional reservations

Here are some tips for taking reservations:

- ✔ Reserve at least one table for special guests. You never know when one of your financiers, the bank managers, the restaurant critic you've been dying to impress, or the latest celebrity power couple may stop in for a quick bite.

- ✔ Get a phone number when you take the reservation. Confirm the reservation with your diners the day before. Doing so is a great way to add a personal touch to their experience and protect against revenue loss from patrons who made other plans.

✔ Make sure you have enough phone lines. If customers are calling your restaurant and the line is constantly busy, they'll give up on it. A few may still want to get in, but most people will go down the street. If your manager is on the line talking to the ad guy, the chef's ordering on another, and your host is talking to a friend, how many other lines do you have to take a phone call? Consider getting an intercom system on your phones to ease the flow of intra-restaurant communication. Also, limit personal phone calls to emergencies only.

✔ Consider getting voice mail or a message machine. Make the most of your message by giving directions, your hours, seasonal promotions, and the reservation number if it's different from the main number.

One twist on the reservation concept that's gaining popularity, particularly in casual restaurants, is *call-ahead seating*. It falls somewhere between a reservation and walking in the door and placing your name on a waiting list. When a person is ready to leave his house, he calls the restaurant to place his name on the waiting list. Basically, the guest shaves the driving time from his home to the restaurant off the wait time. Some restaurants hold the table for a certain amount of time as a courtesy, while others give it away immediately if the diners aren't in the restaurant when their names are called.

Accepting online reservations

These days, if you accept reservations, you must accept them online as well as over the telephone. But don't feel overwhelmed: Online reservations don't require a fancy system and new software. They can be as easy to manage as checking your e-mail. If you have a website (and we recommend that you do), you absolutely should have an e-mail address that allows diners to request reservations. Notice we said *request* reservations. Sending an e-mail to the restaurant doesn't guarantee the diner a reservation. Instead, the diner should expect to receive a timely (within 24 hours) confirmation e-mail from your restaurant. If the restaurant can't accommodate the diner's request, you can recommend an alternate time or date that may work for the diner.

Clearly state your reservation policy on your website so diners know what to expect. Here's our recommendation:

> Please contact us at reservations@yourplace.com to request a reservation. We'll respond to all requests within 24 hours and send you either a confirmation email or an alternate suggested date or time for your consideration. For immediate assistance, please call us at 312-555-1234.

If you want to opt for a one-stop shop in the world of online reservations, OpenTable (`www.opentable.com`) is the big name in fully integrated electronic and online compatible restaurant reservation systems, or *host management systems*. OpenTable gives you the hardware and software to manage your reservations — all your reservations, not just those made through their website. They also put money into marketing themselves and your restaurant, driving new customers to you. And if you use the OpenTable terminal to track all your reservations, the website can make and confirm reservations in real time, saving your new guests time and ensuring that they don't go elsewhere in the meantime. Typically, OpenTable charges a monthly fee for the equipment and a flat fee, around $1, for each reservation booked at your restaurant through their site.

You pay OpenTable only for reservations for guests who actually show up and dine with you. If you have guests who make a reservation and then fail to show up, make sure you note that in OpenTable. The company doesn't charge you, and they note the diner's account. Eventually, OpenTable won't allow diners who don't keep their commitments to make reservations.

Reviewing Restrooms

Restrooms used to be a place to rest and refresh. Nowadays, people usually get in and get out. Decide whether you want employees to share the restroom that your diners use. Also decide whether you want your bathroom open to the public or reserved for customers and staff. Keeping the restrooms solely for guests can be difficult because you risk alienating potential customers. In the following sections, we discuss both options, as well as employee locker rooms.

Make sure that all your facilities are in line with ADA (Americans with Disabilities Act) code (`www.ada.gov`) and are fully handicapped accessible. Check the local code and ordinances when you get your permits.

Providing public facilities

Restrooms are an extension of the front of the house. You must spend just as much attention on maintaining these areas as you do on your dining room. Make appropriate supplies available, including (at a minimum) toilet paper, paper towels, soap, hot and cold running water, and plenty of trash containers. If you have the space, install diaper-changing areas in both the women's and men's rooms. To save space, many new restaurant restrooms offer unisex facilities with "commode closets" and a common sink area.

Conduct regular restroom checks to confirm that your facilities are clean, tidy, and in proper working order. If you want a constant presence in the restroom, consider hiring an attendant. Guests may appreciate the extra service and amenities. An attendant usually offers cologne, hairspray, and a nice selection of hand lotion. But customers may resent the feeling that they need to leave a tip. Decide what's best for your concept and clientele.

Whatever choice you make about maintaining your restrooms, make sure, at a minimum, that you have a schedule for checking it, a person assigned to do it (usually a porter, busboy, or host), and good follow-through.

Decide whether you have room for a lounge area. If you're drawing in families, a couch in your restroom is a nice feature for nursing moms or older kids waiting on moms and dads to finish up with younger siblings.

A full-length mirror is a nice addition to the restroom, especially if formal attire is standard at your place. Diners can confirm that all's well before returning to their tables.

Earmarking areas for employees

Providing separate restrooms for your staff is a good idea. You can post staff notes and reminders on doors where everyone sees them at some time or another. You need to stock the basics in the employee restroom, including soap, hand sanitizer, paper towels, and toilet paper. Make sure hot and cold running water are available at all times.

You must post a sign stating something like this: "Employees must wash hands before returning to work." Depending on your staff, consider getting a bilingual sign. If your employees share a restroom with guests, the sign must go in that restroom. With a separate facility, you can add additional information, like the proper hand-washing technique diagram in Chapter 17. And you may want to include a friendly reminder that you won't tolerate any food or drink in the area.

If you take the next step and add a locker room to the employee facilities, keep the following points in mind:

- ✔ The locker room is not a place to hang out. Employees should change into or out of their uniforms and move along.
- ✔ The locker room is a self-policing area. Make sure that the staff knows that the condition of the room is up to them. They have to clean it themselves.

✔ You can't post cameras or conduct locker searches. Employees legally expect privacy when using these facilities.

✔ Food and drink aren't allowed in the locker room. If you don't implement this policy from the get-go, the locker room will become packed full of dirty dishes and glassware. The next thing you know, it's packed full of pests (of the four-legged or more varieties).

✔ Recommend that employees put dirty uniforms in the laundry hamper as soon as they take them off and then immediately place tomorrow's clean uniform in their lockers. This system prevents employees from rushing when they report for work and keeps the dirty laundry from soiling the clean.

Chapter 10

Setting Up the Back of the House

. . . .

. . . .

Setting up the back of the house is even more important than setting up your dining room. The *back of the house,* or BOH, is any area of your restaurant that a guest can't normally see. If the dining room is the face of the restaurant, the kitchen is the heart. And how it works greatly affects the finished product that guests do see, including how long their food takes to get to the table and what condition the food is in when it gets there. In this chapter, we reveal the first thing you need to consider when creating the back of the house: your menu and how it affects your kitchen. Then we cover the basics of layout, give you some tips on designing from scratch and dealing with an existing kitchen, and offer ideas on the kitchen equipment you need.

Planning a Kitchen with the Menu in Mind

Which came first, the menu or the kitchen? It's tough to say, because you can't have one that works without the other. And you can't be successful without both. Your menu and kitchen should be in perfect harmony or at least be on the same page of the same book. Whether you're designing your kitchen from scratch or working with an existing kitchen, you need to figure out how your kitchen will run based on the menu you're serving in order to set it up right. (See Chapter 8 for info on composing your menu.)

The following sections help you figure out what kinds of equipment you need to fix everything on your menu. We then show you how to put it all together for the best flow.

Figuring out what you need to fix the food on your menu

Look at your menu item by item and determine what equipment you need to prepare it, store it, and serve it, from beginning to end. Make a list of menu items and the related equipment and stations you need to prepare those items — freezers and coolers, prep areas, grills and fryers, a plating area for your expeditor (expo) to check and garnish the plates, and so on. Check out our sample list in Table 10-1. You'll use this info to figure out not only what you need but also how busy each station or piece of equipment will be. (We discuss stations and equipment in the next two sections, and we cover kitchen flow in "Laying out your kitchen.")

Table 10-1	Equipment and Stations Needed in Kitchen	
Menu Item	*Station/Area*	*Purpose*
Fried calamari	Walk-in	Store dairy
	Store Room	Store bread crumbs
	Freezer	Store calamari
	Prep area	Clean & cut calamari squid to desired size, if necessary; bread
	Reach-in	Hold prepped calamari
	Fryer	Bread and finish calamari, cook to order, plate
	Expo	Check plate, garnish dish
Chicken Caesar salad	Walk-in cooler	Store lettuce, eggs, dressing after prep
	Reach-in	Hold prepped lettuce, dressing
	Prep area	Wash & cut or tear lettuce, prepare dressing
	Dry storage	Store canned anchovies, et al
	Grill	Grill chicken breast
	Pantry	Finish salad to order, plate
	Expo	Check plate, garnish, consolidate order

Reviewing the basic kitchen stations

A *station* is an area of the kitchen designed to accommodate a particular cooking technique. So foods that are fried, such as french fries, onion rings, and fried oysters, are prepared at the *fryer station*. Items that are grilled, such as steaks, grilled veggies, and grilled chicken, are prepared at the *grill station*.

A station is defined by the way the food is prepared, not by the kind of food prepared there. The station refers to the main equipment, such as a grill, and the setup and organization of the supplies and products that the cook needs to finish preparing menu items. In the case of a grill, the supplies and products may include the food to be grilled, brushes to clean the grill, side dishes to complete the grill menu item, knives, spatulas, tongs, plateware, and sauces to complete the presentations. Some foods have a variety of cooking techniques. Depending on your menu, a scallop may be grilled, broiled, smoked, steamed, or sautéed, so several stations could prepare scallops.

The *line* is the area of the kitchen where food is prepared, placed on a plate, garnished, and then sent out to the guest. The line is made up of all the stations in the kitchen. When a station receives an order to *fire* an item (cook a dish immediately), it means that a guest has ordered, the server has placed the order with the kitchen, and the kitchen should begin preparing the item.

Grill

The restaurant grill is just a bigger version of the grill you probably have in your backyard. A grill is distinguished from equipment like a broiler or oven by the direction of the heat: A grill's heat comes from under the food being cooked. (An oven's heat surrounds food, and a broiler's heat comes from above.)

You can find two basic versions: a *grated grill* (sometimes called a charbroiler) and a *flattop grill*. Depending on your menu, you may have one type of grill, both, or neither. If you're a steakhouse and want to serve steaks with nice little checkerboard grill marks, go for the grated grill. If you're a diner doing grilled ham and cheese and omelets, consider a flattop grill. If you have room for both, you can be more flexible with your menu offerings.

At the grill station, you need the following:

- Grill (surprise!)
- Cooler for your entree items (such as salmon, kebabs, chicken, and steaks for a grated grill, or eggs, pancake batter, and so on for a flattop)

✔ Seasonings (salt, pepper, signature spice blends, and so on)

✔ Grill brush

✔ Oil rag (to wipe the grill and keep food from sticking)

✔ Water bottle (to squirt down flames)

Sauté

The sauté station is the area you typically see in the open kitchen setup because it's usually busy and exciting. During busy times, several cooks work this station, preparing everything from pasta to poached fish, from sauces to sautéed spinach. If something is cooked in a sauté pan, it's cooked here. Next to sauté pans, tongs are the sauté cook's best friend. Sauté cooks (sometimes shortened to *sautés*) usually use a multiburner range to prepare multiple dishes at a time.

If you have a sauté station in your restaurant, you typically want your most experienced cooks working this station for a few reasons:

✔ Dishes cook quickly here, and you need people with speed and consistency to turn them out on time.

✔ The sauté station is often responsible for the most delicate, carefully prepared dishes on the line, so the items have to be finished with expertise in order to ensure a quality product.

✔ Sautéed items (such as pasta dishes, saucy appetizers, and sometimes the veggie of the day) are usually popular and/or high-volume items, so you need people who can keep up with the pace for the entire shift.

✔ A sauté cook often tastes a dish to confirm consistent seasoning and must do so according to health regulations (this means taste-testing with a clean spoon, which must be sent to the dish area immediately after use — no double dipping!). An experienced sauté cook can take the proper steps to protect you and your customers from violations.

The European sauté station is vastly different from the American system we describe here. The American sauté system involves anything cooked on a gas burner. The Europeans break up this station into anywhere from three to fourteen different stations, each specializing in smaller pieces of the menu. Increasingly, many European sauté stations use *induction* cooktops in place of traditional gas burners. Induction cooking uses electromagnetism to *induce* energy into the cooking vessel, thus creating heat. In addition to being extremely efficient and fast, induction cooking produces very little heat in the kitchen and is much safer than open flame cooking. With recent reductions in the cost of induction technology and new domestic companies entering the market, induction technology is slowly spreading to the kitchens, hotels, and catering trucks of the United States.

Fryer

The fryer is an extremely versatile station. You can use multiple fryers in a single station to finish dishes and supply other stations with a continuous stream of *parcooked* (partially cooked) product to stay ahead during busy times. Look for pressure fryers with lids or quick recovery fryers to speed up frying time if you're planning on doing lots of fried appetizers, or *apps,* and entrees. Always opt for a fryer with a working — and calibrated (accurate) — thermostat so you can monitor the temperature and fry times on your menu items to get a consistent-quality product.

Boiling water in standard electric fryers can damage the heating element. If you want to boil water in your fryer, ask your equipment rep for the specifics on your particular model. If you're taking over an existing location with a fryer, have a reputable serviceperson look over all your equipment and confirm that you can use your fryer to boil water. If you're buying new equipment, you can purchase a *rethermalizer,* a fryer-type piece of equipment that's great for boiling seafood or pasta or blanching vegetables.

Other things that may be part of the fry stations include the fry baskets (for easy retrieval of items), plateware, breading, sauces, sauce cups, a skimmer for removing errant fries, a small reach-in cooler, a reach-in freezer, and anything else your fry cook needs to get the job done.

Broiler

Broilers provide a short burst of high-intensity heat from above. You may use a broiler for melting Gruyère cheese on top of French onion soup, melting cheese on nachos, or providing that super crispy layer on an apple cobbler. A cheese melter is a lower-intensity broiler that warms rather than cooks food. As always, your concept dictates which size of broiler and what heat intensity you need.

Oven

An oven serves a few different roles in the kitchen. It can be a plate warmer or a sauté-pan preheater and can actually cook food. The oven station can consist of any variety of ovens:

- **Convection oven:** This type of oven uses a fan to circulate heat for quicker, more even cooking.
- **Conveyer oven:** The perfect choice for sandwiches and pizzas, the conveyor oven, or *impinger,* usually involves an infrared heat source and forced air, heating food from both above and below. You control the cooking time by adjusting the belt speed and the temperature and by where you place the food on the conveyor belt.

- ✔ **Rotary oven:** This large piece of equipment (the size of a small room) holds five to seven large trays that turn like a Ferris wheel. It may work for you if you're doing house-made bread, pastries, and desserts.

- ✔ **Combination oven:** If your budget allows, you can combine your oven and a steamer by using a combination oven. These freestanding cabinet-style ovens combine convection or conventional cooking, as well as dry heat and moist heat. They can also act as stand-alone steamers.

- ✔ **Programmable speed-cooking oven:** Equipment manufacturers are continually innovating and launching new ovens that combine speed with the efficiency of custom controls and quality production. Many of these new ovens combine microwave, convection, and impingement into a single cooking platform. These ovens, manufactured by leading companies such as Turbo Chef, Manitowoc, and Amana Commercial, are often 10 to 15 times more efficient than traditional ovens. But before you run off and buy one of these angry little ovens, understand that what they offer in terms of speed and efficiency they generally lack in throughput. These ovens are expressly designed and programmed to cook one specific product at a time, limiting their ability to handle high volumes.

Your menu and your concept determine which type of oven you need in your restaurant. If you're a pizza joint, the majority of your menu items will likely come out of the oven. You need a different oven than the Chinese takeout place down the street does. Tailor your choice of oven to your menu needs.

Some restaurants don't have an oven station. Instead, they put an oven in the prep area and hold the already prepared food on the line, in the steam table (see the later section on steam tables). An Italian restaurant, for example, may use ovens in the prep area to bake lasagne, roast large cuts of meat, or braise osso buco over a period of hours. Then it holds the items in batches (with the rest refrigerated) in the steam table on the line for service.

Pastry

The pastry station is typically reserved for dessert items. If your concept doesn't call for a pastry chef or even a pastry station, you can roll desserts into the pantry station. Alternatively, your wait staff can be in charge of *plating* their own desserts (putting them on a plate for service) in a station in the kitchen or in a wait station set up for this activity.

Steam table

The steam table is basically a huge chafing dish that holds cooked items and keeps hot foods hot until they're ordered. The steam table is located on the line. Large and small metal pans fit into various configurations to make up the compartments of the steam table. For example, if you're a family restaurant or cafeteria, your line may consist of a steam table full of vegetables, roasted potatoes, braised meats, fried chicken, and so on, all completely cooked but held at the right temperature until a diner orders them. In this sort of concept, your prep area is where dishes are prepared, and then the entree items are plated on the line.

Pantry

The pantry is the catch-all center for cold food and, typically, a true assembly station. Salads, desserts, cold antipasti, unfried spring rolls, gazpacho, and tuna salad sandwiches can all make their appearance from the pantry. Anything to be cooked for the pantry (whether it's apple pie or hard-boiled eggs) must be done before it gets to the pantry. Even the few hot things that may appear in the pantry (warm bacon dressing for spinach salad or hot fudge for sundaes) are usually already prepped and then held nearby.

Expo

The *expo* is short for *expediter.* It's a station (and a person; if you're *working expo,* you're said to be the expo for that shift) that ensures that all the stations on the line are working in harmony. The expo ensures that all dishes going to the dining room are up to par with your restaurant standards, including those on presentation, portion sizes, temperature, within the specified time for an order to be prepared, and so on.

The expo is the last quality-control check before a dish leaves the kitchen. This station often has some kind of communication tool (commonly a microphone or gopher) with the prep area so that the expo can call for reinforcements — er, we mean replenishments — during busy shifts. Complete this station with a spindle (a metal stake to "stab" completed tickets), a highlighter, pen or pencils, a wet and a dry towel (for cleaning up plates), and any garnishes your expo may use.

The expo is the communication funnel. He protects the individual stations from things they don't need to know about, like waiters' complaints about a missing entree that should've been sent, side dish requests, and special orders. He sets the priorities for everyone working the line and serves as the kitchen's link to the dining room. If the expediter doesn't know everything that's going on in the restaurant, he isn't in control. Without good info flow, a kitchen can crash and burn at 7 p.m. and still feel the effects at 9 p.m.

Specialty equipment

Your concept may depend on a station or piece of specialty equipment that we don't mention. If you're a casual Indian restaurant, you may need a tandoori oven. If you specialize in wood-fired pizza, like Urban Forge Pizza Bar, you need a wood-burning brick oven to create those menu delights. And believe it or not, the microwave isn't just for popcorn anymore. Restaurants, especially large casual chains, are increasingly taking advantage of this tool, paired with the power of food science, to ensure quick ticket times and consistent products.

Sandwich or panini presses have grown in recent years to become a kitchen mainstay in a variety of restaurant segments. These countertop appliances are designed to toast (or in the case of the panini press, grill) sandwiches using direct top and bottom-heated surfaces. Although they may resemble the happy-homemaker sandwich grills made popular by a certain boxer on late-night television, commercial sandwich presses are designed for the rigors of the restaurant kitchen and often require 220 volts of power. People use them to execute a variety of dishes, from their namesake grilled sandwiches to toasted quesadillas and grilled burritos.

Your menu determines which equipment you need. Purchase, lease, and lay out your restaurant accordingly.

Taking control of your prep

You may have noticed that your average restaurant can get a pasta dish to your table faster than you can boil water at home. We assure you that no witches and wizards are hiding behind the curtain. The masters of the culinary world, whether on TV or at your local deli, rely on the time-honored tradition of *prep* (short for preparation) to make quick work of orders as they come into the kitchen.

In fact, most members of the kitchen staff have done some time as prep cooks in their restaurant careers. Prep shifts provide a great opportunity to watch and learn if you're interested in pursuing a career in the culinary arts. And in some of the more prestigious kitchens in the world, working prep is an initiation into the culture that is that restaurant. Prep can be a rite of passage, whether you've painstakingly created 50 pounds of tournée potatoes (little fancy potato footballs), only to see the executive chef turn them into mashed potatoes before your eyes, or you've spent 8 hours meticulously separating 300 quail breasts.

More commonly, though, prep is just a means to an end: getting a product ready to go so you can get finished dishes to the table as efficiently as possible. Most prep is done at off-peak times. If you do a busy lunch and dinner business, your prep staff will likely be working early, say, 6 a.m. to 2 p.m., to get the basics done before the lunch rush starts around 11:30. If you're a busy breakfast place, the prep staff may be in even earlier, maybe 2 a.m., and stay until 10 a.m. Consider a few pieces of equipment as you put together your prep-area game plan. Read on for the specifics.

Coolers

In the restaurant world, a *cooler* isn't something that you use to carry your drinks to the park. *Cooler* is restaurant lingo for refrigerator. No matter what size the cooler is, it's usually called a cooler. Most restaurants have at least one walk-in cooler (familiarly referred to as the *walk-in*) that's the size of a small, medium, or large room. Many stations have their own reach-in coolers to store prepped food that's finished at the station.

Coolers hold anything perishable, from produce to butter to prepared sauces. All raw food, such as eggs or marinating meat, goes in a cooler. Anything wet, like egg drop soup or Alfredo sauce, goes in a cooler. Whether fresh fish, fungi, or something else, any food that isn't canned, dried, or frozen goes in a cooler. Even if you may not refrigerate it in your home (apples, for example), you'll likely refrigerate it here.

Your restaurant's concept (and your purveyor's delivery schedule) dictates how many and which sizes of coolers you need. If you're opening a place that deals mostly with canned or prepackaged foods, you may need only a small walk-in and a reach-in. If you depend on daily shipments of perishables, you may not need much refrigerated walk-in storage and can get by with a single walk-in. If you're part of a franchise that delivers frozen products on a regular schedule, maybe you can get by with a freezer and a couple of reach-ins for the line and a smaller walk-in to thaw frozen products or store thawed products. Take a look at the earlier section "Figuring out what you need to fix the food on the menu" to help you assess your need for coolers and other restaurant equipment.

Freezers

A freezer is simply a place to keep frozen foods. Freezers range in size from large rooms to smaller chest freezers, ideal for ice cream at a dessert station or backup ice in a service bar. Your concept and menu dictate the size of freezer you need. If you pride yourself on serving fresh seafood, you may need only a small freezer area to store things such as french fries and ice cream. If you buy a lot of your food already prepared, a freezer may be an ideal way to save labor and still get a high-quality, consistent product.

When you're figuring out your freezer requirements, don't try to figure in your ice needs with it. Invest in a separate ice machine. You can get freestanding units that produce enough ice to keep up with a very busy restaurant, like the ones in hotel vending areas. Or you can get one that's part of your soda machine setup.

Prep tables

The rows of stainless steel tables known as *prep tables* are essential to a smooth prep shift. You need plenty of work surfaces and sinks for several members of your staff to prepare multiple items at once in a sanitary environment. For example, in one area, Maria may be washing lettuce for salads. At the same time, James may be slicing and weighing tuna steaks. You don't want these two to get in each other's way. If any of the fish bits get near the lettuce, you create a huge food safety issue (see Chapter 17). Depending on your volume, you may need separate workspaces for two to eight people to work independently.

Make sure that the prep tables are at the right prep height, usually a minimum of 36 inches, to ensure comfortable standing while prepping.

Dry storage

Dry storage is the commercial version of your home pantry — a walk-in storeroom that holds all your dry goods. Any food item that's canned (such as canned tomatoes, oil, and canned pudding), dried (beans or pasta), or shelf-stable (vinegar, margarita mix, or spices) can be stored here. You can also keep other disposables here, such as beverage napkins, stir sticks, or candles.

Dry storage can be an organizer's dream or nightmare. Keep your dry storage organized to quickly know what you need to order and stay a step ahead at inventory time. For more tips on managing inventory and purchasing, check out Chapter 13.

Consider creating a cage in your dry storage area if you keep expensive non-perishables on hand. A *cage* is simply a locked cabinet that can hold your saffron, truffles, caviar, or other expensive items securely.

Tilt skillet

A *tilt skillet* is a huge freestanding skillet. It has a handy feature that lets you tilt the skillet (either by means of a manual crank or electric switch) to pour your finished sauce, soup, rice, or whatever into your storage container. You can use it for sautéing, searing, or braising large quantities of foods that don't fit into a conventional pan suitable for use on a range top. For example, you can sear 12 pork loins or 50 chicken breasts at a time, braise 20 osso buco (veal shanks) at a time, or poach 100 eggs at a time. The tilt skillet is an indispensable tool for high-volume restaurants that prepare just about anything from scratch in bulk.

If possible, situate your tilt skillet near a grated floor drain to quickly dispose of used liquid, overflows, and spills. If you're opening a new restaurant or remodeling an existing one, build in drains where you need them now. Doing that job later is costly; you not only have to pay additional construction costs, but you actually have to shut down your business for at least a few days. Drains are also handy for easy cleaning of big pieces of equipment. Just clean them out and dump the rinse water onto the floor and down the drain.

Steam kettle

A steam jacketed kettle (the *jacketed* refers to the steam chamber that surrounds the kettle itself) can be as small as 5 gallons or as big as a hot tub. These specialized pieces of equipment use the even heating of superheated steam to evenly cook soups and sauces in volume. A crank system (similar to a tilt skillet in the preceding section) allows the contents to be carefully poured into smaller containers for storage.

The even heating of a steam kettle is unmatched for preparing things such as stocks, long simmered sauces like bordelaise, and chili for you and 500 of your closest friends. Locate your kettle near a grated floor drain for quick cleanup of spills.

Smoker

A smoker is a piece of equipment designed to do a specialized job. A *cold smoker* uses indirect heat to impart smoky aromas and flavors to the food, thanks to the fragrant wood that fires it. Cold smoking doesn't cook the food; it simply adds the flavor to create items such as smoked salmon or smoky cheeses, including some provolones and cheddars. A *hot smoker* uses direct heat — a smoke box with fragrant woods — to cook and smoke simultaneously. Barbecued items are often cooked in a hot smoker.

Most restaurants don't have a smoker. If you're a rib place or you specialize in wild game, you may consider investing in one. Because of the extensive time it takes to prepare smoked items, the smoker is not a line station. Items prepared in the smoker are held on the line until a guest orders them.

If you want to offer the occasional smoked item on your menu, consider finding a vendor who deals in smoked or specialty goods. Smoked salmon is a good example. If you serve smoked salmon, you likely have a vendor that carries it. Save the labor and the equipment costs by purchasing the product.

Mats

Commercial restaurant floors are usually concrete or quarry tile. Standing on these hard surfaces for several hours a day causes stress on knees, leg muscles, and feet. General work processes can make floors wet and greasy. Invest in some well-designed kitchen mats to alleviate fatigue and eliminate slippery floors. Place mats in prep areas, on the line, behind the bar and host podium, and anywhere else people stand for long periods of time.

Laying out your kitchen

As you design your brand-new kitchen or refurbish your existing one, a single word must be in the top of your mind: *flow.* How are things going to flow? Imagine your meal from delivery of product to delivery of the dishes to your guests. Picture the wine delivery person carrying a case of wine. Can he pass the dish area without falling, getting wet, and disturbing the dishwashers? Take a look at Figure 10-1 for an example of a kitchen layout with good flow.

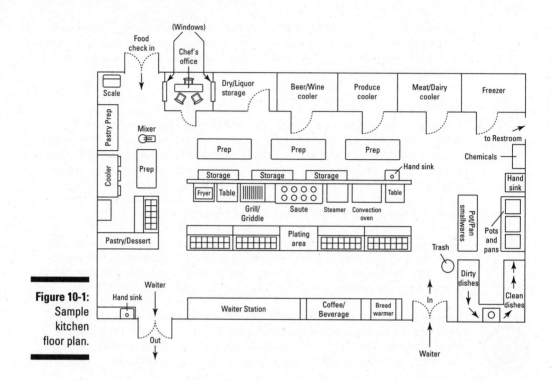

Figure 10-1:
Sample kitchen floor plan.

You and your employees will be on your feet many, many hours each day, so save as many steps as possible by designing an efficient layout. Here are some ideas to help you make sure that your kitchen design goes with the flow:

✓ **Locate your storage area as close to your delivery door as possible.** Doing so saves schlepping time and energy and hopefully keeps storage out of the way of the majority of your prep.

✓ **Determine which stations are getting the heaviest (and the lightest) workload based on your menu.** Look at the forecasted menu mix analysis that you created in your business plan. Your *menu mix analysis,* sometimes shortened to *menu mix,* is a report or prediction of which menu items sell in which quantities. Among other things, it tells you how many orders of Fried Calamari and Chicken Caesar Salad you sell in a given shift. (Check out Chapter 19 for tips on creating a menu mix analysis if you don't have one.)

Pull out your list of menu items and the associated equipment and stations (see the earlier section "Figuring out what you need to fix the food on your menu") and look at how many items in a shift will be coming out of each station. Make sure busy stations have enough reach-in space, counter space, and so on, and share reach-ins and counter space with stations used less often.

✔ **Place reach-in coolers (think of these as the commercial versions of your dorm-room fridge) close to their specific stations to keep products at a safe temperature until use.** In Figure 10-1, the pastry station (left side) has a three-door reach-in cooler; it's dedicated to products that may otherwise suffer from the constant in-and-out of the main coolers, and it's isolated from the heat of the hot line.

Fish files (under-counter refrigeration drawers) are a space-saving way to bring refrigeration to the hot line while conserving space and avoiding the space association problems common with reach-ins.

✔ **Keep your prep area close enough to the line to quickly restock it when needed.** Notice in Figure 10-1 that the prep area is located between the main walk-in coolers (produce and meat/dairy) where food flows to the prep tables and then to the line. Also leave plenty of space for garbage cans around your prep tables. Prep generates lots of trash, including cans, cartons, and vegetable remnants.

Consider your prep schedule and par levels when determining how many prep tables you need. *Par levels* are the goal levels you set for each item on your prep list for a given day based on the amount you forecast using for that day. For each shift, you count your food on hand and then prep to your par level. For example, if the par level for clam chowder on Tuesdays is 3½ gallons and you have only ½ gallon on hand, you prep 3 gallons that day.

✔ **Arrange your stations so that menu items flow down the line and to the expo with ease and efficiency.** The plating area in Figure 10-1 is located in the middle of the line, so plates come in from sides, through the plating area for a check with the expo, and then out the door.

✔ **Ensure that your prep staff can efficiently get dirty plates, pots, and pans off the line and to the dish area.** Keep the dish and prep workers out of each others' paths during busy shifts. Note that the dish area is separate from the prep area in Figure 10-1. The pots-and-pans shelf, where the line cooks can place pans that need a wash, is located at the end of the right side of the line.

✔ **Make sure the wait staff and bussers can get dirty dishes into the dish pit without falling and without hindering someone else's workflow.** Our dish pit is the first stop on the way into the kitchen, with an extended table so waiters won't block the door or anyone else trying to come in. Waiters flow in the "in" door and stop at the dish area.

✔ **Keep the path to the ice machine clear so that bartenders and wait staff have easy access to refill ice wells during peak times.** In our example, you could place the ice machine along the front wall of the kitchen near the waiter station, with easy access for anyone who needs it.

Considering Your Water Supply: Why Water Quality Matters

Anyone who has ever spent time in Dallas can tell you that the tap water has a particular taste . . . and an odor that can change depending on the conditions affecting the water supply. Now we're not leveling a one-off attack on our friends in the Lone Star State — changes in water quality can affect any kitchen, in any state.

You must address water quality if for no other reason than GIGO: Garbage In, Garbage Out. You may have the secret recipe for the very best gnocchi in Little Italy, but if you boil those dumplings in water that tastes like the Swamp Thing took a bath in it, what's the point? Effectively controlling the taste, clarity and smell of the water in your restaurant is a simple yet often overlooked necessity.

An effective water quality assurance program looks like this:

- **Soften the water going to the dishwasher.** This step lengthens the life of the machine and dramatically improves the quality of the job it does on your dishes and glassware. Your guests will notice the difference.

- **Soften the cold water before it gets to the hot water heater.** Softening the water here ensures that your entire food-preparation water supply is free from undesirable hardness, and it saves wear and tear on your hot water heater.

- **Carbon-filter all drinking and ice lines.** The presence of chlorine in the water supply yields unpleasant off-tastes in coffee, tea, sodas, ice, and drinking and cooking water. Install carbon filters on all lines that service the drinking, cooking, and ice water supply.

- **Consider a reverse osmosis (RO) system.** Installing a reverse osmosis system on the restaurant's consumable water supply line ensures that all water served is of bottled-water purity. This step is particularly important in areas where the water supply is subject to variations of taste, smell, or purity.

Have your water checked by a commercial water treatment specialist familiar with the needs of restaurants. These specialists can provide a diagnosis of the quality of your water and a plan (including equipment) to ensure the purity of your water supply.

Adapting an Existing Kitchen

Congratulations! You've found a site, and it already has a kitchen. A big piece of your business plan, including startup costs and equipment, is probably based on not needing to invest in a kitchen because there's one in your space already. But many times, modifying an existing kitchen is more expensive than building a new one. The costs of demolition and disposal, running gas lines, and updating the plumbing, ventilation, and fire suppression systems can really eat into your budget.

Before leasing, have all the plumbing checked out, especially the sewage main to the city lines. Kitchens produce a lot of grease and food matter that can clog pipes. We recommend a thorough jet cleaning of all pipes before you open. Nothing kills appetites like backed-up toilets!

Ask yourself these questions before you sign on the dotted line:

- ✔ Is it the kitchen for you and your menu? Does it have the space to accommodate your food? Can you work with the layout to get the flow you need for your menu?

- ✔ Does the existing equipment work? Can you use it? Is it held together by duct tape and coat hangers? Have a certified restaurant service pro inspect the equipment. If you find that the equipment isn't in top shape and can't be upgraded at the landlord's expense, exclude it from the deal and buy your own.

- ✔ Does the heating, ventilation, and air conditioning (HVAC) system work? A working HVAC system is a necessary asset; one that doesn't work is a liability.

- ✔ Do the wiring and the gas systems meet current building codes? The previous owner may have received a code exemption through a grandfather clause, but now you may have to make major updates to fit in with current codes at your expense.

- ✔ What's the sale price of the kitchen? If the owner is charging a lot for used equipment, you may be better off starting over with your own.

If you choose to include the equipment in your deal, stipulate in writing that the equipment must be in good working order.

An existing kitchen that has a good flow relative to your concept can save you tens of thousands of dollars. But don't get caught up in the fact that a space already has a kitchen and then alter your concept to match. If you've done the work and created a concept you believe in (and have the numbers to back up your plan), fit the kitchen to your concept — not the other way around.

Going into an existing operation can be a little off-putting at first. You may be expecting something that's as clean as the pristine television kitchen. But look at the space with an eye for immovable equipment like plumbing, the line, storage, and so on. You can't move them, so make sure you can work with the current setup. Floors can be cleaned, grease removed, and equipment repainted, so don't let the level of dirt and grime affect your decision. Look for floor drains to make floor cleaning easy.

Acquiring Your Kitchen Equipment

New York has the Bowery. Chicago has Restaurant Row. Most major cities have this kind of restaurant-supply street. Whether the products are new or used, you'll likely buy it here. If you're not located in a major city, going to one may be worth the trip, just for the money you can save and for the used equipment, but bring your bartering hat — and do your homework.

Know what equipment you need for your operation. Use the earlier section "Planning a Kitchen with the Menu in Mind" and Figure 10-1 to create a list of the equipment you need to produce the menu you've chosen. Know what the equipment costs new and used. Shop around. Check out equipment websites, national companies, local companies, and restaurant equipment auctions. Talk to other people in the business about their good experiences and bad ones, and collect names of good companies to work with. If your contacts can introduce you to someone specific, you'll be a step ahead. Be savvy. Know when you're getting a good deal and when you're not.

In a restaurant situation, the simpler the equipment, the better. For example, skip the equipment that boasts internal sensors. They're virtually useless and just another part that can break.

Deciding whether to buy or lease

Finding financing for equipment is tough until you're an established high-volume restaurant. Run the numbers to see whether buying or leasing is the best option for your business.

Looking at leasing

Leasing equipment has certain advantages. You pay for equipment only for the time you use it. When your lease is up, you get a brand-spanking-new piece of equipment with all the latest gadgets by signing a new lease. And when a piece of equipment breaks, fixing it isn't your responsibility.

Spell out all the financial details in the agreement so you're not surprised when the bill arrives. Get the agreement in writing and check your invoices. Things shouldn't change between the time you talk to your salesperson and the billing department sends you a bill, but sometimes they do.

Here are a few items, in particular, that we suggest you lease:

- ✔ **Ice machines and coolers:** Both units have relatively short lives. Their motors and condensers work very hard and burn out. Ice machines and coolers are expensive upfront, and there's virtually no market for used ones. Roll the price over in a lease format for a time so that when your machine is about to die, your lease will be up and you can move on to a new unit.

- ✔ **Dish machines:** This equipment is the restaurant version of your home dishwasher. It's very expensive upfront and usually can be leased through your chemical supplier. Some chemical suppliers give you the machine if you buy your cleaning products from them.

- ✔ **Coffeemakers:** Coffee companies often give you the machine if you buy the coffee from them. You may pay a little more for the product, but this option gives you flexibility and more positive cash flow. Plus if there's a breakthrough technology, you can usually upgrade quickly.

- ✔ **Linens:** Lease, don't buy, all your linens, including entry floor mats, uniforms, towels, tablecloths, and napkins. Usually you pay a single bill to have them delivered, stocked, and laundered.

Depending on your volume of purchasing, food suppliers such as U.S. Foodservice, Gordon Food Service, and SYSCO give you a computer with their ordering software that you can use for other business applications. They want to make placing orders with them as easy as possible for you.

Buying used or new

Wheeling and dealing with equipment can be a lot of fun, but you should be ready, willing, and able to tell the salesperson no and walk out of the store. It's no secret to him or to you (because you've read this book) that you can get the same thing two doors down. Expect to pay between 40 and 60 percent less for used equipment.

When buying restaurant equipment, negotiating is acceptable and expected. For example, say, "I'll buy this oven and grill if you throw in the stainless steel table." You may walk out with a mixer and food processor instead, but you probably need them anyway.

With used equipment, get some kind of a guarantee in writing. You may not get an extended warranty, but you need some assurance that the equipment is going to run for a while. When you buy used equipment, you trade off extended warranties and factory support in favor of a lower price. The only way that used equipment benefits you is by saving you money. If you don't save money buying used equipment, you might as well buy new equipment in the first place.

Don't worry about missing knobs and handles. You can usually add them. Focus on the all-important questions: Does it work? Will it work tomorrow? Is there a guarantee that it will work a week from now?

You can buy many pieces of equipment used, like those in the following list, and sleep soundly:

✔ **Gas ranges:** These appliances are excellent candidates for buying used. Unless you derive some sort of personal satisfaction from fancy equipment, don't go for a copper-clad import from Lyon when plenty of sound products are available that don't command the price.

The biggest consideration when buying a gas range is how many BTUs (British thermal units) it puts out. Most commercial ranges put out between 20,000 and 35,000 per burner. Some European (ring-style) ranges have large burners capable of 40,000 of more BTUs per burner, and commercial woks tip the scales at between 200,000 and 300,000 BTU. The style of cuisine you're serving dictates what you need. If you're boiling a lot of liquids in a large stock pot or need to really sear large joints of meat, you need more BTUs. For general sautéing or slow simmering, you need fewer BTUs. As a general rule, though, you can always turn the flame down — we'd rather have more power than wish we did.

✔ **Ovens:** Gas ovens, like gas ranges, are okay to buy used. But be cautious of purchasing used electrical ovens, because so many things can go wrong with them, including problems with the sensors and temperature controls. Don't buy very specialized pieces of equipment used, such as a combination oven (a combination steamer and convection oven) or a conveyer oven. You benefit from a warranty and complete information on the ideal cleaning and maintenance regimen that comes with a new oven.

✔ **Fryers:** Buy fryers used, but get a guarantee that the thermostat works. Calibrate the thermostat to make sure that the temperature is correct. If you don't know how to change the oil, when to change the oil, how to clean it, and so on, get the information from your salesperson. If you can get a manual with the equipment, even better.

- ✔ **Grills:** Grills are usually okay to buy used, especially the gas variety. But do a detailed visual inspection of wood and gas grills because, over time, the guts eventually burn out. The heat warps and distorts the grill's inner workings. Make sure the grill surface is flat. If the grates are removable, inspect them to make sure that the surface is level.

- ✔ **Smallwares:** You can buy almost all used smallwares (such as tongs, salt and pepper shakers, and soup cups) with confidence.

Moving beyond name-brand equipment

The name of the brand, designer, or manufacturer of kitchen equipment does not always predict the quality, performance, or durability of the tool. Take your time and do your homework researching the specific pieces of equipment, tools, and smallwares your menu requires. You may be amazed at the options and range of prices in the marketplace.

Unless you have an unlimited budget and/or some insatiable need to preference the brand of your grill over its performance, you'll likely find suitable high-performance options for the back-of-house from manufacturers that aren't initially on you radar. Very often these manufacturers choose to put the money that others spend for national advertising, celebrity endorsements, and brand awareness into the quality of their products and their customer service.

Getting purchasing advice

Building a big kitchen is a huge expense, so you may want to hire a consultant to advise you about purchasing equipment. Here's what a consultant can do:

- ✔ Review your concept plan and assist in choosing equipment for your concept. Together, you create a list of the equipment you need, including the quantities of each item, and whether it should be new or used.

- ✔ Develop a sourcing action plan for those pieces of equipment. The sourcing action plan includes using resources (online, network, and trade pubs) to figure out several sources for each piece of equipment, developing a process for evaluating the different options (manufactures, distributors, used equipment dealers, and so on) for each piece of equipment, and creating a schedule for acquiring the equipment.

- ✔ Solicit bids for new equipment. Your consultant should also help you evaluate the bids when they come in.

- ✔ Facilitate purchase of used equipment, including negotiating the purchase price, conducting inspections, clarifying warranties, and scheduling delivery.

Chapter 11

Setting Up a Bar and Beverage Program

· ·

· ·

*W*hether you're looking to open your neighborhood's new favorite pub where regulars become permanent fixtures, the *in* club with the latest music and best drink specials, or an elegant wine bar attached to a chic new restaurant with an up-and-coming chef, this chapter is for you. Here, we cover everything you need to think about when opening your bar, from equipment and supplies to attracting customers.

But don't be so quick to skip past here if your establishment doesn't have an actual wooden bar with stools and all. If you plan to serve alcohol, you'll want to stick around because we also help you set up a beverage program. We give you info on figuring out what you need based on your restaurant concept; tips on stocking, pricing, and selling beer, wine, and liquor; and important information on serving alcohol responsibly.

We can't begin to cover all the ins and outs of setting up a bar in this chapter, so for more information, check out *Running a Bar For Dummies,* by Ray Foley and Heather Dismore (John Wiley & Sons, Inc.). It's brimming with great ideas for making the most of this money-making center of your restaurant.

Setting Up Your Bar

Your bar must match your concept. If you have a bar and restaurant together, the themes should be connected. One global chain of Australian steakhouses is basically made up of bars that happen to have restaurants built around them. Most diners come in and have to wait for a table just long enough to sit at the bar and have a drink. Other successful restaurants have only a service bar (with no stools or counter) that's accessible only to the wait staff.

Before purchasing any bar equipment, think about your goals. Decide whether you want your bar to be the primary source of income for your business or subordinate to the restaurant. This decision helps you determine how much space to dedicate to your bar, your dining room, and all the other front-of-the-house areas. (Chapter 9 covers laying out the front of the house.)

Form and function go hand in hand when setting up a successful bar business. If you have a free-standing bar, spend time considering both factors in your design. The following sections focus on the specifics.

Figuring out furniture

Furniture helps set the stage for your bar. After you've spent some time working on your FOH floor plan and setting up your space (see Chapter 9), you'll have a good sense of what furniture works for your bar. The basic bar furniture list looks a little something like this:

- **Bar and service rail:** Decide where to put the actual bar. Look to Chapter 9 for help in laying out your bar within your restaurant.

- **Bar stools:** If you need bar stools, consider the number of stools you need based on the length of your bar. Each stool should have about 2 feet of dedicated bar space, so if your bar is 12 feet long, you need 6 stools.

- **Racks for hanging glassware:** Installing glass racks above the counters in the bar saves valuable counter space. Of course, if you have 20-foot ceilings, racks for glasses aren't practical. As always, make sure even a utilitarian element fits with your concept before installing them.

- **Tables and chairs:** Consider whether tables and chairs work for your bar area. You can use the same styles you use in the dining room or select something different.

- **Coat/purse hooks:** Hooks are handy for diners and for you. You may save yourself a few chairs for actually seating customers by giving people somewhere specific to hang their stuff.

- **Power outlets:** You may add extra outlets on the customers' side of the bar for diners to recharge laptops and cell phones while passing the time in your establishment.

Selecting equipment

Decide early on where you want the basic equipment of your bar to be. After you set these items up, they'll stay put for quite awhile. The basic bar equipment list looks like this:

- **Payment system:** Tie your bar payment system into your main system. The bar should have a separate cash drawer and computer terminal (if you're using a computerized system). If you plan to serve food at the bar, the bartenders need access to any food ordering system you use. If you plan to use a computerized system, your service bar also needs a printer to print out the restaurant's bar orders as they come in. Take a look at Chapter 14 for help.

- **Pour metering equipment:** Weigh your options for metering, pouring, or strictly controlling the amount of liquor in each drink. Systems range from pour tops added to control the speed the liquor flows to fully computerized systems that dispense the measured amount of alcohol at the touch of a button and keep track of the number of drinks made from each bottle.

  Make sure to check your local blue laws. Some states and counties require metered pouring. Coauthors Heather and Andy lived in South Carolina, and their county required pouring individual drinks from individual 50-milliliter liquor bottles.

  Bar customers like a free pour (pouring the alcohol without using any measuring device). Anything else seems chintzy. Decide how to balance your profit with their perception (see the "Lapping Up Some Liquor Learning" section later in the chapter).

- **Smoke eaters:** If you happen to live in one of the ten counties in this country that still allow smoking in restaurants, install smoke eaters (commercial air-filtering systems) to help control the smoke.

- **Walk-in cooler:** Your bar's walk-in cooler (usually shortened to *walk-in*) should be large enough to hold your inventory of white and rosé wines, your beer kegs, your backup bottled beer supply, and any other supplies your bar uses regularly that must be kept cold.

  If you have the space, consider keeping your beverage walk-in separate from food. You can adjust the temperature to keep each set of items at their own ideal temperatures. Additionally, you can keep high-dollar liquor items at a different level of security than your lettuce and tomatoes.

✔ **Wells:** Each area where a bartender works needs a well. The well holds ice (with a dedicated ice scoop), *well brands* (traditionally, the least expensive brands) of the basic liquors (vodka, gin, whiskey, rum, and scotch), a garnish station, and a soda gun. Figure 11-1 shows what a well looks like.

Don't use glasses to scoop ice — ever, never, not under any circumstances. If your glass chips or breaks in the ice bin, you have to pour hot water in it to melt all the ice (*burn* it, in industry speak) in the ice well, remove the broken glass, and clean and sanitize it. Then you have to restock the ice before you can use the well again. In fact, anytime there's a chance that glass may have gotten into the well, you have to burn the ice and sanitize the well.

✔ **Hand sinks with soap and sanitizer:** Hand sinks are small sinks reserved for washing hands only. Stock the sink with antibacterial soap, paper towels, and hand sanitizer.

✔ **Draft beer system:** Depending on your setup, the kegs can be in the bar or in a separate cooler with lines running to the bar:

✔ **Tap lines:** For cleaning considerations, check with your beer supplier regarding the ideal length of the line for the product you're serving. Make sure to chill the beer lines as well. We've seen beer lines so long that the beer isn't at optimal serving temperature by the time it reaches the customer.

✔ **Beer taps:** The actual tap tower the customers see should match your concept and positioning. Your beer salesperson usually provides the tap handles.

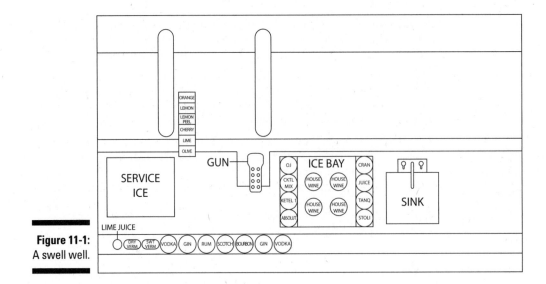

Figure 11-1: A swell well.

Work with the experts to make sure that you're serving the products at the right temperature and pressure. Have the equipment calibrated and cleaned regularly, at least once a month.

✔ **Reach-in coolers:** Reach-in coolers (usually shortened to *reach-ins*) are the professional equivalent of a dorm room fridge. Choose *lowboys* (reach-ins below the waist, typically with solid doors), glass-front display reach-ins for the back bar, or both. And consider a top-opening ice cream style *reach-down* if you're stocking lots of bottled beers. As always, look for the best setup for your operation.

✔ **Soda system:** The bar usually shares your restaurant's soda system, with guns at each well. But double-check your system. If you have to add this feature after the fact, it can be a huge additional expense.

✔ **Wine preservation system:** This system removes the air in a bottle of wine and then seals the bottle until you open it again, keeping the wines in your by-the-glass program fresh. For help deciding whether your restaurant needs a wine preservation system, take a look at the later section "Getting with It about Wine."

✔ **Glass-washing equipment:** Most bars have a system of three sinks designed for washing glasses. The first sink holds the motorized brushes used to clean the glasses. The second contains hot, clean water to rinse the glasses. The third sink contains sanitizer to sanitize the glasses.

✔ **Blender:** This small appliance is sometimes called a bartender's least favorite friend. It's for all those drinks like daiquiris and frozen margaritas that typically take longer to make than a standard cocktail.

✔ **Cappuccino/espresso machine:** Some restaurants place cappuccino/espresso machines behind the bar rather than in the wait station. Consider what fits your concept when deciding where to put yours.

✔ **Specialty equipment for your concept:** Maybe you plan to keep a frozen beverage machine full of margaritas or sangria, or perhaps you need to display the infused spirits you make in-house.

Selecting smallwares

Here's a list of *smallwares* (things like tools, less-expensive equipment, and dishware) that are present in most bars. You probably need it all, but you can set it up in multiple ways and change it as needed:

✔ **Jiggers and shot glasses:** Use these to measure liquor for mixed drinks.

✔ **Cocktail shakers:** Use these items to shake cocktails such as martinis.

✔ **Cocktail strainers:** These gadgets attach to cocktail shakers and strain ice from shaken drinks that are served *up* (without ice).

- ✓ **Garnish tray:** This item holds lime wedges and lemon twists.

- ✓ **Bar spoons:** These items are great for stirring drinks.

- ✓ **Muddlers:** A muddler looks like a small wooden baseball bat. They're used to crush mint leaves for mojitos or fruit and sugar for old-fashioneds.

- ✓ **Glassware:** Choose a variety of glasses to match your beverage program. You may find that one general-purpose wine glass fits your style, or you may instead choose to offer specific glassware designed to enhance the taste, aroma, and visual appeal of various beverages. Beverages that benefit from specific glassware include Port, Belgian ales, aperitifs, and brandies.

  Here's a list of the minimum glassware styles we recommend for most restaurants:

  - • **Wine glass:** One basic wine glass; if you serve sparkling wines, you need a second

  - • **Rocks glass:** Usually a 5- to 10-ounce squatty glass used to serve spirits on the rocks or *neat* (without ice)

  - • **Highball:** A taller glass 8-12 ounces for serving to serve mixed drinks and cocktails on the rocks.

  - • **Pint glass:** An all-purpose glass for serving soda and draft beer

  - • **Martini glass:** Elegant glasses for serving martinis *up,* or chilled and then strained, served without ice

  For a more complete list of glassware options, take a look at *Running a Bar For Dummies,* by Ray Foley and Heather Dismore (John Wiley & Sons, Inc.).

- ✓ **Rail mats:** Bartenders usually make drinks on these mats because they catch small spills.

- ✓ **Floor mats:** These industrial-grade rubber mats cushion achy knees and soothe achy feet. These mats are typically grids of small circles that connect at the edges and can be thoroughly hosed down daily or between shifts. In addition to keeping the bartenders' feet dry, they save wear and tear on the knees, feet, and ankles!

- ✓ **Corkscrews:** Depending on your level of wine service, determine whether you need industrial wine openers for quickly opening bottles.

- ✓ **Bottle openers:** If you do a booming beer business, get the ones with a built-in bottle cap holder.

- ✓ **Knives:** You need these utensils to cut the garnishes.

- ✓ **Cutting board:** Here's where you cut the garnishes.

- ✓ **Silverware and china:** If you serve food in your bar, you need a supply of these items near the bar.

✔ **Sanitizing bucket:** Keep sanitizer mixed (at the proper concentration) and ready to sanitize surfaces quickly to keep from contaminating reach-ins, ice wells, glasses, and other items.

✔ **Containers with color-coded tops:** These containers allow you to keep a supply of bloody Mary mix, orange juice, and the like in your bar reach-in for easy access and to keep contents fresh.

✔ **Ice buckets:** Used for refilling the ice wells in the bar, these containers must be labeled "for ice only." If anything else gets in these buckets, they must be cleaned and sanitized before you use them for ice.

If your ice machine is a long way from your bar, get rolling ice buckets or bins for restocking the ice. The wheels save strain on the staff because they won't need to wrestle the bins through the dining room. Use bins that are small enough that people can pick them up to dump them in the wells without back strain.

Surveying supplies

Supplies are anything you stock and restock on a fairly regular basis. *Disposables,* such as napkins, straws, and hand soaps, are supplies. So are *consumables* such as garnishes, ice, and fruit juice. (Beer, wine, and liquor are consumables, and we cover each later in the chapter. Chapter 13 gives you the lowdown on purchasing and managing supplies.)

Beverage suppliers can be a great source of free supplies like bar napkins, coasters, wine keys, and other swag. Just know that they'll likely bear the brand of the providers, so make sure that works with your concept.

Your supply list will vary, but here's a general all-purpose list:

✔ **Drink menus:** You may have an entire list of different martinis or just a list of spirits that you carry. Be creative but informative.

✔ **Food menus:** Any food available in the bar should be on a menu there. If you have the same menu, keep a supply of dining room menus in the bar. If a limited menu is available in the bar, create a separate menu.

✔ **Soaps, cleaners, and sanitizers:** Get the right cleaners for your equipment. Check with your manufacturer for details.

✔ **Garnishes:** Examples include maraschino cherries, lemon wheels, lemon twists, celery, lime wedges, lime twists, olives, and margarita salt.

✔ **Paper goods:** You need things such as straws, stir sticks, beverage napkins, coasters, and dinner napkins.

✔ **Towels, bar rags, and sponges:** Keep a supply of these items handy to wipe up sticky cordials, overflowing beer taps, and mixer mix-ups.

✔ **Requisition forms:** Employees use these forms to request more supplies.

✔ **Drink recipes:** Your collection may take the form of a binder, recipe-card box, or even a computerized database of drinks. It may be a comprehensive list of every cocktail known to mankind or just a quick reference to your house specialties.

✔ **Food-specific supplies:** If you serve food in your bar, you need other supplies like salt and pepper and condiments.

Keeping Your Bar Clean

Your bar should be just as clean as, if not cleaner than, any other area in the restaurant. Here, your patrons get an upfront, intimate look at the sinks, shelves, counters, and cabinets. If they see dripping, sticky bottles and a mildewed reach-in, how long do you think they'll keep coming back?

Develop a cleaning and sanitation system immediately, before you open your bar. Your bar is subject to health inspections just like any part of your restaurant. We cover cleanliness and sanitation in detail in Chapter 17, but here are a few bar-specific points to consider:

✔ Don't allow any eating behind the bar. Bits of food can get mixed in with supplies and equipment. Similarly, don't allow smoking or drinking behind the bar.

✔ Bartenders should wash their hands often. They shouldn't mix drinks and touch the ice scoop without washing their hands. In addition, after a bartender touches her own mouth or nose, she should wash her hands.

✔ Bartenders must use utensils — not their hands — to stir drinks.

✔ Bartenders should never, ever stick their hands in dirty glasses. Picking up four glasses at a time by placing your fingers inside them and then clamping your fingers together may seem efficient, but each time you do it, it's like sticking your fingers in someone's mouth.

✔ Create a rotation system for garnishes and mixes, especially during slow times. Lime wedges left over from the weekend may not still be useable for Wednesday night margarita specials. Rotation is often more of a problem in the bar than in the kitchen, because kitchen staff members are usually beat over the head with the info from Day 1; Bartenders aren't. Check your perishables and make sure you're practicing FIFO (first in, first out).

Drawing Drinking Crowds

Creative bar owners bring in the crowds in a variety of ways. Behind every busy bar is a reason people come, whether it's music, games, or drink specials. Maintain flexibility in your design so you can reconfigure your space easily as your bar business changes. In this section, we give you some pointers on what you may want to use to both draw and entertain the masses.

Running promotions

REMEMBER

Promotions are events you use to attract customers — and make more money. Your job is to find a balance between getting people in the door and actually profiting from this increased traffic. If a promotion doesn't make money, it's not successful, no matter how many people you get in the door. Planning and analysis are key: Use the same process for forecasting expenses and sales we show you in Chapter 5 to outline the best, worst, and most likely scenarios for each promotion. Then follow up to determine the actual outcome.

Promotions are limited only by your imagination (and all applicable laws, of course). Put yourself in your potential customers' shoes to figure out what will draw them in. Here are a few creative promotions we've heard of, which we include to spark your creativity. We don't recommend that you do or do not use them: Think about what works for the clientele you're going after, what fits with your local liquor laws, and what's profitable for your business:

- ✔ **Sponsor a softball team:** You get advertising space on the jerseys or in the league programs, and the players — and their friends and family — become part of the greater bar family. This approach works with other sporting events (like golf outings) and leagues, too.

- ✔ **Take part in radio station promotions:** Partner with a local station to broadcast from your bar. Give away free stuff such as shirts, other merchandise, and event tickets to improve your chances of drawing a crowd.

- ✔ **Offer a free happy-hour buffet:** Set up an appetizer buffet for a limited period of time, or simply offer complimentary snacks and appetizers at certain hours. You can also charge a small fee to cover some of the costs.

- ✔ **Create a bar event schedule:** For example, you can make Monday football night, Tuesday karaoke night, Wednesday mud-wrestling night, and Thursday $2 draft beer night.

- ✔ **Feature a ladies' night:** Women get two-for-one drinks or no cover charge. Bring in the women, and the men will follow.

Successful bars advertise. Take a look at Chapter 15 for details.

Providing entertainment

Keep your sports ear to the ground and the other tuned to the local music scene. There are sports to watch, games to play, music to hear, and songs to sing. If you're looking for entertainment for your bar, start locally.

If you're running a bar inside a restaurant, think carefully before adding entertainment. If the bar crowd gets rowdy, it can affect your restaurant patrons. Owners of stand-alone bars can be a bit more creative and/or edgy with entertainment options — people go to a bar for a reason, and it's not a G-rated show.

Flipping on the TV

Sports bars are common in most parts of the country. Many have satellite TV packages that let customers watch games from every type of league in every time zone. You need to pay a fee to display the programming for commercial use. Check with your satellite company about the regulations in your area.

Establishing a Wi-Fi Internet hotspot

A Wi-Fi hotspot is an access point that provides wireless broadband network services. Because constantly keeping up with e-mail is a basic need for many people, customers expect to find access in restaurants. If you don't offer Wi-Fi access, people will choose another restaurant over time. Contact your Internet service provider for details on setting up Wi-Fi for customer use.

Don't charge for Wi-Fi access — from a hospitality standpoint, a Wi-Fi hotspot should be an amenity, not a profit center for your restaurant.

Playing games

Besides being a way to draw customers, games such as pool, electronic darts, and video games are actually revenue-generating. In fact, some restaurants rely on the income generated from games to support the business, offering food almost as an afterthought. Grown-up versions of the arcade-with-restaurant-attached are becoming more common. Look for names like Dave and Buster's, Jillian's, and ESPN Zone, to name a few.

Gambling in bars is also becoming more common. Anything from video poker to keno on closed-circuit TV is available. If you're into gambling, you can put together leagues for poker, football pools, and other avenues to drawing customers and increasing profits. But make sure that any gambling you offer is legal. Don't risk your operation by taking illegal bets.

Turning up the music

Adding music to your bar isn't always easy. You can get started with a jukebox. If you're looking to create a dance scene, consider hiring a DJ. DJs usually bring their own collections of music with them and play at your bar. You pay them a fee for their services. The fee can be a flat rate, a percentage of sales, or a percentage of the cover charge, if applicable.

Karaoke allows your patrons to get up on stage and sing along with recorded music. If you're interested in starting a karaoke night, consider renting a machine or hiring a service to run your program to see how it goes. A full commercial-quality system can run anywhere from $500 to $5,000.

If you want to move beyond a jukebox, check out some other bars and restaurants in your area and get to know the local music scene. Live music is a great way to bring in customers. Many local bands have their own followings and bring their fans with them. Expect to pay between $500 and $5,000 to get a decent band in for a weekend night. Some bands charge a flat fee, and others charge a percentage of sales and the full cover charge. Usually, the bigger the band (in number of members and in popularity), the more you pay. Talk to other bar owners to find out acceptable rates.

Offering great bartenders

Bartenders can bring in patrons. Attractive female bartenders bring in men (think *Coyote Ugly*). Attractive male bartenders bring in women who bring in men (think *Cocktail*). But looks are only one way your bartenders can bring in customers.

A knowledgeable bartender can also be a draw. *Mixology* — the art of the cocktail — as a discipline has taken off in recent years. Any bartender you hire should be well-versed in beer, wine, and spirits, with an emphasis on your specialty drinks.

Don't stop with beverages. Educate your bartenders about your food as well. Even if they don't know the full menu, bartenders should know your specialties. If your bartenders know your signature hot sauces, the special cheeses, or the secrets of your simmered sauces, they can build a regular bar clientele and encourage them to bring in friends for meals in the dining room.

Many guests invest time in a bartender. They spend time getting to know the bartenders and, generally, appreciate bartenders who recognize and remember them as regulars. Maybe your bartender is the neighborhood counselor, or maybe he's in the know. Depending on the size of the town or the neighborhood, patrons may follow a bartender if he leaves one bar to work at another.

Get with the (Beverage) Program: Providing Liquid Refreshment

The term *beverage program* generally applies to drinks served in restaurants. Even though nonalcoholic beverages are often inventoried with your food products, they're still part of your beverage program. Typically, things like coffee, tea, and fountain soft drinks are purchased from the same suppliers you get your food from, so they're subject to the same pricing plans (and hopefully discounts and rebates) as your food. If you serve smoothies, shakes, and juices, they're definitely food products (even though you drink them) because they're made from the same things your food products are made from.

In this section, we discuss your beverage program, including info on premium nonalcoholic drinks.

Creating your beverage program

Use the same creative drive in your beverage program that exists in developing your menu (check out Chapter 8 for help). Before you can think about what you need from a beverage program, you must understand your concept and your clientele. Then make choices on what to include on your drink lists based on these factors. If your interior design and menu are taking some risks, your beverage program needs to stand out, too. If you're running a family restaurant offering traditional fare, plan a beverage list to match.

Decide how to focus your list. Are you going to offer boutique vodka, gins, and scotch, or does a basic well (the least expensive brands of basic liquors) do it? Watch your competition. Where's your point of difference from the guy down the street? Maybe being familiar (or edgy) is your point of difference. Do you want to touch on all the facets of the beverage program (wine, liquor, beer, and nonalcoholic beverages) or specialize in one area?

Don't try to support too much from the beginning. It's not a good idea to reduce the number of your beverage choices, especially alcoholic drinks, after your restaurant opens; it's much better to start smaller when you first open and add to your list later. If you serve 15 different domestic bottled beers when you first open but later reduce that list to 2 domestic beers to create inventory efficiency, you risk disappointing customers.

Developing a robust nonalcoholic beverage program

Simply relying on a soda gun as your nonalcoholic beverage program is passé for most restaurants. There are so many good reasons to create a robust nonalcoholic beverage program, and most of them revolve around one key idea: profit. In most cases, premium nonalcoholic beverages are not eligible for free refills.

The demand has never been higher for creative, nonalcoholic drinks. Here are a few common groups of customers that could be lining up for your mocktail creations:

- **Kids:** Kids and parents alike are looking for alternatives to soda.
- **Athletes:** Even amateur athletes often take a break from booze when they're training for an event, like a half marathon or triathlon. Don't miss the opportunity to sell them a premium drink in line with their nutrition goals.
- **Pregnant women:** Many women are looking for something beyond water to drink while pregnant, and a restaurant is the perfect place to treat them. One clever bar owner created a line of materni-tinis to cater to this particular group.
- **Designated drivers:** Many groups include designated drivers who refrain from drinking in order to safely drive the rest of the party around later. Give them a choice beyond a refillable soft drink.
- **Teetotalers:** A significant percentage of adults simply don't drink. You can boost your check averages by offering them a higher-priced alternative to ice tea.

If you agree that your bottom line could benefit from expanding your offerings, consider these categories when creating your nonalcoholic drink menu:

- **Coffee drinks:** Espressos, cappuccinos, lattes, mochas, iced coffees, and their many variations might have a place on your menu.
- **Handcrafted classics:** Consider specialty lemonades and flavored ice teas.
- **Seasonal offerings:** Think about your weather (maybe a specialty hot chocolate) and events (virgin mint juleps for non-drinkers at a Kentucky Derby party) for sources of ideas.
- **Juice-based drinks:** You can leverage trends like organic juices to create your own concoctions.

Consider whether you want to include a nonalcoholic beer or wine on your list as well.

Becoming Beer Brainy

Many restaurants get away with a very limited beer menu. You may consider limiting your beer choices to a domestic beer (such as Bud, Miller Genuine Draft, or Michelob), a domestic light beer (such as Bud Light, Coors Light, or Michelob Ultra), an import (Heineken or Becks), and an imported light beer (Amstel Light). But your concept may require you to dig a little deeper. If you're a German restaurant, you probably have to have a German beer, or three, on your list. You need to know your targeted clientele. Even if your target audience prefers mostly pedestrian selections, you should consider including something out of the ordinary to spice up your list.

Take a look at the beer list we created for our mock restaurant Urban Forge Pizza Bar:

Draft Beers	*Bottled Beers*
Domestic lager	Classic American
India pale ale	Light
Italian	Italian
Regional craft beer	Imported (not Italian)
Seasonal craft beer	Italian-American regional craft

You can approach pricing bottles of beer much like you do wine. See Table 11-1 for an example, in which you charge four times what you pay for the bottle.

Table 11-1	Bottle Beer Pricing Based at Four Times Cost
Cost per 12-oz. Bottle	**Price per 12-oz. Bottle**
$0.60	$2.40
$0.70	$2.80
$0.80	$3.20
$1.00	$4.00
$1.10	$4.40

When you're working with pricing a mug of draft beer, put your calculator away. You'd need to figure the number of ounces per keg and the number of ounces per pour and hope that your keg system is working perfectly. If your gas isn't working properly, you could be wasting lots of beer. Although keg systems require maintenance and incur lots of spillage and waste, they give you huge profits. The average draft beer costs somewhere between 5 and 15 cents an ounce in product.

Because beer is so readily available and people generally know what you paid for it, price it according to market norms — and don't charge too much. You can't charge $6 for a Bud and sell very many (unless you run the concessions at a professional sports venue). People will rebel.

The cost of keg deposits has nearly tripled over the past ten years. The primary reason is the high cost of metals. Breweries saw their kegs disappearing. Some operators were selling their empties to scrapyards and reaping the cost difference.

Winning with Wine

As with most other facets of your restaurant, your wine list choices depend heavily on your concept because it affects customers' expectations for both your list and the food you serve. But whether you're a family-style restaurant or a fine dining establishment, you can use a wine list to your advantage.

Creating your list

A lot goes into creating a successful wine list. You need to make the right choices for your customers and your concept. A wine rep can help you do your research.

Don't put all your eggs in one wine rep's basket. We recommend spreading your selections among several reps. If you don't, you lose your leverage. Keep your reps a little hungry, and they're more willing to help you out. If they "own" your list, they're less motivated.

Considering customer expectations

Many customers know what they want in a wine; others are always open to experimenting and trying something new. A popular strategy for developing a wine list over time is to give your diners familiar choices to start with and then expand your offerings to include similar yet less-familiar choices as you go along. You can introduce guests to new wines and let them explore the unfamiliar ones by the glass.

Anything that makes your customers happy (and keeps them spending money) is a good choice for your wine list. If a customer comes in once or twice a week and wants a particular wine on the menu, give it to her.

Your customers may interpret your use of "grocery store" wines (wines that are extremely familiar and inexpensive) as being too low-end. But, depending on your concept, your clientele may expect these wines. Make sure that you make this type of wine a deliberate choice, not just an easy out.

Matching with menu offerings

The ability to match your wine list to your menu is key to running a good restaurant wine program. Co-author Michael frequents a restaurant where a husband and wife run the restaurant. She does the wine list, which includes only 10 or 12 wines that go perfectly with the menu. She focuses on what's on the menu and pairs accordingly.

If you're just getting started or want to update your list but don't know where to begin, consider having your wine salespeople taste some recipes and help you pair your offerings with their wines. Wine reps love to give their input. Just know that they'll design the list around their own portfolio exclusively.

Looking at the length of the list and quality level of selections

A wine list doesn't have to be long, eclectic, or familiar to be good. And a good wine doesn't have to be serious; it just has to be a wine that someone enjoys. Find a balance between the eclectic and familiar standbys. Don't get too esoteric, or you risk intimidating guests with your offerings.

If people don't recognize the types of wine you're serving, make sure that your staff knows them, can explain them in detail, and brings the diner a sample. Also, if pronunciation may be intimidating, give each wine a number on the menu so guests can order by number; otherwise, guests may avoiding the unfamiliar because they're afraid of looking foolish.

The "grocery store" wines, or wines that everyone knows, are definitely on the way out in restaurants because many diners can figure out what you paid for the bottle, so justifying the price you need to charge to make your margins is tough. But have no fear; plenty of other great wines are available at reasonable prices. Work with your wine rep to find wines that fit with your menu items and that you can buy at a low price and meet your margin.

Teaming up the pros

Having a good rapport with wine reps may help your restaurant. They should help steer you toward the diamonds in the rough, let you know the status of their inventory, let you know about new selections *before* they arrive. When closeouts occur with certain labels and vintages, the reps can make sure that you know about them, and wine reps can help you get a great product before it becomes unavailable. In summary, a wine rep can be key in helping you prepare for wine list changes.

Don't let a wine rep lead you by the nose. Be candid with him. Even if he knows more about wine than you, don't let that dictate how he conducts his business. Your interaction should be mutually beneficial. You don't want to be saddled with inventory that you can't sell.

Work with more than one rep. Exclusives are dangerous. Friendly competition amongst companies vying for your business is an advantage for you.

For our restaurant Urban Forge, we developed an initial wine list. Here's what we want for this list, based on our concept:

- A 2:1 ratio of red to white wines

- Some wines that may not go with our menu specifically but that we know our customers will buy

- Some wines that are perfect for our food but may be unfamiliar to our customers; we'll encourage guests to try these other wines by offering them by the glass

- Some wines that the aficionado will recognize and appreciate

Here's the initial list we came up with, but we intend to expand the list over time. We've covered our bases and can manage our inventory with our opening cost considerations, but we plan to expand the list with our cash flow.

Red Bottle	Red Glass	White Bottle	White Glass	Rosé Glass
Chianti Classico	Chianti	Real Pinot Grigio	Pinot Grigio	Provence Rose
Super T	Dolcetto	Italian Chard	California Chard	
Sardinian Cannonau	Barbaresco		New Zealand Sauvignon Blanc	
Barolo	Primotivo		Vermentino (not Tuscan)	
	Puglian Cabernet		German (Alto Adige) Riesling	
	Pinot Nero		Pinot Bianco	
	Alto Adige Lagrein			
	California Pinot Noir			
	Shiraz			

Pricing your wine

Determining your selling price for wines by the bottle is relatively easy. You simply decide on the factor you want to multiply the cost by. For example, you may pick a factor of two to three times what you paid for it. This system is really just another way to look at food cost. Here you're multiplying; with food cost, you're dividing.

The more expensive the wine is, the lower the factor that you may multiply by. So if you buy the wine from your supplier for $12, you may charge $36 (where you multiplied the cost of the wine by 3). But if you paid $50 for a bottle of wine, you'll likely charge closer to $100 than $150 per bottle. Your percentage is lower, but your profit is higher.

Fifty dollars in inventory does you no good on the shelf. Don't be tempted to overprice your wine — you could price yourself out of a sale. With wine, don't worry about keeping the percentage that you make off your program high. Move wine through your restaurant to keep money flowing instead of tying it up in inventory.

Pricing your wines by the glass is tougher, but you can do it. First decide on the size of your pour, usually either a 5- or 6-ounce pour. A standard wine bottle is 750 milliliters (just over 25 ounces), so you get five 5-ounce glasses or four 6-ounce glasses from each. Then decide on the factor you want to multiply by, just like you do for your bottle program.

The difference in the price you pay versus the price you charge may seem huge. But don't forget that you have to cover all your costs, including waste, if the rest of the bottle goes bad. Take a look at Chapter 8 for details on what expenses you need to cover with your food and beverage prices.

Consider buying wine in a box or by the bag (especially for a house wine) — don't be afraid simply because it sounds suspect or cheap. Increasingly, wineries are using box and bag technology to store a better-quality wine than they previously handled.

Storing your wine

Storage is a huge issue for wine. Wine's biggest enemies are air, temperature, humidity, and light. Most wine cellars are below ground because the temperature underground is constant and cool. Take your cue from these wine cellars and guard your wine against these forces by picking a cool, dry, and dark location for your stock. If your investment in your wine list is sizable, you may want to invest in your own climate-controlled wine cellar.

Store the bottles on their sides or upside down while they're in their cases to prevent the corks from drying out and letting air seep in.

Beyond the bottle storage concerns, many bar owners worry about storing and preserving open bottles for their by-the-glass program. Always date a bottle before opening it to pour by the glass. And if you have an extensive by-the-glass program, consider investing in a wine preservation system. These systems evacuate the air in a bottle, usually replacing it with argon or nitrogen, and then seal the bottle until you open it again. The price for a basic system starts at around $500 and goes up, depending on which gadgets you want and how many bottles you need to preserve.

If you have a high velocity wine-by-the-glass program, a storage system may be more expense and trouble than it's worth. These systems are designed for fairly long term storage for open wine bottles, for up to four weeks.

If you can't afford a wine preservation system, a really competent bartender can be an ally, especially if she works almost every day. She can keep an eye on open bottles, steer bar patrons toward those selections, and help avoid waste. She should also know when to trash a bottle that's been open too long.

Lapping Up Some Liquor Learning

Thanks to the Internet, more people have increased access to smaller distilleries and small-batch liquor producers. Bar-goers are trending to quality niche spirits over volume drinking. Forty years ago, brown spirits, such as whiskey, scotch, and bourbon, ruled the bar roost. But lighter and clearer spirits (vodka, gin, and tequila) — and particularly higher-quality labels of those light spirits — are definitely where the bar business is right now and probably will be for the next few years. Pick the brands that match your concept and watch the trends to adjust your offerings accordingly.

Avoid the urge to overstock. Allocate your valuable bar space to stuff that moves. You can probably skip Bénédictine herbal liqueur and sloe gin, no matter what your liquor rep says. And resist the sales pitch that promises free bottles of stuff you don't use. If the free liquor is only a dust collector, how does that help you?

You can't *marry,* or consolidate, bottles of liquor. Doing so is illegal. You may think that you're being efficient by adding your half bottle of well vodka from the south well to the bottle of well vodka from the north well and then stocking a fresh bottle in the south well. But you can't. Basically, the government is trying to protect consumers from fraud — bartenders putting cheap vodka in a high-end bottle and charging more.

Pour size and pricing

Your *pour size,* or how much liquor you pour into each cocktail, is important. It determines what the finished drink costs you, how much you can charge, and how much profit you make on each drink.

A typical serving of liquor in a mixed drink is 1 to 1½ ounces. If you pour 1 ounce per drink, you'll get 33 drinks from each 750-milliliter bottle. If you pour 1½ ounces, you'll get 22 drinks from each bottle. So if you pay $20 for a bottle of booze, those same shots will cost you 61 cents and 91 cents, respectively. Add in another 10 cents for each for ice and the mixers. So if you want to achieve a 20 percent cost on your liquor, you should sell a 1½-ounce drink made from a $20 bottle for $4.59. You probably want to round these up a bit because, honestly, who can keep track of a drink that costs $4.59? Round it up to $4.95. For more on why you round menu prices, check out Chapter 8.

You charge more than the drink costs you to make because you have to account for your profit and various other costs like *buybacks* (buying the occasional drink for regular diners or for guests spending lots of money in your establishment), overpouring, spillage, breakage, employee drinks, the occasional unscrupulous bartender.

Pricing mixed drinks is more like pricing food than pricing beer and wine. Because the ingredients in a mixed drink can vary so much, you really need a formula (much like the one we provide in Chapter 8 for food) in order to determine the full cost and then the price of cocktails. It costs you more to sell a martini served with three jumbo olives stuffed with blue cheese than a martini served with a plain olive, so you should charge more.

Liquor lingo: Understanding cost and quality

Terms like *well, call,* and *premium* refer to the cost, and presumably the quality, of the ingredients in a drink and, ultimately, what the customer pays for the drink. If a customer doesn't ask for, or *call,* a specific brand of liquor, you use what you're pouring from your *well,* which are the cheapest house brands. The pricing-tier system of vodka looks like this:

Tier	*Common Brands*
Well	Popov, Dark Eyes, Georgi, Alexi
Call	Smirnoff, Absolut, Stolichnaya, Skyy, Finlandia
Premium	Grey Goose, Effen, Chopin, Belvedere
Super Premium	Imperia, Ultimat, Elite Stolichnaya, Tru Organic

You determine the price you need to charge your customers to hit the margins you've set based on the pricing you get from your suppliers. Even if the percentages you make from each drink are equal, the dollar amounts you make from calls, premiums, and super premiums are much higher, so encourage your staff to know their liquor brands (liquor distributor sales reps can help train them) and to recommend the better liquor brands to your diners.

Serving Alcohol Responsibly

If you serve alcohol to the public, you need to be aware of the risks you're taking and take steps to minimize them. Use your local liquor licensing authority for specific guidelines on what you can and can't do. Take this agency's recommendations and stated penalties seriously. (Check out Chapter 8 for information on finding out which agency handles licenses in your area.) Here are a few tips that can help you and your staff keep your customers safe:

- ✔ **Promote safe transportation.** Keep the phone numbers of several taxi services handy, and set up a program for designated drivers. Maybe you can offer them free nonalcoholic beverages all night long.

- ✔ **Encourage bartenders and waiters to attend training on responsible alcohol service.** In some areas, the law requires specific training for all supervisors and staff members who deal with alcohol. Even if it's not required in your community, these classes are great tools for training your team.

- ✔ **Keep patrons in the safe zone as far as blood alcohol is concerned.** Table 11-2 shows how standard-sized drinks affect blood alcohol concentration for people of various weights. The legal limit in most states is either 0.08 or 0.10 — make sure you know your local laws.

- ✔ **Check with your insurance company for recommendations they may have on ways to lower your liability.** Your insurance company may recommend signage (for example, reminding patrons to give their keys to a friend) that you can visibly post to lower your liability and help keep your customers safe.

- ✔ **Be vigilant about potential problems.** For example, don't assume that you can give people darts and alcohol and expect nobody to ever get hurt.

- ✔ **Decide whether to hire bouncers.** If you have a rowdy crowd, bouncers can help deter dangerous behavior. *Warning:* Be careful when hiring and screening bouncers. They can be the catalyst, instead of the deterrent, for violence. Conduct thorough background checks on them to discover any arrests, criminal convictions, or even complaints filed against them. You can be sued if your overly aggressive bouncer decides he needs to punch someone to keep him in line.

- ✔ **Develop a system for consistent *carding,* or checking IDs.** Confirm that your patrons are of legal drinking age, which is 21 in most places.

Table 11-2	Percentage of Blood Alcohol Concentration (BAC)				
Weight	*Number of Drinks in Two Hours*				
	2	*4*	*6*	*8*	*10*
120	0.06	0.12	0.19	0.25	0.31
140	0.05	0.11	0.16	0.21	0.27
160	0.05	0.09	0.14	0.19	0.23
180	0.04	0.08	0.13	0.17	0.21
200	0.04	0.08	0.11	0.15	0.19

No matter what advice they receive, some owners insist on walking the line between what's legal and what they think they can get away with. Our advice: Toe the line. If you're open when you're not supposed to be, you could risk your business. If you consistently have underage drinkers in your bar, you'll eventually get caught. At best, you'll get points counted against your liquor license. At worst, say goodbye to your business.

Chapter 12

Hiring and Training Your Staff

· ·

· ·

A chain is only as strong as its weakest link. You've heard this idea related to business a million times. Choose a good team and train them the right way to maximize your chance for success. Whether you're starting a new restaurant from scratch or revitalizing an existing one, the information in this chapter can improve your staff development today.

Deciding Which Roles Need to Be Filled

Before you can figure out who you need to help you operate your restaurant, you need to fully develop your concept (see Chapter 2) and menu (which we cover in Chapter 8). Then put on your operations cap and think about which jobs you need to fill. If you're a fast-food restaurant, you don't need a host to help people find a table or take reservations, but you do need some cashiers to take orders and make change. If you're a fine dining restaurant, you need at least two hosts, one to kiss each set of cheeks, but no cashiers. Use our suggestions in Table 12-1 (and the descriptions throughout this section) to determine the employees you need based upon your concept.

Different jobs in the restaurant world require different personalities. For example, a fry cook doesn't need an outgoing personality. You don't want him to be so chatty that he can't focus on what he's doing. And a hermit at the front desk will alienate customers. You need people to be friendly when they interact with guests but focused on productivity where you need production. And you probably need a drill sergeant to make sure it all gets done.

Table 12-1	Employees Needed for Each Shift
Type of Restaurant	*Positions to Fill*
Casual/family style	Hosts or hostesses Servers Bussers and barbacks Dishwashers Line cooks Prep cooks Cashiers Food runners Delivery Bartenders
Fast food with a centralized menu	Cashiers/order-takers Line cooks Delivery Dishwashers
Fine dining	Hosts or hostesses Servers Bussers and barbacks Dishwashers Line cooks (several with different specialties) Wine stewards (who pour and serve wine) Bartenders Sommelier(s)
Bar and grill	Servers Bussers and barbacks Dishwashers Line cooks Bartenders Delivery

In the following sections, we give you an overview of what to look for in potential employees. We break up the information by position, detailing the scope of the responsibilities for each one.

True hospitality is everyone's job. You need employees who understand the mantra "If you see something, do something." No matter which position an employee holds, each is an ambassador of your restaurant and should act accordingly. All employees should

✔ Acknowledge customers

✔ Yield to customers as they cross paths

✔ Respect the neighboring businesses and tenants

✔ Pick up trash inside and outside the restaurant

✔ Tidy up public areas including the bathroom

We've included a sample organizational chart, Figure 12-1, to show you how everyone fits together.

Create your own formal job descriptions for each position, preferably before you hire the people to fill them. The process of creating job descriptions can help you immensely during the hiring process by clarifying who you need for your operation and defining their responsibilities.

To keep everything running smoothly, don't usurp the authority of your managers or chefs by letting their people bypass them to have your ear. Be understanding about whatever they bring you, but point them back in the right direction and give the manager a heads up as to what's going on.

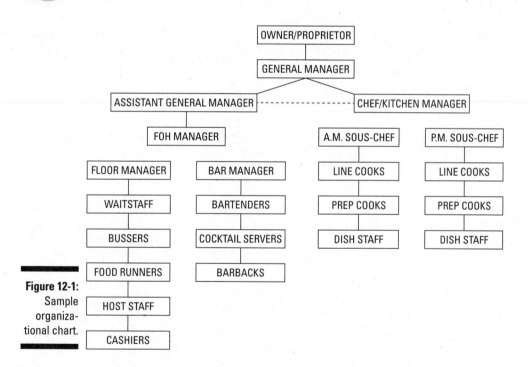

Figure 12-1: Sample organizational chart.

Managing your quest for managers

Managers set the tone for the rest of the staff, so hire the best people for the job. They affect how smoothly your operation runs, how your staff controls the chaos and treats the customers, and how much money you'll ultimately make. In the following sections, we let you know about some key things to watch for when selecting the best people for your management team.

You should like the managers you hire, at least on some level. You're together for at least 12 hours a day, so you'd better get along.

Cross-training management team members is a good idea. Your bar manager, for example, may not need to know how to run the dining room, staff the kitchen, or expedite orders coming from the kitchen, but in most cases, the more cross-trained your managers are in each position, the better. You gain more flexibility, you respond rapidly to changes in business levels, and you're better equipped to deal with the inevitable vacations, sick days, late arrivals, and no-call/no-shows that your staff will take at the most inopportune times.

General manager

In any business, a *general manager* (GM) must have a grasp of all facets of the operation. You can hire a GM, but many owners choose to serve as the GM. They may or may not use the title, but they perform the duties and save an extra salary. If you've never waited tables, checked coats, fried fries, or tended a bar, get yourself a quick education. If you don't, the employees in those areas will dictate the business. That may be okay, but think about this: If your chef says he has five guys but needs eight, how are you going to know if he's on target or asking for more than he needs? He's asking you to increase your labor costs by 60 percent for a single shift. You need to know enough to make an informed decision. Otherwise, your productivity goes down, your labor goes up, and your profits go out the window.

The GM is ultimately responsible for the staff's knowledge and commitment. He must lead by example. He must have a handle on the financial forecasts, budget objectives, and all the other numbers. Control of the restaurant is important as a means of maximizing profitably and maintaining cash flow.

The GM represents the restaurant not just while he's in the restaurant but out in the community as well. If he goes out and gets hammered down the street, sleeps with a competitor's wife, cusses out the mayor, and runs someone over on his way home from the bar, you won't have good community relations.

Assistant general manager

The *assistant general manager,* or AGM, is the heir-apparent to the GM, or next in line. (See the preceding section for details on traits of a good GM.) The AGM should be aspiring to be a GM, trying to do the job before she gets the job. The GM delegates responsibilities to the AGM to prepare for an eventual promotion. The AGM either knows or is learning how to be the GM. As the owner, you may be attending to the GM's responsibilities without the title, and your GM may be acting as an AGM.

The titles matter less than the responsibilities. You need someone to be in charge and someone right behind him serving as a backup, the next in line, and learning all the ropes. Some GMs may be reluctant to show the "heir-apparent" all the ropes for job security considerations. A good owner should allay his fears and encourage cross-training.

Chef

Many restaurants don't need a true chef. Base your search for a professional chef on your concept. Anticipate your volume of business, the technical difficulty of your menu, and whether you want the chef to be part of your public relations push. Then narrow down your hunt. You can categorize chefs by their specialized cuisines or the types of operations that they have experience in.

A chef brings creativity, expertise, and leadership to your kitchen. Be aware that many people call themselves chefs when they really don't know which end of a knife to hold. The title has been somewhat diluted in recent years. A true chef has a proven track record of the following:

- Managing, training, teaching, and developing a staff
- Developing a menu
- Running efficient, profitable, and clean kitchen operations
- Receiving accolades, awards, and positive critical reviews
- Demonstrating specific knowledge of service, wine, and spirits and how to apply them to your concept

If you don't need or want someone else to be that involved, consider hiring a kitchen manager (KM) instead of a chef. (See the KM description in the "Staffing the kitchen" section.) Then you can hire a consultant to make scheduled menu changes seasonally, something that a chef would handle.

Here are a couple of things to be wary of when interviewing chefs:

- Be wary if your chef candidate says "No special orders." Diners who request special orders are by definition finicky, and they go where they can get what they want. A good chef is in his diner's psyche. He is current with food trends. He has the adaptability, creativity, and passion to see an opportunity where others may not bother with "difficult" diners.

- Be wary of a candidate who waxes poetic about his latest White Alba Truffle Ragoût with Duck Confit and Microgreens finished with a 1947 Châteaux Lafite Reduction while being unable to discuss the food cost percentages, labor rates, and waste numbers that he has historically run. With popular attention being paid to all things culinary, any kid with a cookbook and a couple of squeeze bottles has awareness of avant-garde cuisine, yet far fewer understand the business of running a profitable and efficient back-of-the-house operation.

Your chef is a manager, just like any other restaurant manager. He should conduct himself in the same way you expect every other manager to behave. The restaurant is a tamer environment than it was 20 years ago, and behavior like boozing and yelling are no longer tolerated. Make sure that your chef got the memo!

Take a look at Chapter 18 before you start hiring to make sure your potential chef and staff members have what it takes to help you build and maintain your customer base.

Staffing the kitchen

We list kitchen staff positions in order from the unsung heroes (dishwashers) to the more specialized positions (the sous-chef or kitchen manager). Someone must be in charge of the kitchen, but you may have a single manager in charge of every restaurant employee, not a kitchen-specific manager. But no restaurant can survive for long without a dishwasher.

Dishwasher

The dishwashing job is very physical labor. Boots and an apron, preferably waterproof, are the standard uniform. Dishwashers are the serfs of the restaurant world, but most experienced chefs and managers agree that they're among the most important people in the building. The most amazing food in the world does you no good if you don't have a clean plate to put it on or a clean fork for guests to eat it with.

Promotion from within your organization is an ideal way to sell an employee on working in the dish area. Many cooks and kitchen managers start out in the dish area. If they have the desire, dishwashers can move from dish to prep to line to sous-chef (or elsewhere in the organization). Motivating someone to "bust suds" and dig his elbows deep in discarded food is tough. Promotion can be the carrot dangling out in front of the employee. If you're able to hang on to your dish guy and move him up the ranks, you and he will both have a great story to tell and be better able to recruit for the position.

After you get some dishwashing candidates in the door, make sure they have the following traits before hiring them:

- **Good work history (if they have a history):** Don't discount applicants just because this is their first job, but if they've been fired from their last five dishwashing jobs, you may not want to give them the sixth.

- **Punctuality:** If applicants are late for the job interview, that could be a sign of things to come. You want a dishwasher you can count on to show up on time.

- **Organizational skills:** Keeping the dish area neat and organized is important in order to keep dirty dishes flowing in and clean ones flowing out. Make sure the person you hire is up to the task.

> ✔ **Necessary physical attributes:** Dishwashers must be able to stand for long periods of time. They have to be able to lift heavy loads, such as stacks of plates or full garbage bags. They should also be fairly dexterous and not clumsy. They should be able to maneuver a rolling cart of glass racks through a busy kitchen without getting in someone else's way.

Prep cook

Prep is short for preparing, or making preparation. It's the root system of the kitchen. Your prep cooks are the unsung heroes of the kitchen, the ones who do the daily grunt work. Prep cooks touch every part of your menu and kitchen, whether they're cutting steaks off the side of beef; chopping lettuce; making soups, bulk sauces, frosting, or pizza dough; or wrapping and freezing compound butters. Prep cooks prepare your kitchen for the shift to come.

Many people believe that prep is the most important part of the cooking. If it's not done right, nothing can fix it. Take soups, for example. Soups aren't cooked to order. They're prepared early in the morning so flavors are melded by lunch or dinner. When a diner orders a piping hot bowl, the waiter serves up a ladleful and goes on her way. If the soup isn't prepared right in the prep stage, you can't do much to fix it after it's ordered.

In other cases, your prep cooks start the process, and your line cooks finish it. For example, your prep guys peel and devein shrimp for salad but don't assemble the final product.

Prep cooks should have a working knowledge of the storerooms and coolers so they know where to find all the ingredients they need for whatever they're making. They also need to know how to operate many kinds of equipment — a Buffalo Chopper (bowl cutter/food cutter), food processor, tilt skillet, fryer, or even the grill. Prep cooks could be roasting corn for a salsa and then frying noodles for a garnish — all within the same shift.

Look for the following traits and characteristics in a good prep cook:

✔ Punctuality and dependability

✔ Ability to take direction, criticism, and instruction well

✔ Organizational skills

✔ Ability to complete tedious, repetitive tasks over a long period of time

✔ Ability to read a recipe and apply basic math skills

✔ A real desire to be in the business (an applicant in it just for the money could be gone next week, searching for that extra 25 cents per hour)

✔ Ability to stand for long periods of time and lift and move cases of food with relative ease

Experience in other restaurants is always a plus. If prep cook applicants don't have experience but seem like they could be good employees, consider them as candidates for the dishwasher position.

Line cook and expediter

A line cook is assigned to a station on your *line* (the section of the kitchen where food is finished, or cooked when ordered). The line is made up of kitchen stations dedicated to different preparation techniques, such as the grill, sauté, fryer, and so on. See Chapter 10 for the full scoop on kitchen stations.

Most line cooks should have some kitchen experience before working on the line. Many people start in prep and work up to the line. Depending on your concept, you can start inexperienced line cooks on a cold station, such as the pantry or pastry, and then cross-train them on other stations as their abilities and interests develop. Usually, cold stations have a more limited menu than the hot stations and require fewer skills to run. Typically, the sauté cook needs the greatest amount of kitchen experience because this station has the most volume and requires the most expertise.

The key traits of a successful line cook are

- ✔ **Punctuality:** As with any employee in the restaurant, line cooks need to show up on time.

- ✔ **Willingness to learn:** From what goes into the menu items to plate presentation, a line cook is always learning. She may be getting to know her station or learning to run the one next to her.

- ✔ **Previous experience:** Line cooks need to have some experience before they start on the line. Figure out which particular station they're suited for by comparing their past experience with your needs and concept.

- ✔ **Positive attitude:** Because busy times in a restaurant are so hectic, you need cooks who can keep their cool and go with the flow. You also need employees who can follow instructions and follow the directions of their supervisor, especially during shifts.

Having cross-trained employees is ideal on the line, especially during slow business levels. If one guy can work one end of the line that consists of the oven and the fryer, plus he knows his way around the pantry, you have the flexibility to *cut* (send home early) some of your other staff. You save labor dollars but maintain your full menu and service levels.

If you have an *expediter*, often shortened to *expo*, she's the end of the line. Basically, she gets all the line cooks working together on an order at the right time. See Chapter 10 for the duties of the expo.

Sous-chef

The *sous-chef* (pronounced *sue,* French for "under") is the kitchen's second in command. He's usually in charge when the chef isn't around. The sous-chef is sort of the executive chef in training, but he may still train the underlings. A sous-chef is in the process of learning ordering, inventory management, and food costing. Also, the sous-chef is likely trying to pick up on the creativity of the chef, understanding his style of cooking and food philosophy. Some chefs use them as assistants. But other sous-chefs actually run the kitchen, and sometimes several sous-chefs work in a single kitchen.

Kitchen manager

A kitchen manager, or KM, knows the nuts and bolts of running the kitchen machine. She may do the ordering and manage the staff, but she may not have advanced culinary training — and she may not need it for your concept. KMs are great at maintaining consistency. A good KM knows the standards and can follow production manuals, but she doesn't have to be creative or focused on technique. She can teach the staff the basics. She should be very production-focused and efficient.

Filling the front of the house

The *front of the house* (FOH) is restaurant-speak for any area of the restaurant where a diner can be. (For details, check out Chapter 9.) FOH employees have regular contact with your diners.

Host

You may call them *hosts* or *hostesses, greeters, seaters, reservations desks,* or a host (pun intended) of other names. Whichever name you use, the basic function is the same. These folks greet your diners, show them to their tables, and start their meal and experience on the right foot. Hosts are also the last faces that guests see on their way out of your restaurant. You want hosts to thank everyone and send diners off with a great final impression.

Look for composed, friendly, and organized people to fill these positions. They're essential to your success. This is one of the most difficult jobs in a busy restaurant. The nicest person in the world doesn't appear nice to prospective diners if she can't control the phones, deal with the customer who hated his soup, get the complaining waiter in Station 4 back on track, and deal with the smoke coming out of the kitchen, all while maintaining her composure. And if your host isn't taking down the correct time, number of people, and names for the reservation, it can be a disaster. Enough chaos will develop in the restaurant; you don't need a host staff contributing to it.

You don't need a beauty queen or Adonis to serve as your host, but your host does need to capture the mood of the restaurant. Hip, trendy restaurants should have hip, trendy greeters. And communication skills are a must. Knowing when to communicate with the floor manager or the kitchen can keep the night running smoothly. Effective communication with the diners means going beyond friendly; a host must be able to observe the diners, pick up on their moods, and adjust the game plan accordingly.

Waiters often try to manipulate the host staff to seat them in a favorable way. Make your staff aware of the potential problem and give them tips to avoid it. If you're going to screw up the seating, do it on your own. Don't let a waiter do it for you.

Coat check

Coat check is often a function of the host staff. On busy nights, you may employ a designated coat-check person. This staff should be organized and methodical in how they take the coats, label the coats, and so on. The success of the coat check is determined by the equipment that you give them. If you have the right tools (such as hanger tags, as well as labels for accessories such as hats, umbrellas, bags, and so on), you should have a smooth operation.

If you don't have a good coat-check system, you *will* have problems that involve claims against your establishment for missing or damaged goods. You'll probably find yourself settling these claims in the spirit of goodwill, at a not insignificant cost. Copy whichever successful system your favorite upscale chain restaurant or steakhouse uses. These establishments have risk-management people in their organization who've figured it out for you.

Cashier

Cashiers should be honest, organized, and friendly. If the cashier is the same person who deals with tipping out wait staff, she needs to be strong-willed and resistant to games that waiters may play.

Waiter

Waiters are salespeople. They're the most direct connection between your diner's wallet and you. They should be friendly and able to relate to people. Successful waiters are able to make judgment calls about what kind of customer they're waiting on and what their diners' expectations are. They should be able to read their diners and react accordingly. They should know when to chat people up or leave them alone. Is the couple that's been married for 40 years simply quiet but otherwise happy? Are they involved in an intense, private conversation? Or maybe the group is out to celebrate and want the waiter to entertain them.

As salespeople, waiters should know their product (the food and beverages your restaurant serves) inside and out. They should know ingredients, preparation methods, and taste. Take a look at the section "Training Your Staff" later in this chapter for more information.

Waiters should be able to smile no matter what happens. Coauthor Mike tells waiters, "Pretend this is a stage and you're entertaining these people. Don't let them see your problems. Don't let them even know you have any. They're supposed to have a good time, so let them."

Food runner

Depending on your service, you may include food runners on your schedule during busy shifts. Runners help get hot food out of the kitchen and to your diners quickly. They may be assigned to a particular section or can be available to help anyone who needs it at any point. Sometimes runners are waiters in training. They may be learning the ropes or are too young, based on local laws, to actually wait tables if beer, wine, and liquor are served. Or they may be waiters who take turns in a shift rotation to run food.

Runners should be knowledgeable about the food, the dining room layout, and your concept. Being a runner is a great way for an employee to get to know your restaurant and your food. A runner should be able to recognize dishes but may not be able to tell a guest every ingredient or preparation method.

Delivery person

Much like a food runner, a delivery person should have a good knowledge of your food, how it should look, and how it should be presented. Delivery persons should have a good sense of direction (or a GPS) so they don't get lost delivering orders. Lost delivery persons mean cold food to your customers. Additionally, a delivery person needs to have good payment handling skills because he may be accepting payments when dropping off deliveries.

Busser

A busser's job is to keep service flowing. Bussers clear and set tables to prepare them for the next set of guests. Some bussers may also be assigned to start service at a table. For example, they may pour water and bring bread and butter or other complimentary items to the table.

Bussers may have aspirations of being waiters. Like food runners, they may not be old enough to serve alcohol. Some bussers move from the back of the house to the front. Bussers should be quick and organized. They should know the proper table setup for your concept and their way around the dish area. They usually aren't required to have extensive food knowledge, but they should know your points of service and expectations for guest courtesy. They need some sophistication about when to clear and when not to clear dishes.

Don't call bussers *busboys*. Some people consider that term disrespectful, and you don't want to set an unprofessional tone in your restaurant.

Bartender, service bartender, and barback

A bartender should have an extensive knowledge of making cocktails, especially those that are associated with your concept. If you have a Mexican restaurant, the bartender needs to know how to make many kinds of margaritas, for example. She should also be likeable and friendly with guests. (We cover good bartending traits in detail in Chapter 11.)

Don't jump to hire a graduate just out of bartending school. Bartending is a skill that you learn from hands-on experience.

The *service bartender* makes the drinks for the waiters, helps other bartenders, and assists in prep work. The service bartender usually doesn't have much contact with guests. A bartender may use a barback during busy shifts. The *barback* can do anything except make drinks and handle money — stock glasses, ice, liquor, and other supplies and maybe wash glasses and empty the trash.

Cocktail server

Cocktail servers, stereotypically women, specialize in drink service. They usually wait on tables in the bar area of the restaurant. The cocktail server should know your menu if you serve food in your bar. She should definitely know the specifics of your liquor, beer, and wine lists. If you have any entertainment in the bar, she should have an idea of the schedule (such as what time the band starts and who's playing tomorrow night). Depending on how busy your bar is, you may need a very experienced cocktail waitress who can handle multiple tables of patrons. If your bar isn't terribly busy, restaurant waitresses may be able to take on the task of cocktail shifts.

If possible, don't require a diner to pay his tab when moving from the bar to the dining room for dinner. Just add his bar tab to his dinner check. Making people pay two tabs usually makes diners angry, and using one check doesn't necessarily reduce the amount of a cocktail server's tips. People often leave a cocktail server a cash tip when transferring their bar tab into the restaurant.

Staffing the office

The office is the nerve center of your restaurant where all the information in the restaurant gets tied together. Your POS (point of sale) system, payroll records, and telephone systems are usually housed here (see Chapter 15).

Staffing the office can be as complicated as staffing any other part of the restaurant. Depending on the size of your operation, different people wear different hats. In fact, until you can support the expense of hiring people, you may be wearing all the hats! The same person may handle marketing, reservations, and accounting. You, as the manager, need to know how your office runs, inside and out. If not, people may rob you blind. If you think the bartender can do it by giving away free drinks, just wait until someone in the office scams you.

Office staff should be honest because they provide the checks and balances for both the physical cash that moves through your restaurant — counting *banks* (usually cash drawers set up to give change at the bar and cashier station) and *drops* (cash deposits ready to go to the bank) and monitoring FOH cash handling — and the financial records. You may hire an outside accountant to come in to audit annually, quarterly, monthly, or more often if you feel it's necessary.

Accounting

Your accountant may have no idea of what the business does, but she is responsible for checking numbers. The best bookkeepers understand the numbers and can give you info on how they apply to your business's past performance and future needs. If you're new to the restaurant business, you need someone with this type of experience. Find an accountant who does the books for other restaurants. If you have your accountant set up your books according to industry standards, comparing your operation to others will be easier. See Chapter 8 for info on accountants.

Payroll

Many restaurants *outsource* (hire an outside firm to do a job) some of their payroll processes. But you can't just turn payroll over to an outside company and assume that it will run without a hitch. Usually, someone in the restaurant confirms hours worked, pay rates, and so on and then sends the information to the payroll company, which just cuts the checks. The same internal person usually double-checks the checks against the data sent to the payroll company, verifies the payroll deposit has been made, and so on. This person is an initial investigator who identifies the discrepancies, asks the questions, finds the reasons, and conveys the potential problems to management. For details on planning for payroll, make sure to visit Chapter 15.

Marketing

Someone in your organization should be in charge of marketing, even if you get help from an outside source. In some cases, a general manager or owner serves as the liaison between an outside marketing consultant and the restaurant or may choose to perform the duties himself.

If you hand off this job to someone else in your organization, pick someone who knows the operation and the concept behind the restaurant. If this employee doesn't know your business thoroughly when she starts, she has to get to know it quickly. If you hire someone without an interest in how the lamb is getting to the table with its special Armenian mint, what are the chances this person will have an interest in the long-term success of your business? Your marketing person should understand your passion and the nuances of your concept. Take a look at Chapter 16 for details on marketing and promoting your business.

Technical expert

You can hire outside people or outside firms to maintain your computerized point-of-sale (POS) system, but you need someone in your operation to watch over them. Even if you sign up for a 24-hour support team available to you with your newly purchased system, you need someone on your staff to be the liaison with them. You need someone who can handle the situation. This person may not have specialized training to handle the systems, but if he has an aptitude and an interest in helping out, you'll be a step ahead.

Finding the Right People: Placing Ads and Sifting through Résumés

When you're looking to hire people to staff a new restaurant, start by placing an ad in the newspaper. Make the ad as descriptive as possible for the criteria you're seeking. Newspaper ads advertising new restaurant jobs get a *huge* response. The industry is full of job jumpers. If you're the newest restaurant on the block, servers assume you'll be busy, so you'll get swamped with applicants who jump from one opening to the next. Organizing your recruitment process to account for this volume of response is important to stay afloat in the sea of "people persons" and dependable, hard-working people who wonder if they can have Friday and Saturday off.

For entry-level positions in your restaurant, newspaper ads (and the corresponding online job posts) generally get a good response from qualified candidates. Also consider word of mouth. For example, if you have a good employee who recommends a friend or relative for a dishwashing position, definitely consider that person.

Job search sites and search engines have come a long way since the first edition of this book in 2004. They are easier to use, give more targeted results, and are more secure for applicants and hiring organizations. Consider sites like Monster (www.monster.com) and even Craigslist when looking for employees, including managers. Also, take a look at Hcareers (www.hcareers.com) for a good website focused on hospitality-industry employment.

Hiring a recruiter to help you look for restaurant managers is an option. Recruiters usually charge you, the employer, anywhere from 10 to 25 percent of the new employee's salary for their services, but recruiters can really cut down the length of your search and improve the quality of your candidates. But make recruiters earn their keep. Simply feeding you candidates is only one aspect of their service. They should provide some due diligence. They should not simply review a résumé and pass it on. A good recruiter personally interviews each candidate and does some background checking for you, especially with references.

Use quality chef recruiters to find a quality chef. Newspaper ads and generic job websites have limited success at this level, but they may work if you're located in a large metropolitan area. Your choices may be more limited if you're in a smaller market. If you use a typical newspaper ad and corresponding job-posting website, the response won't be very targeted. You'll get résumés from every joker with an apron in your market. A recruiter can scour the country quickly for candidates that match your concept and budget, checking references and saving you time.

If you see obvious errors or red flags on a résumé or application, don't bother to interview the applicant. If someone says she's an expert on Rhône wine but she misspells *sommelier,* that's probably a red flag. Or if she's worked three months at each of her last ten jobs, skip her.

Interviewing the Candidates

When hiring, do your best to make a sound decision based on the facts and your gut instinct, but don't beat yourself up if something doesn't work out. In the restaurant business, lack of experience isn't always a good reason to not hire someone. The only way people really learn a job is to do it. If you think someone has the right attitude, give him a try.

For most positions, we recommend doing at least two interviews for each candidate with at least two different people in your company. Use the first as a screening interview to get a feel for how the person fits into your organization. Many second or third interviews involve an audition or tryout, especially for kitchen and bartending positions.

Coauthor Mike says, "You can't train 'nice.'" Once when staffing a new restaurant, he looked for candidates who had outstanding natural hospitality. The restaurant had an extensive (2-week) training period, and Mike figured that he could train the staff in that time. Even during the restaurant's dry run opening, the staff received outstanding feedback, even though they weren't technically excellent. People are much more forgiving when they're treated well.

If the risk doesn't work out, cut your losses right away. Consider including a probation period, usually 60 to 90 days, for new hires. That way if someone really isn't working out, you can get rid of him quickly with very little trouble later.

Consult your state labor laws regarding probationary periods and unemployment laws. If you've never managed a business (or even if you have), you'd be very wise to find an expert labor attorney. This legal expert can save you untold dollars and possibly even your business. The really good ones are expensive, but this is truly a case of getting what you pay for.

Round 1: The meet and greet

Use this round for screening out people whom you *definitely won't hire.* Keep your questions short. Have the applicants fill out applications, get their background information, and get a feel for how they answer questions. You won't have a lot of people whom you definitely extend an immediate offer to at this point — save that for Round 2. Here's a quick list of good Round 1 questions:

✔ What's your employment background?

✔ Why do you want to work here?

✔ What are your strengths? Your weaknesses?

✔ Why did you leave your last position?

✔ What do you think is the most important aspect of the job you're applying for?

✔ Why are you equipped to succeed in this position?

✔ Are you looking for a career or a job?

Cull it down to the few applicants you'd like to find out more about. For FOH positions, put yourself in the guest's position. Do you want this person talking to you? Is she engaging? Is her voice nice to listen to? For BOH positions, does an applicant present herself as eager to learn? Is she modest, or is she very impressed with herself? Beware the hotshots in the kitchen; they're often resistant to training specific to your concept. Good candidates are attentive, willing to learn, and physically capable of doing the job.

Round 2: Comparison shopping

Make a list of the available positions and add spaces for the number of people you need in each position. During Round 2, build a roster of candidates to fill the available slots. Use paper, a chalkboard, a dry-erase board, an emery board, whatever works for you. Think of it like the NFL draft. By the end of Round 2, you start to build a roster of your first, second, and third picks for each position.

The goal of the second round of pre-opening interviews is to ask the hard questions and get to the core of who the applicant is, in 15 minutes or less. Let the applicants know the good, the bad, and the ugly of the available position. Assess whether this discussion should continue to the next phase. Scare off the weak. Find out why candidates want to work at your restaurant — and it better be for reasons other than because you're hiring.

Get specific with the applicants' past background, job-related skills, techniques, and specific knowledge. Field their questions. Discuss pay rates, as appropriate. By the end of this round of interviews, you should start to feel comfortable making offers of employment.

When making your final hiring decisions, make sure that all applicants

✔ Have the applicable specific experience you're looking for

✔ Meet the specific criteria you've established for the position they're applying for

✔ Are available to work the number of hours you need them

✔ Have a solid work history (or no work history for entry-level positions)

✔ Have a positive attitude, desire to learn, and enthusiasm for your restaurant

✔ Mesh with your concept, brand image, company culture, and work style

Never ask candidates about their religion, marital status, sexual orientation, age, gender, race, political affiliation, national origin, or disability or whether they have children. Answers to these questions could be construed as a reason that someone didn't get a job and set you up for a lawsuit. Visit the U.S. Equal Employment Opportunity Commission website at www.eeoc.gov for details. Make sure that everyone in a position to hire on your behalf understands these rules. You're liable for their actions if they're on your payroll.

Bonus rounds: The inevitable re-staffing

Turnover in the restaurant business is about twice the national average for all businesses. So it's inevitable that at some point, you'll have to hire for some positions again. When you do, the process tends to go like this:

1. **Do a phone interview.**

   Unless you've placed an ad that specifically tells prospects to just show up at a certain time, you'll likely get a phone call first. The first phone call gives you a chance to assess conversation skills, ask questions about previous experience, and set up the next interview. Typically, you don't say, "Yes you're hired," on the basis of the phone interview, but you may say "no." If the applicant is applying for a server position yet is rude and interruptive or can't hold a conversation, you may not be inclined to bring her in for a face-to-face interview.

2. **Complete a face-to-face interview.**

   At this interview, have the prospect arrive early to complete an application if she hasn't already done so. If possible, have the prospect meet with two interviewers to get differing perspectives.

3. **Take the applicant for a test drive.**

   If you feel like the prospect has potential, have her come in for a *trail* or shadow shift. During a trail shift, the applicant follows a senior staff member throughout the course of a real shift in the restaurant to learn the systems. In this all-important restaurant staple, the interview takes on an anonymous component. You can have a senior staffer evaluate the candidate in a real-life scenario.

Forms for new hires

After you pick your staff, they need to complete some basic government forms. Give them their employee manual and have them sign for it. Also have them complete any helpful forms, such as emergency contact information, at this time. Here's a quick list of the forms to keep on hand for new employees:

✔ **I-9:** The required I-9 form documents eligibility to work in the United States. It's a required document for every person in your employ, whether a U.S. citizen or an alien.

✔ **W-4:** The IRS-required W-4 forms allow employees to declare their number of withholding allowance to take from their pay.

✔ **Attendance calendar:** This allows you to quickly document any attendance discrepancies, calculate vacation days, and the like.

✔ **Emergency contact card:** This card is handy in case the unexpected happens in your restaurant. If you have to take an employee to the hospital, you'll be glad you have the name of a close friend or family member to call.

Keep a file on each employee in which you retain all of these forms, along with the person's initial job application and/or résumé. Doing so isn't just a good business practice; it's essential in case of a government audit.

Hiring Foreign Nationals

Immigration is a hot-button issue for many Americans, and the restaurant business is no exception. Whether your restaurant is in an urban center or a small Midwestern town, your workforce likely is made up of a significant immigrant population. With higher fines and tougher penalties (including possible loss of your business license), compliance with local, state, and federal laws in hiring eligible workers is essential. In this section, we include tips to help you ensure that you're hiring only employees who are legally eligible to work in this country.

Double-checking the documents

Familiarize yourself and your hiring staff with the proper instructions for completing the I-9 Form. This form is designed to ensure that the employer has the proper documents to verify employment eligibility.

In 2010, U.S. Citizenship and Immigration Services (USCIS) redesigned the *Permanent Resident Card,* more commonly known as the *Green Card.* Among the many security updates, the most obvious change is that the card is now actually green.

USCIS replaces Green Cards already in circulation as individuals apply for renewal or replacement, so both designs (old and new) are in circulation, and both will be valid for some time. Check out www.uscis.gov for more information on required documentation.

Evaluating the E-Verify system

E-Verify is an Internet-based system jointly operated by the Department of Homeland Security and the Social Security Administration. It allows businesses to determine the eligibility of their employees to work in the United States. Subscribing companies can quickly input prospective employees' identifying documentation into the online system and receive a quick verification that the employee is eligible or ineligible to work in the United States.

Several states require private employers to use the E-Verify system, and it will become a requirement in more states soon. For information on using this free system, go to www.uscis.gov and click on the E-Verify link.

Petitioning for an employee

In rare instances, you may find it necessary or desirable to hire an employee who is not yet qualified to work in the United States. Say, for example, that your new Italian trattoria concept just *must* have a genuine Italian chef behind the stove. As an employer, you may file a Petition for a Nonimmigrant Worker petition (known as an I-129) with the USCIS on behalf of a prospective foreign citizen employee. If the petition is approved, the prospective employee may apply for admission to the U.S. to temporarily perform work. This process is expensive and complex, so make sure you're ready for a lot of work and wait.

Training Your Staff

Assume that, when you hire your staff, they have no preconceived knowledge about your business. The more information you give them about the way your business runs, your expectations, your concept, your menu, and so on, the better they'll be as employees. Training is expensive. Teaching employees about your operation uses up labor dollars. Printing out manuals uses up supply dollars. Putting all the materials together uses up manager time. But think about how much a poorly-trained employee can cost you in terms of wasted products and supplies, broken equipment, and lost customers. In the following sections, we discuss employee manuals, operations manuals, and your training schedule.

The employee manual: Identifying your company policies

An employee manual is your chance on paper to spell out for your employees what you expect of them in terms of performance, behavior, communication, appearance, and so on. You need to make sure everybody gets one so every employee is on the same page.

Get each employee to sign and date the manual, acknowledging that they've read it and have been given a copy for their personal records. Make sure the general manager (GM) reads and signs a copy, too. If their signatures are their statements that they've read, understood, and agreed to abide by the contents, give them a chance to read the manual thoroughly before signing. You'll eat it in court if you don't. Be sure to tell employees that they should keep it and refer to it as necessary. Any changes that you make to the manual need to be handled the same way. The changes must be given to all employees and signed for.

Use the manual to get your new staff excited about your restaurant. It's an opportunity to show your employees that they all contribute to the big picture and explain to them why they're important. Show them what safeguards are put in place to make sure the big-picture things happen.

The employee manual serves as documented proof of your policies. You can easily tell a server to remove his earring if you've written in black and white that earrings aren't permitted. You have a consistent way to handle situations. If you have employees' signatures on file saying that they've received and read the manual, you have some protection if they sue you for terminating them based on something clearly spelled out in the manual.

No one employee manual suits every operation. Each is as different as the operation you run and the goals you set. If you're new to the business, don't let your GM write the manual because he has restaurant experience and you don't. This is one of those things you can't delegate: If he leaves in six months, you want the manual to reflect you and your philosophies.

Have an expert labor attorney review the manual before it gets issued to any employee. The money spent here will be minimal compared to the potential damages paid later.

Operations manuals: Understanding specific job functions

An operations manual helps you train employees to perform specific duties for each position, from pot scrubber to maitre d', from fry cook to general manager. Thoroughly explain each position, including duties, standards, and objectives. Tell employees what they're here to do, how to do it, when to do it, what your quality standards are, and so on.

The more detailed you can be in your operations manuals, the more successful your training will be. Outline in black and white what you want employees to do. You may feel like you have to spend a lot of time putting your operations manuals together, but you'll more than make up for it by not having to take time to re-explain how to do things, when to do things, and so on. With the details written down for employees, their training time shrinks and they're up and running much more quickly.

Certification-based training, such as TIPS (Training for Intervention ProcedureS, a safe alcohol service, www.gettips.com), ServSafe (food-safety training, www.servsafe.com), and HACCP (Hazard Analysis and Critical Control Points food safety training; www.fda.gov and then search for HACCP training), complement in-house training programs. Often, local health departments sponsor these training sessions at little or no charge. Encourage your staff to attend whenever possible. The info is valuable to every food-service professional.

Creating a training schedule

Create a training schedule, including these specific training sessions:

- Steps of service (what to do when a guest sits down, when to offer bread, or how to present the dessert tray)
- Product training (info on your menu, beverages, restaurant concept, and so on)
- Point of sale (POS) system operation
- Menu tastings
- Equipment training (dishwasher, food processor, slicer, coffee and espresso machine, and any other equipment you have)
- Sanitation, cleaning, and energy usage

If you're opening a new restaurant, coordinate BOH and FOH job-specific training. Both teams should train on similar concepts at the same time. When you have your menu tasting, your kitchen should already be able to cook the food, and your wait staff should have an understanding of what your concept is. When it's time for your dry runs, everyone should be on the same page. If the kitchen is ready but you haven't hired your wait staff, you've wasted kitchen time.

Doing a dry run

About a week before opening, conduct your first *dry run*. Some people call them *trial runs, soft openings,* or a host of other names. Before you open, invite employees' families, friends, investors, advisers, consultants, and others to eat in the restaurant. Treat them just like regular diners. They order off the menu, and the kitchen prepares the orders. Everything is the same as a real dinner shift, except the customers aren't paying.

The dry run is a chance to go through a practice shift and see how everything works together. You'll likely have a few things to iron out between your trial run and opening day, which is why you do it. Every restaurant should do at least one dry run, but do as many as you can afford to schedule-wise and money-wise. Trial runs aren't cheap, but they're well worth the money.

Ongoing training

Don't think that because someone's training period is over, he's trained. Training is an ongoing process. Keep products fresh in your employees' minds. Include training on current specials, new wines, or whatever else your staff needs every single shift. Hold weekly position-specific meetings and monthly all-employee meetings to go over important information with the staff. Regularly scheduled meetings keep lines of communication open and prevent misunderstandings. See Chapter 16 for more info on the subject.

Cross-training is important. Your fry cook should be able to work the grill; your pantry cook should be able to sauté. If you notice someone who's trying to learn more — a prep cook who wants to learn the line, for example — never discourage his efforts. Consider allowing him time during his regular workday to assist or learn the ropes. Not only will you be encouraging his interests, but you'll also have a possible substitute in case someone can't make it in one day or leaves.

Chapter 13

Purchasing and Managing Supplies

In This Chapter

▶ Getting control of purchasing

▶ Picking the right suppliers

▶ Working with prices, quality, and service

▶ Developing a solid inventory system

A wise man once said, "You make more money buying than selling." That adage is true in any business, particularly a competitive one like a restaurant. Purchasing takes vigilance and enthusiasm. You must be diligent in your research, knowledgeable about what works for your concept, current on the latest food trends and production techniques, and confident in your volume of goods purchased. Good purchasing decisions result in positive bottom lines.

In this chapter, we take you through purchasing from start to finish. We show you how to figure out what you need to buy and who you need to buy it from. From an inventory standpoint, you need to develop a system for confirming that you got what you ordered, that it's stored in its appropriate location, and that it stays there until you're ready to use it in your restaurant.

Preparing to Stock the Supply Room

Before you order that first supply, you have to understand your concept (see Chapter 2), your menu (see Chapter 8), the time needed to prep menu items and their corresponding shelf lives, and the number of people available to produce them. The decisions you make in regard to all of the above ultimately affect how, when, and with what you stock your supplies.

So how do you figure out what you need to order? Start by researching products: Go out to eat and try new things — new concepts, new drinks, new styles of service, and so on. Read the industry magazines (see Chapter 21 for a list of resources). Any information you can get helps you make better decisions.

Purchasing entails buying anything you need for your restaurant: food, beverages, equipment, paper goods, furniture, office supplies, smallwares, services, and everything else. After you purchase the basic equipment for your restaurant start-up, you spend the majority of your purchasing time buying food and beverages. If yours is like most restaurants, you not only invest lots of time but also lots of money buying these types of supplies, so we focus our examples in this chapter on food and beverage purchasing. But you can definitely apply these same principles and tips to purchasing just about anything else you need for your restaurant.

Listing what you need

Make a list of all the food and beverage supplies you're going to need according to your menu. Start by listing each menu item and every ingredient needed to make it. Then organize the list by category, as we've done in our example in Table 13-1. You need to have this list in hand before you start locating and interviewing suppliers. (Although our example deals exclusively with food and beverage items, you can use this approach for every purchase, including bar equipment, paper goods, and linen.)

Use a good spreadsheet application, such as Excel, to make your master list. You can sort and filter the information according to different categories to make the list-making process much easier.

The categories in the table are organized according to how most purveyors specialize. You may have a meat guy, a seafood guy, and a *broad line* supplier (a large supplier who carries a variety of goods across many product lines). The list in Table 13-1 is by no means comprehensive. Your list will be based on your menu.

Be specific with your final list. Don't just write "beef tenderloin." Instead, write "beef tenderloin, grass-fed, organic, block ready, 5½ up [5.5 pounds and greater in weight], silver skin removed, prime," if that's your specification. If you just say "beef tenderloin," the supplier could give you a price on no roll (ungraded) or select (instead of prime) beef tenderloins that look great from a price standpoint but that may not be the right quality match for your concept.

Deciding on your menu, recipes, and desired end results before you draw up your list is a real plus when you're not sure about the exact product you want. You can then turn to your supplier for guidance. For, example, tell him that you need chicken fingers but want to taste all his company's chicken fingers side by side. You can look at 2, 10, or 20 products side by side and discern why something works for your application and why it's the best choice for your operation.

The sample supplies list in Table 13-1 can help you get organized now and stay organized later. After you're up and running, fill in the amount of each item you expect to use (Projected Volume). Subtract the amount you already have (On-Hand) to figure out how much you need to order (To Order).

Table 13-1		Sample Supplies List			
Item	*Category*	*Unit*	*Projected Volume*	*On-Hand*	*To Order*
Bread, French roll, 1.5 oz.	Baked goods	Case, 144 ct.			
Bread, roll, herb garlic, 1.5 oz.	Baked goods	Case, 144 ct.			
Bread, 3-ft. loaf, Italian	Baked goods	Each			
Pizza dough balls, 20 oz.	Baked goods	Case, 24 ct.			
Bread, sticks, 2 oz.	Baked goods	Case, 96 ct.			
Bread, wheat, French roll, 1.5 oz.	Baked goods	Case, 144 ct.			
Butter, unsweetened, 1 lb.	Dairy	Case, 36 ct.			
Butter, whipped, 5-lb. tub	Dairy	Case, 6 ct.			
Cheese, Asiago, shredded	Dairy	Case, 15 lb.			
Cheese, Bleu, crumbles	Dairy	Case, 20 lb.			
Cheese, Cheddar-Jack, shredded	Dairy	Case, 15 lb.			
Cheese, cream, 3-lb. tub	Dairy	Case, 3 ct.			
Cheese, cubed	Dairy	Case, 20 lb.			
Cheese, mozzarella, fresh	Dairy	Tub, 8 lb.			
Cheese, Parmesan, shredded	Dairy	Case, 15 lb.			
Cheese, provolone, longhorn	Dairy	Each			
Cream, heavy, 40%, 1 quart	Dairy	Case, 12 ct.			
Cream, sour	Dairy	5 gal. bucket			

Considering premade items

Here are a few examples of premade products that can make your prep labor dollars go further:

- ✔ **Sauce bases, such as demi-glace and pesto:** You purchase the base and add a few other ingredients to finish them as you need them.

- ✔ **Meats that are cut, portioned, and individually sealed:** These products are more expensive, but you may have less waste and spoilage. Use them if you don't go through a lot of meat or don't have the skill to cut it yourself but want to keep some beefy options on your menu.

- ✔ **Baked goods, including breads, pastries, and other desserts:** Many good products are available prepackaged these days. Work with your purveyors to see what may work for your concept. Consider partnering with a local bakery to get locally known breads, pastries, and desserts.

Before you make a final decision to put prefab items on your menu, taste them and determine whether they fit your concept. Decide how close the quality of the commercial product is to the from-scratch version and whether the savings in labor is worth any sacrifice in quality. Ultimately, if your diners don't like something or it tastes like it came out of a box, they won't come back. We discuss working with suppliers in the next section.

Finding and Working with Purveyors

When you know what you need, find out which *purveyors* (also called suppliers) have those products.

Keep in mind that there's a fine line between working with your sales rep in a partnership that benefits you both, known as *consultative selling,* and letting the sales rep run your show, known as *getting taken for a ride.* As often as possible, figure out what you need before the sales rep tells you what you need. Sales reps won't tell you about their competitors, so don't use them as your only research source.

In this section, we help you interview purveyors, decide who to work with, and make sure everything goes as smoothly as possible.

Finding and interviewing suppliers

Make a list of supplies you need and, next to each item, write the name of the suppliers the competition is using for each category (ask the purveyors, ask your competitors, or simply watch who's delivering to other restaurants).

Start with no fewer than three suppliers (also referred to as *houses* in the restaurant industry) in each category for the interviewing stage. This process works in all categories, from cleaning supplies to specialty foods.

With your list in hand, pick up the phone, call each supplier, and get a *sales rep* (salesperson) assigned to you. Set up times to interview each one. Have the meeting at your restaurant if possible. You may also choose to tour the supplier's facility to observe the sanitation level, the size of the operation, and how its warehousing systems work.

Engaging in your first conversation

When you talk to suppliers on the phone, tell them who you are and describe your situation. Let them know whether you're new ownership, new management, or a brand-new restaurant. Maybe you have an existing restaurant and want to interview potential alternate purveyors.

Get the supplier's sales rep *and* her boss into your restaurant for the meeting. That way, your salesperson has a clear understanding of your objectives and her boss gets the same info firsthand from you. Often, the real power in negotiating prices doesn't lie with the sales rep. Usually her boss or boss's boss gives the thumbs up or down on special requests. If the supplier knows that you're professional and organized, with concise needs and wants, the whole process goes much more smoothly, and you can cut out much of the game playing before getting to the real pricing.

Conducting your first meeting

Be concise in your first meeting with the supplier. Your goal is to educate the supplier about your concept, your specific needs (and limitations as you see them), your concerns, and what you expect from a supplier. Show suppliers your kitchen, your equipment, your delivery dock — basically the whole operation — so you can make them aware of all the logistics.

When you have that initial meeting, bring copies of your whole supply list sorted into categories (see Table 13-1 for a sample list). Purveyors may surprise you with a broader inventory than you expect. Coauthor Andy worked with a dairy supplier who noticed that Andy was using a lot of imported olive oil and specialty goods. Two years earlier, the dairy supplier had quietly amassed an inventory of these items and was selling them at a significantly reduced cost compared to the local specialty house. This chance meeting became an exclusive purchasing arrangement for dairy and select specialty products at a big savings over the previous supplier.

Go through the list item by item with each supplier, starting with the supplier's specialty. Explain what you're looking for in terms of flavor, performance, packaging, and cut, and provide an estimate of how much you'll need in a given week.

Keep in mind that suppliers are coming to sell you products; the more you buy, the more they make. Before you enter into *primary* (or *preferred*) *supplier agreements* with a vendor, make sure doing so helps you. In these contracts, a restaurant agrees to purchase selected items from one vendor in exchange for fixed prices, volume-based rebates, and the efficiency of having a minimal number of vendors.

Make it clear that you're looking to establish primary supplier agreements and that you're going to buy a certain group of items from one company. If a supplier walks away understanding that it gets all or none of a group of items, you'll be amazed to see what a supplier can make happen in terms of prices, discounts, delivery, and special orders.

Don't assume that a company can't bring something in for you packaged a certain way. Sometimes a supplier really can't, for lots of reasons. But maybe the only thing a supplier needs to do to get all your business is bring in a couple of additional products, take a loss of a couple cents on the pound, or split a case of a product that comes only in a quantity that's more than you need.

The supplier may interject and say things like "We don't carry that, but we carry this kind instead" or "Ours is in a 15-pound case, not a 5-pound case." Your response should be a version of "I understand. My decision is simple. I'll give my business to the company that can service the needs on this list. I'm going to spend money, and this is what I'll spend it on. If you want my money, get what's on this list done for me. If you don't want my money, I'll find someone who does."

Then the supplier has to decide whether your volume of business is worth the additional inventory, reduced margins, and increased customer support. Not all restaurants qualify for these types of programs, but all restaurateurs need to understand that these volume-based incentives exist and that in most cases you get only the discounts, pricing structures, delivery schedules, and products that you *ask* for.

If suppliers aren't interested in getting your business, they aren't going to be interested in servicing your business. Make it clear to them that you want them to understand your restaurant and how you want it to work. You're setting up an ongoing relationship, not just buying groceries once a week. The best purveyors understand their clients' business and bring them ideas, new products, and opportunities in the marketplace that can benefit their business. They must understand your goals, business, costs, order and delivery requirements, and where you want to position yourself in the marketplace. If they can understand your business and maintain and increase your quality, while maintaining or decreasing your costs or your labor, then you're likely to buy that product from them.

Giving suppliers a chance to respond

At the end of each meeting, send the supplier on her way with your list, an understanding of your objectives, and an understanding of your desire to have a purchasing program with a purveyor in this category. Remind her that the purveyor who can meet most of your needs will get the lion's share of your purchasing business. Give the supplier a definite timeline to get back to you. Make it clear that you're interviewing several purveyors in your category, and mention the competitors by name. Let the supplier know that you're willing to engage in a preferred provider agreement with her company, provided that she comes back with the best possible price guaranteed for one year based on your expected volume. This step shows the supplier that you know what you're doing and you're confident in your research.

Request your sales rep's office, mobile, and home phone numbers. Ask for her boss's office and mobile numbers, too, but make sure that the sales rep is aware that you've asked for the boss's contact info. Taking this step gives her the courtesy of not being blindsided if you call her boss, and keeps the pressure on because she knows that you may call.

Comparing prices, quality, and service

After your purveyors get back to you with their prices on the stuff you're interested in, evaluate their bids. Their response should include more than just their pricing strategy. It should specify their terms of service, delivery schedule, credit terms, ordering process, any extras you've asked for, applicable rebate programs, and so on. If the agreement is to be *contractual* (agreed upon by a written contract with specific order volume or a specific time period), get your attorney involved to review the contract.

Now's the time to iron out any logistical details as well. If you need your product before 8 a.m. every day, tell the supplier that and make sure that the commitment is in writing. If you need net 90-day payment terms (90 days to pay the bill), you both should agree to that upfront. You're building relationships and goodwill with your purveyors, but not completely relying on the purveyors. You both should be comfortable with the relationship, but the supplier shouldn't get too comfortable.

How fast you pay often dictates what your prices are.

Considering the size of suppliers

Working with a large supplier has a major upside. Because large suppliers buy in bulk, they get better pricing than smaller companies and can pass those discounts along to you. They usually carry more categories of stuff, and within those categories, they often offer many choices. They probably carry thirty brands of tomato sauce, while a smaller company may have only five.

Larger suppliers often have additional bonuses and incentives for agreeing to sign with them for a particular volume. They may be able to schedule daily deliveries if you need it because they have a larger trucking fleet than the little guys. They may give you a computer, complete with their ordering software, which you can use for other office functions as well.

The big downside when working with major suppliers is that you're one of many customers. They take your money but won't go out of business without it. They may be less likely to give you a generous pricing program unless you can give them a guaranteed volume. They can be a bit flakier with their deliveries, invoicing, and the like. As with any large company, considerable red tape is usually involved, and often what you and your rep discuss doesn't make it to the accounting department. A problem can take weeks to get straightened out. And major suppliers have been known to bully a customer here or there, especially when it comes to a verbal agreement. Get all agreements in writing.

Small purveyors offer excellent service. They have to, or they'll be out of business quickly. With a small purveyor, you *are* his business. Small suppliers will often go above and beyond to make sure that you're happy and satisfied with your service. You can often build business relationships that last decades.

Getting the right quality at the right price

Pricing figures prominently on both sides of the equation — buying and selling. Your goal is to get products that match your concept and meet or exceed your guests' expectations at the lowest price possible. Then you work to sell your menu items at a price that matches your guests' expectations, covers all your costs, and leaves you a nice, tidy profit.

Twenty different kinds of breaded chicken tenders may be available from your local broad line supplier. The top-of-the-line product is all-white-meat, single-muscle chicken breast breaded with focaccia, Parmesan cheese, and herbs. The lesser-quality product is a chopped and formed mystery meat with extenders, phosphates to keep it moist, and a nondescript flavorless breading. One is cheaper than the other, but which one matches your quality standards?

Here are some tips to keep in mind:

- ✔ **Minimize your physical inventory but maximize the ways you can use what you get.** Find ways to use raw materials across the menu. If you bring in beef tenderloin for your entree menu, think about where else you can use it. Can you bring the tenderloins in whole so you get a better price and then use the scraps for beef bourguignon, a stir fry, or salad? This type of purchasing helps you get more utility for the same product, increasing your volume and decreasing your cost.

✔ **If you can't take control of the market with volume buying, take control of your menu to take control of the market.** If one company sells shredded cheddar cheese, one sells block cheddar cheese, and another sells sliced cheddar cheese, why store three different varieties of the same cheese and hope that the respective menu items sell? Instead, bring in the core item, the block cheese, and then slice or shred it according to your needs, as part of the prep. You're buying more cheese from one person, driving costs down, and fulfilling the needs of your menu.

Getting what you ask for the way you ask for it

After you set up your purchasing plan, you buy things a certain way for a good reason, maybe several good reasons. Nail down specific delivery times and any other special instructions before you make your first order, and hold the purveyor to them.

If the products you order aren't the products you receive, you have a problem. If you get bone-in chicken breasts priced at the boneless, skinless price, you're not only paying more for the product, but you'll throw good money after bad with labor dollars to debone the chicken. If you get a great price on liters of gin but receive fifths (which contain 25 percent less liquor) instead, you may not be getting a deal at all.

If you're signing for a product, know what you're signing for. You can't just order things, think that you got a great price, and assume that everyone along the line will perform flawlessly and the whole process will run smoothly. More often than not, mistakes occur because of honest human error, either on the ordering end or at the purveyor's location.

When trouble occurs, how do you resolve it? Your first call should be to your sales rep. For example, suppose that the supplier's delivery driver doesn't bring you everything you ordered on a certain day. If the rep wants to keep your business, he'll resolve the problem for you. Don't accept excuses. If suppliers promise to deliver in a certain way by a certain time, they should resolve any problems for you, making the delivery themselves if necessary.

Building an Efficient Inventory System

Your *inventory* is the stock of supplies you have on hand at any given time. It's an investment, and you get no return on that investment until that product sells. You want as little money as possible tied up in inventory but still want to be able to efficiently run your business. You do need to have an adequate supply of product on hand for an unexpected upsurge in business. Not having a menu item can be bad for business. People understand that you may occasionally run out of a menu item, but they'll go elsewhere if you're inconsistent in your offerings.

Inventory is also a warehouse of your cash flow. Excess inventory ties up money that you can't use for other necessities until the products sell. Inventory inversely affects cash flow. Not managing it properly is the failing of many a restaurant. You want your money where it can work for you, not tied up in the skid of sugar packets that you got for half price and that's now taking up space in the storeroom.

Salespeople love to come up with incentives for you to buy in bulk, but examine the offer closely. For example, they may say, "If you buy 100 cases of water today, you'll save $2 a case." Take a look at that deal. If you buy 100 cases of bottled water at $20 per case, you've invested $2,000 in bottled water. Suppose that it takes you two months to sell this water, but you're on net 15-day terms with your vendor. In the meantime, at your margin of 50 percent (which means half the price to your customer goes to cover what you actually paid for the water) on bottled water, it will take you a month to break even on the investment and two months to realize your profit, all to save $200. For two weeks, you're in the red on that investment, meaning that you paid more than you made. If this is a pattern in your purchasing system, your money is tied up in inventory. Meanwhile, you have payroll to meet, a lease to pay, and repairs to the toilet that backed up during the Saturday night rush.

Managing the inventory

Many systems exist for tracking inventory. Some are high tech (such as scanner guns and bar codes that automatically update the system), and some are low tech (monthly hand counting your stock on hand). Some systems are fully integrated, tracking products from the time they're delivered, through the preparation process, to the time they make it to the customer. Other systems can automatically count down your inventory as you use products. If you're missing a single can, it shows up. The systems work well if you're planning on having an exceptionally stable menu. If you're planning any kind of a change, systems that are completely automated can be more work than they're worth.

Establishing your par levels: Keeping enough product on hand

Most restaurants resort to the tried-and-true process of manual counts for inventory purposes. In most cases, food is counted on a shift-by-shift basis. Use *daily par sheets* (itemized lists of the amount of prepped inventory you need to have on hand until your next prep period), like the one in Figure 13-1, to count your food and set up your prep schedule. For example, in the kitchen you may set a par for the amount of Alfredo sauce to have on hand or the number of steaks ready to hit the grill. In the wait station, you set a par for the number of lemons to cut for iced tea. The bar keeps a par for everything from margarita mix to beverage napkins.

Daily Par Sheet

DATE <u>January 25, 2005</u> DAY OF WEEK <u>Tuesday</u>

POSITION <u>Prep</u>

Menu Item/ Product	Amount on Hand	Par Levels		Amount to Prep	Shelf Life	Container	Comments
		Mon - Wed	Thu - Sat				
Shaved Beef for Philly Sand	5.5 lbs.	15 lbs.	25 lbs.	9.5 lbs.	3 days	6 inch plastic tray	Add 1 lb. Peppers and 1 lb. Onions.
French Onion Soup	2.5 gal.	4.0 gal.	8.0 gal.	10 gal.	4 days	5 gal plastic tub	Prep through the weekend.
Chicken Wellington	6	16	30	10	2 days	Third pan	See chef for recipe change.

Figure 13-1: Sample daily par sheet.

Build a functional inventory by analyzing your recipe ingredients and historical or projected sales of an item. For example, if an ingredient is in your number-one selling item, you'll use a lot of that item, so you need to have a lot of them on hand. If you're McDonald's, you'll need more fries than apple pies. That information becomes the basis for your *ordering par sheet,* an itemized list of the amount of inventory you need to have to keep you up and running between orders.

Keeping par levels and doing *shift counts* (counting your products before or after every shift) help you stay on top of your inventory. Don't wait until the end of the month to find out that you're missing supplies.

Counting your inventory

As part of your monthly income statement (which you can read all about in Chapter 4), you count your inventory. Even if you have an accountant prepare your reports, you must provide the inventory count to the accountant. This count is a full and complete account of all supplies in your restaurant. *Supplies* include any items that are restocked or replaced on a regular basis.

Don't include *equipment* — things that are part of your restaurant for a long time, such as tables and chairs — in your inventory. You're reconciling your assets on hand (your inventory) against the liability of the invoices (the bills you've paid or must pay).

Use a spreadsheet program like Excel to help you calculate the value of your inventory. Do a physical count of the products you have on hand and then multiply that by the price you paid for them. This figure gives you the value for each item on your inventory. Add up the values you paid for everything you still have on hand (from lettuce to liquor), and you have your total value of inventory. This number will be listed as an asset on your monthly income statements. Check out Table 13-2 for an example. (We use just the dairy section of Table 13-1 to show you how it works.)

Table 13-2	Sample Monthly Inventory Worksheet			
Item	Unit	Unit Price	On Hand	Value
Butter, 1 lb., unsweetened	Case, 36 ct.	$75.00	0.75	$56.25
Butter, whipped, dairy, Tub, 5 lb.	Case, 6 ct.	$38.52	0.05	$1.93
Cheese, Asiago, shredded	Case, 15 lb.	$53.70	0.1	$5.37
Cheese, Bleu, crumbles	Case, 20 lb.	$49.00	0.8	$39.20
Cheese, Cheddar-Jack, Shredded	Case, 15 lb.	$39.80	1.2	$47.76
Cheese, cream, 3-lb. tub	Case, 3 ct.	$17.00	0.66	$11.22
Cheese, cubed	Case, 20 lb.	$47.73	0.25	$11.93
Cheese, mozzarella, fresh	Tub, 8 lb.	$9.91	0.5	$4.96
Cheese, Parmesan, shredded	Case, 15 lb.	$16.69	0.66	$11.02
Cheese, provolone, longhorn	Each	$8.50	0.75	$6.38
Cream, heavy, 40%, 1-qt.	Case, 12 ct.	$29.72	0.5	$14.86
Cream, sour	Bucket, 5 gallon	$24.00	0.25	$6.00
Total value of inventory				$216.86

Using requisition sheets

A *requisition sheet* is a form that you use to track requests for supplies. Your bartender can use a copy of the wine list to request a new stock of wine. Your sous-chef can use a par sheet to request more olive oil. Or maybe you actually create a separate form that people who need stuff fill out and give to the buyer for the restaurant.

Whatever system you use to track requests for supplies, make sure that it's a written system, understood by everyone involved. It's tough to keep track of who needs what if you carry 50 wines by the glass or 15 different kinds of cheese. A written system provides an excellent way to communicate requests and start a paper trail for your supplies.

Requisition sheets also provide one more check to make sure that products are staying on the shelves until they're sold — and not walking out the door or being misplaced. If your chef needs a 5-pound bucket of liquid margarine but your purchaser just got one in the day before, a requisitions sheet can help start the search for the product.

Reducing waste

Waste costs money, plain and simple. Waste occurs in many places: perishable food, utilities, labor, and so on. Spend some time analyzing your operation. Identify areas where waste occurs.

The easiest way to reduce waste is to be organized and be vigilant. When you're visible, your employees are less likely to leave the water running, steal something, or forget FIFO (first in, first out; see Chapter 17 for details). Train your trainers to have your eyes for waste. Financially motivating your employees to help control expenses benefits you immediately and forever.

Here are a few key ways to reduce waste:

- ✔ **Keep your utility usage in check.** Maintain your equipment. Close the cooler doors. Turn off lights in storerooms and coolers when no one's working in them. Saving energy is good for both the environment and your bottom line.

- ✔ **Keep tabs on the use of office supplies.** Sticky notes, pens, paper, and menus add up. Don't let your employees stock their home phone centers and offices with your office supplies, which are the most stolen items in a restaurant. They're small and aren't usually tracked.

- ✔ **Ration your linens.** Ration your towels and aprons. Each kitchen or bar employee gets, say, two towels to last them the whole day. Also, clean up floor spills with dirty linen, not clean linen. It's much more efficient to clean up spills with dirty linen and then sanitize the floor with a mop.

Waste can be as simple as serving food portions that are too big. If your specification is 4 ounces of fresh vegetables on the plate, don't give diners 8 ounces. If you've done your homework and studied your food costs, put your knowledge into practice.

Eliminating spoilage

Begin with an attitude that food spoilage is unacceptable. Here are some ways you can prevent it:

- ✔ **Order only the amount that you'll use well within the item's shelf life.** Establish your pars and get organized about your ordering amounts (see the earlier section "Building an Efficient Inventory System"). You may find that you need to order berries twice a week or fresh fish three to four times (or more) each week.

- ✔ **Take advantage of storage technology.** Equip yourself with the means to properly store, handle, and extend the shelf life of foods. Vacuum sealing, individually frozen or ready-to-cook portioned food items, and advancements in shelf-stable technology are improving food safety and eliminating the risk of spoilage.

- ✔ **Invest in the proper stackable food storage containers.** Use clear containers for ease of inventory and quality checks (unless the product in question can be damaged by exposure to light). See your equipment or broad-line food rep to purchase these containers.

- ✔ **Make sure that items in your cooler are covered, labeled, and dated.** See Chapter 17 for details on setting up a safe kitchen, rotating products, and establishing an effective sanitation system.

- ✔ **Remember that beer and wine are perishable.** To slow the perishing process, store them at a consistent temperature under the proper light conditions. If you buy 20 cases of wine and your storage area has a fluctuating temperature or is too bright, you'd better be going through your stock quickly, or the wine quality will decline.

- ✔ **Be vigilant and visible.** The chef and the owner should check the coolers and storage areas several times a day to confirm that food is properly stored and labeled at all times. Fresh products are more prone to spoilage.

- ✔ **Investigate spoilage that happens outside your restaurant.** Spoilage can happen before the product even enters your cooler doors. Did the delivery person handle it wrong, leaving your case of lettuce on the sidewalk for an hour while he delivered to another restaurant? Were your quarts of cream mishandled from the plant? After you find the cause, correct the problem. And make the person responsible for the mistake accountable for his or her actions.

Spoilage from the purveyor is more likely for restaurants that don't order in case quantities. Some purveyors (certainly not all) seize opportunities to pawn off less-than-fresh products on case-breakers. But don't ask for full cases if you don't need them. Order what quantities you need, but insist upon products at the height of freshness when you do.

Chapter 14

Running Your Office

*Y*our office is an important part of your restaurant. More often than not, however, restaurateurs give very little thought to the office's setup and location. But much of the important management of the business takes place in this space, so set it up right to maximize your productivity, maintain proximity to your diners and staff members, and protect your valuable data.

Deciding Where to Put Your Office

Your office size and location, along with the number of offices you have, are a direct result of the size of your operation. Most restaurants have a main office that's relegated to the least-valuable storage space and that serves as a shared office for all managers. Sometimes a chef or kitchen manager gets a desk in the *dry storage area,* the kitchen area where you store dry goods and canned goods, so he can be closer to the kitchen and to his staff.

You'll likely be stuck with an existing office or have little choice of where to locate your office. But if you have the luxury of deciding where to put it, determine who will be using office space before you choose its final location. If your managers (rather than just an office staff) are using the office, its location should give equal access to the various departments. You and your managers should be as accessible as possible to your respective responsibilities.

If your office is in the kitchen, consider having lots of windows looking into the kitchen so you can see what's going on there while you're in the office. You can add adjustable blinds for occasional privacy.

Creating a Communications Hub

The office is the central place through which all internal communications (among managers and staff) and external restaurant communications (with customers and suppliers) flow. And in the restaurant world, open lines of communication are key — no matter what you've seen from screaming chefs and temperamental managers.

Counting on your computer

For most restaurateurs, computers are essential for administrative and management tasks. Computers mean efficiency in all areas — ordering, tracking sales, doing financial analysis, menu planning, communicating with customers, staffing, you name it.

You may find laptops more useful than standard desktop computers. Laptops save space and are easily portable if you want to work in the bar or the storeroom, for example. (If you have a secured company Wi-Fi [wireless] network on site, you can literally work from anywhere in your restaurant.) But computers can get lost, stolen, or damaged if you move them around, so take proper steps to protect your equipment.

In addition to the actual computers, you need the following items to get your computer systems running smoothly:

✔ **Software:** You need a variety of software programs, including programs that protect your computers from outside attack (such as firewalls and other security software), total your sales and sales tax received and owed, track your wait staff's sales and declared tips, and reconcile credit card receipts. You also need the following software:

- A word-processing program, such as Microsoft Word (for menu creation, business correspondence, and so on)

- A spreadsheet application, such as Microsoft Excel (for tracking inventory, ordering, and figuring daily food counts)

- An accounting program, such as Intuit QuickBooks (for tracking your accounts, writing checks, and managing receivables)

✔ **Printer(s):** You need to print out all the reports, spreadsheets, menus, letters, checks, and so on.

✔ **UPS:** No, not the brown company. The UPS we're talking about is an *uninterruptible power supply,* which helps keep your computer's data intact in case of a power outage. Most also have surge protectors built right in to protect your system in the event of a power surge.

Picking up the phone

Get with a reputable, authorized phone system dealer to help you pick the right system for you.

Call your local phone company to ask about business rates before you select a system. Sometimes phone companies offer different rates for different kinds of systems, and the price difference may affect your buying decision. Ask about rates for Small Office/Home Office (SOHO) key systems (KSU) versus private branch exchange (PBX) phones. The differences between the two are technical and deal with how the phones work with the phone lines, but they don't really affect your daily use of the systems. Your decision can, however, affect what you pay.

Ask your dealer about used or refurbished systems. In most cases, restaurants don't need so many extensions and features that they demand the latest phone technology, so take advantage of a better price.

Using e-mail and online services

E-mail is a necessity in the restaurant business, just like any other business. Here are three ways in which the Internet and e-mail can benefit your business:

✔ **Patrons can contact you.** Diners can use e-mail (and websites) to make reservations, communicate satisfaction and dissatisfaction, and place orders for takeout and delivery. In some large metro areas, e-mail and online reservations are so ever-present that some diners make reservations via e-mail only. If you don't offer this service, they won't dine at your place. Check out Chapter 9 for info on setting up a reservation policy.

Have a designated staff member who's in charge of online customer interaction. Someone needs to manage these experiences and respond to questions, comments, and complaints quickly. Consider setting up an automated message that responds immediately with a generic thank-you message each time someone e-mails you — something as simple as "Thanks for using our website. Someone will respond to your question as soon as possible." But you still have to follow up quickly.

✔ **You can contact suppliers.** Having e-mail and Internet access for your managers can increase efficiency and productivity, speeding up must-do day-to-day tasks such as purchasing and ordering. Many large food brokers accept orders via e-mail or their websites. If you develop your own spreadsheets, you can often e-mail them to your vendors to show which items you need and in what sizes and quantities.

✔ **You can contact customers.** Use social media to build your brand online. Develop a database of customer e-mail addresses when customers contact you. Then you can send electronic advertising, mailers, special offers, and other promotional material to diners who are likely to take advantage of that info. You can even encourage your diners to register to receive promotional materials in exchange for a drawing for a free dinner. See Chapter 18 for info on using mailing lists, social media, and other methods to build a loyal customer base.

Tracking sales with a point-of-sale system

A *point-of-sale* (POS) system is essential for just about any restaurant or bar. Manual cash registers mean inefficiency and botched cash handling. But a POS system is much more than a cash register — a POS system can be your time clock, your ordering system, your credit card processing unit, your inventory manager, your calculator for food cost percentages, and so on. If you can, invest in an integrated system to ease the burden of watching your numbers.

POS systems allow you to track sales of particular items, sales made by particular employees, and special orders and to organize credit card transactions. You don't have to be able to perform a hostile takeover of the Federal Reserve with the thing, and it doesn't even have to be brand-new (if you're trying to save money, look for used systems). At the low end of the operational scale, you simply need something to track the basics, things such as sales, tax, and labor hours. With a good POS system, you know not only how many people ordered the ahi tuna but also how many people ordered it rare with an extra side of wasabi. Many systems allow you to manage the business in real time instead of requiring you to analyze things after the fact.

A POS system comes with some basic standard reports. These reports can get you started and allow you to spot and analyze general trends in your business. Generally, they provide a big-picture view of your operation. But you'll likely need more targeted and segmented info so you can watch specific areas of your business in specific ways. If you want to track how much fish you're selling compared to beef, you need to add that report.

Make sure that the system you buy has some customization features. Sometimes, you or someone on your team can customize the reports, but often you must work with the POS distributor's programming team to create the specific reports.

Here's a list of some of the data your POS should be able to provide for you:

- ✔ **Good basic info:** This includes info such as entire check average (the average total check for each table), per person average (the average amount each guest spends), per person liquor sales (the average amount of beer, wine, or liquor each person orders), dessert average (the average amount of dessert ordered by each person), and average entree price.

- ✔ **Sales trends by both major and minor categories:** Say that you have a major category such as wine. You also have several minor categories, such as white wine by the glass, white wine by the bottle, red wine by the bottle, red wine by the glass, sparkling wine by the glass, sparkling by the bottle, and so on. Your system should be able to break up your sales info in many different ways, such as all bottle sales, all glass sales, all red sales, and so on.

- ✔ **Sales by different cost centers:** A *cost center* is a different area of the restaurant that takes in money. Your system should be able to set up each drawer of the bar as a separate cost center, each server as a separate cost center, and so on. The system should also be able to combine the cost centers to look at the bar or all the servers as a whole. Another feature of the system enables you to see what these groups or individuals sell during specific times and shifts.

As you refine your reporting and better understand your business, look for specific trends. You may find that a customer who orders a bottle of wine also orders 20 percent more appetizers than a customer who doesn't order wine. Maybe when Joe the manager is on duty, you tend to be busier than when John's on. Then you can use the numbers to make adjustments. Janice has a higher check average than anybody. Don't you want her in the sections that serve the most people? If you discover that you're selling only three veal osso buco dinners each night, maybe you should stop offering it. All this info is available if you track and analyze your sales numbers.

Look for brand names like POSitouch, Aloha, and Micros when you're looking at POS systems. Many systems, such as Aloha, can integrate your scheduling, inventory, labor costs, accounts receivable functions, and so on into a single system. (For more on integrating all the electronics in your office, check out the following section.)

When shopping, make sure that the paper that works with the POS printers is readily available and relatively inexpensive. If you're saving a ton on the system but spending a fortune in your monthly paper supply, what are you really saving?

Interfacing your different systems

The best time to think about interfacing, or connecting, your systems is before you buy them. The most likely candidates for connectivity are your inventory and sales systems, your scheduling system and time clock, and your online reservations and your phone reservations. Think about what you want from your various systems and how you may be able to save time by connecting them. Working with an authorized POS dealer is a great first step. Your sales rep should be able to help you interface anything you're willing to pay for. The easiest way to get your systems talking is to buy software that already works together. Such software isn't always the cheapest way to go, but you can expect that the systems have been tested together and are compatible.

Hardware (the Old-Fashioned Variety)

It may be the information age, but you still have to sit on something. Here are some un-techy things you need for your office:

- **Desk and chair:** Restaurants are notorious for bad furniture, especially in the office. The importance you place on comfort determines how much you spend.

- **Copier/scanner:** This unit can be an all-in-one fax machine/copier/scanner. Customers sometimes request itemized and signed receipt copies.

- **Postage machine with scale:** This item may not be essential, but it's a huge help for mailing paychecks, checks, marketing materials, and so on. However, it pays for itself only if you mail lots of items. Weigh the overall cost against the convenience of having the machine before signing for it.

- **Calculator:** You need a 10-key calculator with a roll of paper that keeps a hard-copy record of your calculations. This old-school device is still the standard for balancing drawers, checking out servers, and so on. It's a must-have item in any restaurant office.

- **File cabinets:** Make sure that they have locks to protect sensitive info, such as employee records.

- **Safe(s):** Your safe doesn't need to be huge. It should be able to hold however many cash drawers you use plus at least one extra, a supply of gift cards, credit cards accidentally left by diners, and deposits until you can get to the bank.

Some restaurants use a second safe (or a second compartment within the primary safe), called a *drop safe,* for holding deposits. This safe functions sort of like a public mailbox; you can drop your deposit through the slot, but no one except the armored car driver can open it. These drop safes are a good deterrent to guard against employee theft or an inside-job robbery (because insiders know you can't get to the money), but they can be very frustrating to an armed robber who may not believe you can't access the money.

The fewer people with the safe combination, the better. Make sure everyone who has access to the safe has his or her own combination code. And remember to deactivate codes for any former employees.

Here's a list of some basic office supplies you need to start with and that you'll replace as time goes by:

- ✔ **Paper:** You need legal pads, message pads, the paper you print your menu on (if you do it yourself), letterhead, paper rolls for POS printers and the 10-key calculator, and so on.

- ✔ **Envelopes:** Your supply should include legal envelopes with or without the company logo, larger envelopes for mailing banquet pricing proposals and press kits, and envelopes to match your checks.

- ✔ **File folders:** Usually letter-size folders do the trick.

- ✔ **Forms:** Keep a supply of employment applications, I-9 forms, W-4s and all applicable tax forms, time cards, deposit slips, and so on.

- ✔ **Miscellaneous office stuff:** Don't forget things such as paper clips, scissors, sticky notes, tape, pens, pencils, trash cans, clipboards, staplers, staples, staple removers, and the like.

- ✔ **Mailboxes:** Each manager needs a plastic tray, cubby, or some kind of bin. You use these mailboxes to disseminate written info, such as schedules, new policies, and department-specific paperwork.

Processing Payments

Payments are the lifeblood of your restaurant. They provide you with the means to settle your bills, buy the supplies you need, and pay your employees. Diners have more payment methods at their disposal than ever before, and more options are becoming available regularly. We can't cover all the possibilities in this book, but in this section we include details about the most typical payments you run across in the restaurant business.

Credit and debit card transactions

Not all credit and debit card processing companies are created equal. Shop around to get the best rates and service. Never be complacent with your purveyors, including your credit/debit card processor, when evaluating both what they provide and how much they charge. Over time, they may raise their rates, change the services they provide, or even unilaterally add a service (that may or may not benefit you) and charge you for it. Be vigilant!

Look at these resources for help in choosing a credit/debit card processor:

- ✔ Your POS provider
- ✔ Your local restaurant association
- ✔ Your local chamber of commerce

And continue to shop. If your business grows, don't sit and wait for someone to give you a better rate just because you may be eligible.

You may also want to accept debit cards from nonfinancial entities such as nearby universities. Participating in such programs has obvious promotional upsides, but make sure you're able to interface the organization's system with your POS.

Gift cards

The gift card has gradually replaced the gift certificate in the restaurant industry. The cards essentially perform the same service as the certificates for your customers (allowing your diners to give the experience of your restaurant and its services to their friends and family), but gift cards offer many distinct advantages over the certificate for both you and your customer — chiefly, speed and accuracy.

Taking advantage of the gift card option

The process for using a gift card as a method of payment is exactly the same as using a credit or debit card for your diner. The customer presents the card to pay her bill. The server or bartender swipes the card, applying the gift card amount to the bill. Any remaining balance stays on the card for another use. As fast as the gift card is swiped, your POS computes the amount of the transaction and the resulting balance on the card. (To compare, using a gift certificate requires the server to break out the calculator, figure out what the remaining gift balance is, have your customer agree to it, and have your manager-on-duty initial approval.)

If you opt for preset gift cards, keep a few in popular denominations (such as $25, $50, and $100) ready to go in an easy-to-access yet secure spot at your front desk or as a component of your till. The rest can remain tucked away in your safe until they're ready to use. (Don't forget to count and verify these cards each shift, just like you do cash.) On the other hand, you may choose a service that allows you to set up an individual gift card with any amount. The bonus is that blank cards have no cash value until they're authorized, making them much less likely to walk off.

During popular gift-giving times like Christmas and Father's Day, have your gift cards in as convenient a spot as possible. Customers don't want to wait; if buying a gift card is a hassle this time, they may not bother with a next time.

In many states, neither gift certificates nor gift cards are allowed to expire unless those balances are turned in to the state as unclaimed funds. As always, check your local laws.

The cost of offering gift cards

As you may expect, you incur some costs for offering your diners gift cards. Depending on how and from whom you purchase the cards, your costs can be front-loaded, incremental, or based on percentage (or a combination thereof).

Here's a list of the typical costs associated with gift card programs:

- Graphic design and layout of the gift card
- Production of the actual gift cards
- Setup fee (which usually covers programming your terminals, training your staff, and so on)
- Redemption terminals with software, or software that runs on your existing POS (having a stand-alone terminal for gift cards may be cheaper than integrating with your POS system, especially if you're using an older POS system)
- Monthly processing fees

You may choose to purchase the cards in bulk and pay for them and their corresponding software once. You may opt for buying them in smaller amounts from your POS (or other) service provider and having those folks maintain the software and any ensuing upgrades. In this case, the provider may charge you with each swipe of the card or charge you a percentage of the dollar amount used on each transaction.

Wow! How can you expect to afford gift cards? The cost of maintaining such a program outwardly seems to suck your profits right out of your transaction.

First, understand that you should consider some of this cost as marketing. Having one of your logoed gift cards in a wallet or purse is worth something.

Another way to offset your cost is to pass it (or at least part of it) on. Gift cards (and not just restaurant gift cards) are often subject to a *maintenance fee*. These charges kick in if a card is inactive for at least a year. They effectively make up some of your costs by debiting money from a lost or forgotten gift card. If the card is inactive for an extended period of time, these costs eventually bleed the balance down to zero.

Contactless and proximity payments

Sometimes called "wave and go" or "touch and go," *contactless payments* are becoming increasingly popular and are guaranteed to become more popular in the future. *Radio frequency identification* (RFID) chips are embedded into a variety of devices such as credit cards, student ID cards, key fobs, and even smartphones. These devices are passed near an antenna on your POS system, and then the secure payments are processed much like a credit card transaction. The benefit is that customers don't need a PIN or signature at each transaction, which speeds up transactions significantly. In most cases, transactions are limited to $25 and under and periodically require a user to enter a PIN.

Contactless payment cards offer features that can make your transaction even faster than a swipe. If your restaurant concept is reliant on moving customers along as quickly as possible, consider this feature as an option.

Preparing for Payroll

You should have two bank accounts:

- ✔ **Operating account:** You pay all your bills from this account.
- ✔ **Payroll account:** Use the money in this account to pay payroll checks only.

Shuttle money *from* the operating account *to* the payroll account, never the other way around. After you put money into the payroll account, it's gone. Even if it stays there and an employee doesn't cash his check, that's his business. Resist the urge to "borrow" from this account even if things seem tight.

As soon as you hire someone, have the new employee fill out the necessary paperwork, such as the I-9 and W-4 forms (see Chapter 12 for the list), so you can properly process his or her paychecks. You have to pay employees if they work for you, but you can't pay them without the right paperwork. This situation is the *ultimate* case of dotting your *i*'s and crossing your *t*'s. If your records are audited and you don't have the proper paperwork, you may face devastating fines or worse.

Farming it out or doing it in-house

Depending on the size of your operation, you may opt to do all the payroll duties yourself from start to finish (or assign them to someone in your operation) or outsource some of the work to a payroll company. If you keep everything in-house, typical duties of the assigned payroll guru for each pay period include the following:

✔ **Calculating and verifying hours:** If you use an integrated computerized system to track hours worked, you should be able to print a report to verify the hours worked by each employee. If not, collect those time cards and start adding.

✔ **Confirming employee pay rates:** Computers are only as flawless as the people who program them. Data entry errors are common, so a human needs to double-check this important piece of info if your time clock is computerized.

✔ **Crunching the numbers:** You have to calculate gross pay and take out taxes and FICA (Federal Insurance Contributions Act) contributions for each employee.

✔ **Tallying the total deposit for the payroll account:** Figure out the full amount of net pay (the amount owed after all the withholding is withheld) that you owe your employees.

✔ **Transferring the payroll deposit from the operations account to the payroll account:** In most cases, both your accounts will be held at the same bank, so you can make a phone call or an online transaction to move money from one account to another and post it by the end of the day.

✔ **Cutting checks for each employee:** Print a separate check for each employee. Make sure that each check includes details about the number of hours the employee worked, his gross pay, and any deductions. (Prefer to go paperless? We discuss direct deposit in the later section "Choosing a method of payment.")

✔ **Distributing checks to employees on payday:** Establish a scheduled time, usually between the lunch and dinner rush, to distribute checks.

Payroll companies generally calculate the amount of withholding tax, Social Security contributions, and so on and cut the checks.

Even if you hire a payroll company, you still need someone in house to double- (or triple-) check the records and perform the functions (listed earlier) that the vendor doesn't cover. So decide whether that service is worth the amount of money you'll pay for it. Check with a payroll company such as ADP, Paychex, or PayMaxx for quotes and details of the services it can provide.

Deciding on a payroll period

There's no right or wrong payroll period, but once a week or every other week is pretty standard for restaurant pay periods. Every choice has its advantages and disadvantages. Pick the period that works best for you.

- ✓ **Weekly:** You keep a fairly consistent expense each week, but your payroll management time (verifying hours, cutting checks, and so on) increases.

- ✓ **Every other week:** You have no payroll expense one week and then a big expense the next week. Paying less often cuts your payroll management time virtually in half compared to paying weekly.

After you pick a pay period, pick a day to hand out or mail the checks. If your pay period ends on a Saturday, maybe you hand out checks the following Wednesday or Thursday. If you're using an outside company to cut the checks, make sure that it commits to delivering the checks by your payday. Also, always deposit money into your payroll account before you hand out the first check.

Not paying your employees on time is a telltale sign that the restaurant is in its death throes. If the employees aren't getting paid on time, everyone will know about it. Set a pay period and stick to it.

Choosing salaries or hourly wages

A *salary* is a regular wage that doesn't change no matter how many hours the employee works. *Hourly wages* are paid to employees at a set rate for each hour worked. Here's a list to help you decide which system works best for your employees (see the job descriptions in Chapter 13):

✔ **Salary:** Team members with managerial, supervisory, or accounting-type functions are usually salaried. They include the following positions:

- **Back-of-the-house employees:** General managers, assistant general managers, accountants, bookkeepers, controllers, kitchen managers, chefs, and sous-chefs

- **Front-of-the-house employees:** Front-of-the-house managers, floor managers, bar managers, the maitre d', and possibly cashiers whose cash handling and money management responsibilities are extensive

✔ **Hourly rate:** Some staff members clock in and out at the beginning and end of each shift. Tipped employees make less of a wage than other hourly employees, usually half of minimum, and make most of their money in tips. Here are some hourly positions:

- **Back-of-the-house employees:** Line cooks, prep cooks, and dish staff

- **Front-of-the-house employees:** Wait staff, bussers, food runners, host staff (except the maitre d'), most cashiers, bartenders, cocktail servers, and barbacks

Choosing a method of payment

You have several payment methods available to you. The most common form of payment is a physical check, but many restaurants opt for the other forms as well.

Physical checks

Paper checks are the most mainstream form of payment for restaurants. The check should itemize the hours worked, taxes withheld, Social Security taxes paid, deductions for insurance payments or 401(k) contributions, and any other deductions relevant to your benefits plan.

Direct deposit

Direct deposit is a service you may want to consider extending to your employees. Instead of a physical, depositable check, the employee gets a receipt that shows her hours worked, deductions, and the amount automatically deposited in her account. Salaried employees are the best candidates because their pay amounts are the same, and their Social Security, FICA, health insurance, and other deductions are the same each pay period.

Cash

Cash is kind of an old-fashioned method of payment, but it's completely legal. Most restaurants are cash businesses. Nowadays, banks charge businesses for converting checks into cash and vice versa. If you're doing it the right way, why pay the penalty, also known as the *fee,* and go through a bank? It's almost an incentive to use the cash because you have it. Cashing a check may be tough for an employee, especially one new to the area or the country. If an employee can legally work in the country, he still may not have a bank account.

Even if you pay employees in cash, you still must withhold the proper amount of IRS-required tax and so on from their pay. Keep good records regarding all this information because you're required to pay your portion to the government and report all the employees' wages for tax reasons.

Saving, Storing, and Protecting Your Records

Record-keeping is an important part of any business. Various government agencies require most businesses to save certain information for a certain period of time. Check out Table 14-1 for our recommendations.

Table 14-1	Recommendations for Keeping Records
Records	**How Long?**
Balance sheets	Permanently
Bank statements	7 years
Cash receipts	Permanently
Cash sales slips	3 years
Credit card receipts	10 years
Contracts: Employee, government, and labor union	Permanently
Contracts: Vendor (after expiration)	9 years
Equipment leases (after expiration)	6 years
Equipment repair records	Life of the equipment
Financial statements	Permanently
Franchise documents	Permanently
Garnishments	6 years
General ledger	Permanently
Inventory records	3 years

Records	How Long?
Inspection reports	5 to 10 years
Invoices	7 years
Job applications, nonemployee	1 year
Leases	Permanently
Payroll records (after termination)	10 years
Mortgages	Permanently
Income statements	10 years
Permits and licenses (fire, elevator, liquor, and so on)	Current on file
Tax records	7 years

Depending on the office and storage space your restaurant offers, the length of time you'll be storing particular documents, and the amount of access you'll need to the document, you can store your records on- or off-site. Wherever you store them, though, remember that temperature and moisture can be the enemy of both paper records and computer disks. Make sure your long-term storage area protects them from excessive heat and the possibility of flooding or fire.

You also have to ensure that the information stays out of the hands of prying eyes. Here's our advice:

- ✔ **Secure the office.** You probably keep many records stored in your office, either on the computer or as hard copies in a file cabinet or safe. Job one, then, is to secure this area. Make sure that your door has a heavy-duty lock.

  If you have a security system with cameras, you can train one camera on the office itself. You may even consider putting the recording device in a safe in the office so it can't be erased or damaged.

- ✔ **Lock all file cabinets.** Ultimately, if someone wants to get into your file cabinet, he will. Locks don't keep criminals and thieves out of your stuff, but they do keep honest people honest. Lock up your employee records, bank account numbers, and credit card numbers.

- ✔ **Use passwords.** Make access to computers password dependent, and give access to only a limited number of employees. Also, make sure that all managers promptly log off when their computer sessions are finished. As an added security measure, set your machines to automatically log out users after a period of inactivity — for example, two to five minutes.

- ✔ **Install firewalls.** A *firewall* is a software application that protects the restaurant *and* its clientele from hackers attempting to gain access to your computer records to either destroy them or use the information for illegal gain. Talk to the sales rep who sells you your computer systems about the best plan for protecting your system.

✔ **Secure credit card transactions.** Hackers can attack your credit card system as well. Use a reputable credit card company and make sure it has protection, insurance, and *encrypted* (secure) systems. Talk about what services the company can offer, and pick what's best suited for you. Be sure that your POS and your record-keeping are in full compliance. If your POS hasn't been updated since 2008, you're likely not compliant with current Federal Law.

Chapter 15

Getting the Word Out

. . . .

. . . .

*Y*ou may have the most incredible menu, the hippest atmosphere, the most attentive wait staff, the hottest chef, or the deepest wine list in town. If no one knows about it, however, your restaurant will fail. Getting the word out about your new place isn't as easy as telling your friends and family and waiting for the word to spread around town.

Using public relations (PR), advertising, and social media to your advantage is essential to your restaurant's success. Pick the message that you want your potential diners to hear and make sure that it gets to them loud and clear (and over and over again). Of course, you have to live up to your own hype, or your guests won't come back. But the first hurdle is getting them in the door. This chapter gives you the details for creating your own marketing machine to bring them in.

Customers return to your business because they like it. You may get them in the first time because you sent out coupons or offered a buy-one-get-one-at-half-price night, but they probably won't come back unless they enjoyed their first experience. We get them in the door in this chapter. Check out Chapter 18 for tips on how to keep them coming back.

Defining Your Message

Purposefully crafting your *message* (what you want people to remember about your restaurant) is the key to marketing success or failure. Understand what you want to say, who you want to say it to, how you reach this group or groups and why, operationally, you're choosing this particular strategy. A *marketing plan* is your plan to deliver your message to the group you want to reach.

Success is rarely an accident. It's a function of motivating the buying decision of the potential customer. Efficient operational practices, consistently delicious foods, and an attractive, accessible location don't guarantee success. With all the dining choices available, consumers expect those things at a minimum. You, therefore, have to clearly communicate your message to your audience. Build your message to speak to these components:

- ✔ Preferred clientele
- ✔ Concept
- ✔ Competition within that segment
- ✔ Desired business outcomes

Simply put in restaurant lingo, marketing is all about butts in seats. Unless you attract a consistent flow of paying guests to your tables, you'll have a For Sale sign in your windows before you can say, "Table for none."

Focusing on the consumer and tailoring your message

One size doesn't fit all for restaurant marketing. Just as neighborhoods and cities feature cultural and economic differences, your marketing plan should address the varied needs and wants of your consumer, whose dollar you're competing for. Each scenario requires an individualized marketing plan.

The simplest marketing plan is the shotgun effect — you throw it all out there, anywhere, and see what happens. But that's not the most successful approach. Some consumers don't care, and others will hear it, see it, or read it, and then reject it. Still others won't pay any attention. So the most successful marketing plans target specific consumers.

To run your marketing and promotions program well, you need to understand your clientele. Big restaurant companies spend millions to understand the demographic (who they are) and psychographic (what they think about) profiles of their consumer. In Chapter 3, we provide you with concrete suggestions and resources for researching and defining your potential customer. After you have a handle on who your potential customers are, they become your *target audience* for marketing purposes. You need to craft your message with them in mind.

The audience for a restaurant can be pretty broad, but you can segment it and tailor a different message for each target audience. Identify both primary and secondary target audiences, and develop multiple messages based on the differences of your consumers. You can break up potential customers categorically to focus on gender, geography, income levels, age, interests, or any other demographics of your consumers.

Communicating your concept

Your *concept* is the combination of your type of restaurant, your menu and prices, the ambience you offer, and the style of service you provide. To get folks in your door, you have to tell them the following:

- Who you are
- What you're offering
- Why they should care

We help you establish your initial concept in Chapter 2, and your concept will likely become more concrete as you analyze your local market (as we explain in Chapter 3).

Keeping up with the competition

You're competing for just one thing: the discretionary food service dollar of the consumer. Those food service dollars are owned by a spectrum of consumers more or less likely to use your concept, with varying frequency. Your job is to identify your competition, determine their strengths and their weaknesses, and determine your points of difference. (We guide you through both processes in Chapter 3.) Simply put, a *point of difference* is how you're different from your competition. At that point, you're ready to tailor your marketing plan to counter your competitors' strengths or attack their weaknesses in an attempt to attract a segment of the market.

Emphasizing points of difference

Your message can focus on a clear-cut point of difference versus your competition. This tactic is extremely common, but you have to decide how aggressively you want to point out your competition's weaknesses, instead of simply emphasizing your own strengths. "We don't microwave our burgers" clearly conveys the fact that the others do, so diners should choose you over them. Or your message may be a more subtle statement of a great feature of your concept that leads the consumers to compare your features with another place's. For example, at Urban Forge Pizza Bar, "We cook our pizza to order in a wood-fired oven." We're not saying that the other guy doesn't, but we're leading customers to think about how the pizza they had delivered yesterday was cooked and how it could've been better had it been freshly wood-fired.

When you're defining your own point of difference, think about the burger wars. McDonald's, Burger King, Wendy's, and Hardee's all have similar menu items on the surface: burgers and fries, basically. But for years, they've focused their marketing on a point of difference, such as the following:

✓ **Price:** Enter the 99-cent menu.

✓ **Value:** The combo meal concept is an example.

✓ **Quantity:** Think super-size.

✓ **Quality:** Flame-broiling versus frying may be the difference.

✓ **New menu offerings:** Examples include premium salads, smoothies, and turkey burgers.

These companies spend millions each year trying to leverage their individual points of difference — whether it's their combination of offerings, size of portions, extended hours, kids' toys, co-branding with the hottest new movie, or exotic bikini-clad hotties — and make them resonate with consumers. These companies answer the needs and wants of their targeted consumers and shape the future market by centering their marketing campaigns on emerging trends and the development of new products that their competitors will have to respond to in order to protect their market shares.

After your restaurant is established, don't fall into the trap of just marketing to your strengths. You don't need to target the market segment that will visit your restaurant whether you advertise or not. In a competitive marketplace, you must highlight the "wow" (the new and exciting parts of your business) to attract a constant flow of new diners looking for variety.

Facing off head to head

You can always choose to go head to head with your competition. "My secret family recipe fried chicken will kick your fried chicken's butt, Colonel!" Your competitor launches a French toast breakfast sandwich, so you counter with a sausage, egg, and cheese grilled waffle panini. Just don't make the mistake of always being the copycat. Create your own point of difference instead of taking a me-too approach all the time.

Conceding strengths

One approach is to concede a competitor's strength and focus on something it doesn't do at all, such as breakfast or steaks. For example, Arby's served basically only hot roast beef sandwiches for years. Then, instead of going after the traditional burger market, Arby's got some really good bread and developed its cold sandwich program, the *Market Fresh* program. Domino's Pizza also tried something new. Instead of relegating itself to being just another pizza joint, Domino's branched out with its delivery options. It added chicken wings and dessert items for more variety.

In your case, suppose that two identical restaurants are located on the same block, but one offers a 15-minutes-or-it's-free lunch menu. Instead of adding your own 14-minute menu, maybe you offer a lunch buffet.

Getting tactical

You can craft your message to achieve strategic results. For example, if you were fortunate enough to lock in a great price on 500 kilos of free-range, all-white-meat chicken nuggets hand formed into the lifelike image of Michael Jordan, you may design a marketing strategy to drive sales of these signature items and take advantage of your razor-sharp business acumen.

You see examples of this type of strategic marketing everyday. Simply consider the strategy behind "value meals," "super-sized" menu upgrade options, and "add a side of popcorn pigeon for $1.99." These suggestions appear as attractive discounts offered by a generous operator grateful for your patronage. In reality, they're carefully crafted strategic marketing decisions designed to increase customer traffic, maximize profitability, and drive customer purchases toward high-margin menu items. In short, it works like this: "I'll discount the soda that costs me 10 cents per serving if you purchase the 'Half-Pound Holstein Melt' that I make nearly $2 on."

Look at your marketing plan as your best opportunity to control the buying decision of your customer. A well-designed, purpose-driven marketing message can both increase your operation's top line by attracting new customers to your restaurant and increasing the frequency-of-use by your existing customer base; the same plan can also increase the all-important bottom line by inducing patrons (consciously or unconsciously) to select those items on your menu that are the most profitable.

Building Public Relations

The goal of *public relations,* or PR, is developing a positive public perception of your restaurant with the local community and the media.

Planning for the good and the bad

Good publicity is a fantastic asset. If you have a good PR machine working, you spend less time and money on other promotions, including advertising. If everybody already wants to come in, then you don't need to advertise in the local dining magazine every week or hold special events.

But publicity can also hurt you. If you have a British burger joint and Mad Cow disease is running rampant in the press, that's bad publicity; it will hurt. Sometimes media stories are political, overhyped health concerns, but no matter how true or false, they alter public perception, which affects your business. If you get a bad review from a critic, it can hurt. If people haven't been to your restaurant before, the bad review may be this first thing they hear about you. If you don't make a good first impression, you may never get a chance to make another one.

Positioning positively: Assembling a marketing kit

Your *marketing kit* is the package of promotional materials that you have at the ready to send to people who want details about your restaurant. You can hand a kit to a bride-to-be looking for the perfect restaurant to host her wedding reception or send one to a new hotel concierge to let him know about your facilities.

Your marketing kit should contain all pertinent info about the restaurant, including the phone and fax numbers and website and e-mail addresses (we discuss your website later in "Creating a Compelling Restaurant Website"). Include information about designated contact people, such as the chef, general manager, PR person, owner, banquet planner, and so on. Any positive press clippings about your place should make an appearance. Add a summary of your restaurant's history or goals and specifics about your cuisine. Detail your mission statement. Include business cards, a copy of your menu, and something that tells someone what the restaurant's about, such as a postcard if you're in a scenic area or a matchbook if you're a cigar bar. In general, unique is better. Put it all in a sturdy folder, preferably one with your logo.

Preparing for the worst: Contingency planning

Drawing attention to yourself is good. But after you're up and running, you become a target. You need to have a game plan for handling negativity, whether it comes from the competition, a disgruntled critic, or a disappointed customer. Role-play or run through different negative scenarios with your staff and your managers. Ask specific questions related to your concept. Here are a few to get you started:

- ✔ What do we do if we have an underage drinker in the bar?
- ✔ What do we say if people get sick from a contaminated green onion?
- ✔ How do we handle an aggressive newspaper reporter asking about our employee strife?
- ✔ How do we respond to a less than glowing review? Or do we?

Make it a regular practice to anticipate bad scenarios. The exercise helps you prevent a situation by taking the precautions against it. It heightens awareness of potential issues, improves food safety, and ensures product quality enhancement. And it helps you to be better prepared for dealing with the customer or press questions.

Your PR campaign: Going it alone

As with most things, you can manage your PR yourself, hire someone to do it, or hire someone to do part of it. Depending on your budget, you may start doing it yourself and then work up to hiring others after you're running a 150-restaurant conglomerate.

The do-it-yourself (or with your team) approach can work very well. You know your product and your concept, and you can make quick decisions about specials, promotions, and incentives. You save money because your time is paid for already, and you save time because the communication is more direct. The downside: Tons of work and another serving of stress to your already full plate. Plus, you don't get the different perspective of your operation that an outsider can bring — a fresh pair of eyes and some new ideas.

Getting noticed in the community

PR involves the public perception of both your restaurant and the most visible people in your restaurant, most likely you. Our best advice is to simply do things the right way. The goal here isn't to avoid attracting negative attention. Your goal should be to make a positive contribution to your community — a positive *visible* contribution to your community. The rewards are twofold: You make a difference, and you generate goodwill for your business.

Have the restaurant participate in charity events, including silent auctions or special dinners. Encourage your chef to teach cooking classes on occasion at the local community college or gourmet shop. You can build community relationships and relationships with other restaurant peers.

Make the most of these opportunities to let people try your food. Be in the booths at the major events in your area, like charity events, neighborhood or community events, or street fairs — whatever is appropriate to your business.

You, personally, have to make the effort as well. Volunteer for a board or join the Chamber of Commerce or the food service advisory board for a country club. Find something that gets you noticed within your clientele group. Or even better, join the group that your clientele wants to be. Coauthor Mike is on the board of Grand Central Neighborhood Association, a social services organization that feeds, shelters, and gets work for the homeless in the Midtown area near his restaurant. Coauthor Andy served on the board of Second Helpings, an Indianapolis-based food rescue organization that repurposes food that restaurants and caterers donate for homeless shelters and missions, as well as provides culinary training for the homeless.

Generating positive PR from the inside

Consider your employees to be one of your target audiences in your PR campaign. You want them to be proud of your place so they can pass on the good vibes to the guests. The ideal situation is to have a staff that works as a mini-PR machine. Bartenders build up the waiters. Waiters talk up the chef. The chef meets people at the tables or has an after-dinner drink in the bar. Good service equals good PR.

These examples aren't only ways to generate good internal PR; they also generate word-of-mouth PR — the good word about your restaurant that spreads outside the restaurant. Social media is a key component of word-of-mouth PR. Word-of-mouth PR includes diners telling their friends about their experience at your place and talking about your ads, location, and so on. Basically anytime anyone is talking (or posting, checking in, or sharing) about your establishment, it's word-of-mouth PR.

Courting your neighbors is a good (and necessary) first step because you get them on your side. But be careful: Don't exclusively target your neighborhood unless it can fully support you. You may suffer from "secret syndrome" — neighbors don't want to share your restaurant with the outside world. Long-term success comes from a balance of neighborhood support and extra-neighborhood support. If you make your restaurant a destination, as word spreads, it'll become bigger than the neighborhood.

You can generate a ton of talk and a huge buzz, but to move from being the "in" place of the moment to a perennial favorite, you have to deliver on your promises and exceed your guests' expectations (see Chapter 18).

Getting some help with PR

A PR firm should have connections already. In addition to talking with several people at the firm, speak to the person who's actually handling the account before signing with the firm. If you don't feel comfortable with the account rep, pick another person or even a new firm. You're looking for someone who's personable and charismatic. If you don't enjoy talking with someone, how will your potential diners feel? Additionally, a firm should have social media specialists on staff. They can develop and run an effective and coordinated campaign across multiple services. See info about social media later in "Sounding off on Social Media."

Paying someone by the event

Say that you're having an event in your restaurant and inviting all the major chefs in town. Or you're having a blueberry-pie-eating contest and promoting it in the media. A PR rep or firm can help you spread the word. Maybe you're trying to promote a holiday dinner or a recipe, and you just want someone to get this one thing done. Use it as an opportunity to audition a PR company. Start small with a single event and then add a few things to the firm's plate.

Some PR companies specialize in restaurants in large cities. In smaller areas, you may find a more general PR company who may do PR for the local hospital, charities, a new gym on the west side, and a few restaurants as well.

Hiring a person or firm for full-time work

Even if you source out your PR work, you must remain actively involved in the process. You get as much out as you put in. A PR professional is the multiplier of your effort. If you put in zero effort, you still get zero out of it. Confirm that everything is meeting your expectations and approval. Review all press releases. Stay on top of things.

A good PR agency probably has a well-oiled PR machine already working and a system already in place and is fitting you in as a client. Such a business won't be reinventing the wheel or using you as a guinea pig. You should be able to get fairly quick results, compared to doing it all on your own.

Creating an Advertising Plan

An *advertising plan,* the plan you use to inform the world about your restaurant, is as unique as your restaurant. Advertising differs from PR in that you always pay for advertising. No one plan works for everyone. And the same formula probably won't work for your restaurant from year to year or season to season. What works in January doesn't necessarily work in July. Maybe in 2000 your $50 burger was a great idea, but a few years later, the economy was completely different, and people were looking for value.

Developing an advertising plan is an investment in both time and money. Make sure that you're managing advertising like any other expense of time or money. It should be efficient and offer the greatest return on your investment. But unlike other expenses in your business, it's a *speculative* investment, meaning you're rolling the dice and saying, "I'll make this investment in hopes that I'll see a return in the food service dollar."

After you know your target audience to a T (see the section "Focusing on the consumer," earlier in the chapter), figure out where to reach them. Many of the same sources you initially look at to research these folks are the same places you use to reach them — local newspapers, foodie magazines, TV, radio, and other sources we provide you with in Chapter 3.

Make concerted decisions about which outlets you choose to convey your message. You should know which section of the newspaper to put your ad in. If you're opening a sports bar with beer pitcher specials and the obligatory "I ate the whole thing" t-shirt you win for eating the 40-ounce steak, don't waste your ad dollars in *Ladies' Home Journal.* Find out enough about your potential consumer to know that if you're in the Upper Peninsula of Michigan, you may well reach more people in the hunting and fishing publication than on the local sports scores and stats page. (And if your ad includes a picture, show somebody just like your desired clientele.)

Put together a plan to reach your clientele in as many ways as you can. Think about the reach of really big companies. Ask yourself what age you were when you knew every component of a Big Mac (two all-beef patties, special sauce, lettuce, cheese, pickles, onions on a sesame seed bun). These folks have reached you since you were born. They continue to speak to you, consciously or unconsciously throughout your life, and it's no accident.

Here are some successful strategies we've used to get people in the door:

- ✔ **Use incentives:** Send coupons to your targeted clientele. This approach traditionally works for casual concepts, diners, and family restaurants. You can offer 2-for-1 entrees, a free appetizer, a kids-eat-free meal with paying adult, or anything else relevant to your concept and clientele.

- ✔ **Run TV commercials:** This approach can be expensive. You pay for the creation of the commercial (including actors, writers, a director, and production personnel) and the airtime to run the commercial.

  Warning: Run only quality TV commercials. TV production is not a DIY option. Think about all the bad automobile dealership ads that feature the owner with the made-for-radio looks and the sad clip-art graphics. If you're not doing it right, this money would be better spent in other advertising channels.

- ✔ **Place print ads:** Use local newspapers and magazines and dining or entertainment papers. If your potential diners are reading the periodical, let them see your restaurant. Alumni newsletters are an idea — former classmates may be interested in checking you out.

- ✔ **Sponsor a local athletic team or event:** Don't just consider softball and bowling teams. Consider peewees to blue hairs, fishing tournaments to soccer leagues.

- ✔ **Find exposure on buses, trains, or cabs:** If your potential patrons use these modes of transportation, you may find an interested audience.

- ✔ **Go global on the Internet:** There are innumerable ways to promote your establishment on the Internet. See the section "Sounding Off on Social Media" later in this chapter for information on advertising on these sites.

Considering developing QR (Quick Response) or Data Matrix codes and include them on any printed advertising, to-go cups, business cards, and beverage napkins. Potential diners can scan these with one of the many QR apps on their cell phones and go directly to your website, call the restaurant, or receive information from you. Scan the code in Figure 15-1 to go directly to the online Cheat Sheet for this book.

Your message should speak to your to your target audience and tell them

- ✔ Who you are
- ✔ What you serve
- ✔ Where you fit into the local dining scene
- ✔ Where you're located
- ✔ When you're open
- ✔ How they should respond to your ad

Figure 15-1:
Scan this
QR code
with your
smartphone
to go
to our
online Cheat
Sheet at
Dummies.
com.

Creating a Compelling Restaurant Website

Unless you have a day job as a web designer and programmer, we strongly recommend that you seek professional help to create your website. According to the National Restaurant Association, at least 40 percent of customers choose a restaurant through the Internet. Your website cannot be an afterthought. Don't leave it for your junior manager and a copy of FrontPage to slap something together and throw it up online.

SEO (or *search engine optimization)* is essential in website development. In a nutshell, SEO is the way that search engines (such as Yahoo! and Google) find a particular website. It involves a little bit of brainstorming on your part (to create keywords for your website) and fancy programming on your web developer's part. Any programmer worth her caffeine should be well-versed in its nuances and can guide you through the process.

Even though you're hiring an expert, you should have an idea about what you need. Include the following on your website:

✔ **The physical address of the restaurant:** Yes, the whole thing, including your zip code. Search engines love that stuff.

✔ **A map and some general directions:** People who aren't looking at your website with a smartphone with mapping capabilities will appreciate the gesture.

✔ **Your menu:** Even if your menu changes regularly, include a sample online so people have an idea of what they're getting themselves into.

- ✔ **A blog:** Although you may not have daily blog entries, you need the ability to create and post updates without paying a programmer for every character and @ symbol. Work with your web designer to choose the right blog for your site.

- ✔ **A link to sign up for updates or a newsletter:** If people are already at your site, they're likely interested in what you have to say. Make staying in contact with you easy for them. For tips on setting up an e-mail newsletter and marketing campaign, take a look at Chapter 18.

- ✔ **A contact e-mail address:** Sometimes people need answers but they don't want to actually speak to a human. An e-mail is the perfect compromise.

- ✔ **Reservation information:** See Chapter 9 for our recommendations for managing reservations, on- and offline.

- ✔ **Links to your social media pages, such as Facebook and Twitter:** Both services make widely recognized buttons that you can place on your website. Use theirs; don't create your own. You'll just embarrass yourself.

- ✔ **Your positioning statement:** What makes your restaurant special? People need to see it. For help developing and refining this key element, see Chapter 2.

- ✔ **News and press:** Because you do such a great job running your restaurant, you're sure to win awards, get voted "Best of," and get noticed for your charity work. Check out Chapter 18 for ideas to populate this section of your website.

Make sure that your developer creates a mobile-friendly site. Many, many potential customers choose a restaurant online without a computer. This number is sure to grow, so plan for it now.

Sounding Off on Social Media

Increasingly social media is *the* way that people connect with each other, celebrities, brands, products, and yes, even brick-and-mortar restaurants. People go online to get and share information and opinions about what they're doing, where they're going, and who they're with. Restaurants are firmly entrenched in the everyday life of Americans, so it's no surprise that people talk, post, and tweet about restaurants. Sometimes referred to as *word of mouse* advertising, this medium is even more powerful because it legitimizes reviews and gives people a recognized platform to vent, rave, prop up, or drag down businesses.

The old adage "a happy customer will tell one other person about their experience; a disgruntled one will tell ten others" used to be true. With social media, that number increases exponentially, so it's essential that you be out front, managing your restaurant's online presence and reputation.

You can find a consultant to help you tackle any piece of your social media plan. Experts can help you formulate a plan, build your profiles, create your specials, and even send your status updates or tweets for you. It's a balancing act between what you need and what you can afford. To find a social media expert, look at targeted websites like www.elance.com or www.social mediajobs.com or even more-general sites like Indeed (www.indeed.com).

Investigating your options

We could fill books with details about an almost infinite number of websites and services that allow people to share information about restaurants. But alas, we all have day jobs, so instead, we cover the most relevant services for restaurant owners and managers: Facebook (www.facebook.com), Twitter (www.twitter.com), and foursquare (www.foursquare.com). All these services offer free accounts to both individuals and businesses. If you have the budget, you can pay to advertise on them as well. Contact the individual companies for their specific rates and program information, but get started by setting up a free account right now.

Regardless of which service(s) you use, social media is best when it starts a dialogue with your customers. You want them to respond to what you say. You want them to share their experiences at your restaurant with the world. You want them to contact you directly with their ideas. For details on creating an effective online community, take a look at Chapter 18.

If you sign up for more than one service (or have more than one account on one service), and we recommend that you do, consider using a *dashboard* (software that connects social media profiles together) like HootSuite, TweetDeck, or Seesmic. All work on multiple platforms (Mac and PC) and across many platforms, including iPhone, Blackberry, and Android. And all are free for a basic account that allows you to write once and post across all (or selected) profiles, schedule posts for delivery in the future, and analyze your traffic across multiple sites. Good stuff!

Setting up your space on Facebook

Facebook is more than just a way to reconnect with friends before your next high school reunion. In fact, with hundreds of millions of subscribers, it's a strong platform for marketing your business. Facebook has developed a fairly robust insights tool that helps you track your number of users over time. And it's free. What's not to love?

Facebook is a great choice for

- ✔ Creating a robust connection with your customers
- ✔ Posting pictures of people enjoying your restaurant
- ✔ Creating polls for customers to give you feedback on ideas
- ✔ Displaying your full menu online
- ✔ Announcing events, special dinners, and parties complete with an RSVP feature, photo posting, and event descriptions

Setting up a specific business page is simple. Here's how you set up a basic page for your restaurant:

1. **Go to the Facebook homepage, `www.facebook.com`.**

2. **Click the link "Create a Page for a celebrity, band or business" (under the green Sign Up button).**

3. **Click the "Local business or Place" icon.**

4. **Choose the appropriate category from the dropdown box.**

   Your most likely category is Restaurant/Café or Bar.

5. **Enter your contact information.**

   Then you can link your personal Facebook account to your business page. In fact, you must have a personal Facebook account in order to administer your business page.

6. **Modify and customize your page.**

   You can add photos of your restaurant, food, staff, patrons, or anything else that's relevant to your business. You can update your hours of operation, attire, food style, and payment options and include the names of the management or culinary teams. You can also include your website address (see the earlier section "Creating a Compelling Restaurant Website" for info on setting up a website).

7. **Import customer contact information into your account so you can let customers know when your page is up and running.**

   Until your page is really ready for the world to see, keep it private. Go to Edit Page→Manage Permissions→Page Visibility and confirm that the box labeled "Only admins can see this page" is checked. You wouldn't open your doors with misspellings on your menus or boxes of glassware in the dining room. Your virtual restaurant should be no different.

After you complete your page, keep the content fresh and compelling. You can post your lunch specials as your status, letting anyone who has "Liked" your page know what's on the menu. Or you can quickly send a more targeted update about Ladies' Night to just the women in your city between the ages of 21 and 35 who have "Liked" your page. So many possibilities!

Get a copy of *Facebook Marketing For Dummies* by Paul Dunay and Richard Krueger (John Wiley & Sons, Inc.) for details on making the most of your Facebook account, including details on setting up your business profile page and monitoring the success of your marketing campaigns and traffic.

Tweeting your way to a following on Twitter

Twitter is a social media service that asks you to answer the question "What's happening?" As a restaurateur, you could probably answer that question 20 times a day and never give the same answer. But to use Twitter effectively, plan your Tweets and don't overwhelm your followers.

A few quick Twitter-specific jargon things: A *Tweet* is a message you send from your Twitter account. A Tweet must be less than 140 characters but can contain links to longer posts at your website or blog, to pictures, and to video. The term *followers* (sometimes referred to as *tweeps*) refers to people who want to receive your Tweets. Your Twitter username is the @ symbol plus the name you choose, so co-author Heather's twitter username is @heatherdismore. (Feel free to follow her). And finally, a *hashtag* (known visually as #) is not the number sign in the Twitterverse; it's more like a theme for your tweets. People on Twitter search for Tweets with a particular hashtag (like #happyHourNYC) to find out what other users are saying about the topic (like 30 separate posts that suggest a version of "Let's meet up @UrbanForge for #happyHourNYC).

Your restaurant can benefit from using Twitter for

- ✔ Sending out quick shareable bursts of information in the form of Tweets
- ✔ Encouraging your followers to send your Tweets out to their followers (and so on, and so on), known as a *retweet* (RT)
- ✔ Taking a snapshot of trends people are talking about
- ✔ Responding to customer compliments and complaints in real time and in public
- ✔ Tracking people who mention your restaurant online

To get started with a Twitter account for your restaurant, follow these easy steps:

1. **Go to www.twitter.com and look for the boxes under "New to Twitter? Sign up today!"**

2. **Sign up with your real name, a verifiable e-mail address, and your desired password.**

3. **Choose a user name.**

   Twitter often suggests something close to your name or e-mail address, but we recommend choosing the name of your restaurant, because that's what your customers will look for. If for some reason that name is taken, consider adding a geographical component. For example, if your coffee shop is named *The Daily Grind* and is located in Indianapolis, you may consider @thedailygrindindy or @indydailygrind. Just remember you don't want to get too creative, because you want your tweeps to find you.

4. **Set up your profile and customize it.**

   On the left hand side of the screen, you see your Tweets (after you've made some) and the Tweets of the people you follow. On the right side of the screen, you see instructions for adding a profile picture, writing a bio, and so on.

   Include your contact information and link to your website. Choose your profile picture wisely. Make sure that it looks good both large and small because it accompanies all your Tweets.

5. **Choose whom to follow.**

   If you have customers who use Twitter and you have their Twitter usernames, follow them. You can also follow other restaurants, chefs, business experts, liquor brands, and so on. A few restaurant industry people to check out on Twitter include @fohboh, @NRNonline, @Eater, and @HuffPostFood.

   Pay particular attention to the @Mentions and the Retweet tabs on your Twitter homepage. Anyone on Twitter, whether following your or not, may mention you, especially if you use an obvious username (which we encourage). For example, someone may say, "Ate dinner last night @UrbanForge. Killer pizza!" We definitely want to know that someone ate at our pretend wood-fired pizza place. And we'd definitely reply with "Thanks so much!" or something to that effect. We can go to the @Mentions tab to see who's talking about us. The Retweet tab lets us know when someone retweets our Tweets like "Come see us @UrbanForge tonight for 2 for 1 Negronis and Peronis!"

Finding friends on foursquare

Foursquare is a location-based social media site. A user looks for foursquare businesses near his present location, likely on a smartphone. With a foursquare app, he can see other users near him, figure out which of his friends are at his favorite bar, or read reviews and tips from other users. Foursquare users are encouraged to check in at their favorite places by earning points in a variety of ways (like being the first of their friends at a venue or visiting a pizza place for the first time). Additionally, if a user is the person to check in the most often at a particular venue over period of time, that user becomes The Mayor. It's sort of a game in which you compete against friends to earn the most check-in points and win the most mayorships.

As a restaurateur, foursquare is for you if you want an easy way to

- ✔ Track the number of times patrons check in at your place
- ✔ Encourage customers to bring their friends by offering specials that can be unlocked only when a minimum number of users are present
- ✔ Bring in new diners by offering specials for first-time diners
- ✔ Create flash specials that are only good for a few hours, encouraging diners to come in to your place *now*

Here's how to set up your foursquare account:

1. **Go to www.foursquare.com and click the "merchants" link, near the bottom of the right-hand column.**

2. **Click the "Search and claim your venue" button.**

3. **Enter your restaurant's name in the search box, making sure you list the correct city and state.**

4. **After you find your listing, look for the "Claim this venue" link, at the bottom of the right-hand column.**

5. **Carefully read their Authorized Platform terms of use and make sure you are authorized to make the promises listed in the agreement. If appropriate, agree to the terms of use.**

6. **Create specials to bring people in the door.**

   Take a look at some of our ideas in Chapter 18.

Managing your other online profiles

You need to keep an eye on your profiles on restaurant review sites like Yelp, Urbanspoon, and Citysearch. These sites allow users to review, recommend, and even rant/rave about their experiences in restaurants, bars, nightclubs, and the like. Typically, restaurant review sites use a database and some fancy programming to create listings on their sites for all businesses in a given area, yours included. Users then upload pictures, offer opinions and tips, or post reviews and ratings.

Instead of going to the websites on a computer, many people use these sites through proprietary mobile applications (more commonly known as *apps*) installed on their smartphones. Often, users are in an unfamiliar area or want to try something new, so they shake, spin, and search their way to reviews of nearby restaurants in many cities worldwide. As a restaurant owner, you want to encourage potential customers to choose yours rather than someone else's, so you need to shape the dialog about your restaurant.

Here's an incredibly brief rundown on some of the most popular sites and how you can use them, as the verified business owner:

- ✔ **Yelp:** Yelp (www.yelp.com) offers free business accounts. You must unlock your account with a computer and a quick telephone-based authentication process.

- ✔ **Urbanspoon:** Go to www.urbanspoon.com and search for your restaurant. Click on the "Is this your restaurant?" link at the top right-hand corner of the restaurant's listing. Then click on "Claim Your Restaurant Now," and they'll call you at the number included in the online listing to verify that you're the legitimate owner or manager.

- ✔ **Citysearch:** The process at Citysearch (www.citysearch.com) is easier but scarier. There's no verification process; instead, you find your restaurant's listing and then click an online agreement stating that you're authorized to claim a restaurant as your own. The agreement includes language threatening a hefty legal bill and fine to discourage online jokesters.

Go to these sites and, at a minimum, confirm that the basics are correct. Even if you're not ready to upload photos, set up specials, and create marketing messages, make sure your restaurant's address, phone, number, web address, and directions are all correct.

Responding to reviews both positive and negative

Because the world is watching and everyone with a keyboard or a cell phone is empowered to share their opinion, good or bad, responding to compliments and criticism can be a tricky business. Respond enthusiastically to praise, and you may come off as a cheeseball. Respond in any way to criticism, and you risk sounding defensive. So weigh your options carefully.

You can retweet positive comments on Twitter; in fact, people expect it. On any other social media sites, we recommend a simple "thank you."

Here are our recommendations for handling negative and oh-so-public complaints:

- ✔ Breathe. Let the comments (and your blood pressure) settle for a bit and really consider the feedback before dashing off a potentially ouchy response.

- ✔ Remember that the person complaining was a paying customer in your restaurant and could be again.

- ✔ Remember that electronic communication lacks the body language and tone that a face-to-face conversation may have, so proceed with caution.

- ✔ Consider a neutral response, such as "Thanks for coming in and sharing your feedback with us." No need to get into a point-by-point defense of the review.

- ✔ Acknowledge changes resulting from the review, if appropriate. If the customer gave you some constructive feedback and you improved your restaurant because if it, let him (and the world) know.

- ✔ Take the conversation private. Almost all social media services have some private or direct messaging feature. Politely contact the customer to acknowledge her review and see what you can do to improve the situation. Take a peek at Chapter 18 for tips on handling complaints.

- ✔ Do not publically or privately engage in a personal attack. Period.

✔ If the review is completely false, attempt to resolve the situation privately and ask the user to remove his review. Hopefully, there's just a mix-up that you can solve quickly and quietly. If that's not possible, you can post a public response, but always remember that potential customers will be reading your response. Make sure you make a good impression.

If you have any concerns that your response *might* be too harsh, abrasive, or ouchy, do not post it or send it. Again, you don't want to make the situation worse. Many potential customers can overlook a negative review, but few will tolerate a rude restaurant owner or manager.

Part IV
Keeping Your Restaurant Running Smoothly

The 5th Wave   By Rich Tennant

"Our customer survey indicates 30% of our customers think our service is inconsistent, 40% would like a change in the menu, and 50% think it would be real cute if we all wore matching colored vests."

In this part . . .

*W*hether you're currently running a restaurant or
you're still in the planning stages, this part is for
you because we focus on maintaining and building on your
current operation. We offer suggestions that can help you
improve your style of management, retain long-term
employees, take another look at cleanliness and food
safety, attract a loyal customer base, build your brand, and
crunch the numbers to improve your financial standing.

Chapter 16

Managing Your Employees

*B*usiness would be great if it weren't for people. We say this with tongue firmly in cheek, but some days, it definitely feels that way. When you have three servers clamoring for the same Saturday night off, your dishwasher didn't show up, and you discover that an expensive bottle of wine is missing, you just might agree. In this chapter, we help you work through some of the common obstacles that come up while managing employees, and we give you tips on how to avoid most of them (the obstacles, not the employees).

Selling Employees on Your (or Their) Restaurant

Whether you're opening your doors for the first time or ten thousandth time, your success is intrinsically linked to the performance of your staff. And the way to get a top-notch performance out of your employees shift in and shift out is to make sure that they feel like they're part of something special. You have to continually sell your vision, your restaurant, your food, and the employee's vital role in the process to every staff member.

Simply hearing about your enthusiasm for your business and concept only takes you so far with employees. You must talk the talk, but you also have to walk the walk. Make sure they see you consistently exhibiting your standard of guest service, insisting on meeting and exceeding diners' expectations, and maintaining high food-quality standards. Don't just tell employees how they should perform; show them every single day, every single shift.

Educating your employees

Continuous employee education keeps your staff informed about and interested in your business. Correct training from Day 1 is essential (see Chapter 12 for details). But *educating* your employees entails more than initial training programs. Use weekly, monthly, and daily staff meetings to educate, inform, and motivate your employees. Share as much information about your business as you can. Investing the time to train and educate them properly shows that you view your employees as an important asset to your business.

A good place to start the education process is with the food and the beverage program. Here are some training options:

✔ **Periodic menu tastings:** If you're just opening your restaurant, have a complete menu tasting. You train two teams at once: The kitchen trains on preparation and presentation, and the wait staff gets lessons on the taste and appearance of the food. Let the wait staff develop subjective opinions about the menu by describing, in their own words, how they feel about the offerings. You run the risk that they'll impart personal preferences on the diners' experiences, but if your wait staff consists of good salespeople, they can find a pleasant, honest way to describe any dish.

  If the restaurant is in operation, conduct mini menu-tastings on a regular basis. Once a day, or at least a couple of times a week, bring out items that are on your regular menu, not just the daily specials. These tastings affect food cost but give your wait staff more knowledge and confidence in what they're serving, and that leads to better service (and sales).

✔ **Ongoing beverage training:** Any day's a good day for employees to find out more about your beverage program. Your beverage sales reps should be willing to come in and talk with your staff about any category of liquor, beer, or wine (on their own dime). Just as with food, the more your staff knows about a particular selection, the more likely they are to sell it.

  Let your staff taste different vodkas side by side or introduce your employees to the nuances of scotches or ports. Pair wines and beer with your food and let your staff taste them together. Beer and wine sales reps should provide you and your staff with good basic information about their selections, such as the terminology used to discuss it, as well as details about the specific wines in their portfolio.

✔ **Service drills:** There's always room for improvement on service. Your best waiter or your most knowledgeable bartender (and even you) can benefit from ongoing service training. You may have staff members who excel with technical applications, hospitality, or even etiquette rules of thumb, but only the rare individual nails all three all the time. Role-play with specific service situations to give your staff insight into the proper and improper ways of handling those situations.

If you have employees who don't speak English as their first language, consider offering a bonus if they successfully complete an ESL (English as a Second Language) program. They'll be better able to understand your ongoing training and articulate your products and offerings to your customers with improved English skills.

Motivating your staff

Keep the momentum going by praising your employees often, encouraging them to praise each other, and displaying a positive attitude. Keeping morale up is key. Here are some ways we've found to be effective in boosting and maintaining morale:

✓ **Encourage communication.** Keep an open-door policy. Make yourself available to listen to staff members when they have something to say without breaking the chain-of-command. And encourage them to communicate with each other. Their feedback may not always be positive, but if staff members get some say in resolving a problem, they're likely to stick with the solution.

✓ **Offer constructive criticism as well as praise.** Clear, concise feedback to employees on their performance is essential, and often, the message is that they need to improve. But don't beat them up with the criticism. Get your point across in a way that also encourages employees to perform at a higher level. And remember to pat them on the back for a job well done. If they receive only negative feedback, you're the one doing something wrong.

✓ **Know your staff.** Demonstrate a real interest in (and knowledge of) what's going on in employees' outside lives (such as tests, school, and other jobs). Talk to them and ask specific questions, such as "How's that Juliet part going?" or "Did you get that gig at the Sly Fox?" Such questions show employees that they matter to you and that you're paying attention. Small things, like acknowledging birthdays, also go a long way toward building morale. (Add the birthdays to your calendar as recurring annual events.)

 Asking your staff personal questions can be a minefield. Don't get too personal or ask questions that could darken their moods. Understand each person's individuality. What one person may appreciate another may consider an intrusion or an insult.

✓ **Encourage camaraderie among your staff.** Look at how the informal hierarchy treats different people, both veterans and newbies. When new people are treated well, they're much more enthusiastic about their training and tend to stay longer.

The pecking order should have zero impact on how you treat your staff and the amount of respect you pay them. A kitchen can't run without a dishwasher, and don't forget it.

- **Encourage apprenticeships, either formal or informal.** You want experienced staffers to take the new ones under their wing. When possible, give perks, such as preferred schedules or free lunches, to trainers and mentors.

- **Don't lose your cool.** Employees (and customers) can smell fear. If they see you act rattled or distressed during busy times — or feel that you're not in total control — your behavior may be infectious. The people around you may start feeling uncomfortable and become upset. Don't let it show if you feel out of control. Staying composed is half the battle.

- **Implement specific staff incentive programs.** Friendly competition and small-scale incentive programs are a tried-and-true path to boosting morale.

Don't focus staff incentive contests on general stats, such as overall sales for a shift. Instead, get your staff focused on specific products or categories of products to build enthusiasm. Do a training session on your wine-by-the-glass program and coordinate that with sales contests and incentives during the following shifts. Get creative with the prizes: Give winners a bottle of your house wine, a preferred parking space, or an extra day off. Motivating your staff doesn't have to cost you lots of cash.

- **Watch for animosity between front-of-the-house (FOH) staff and back-of-the-house (BOH) staff.** If you've spent more than a minute working in a restaurant, you know that this problem is all too common. The best way to combat it: Keep the lines of communication open. Have meetings that include both FOH and BOH staff to ensure that everyone hears the same info delivered the same way. Don't favor one department over the other. Keep in mind that the chef is more likely to side with the cook rather than a waiter, and a dining room manager is more likely to see the waiter's point of view than the cook's. To succeed, both departments need to work together.

Cross-training your department heads can go a long way. Although there may be initial resistance, try inserting your chef or kitchen manager into the FOH once in a while. Similarly, have your manager/host expedite or even work a shift on the cook's line. Both people can get a feel for the processes and people the other interfaces with. (Just don't try this on a busy Saturday night.)

- **Turn the mirror on yourself.** What you do is reflected in what your staff does. You can't expect the cook to be nice to the waiter if you're not nice to the cook. You can't expect friendly service from your busser if you're not smiling at him. And don't forget that managers are staff, too. How you treat them affects how they treat the rest of the staff.

Making Staff Schedules

Creating a schedule is a necessary step for any business that relies on shift workers with changing hours. A posted, written schedule communicates who will be working and when they should be in the restaurant. Making schedules for the wait staff in the restaurant is one of the toughest jobs in the working world. You're dealing with part-timers, many of whom have other jobs, attend school, are aspiring actors, and so on. Many employees may have scheduling needs that change from week to week. Back-of-the-house employees tend to be a bit more consistent in their schedule expectations.

Adding it all up: How many workers you need

The best way to create your schedules is to start with a job slot list. A *job slot list* is a chart that helps you determine the number of people you need doing a particular job at a particular time. Your job slot list will change for different shifts (or meal periods like breakfast, lunch, and dinner) and will change based on the days of the week, weeks of the month, and months of the year, just as your business levels change.

Check out the job slot lists in Figures 16-1 and 16-2. These job lists are for the back and front of the house for our fictional restaurant Urban Forge Pizza Bar. First, a bit of background: We serve inspired, wood-fired cuisine to a younger, hip crowd that flocks in for our Neapolitan pizzas, pastas, salads, and menu of specially paired beverages. *Cover counts* (the number of diners in the establishment) for dinner are steady during the week and peak on the weekends, when the pre-theatre rush brings in large groups of diners who enjoy our menu of sharable food and our social vibe.

	Monday	Tuesday	Wednesday	Thursday	Friday	Saturday	Sunday
	Average Covers Lunch/Dinner	*Average Covers Lunch/Dinner*	*Average Covers Lunch/Dinner*	*Average Covers Lunch/Dinner*	*Average Covers Lunch/Dinner*	*Average Covers Lunch/Dinner*	*Average Covers Lunch/Dinner*
	60/100	*60/100*	*60/100*	*75/120*	*80/165*	*100/165*	*100/60*
Job Classification	*Employees Required to Fill Position*						
Dish	0.5/1.0	0.5/1.0	0.5/1.0	1.0/1.0	1.0/2.0	2.0/2.0	1.0/1.0
Sauté	1.0/1.0	1.0/1.0	1.0/1.0	1.0/1.0	1.0/2.0	1.0/2.0	1.0/1.0
Fry	0.5/1.0	0.5/1.0	0.5/1.0	0.5/1.0	1.0/1.0	1.0/1.0	0.5/1.0
Broiler/Grill	0.5/1.0	0.5/1.0	0.5/1.0	0.5/1.0	1.0/1.0	1.0/1.0	0.5/1.0
Pantry	1.0/1.0	1.0/1.0	1.0/1.0	1.0/1.0	1.0/1.0	1.0/1.0	1.0/1.0
Prep	1.5/0.0	1.5/0.0	1.5/0.0	1.0/1.0	1.0/1.0	1.0/1.0	1.0/0.0
Totals	**5.0/5.0**	**5.0/5.0**	**5.0/5.0**	**5.0/6.0**	**6.0/8.0**	**7.0/8.0**	**5.0/5.0**

Figure 16-1: Job slot list for the back of the house.

Urban Forge Pizza Bar, via Figure 16-1, provides examples of common staffing techniques that you can use to conserve labor and maximize productivity:

- **An overall buildup of labor commensurate with anticipated business levels:** Traditionally in the average restaurant market, here's what you find:
  - Thursday is busier than other weekdays.
  - Friday and Saturday are busy all day.
  - Sunday is busy early; business then tapers off in the early evening.

- **Job sharing during slower shifts:** Some stations are shared on some lunch shifts. One employee works the fryer and the broiler for early week lunch shifts. The dishwasher and prep share some duties on Monday.

- **Concentration of morning prep labor early in the week:** This scheduling gives the staff time to prep items such as salad dressings, desserts, and soups for the whole week. And notice that more prep people are scheduled for lunch than dinner. Most prep takes place during your slower periods so that you can gear up for your busy times. See Chapter 10 for details on prep and the stations in the kitchen.

The job slot list in Figure 16-2 is also based on business levels that increase toward the weekend, through a busy lunch on Sunday but earlier dinner. In the front of the house, you may make other adjustments as well. For example, you may need only five waiters to handle your Friday night dinners if the waiters are experienced and reliable. If you have newer, less experienced people, you may need seven waiters.

As with the back of the house, always look to save FOH labor dollars during traditionally slow shifts. In Figure 16-2, notice that a morning bartender is scheduled on Monday to put away the big weekly liquor order, and then none are scheduled again until Friday. Managers can handle any guest orders for alcoholic beverages during these shifts.

	Monday	Tuesday	Wednesday	Thursday	Friday	Saturday	Sunday
	Average Covers Lunch/Dinner	*Average Covers Lunch/Dinner*	*Average Covers Lunch/Dinner*	*Average Covers Lunch/Dinner*	*Average Covers Lunch/Dinner*	*Average Covers Lunch/Dinner*	*Average Covers Lunch/Dinner*
	60/100	*60/100*	*60/100*	*75/120*	*80/165*	*100/165*	*100/60*
Job Classification	*Employees Required to Fill Position*						
Wait staff	3.0/4.0	3.0/4.0	3.0/4.0	4.0/5.0	5.0/6.0	6.0/6.0	6.0/4.0
On-call wait staff	0.0/0.0	0.0/0.0	0.0/0.0	0.0/0.0	0.0/2.0	0.0/2.0	0.0/0.0
Bartender	1.0/1.0	0.0/1.0	0.0/1.0	0.0/1.0	2.0/2.0	2.0/2.0	2.0/1.0
Bussers	1.0/1.0	1.0/1.0	1.0/1.0	1.0/2.0	2.0/3.0	2.0/3.0	3.0/1.0
Greeters	1.0/1.0	1.0/1.0	1.0/1.0	1.0/2.0	2.0/3.0	2.0/3.0	3.0/1.0
Totals	**6.0/7.0**	**5.0/7.0**	**5.0/7.0**	**6.0/10.0**	**11.0/16.0**	**12.0/16.0**	**14.0/7.0**

Figure 16-2:
Job slot list for the front of the house.

Schedules aren't set in stone. You can make adjustments later based on experience (yours and theirs) and business levels. During each shift, you cut one or more employees (end their shift early) if your sales don't meet your projections during a certain time of the day.

Consider implementing an on-call system if you have very dynamic business levels, especially until you establish some patterns. An *on-call employee* calls into the restaurant an hour or so before a scheduled shift to see whether he or she is working that night. If other employees call in sick or you get slammed with traffic you weren't expecting, having this extra person on the schedule can be a lifesaver. If you don't need that person, she gets a bonus night off. Be sure to rotate this duty, especially if you don't need the on-call staff very often. Most employees work because they need the money.

Putting names to numbers

After you complete your slot lists and know how many people you need for each position, shift, and day, insert specific employees into those slots. At this stage of the game, you turn your attention to employee schedule requests. Decide how you want to run your system for requesting days off. Many people use a master-calendar system combined with a request book. Employees place their names in the request book by the days they want off. Allot space for them to write a reason for a special request, such as a birthday, so that the person writing the schedule can take it into account.

Be consistent in how you resolve conflicts regarding scheduling. Have a policy in place for priority of requests. Many new restaurants use a dibs system, meaning that whoever requests a day off first gets it. More-established places use seniority systems effectively. You can base seniority on either hierarchy or tenure with the company.

Then start filling in the blanks in a table or spreadsheet like the one in Figure 16-3. We use the wait staff for Saturday at Urban Forge Pizza Bar as an example. We filled in a couple of names so you can see how a double shows up on the schedule. A *double* occurs when an employee essentially works straight through, or works two back-to-back shifts in a single day. In this case, Steve and Loretta are working both lunch and dinner. Also, this schedule is based on the first-in, first-out philosophy. Some operations reward openers with longer shifts, which mean more tables and usually more money.

Save yourself some time by setting up a schedule like the one in Figure 16-3 in a spreadsheet or other computer program. You can keep track of expected hours worked, planned time off, and so on much more easily.

You have to find a balance between your business levels and staffing levels. Good waiters won't stay where they can't make money. While you're getting a feel for business levels, you'll probably be *overstaffed,* or have too many people for a given shift. Try to make corrections as soon as you can.

Don't get complacent when writing your schedule. You must adjust your schedule to the business on particular weeks or days of the weeks, in particular weather, and so on. Holidays, traditional vacation times, ethnic or religious occasions, sporting events, and the like all affect your business, either positively or negatively. The degree to which they affect your business varies from concept to concept. During Super Bowl Sunday, many restaurants are dead, but if you're a pizza delivery place or a sports bar, you should be rocking.

Lunch		
1.	Open	9a.m. - 3p.m.
2.	Open	9a.m. - 3p.m.
3.	Open	9a.m. - 3p.m.
4.	Close	11a.m. - 5p.m.
5. STEVE	Double	12p.m. - 7p.m.
6. LORETTA	Double	12p.m. - 7p.m.
Dinner		
1. STEVE	Double	12p.m. - 7p.m.
2. LORETTA	Double	12p.m. - 7p.m.
3.	Setup	4p.m. - 9p.m.
4.	Setup	4p.m. - 9p.m.
5.	Close	6p.m. - 11p.m.
6.	Close	6p.m. - 11p.m.
On Call		
1.		
2.		

Figure 16-3:
Wait staff schedule worksheet (Saturday).

Setting Up Policies to Live (or Die) By

The best way to establish your policies is to write them down and then consistently implement them. Be as specific as possible and try to anticipate most potential problems. When appropriate, make sure to include the consequence for infractions, up to and including termination. Put all your policies together in one easy-to-use reference called your *employee manual.* (Check out Chapter 12 for details on creating and maintaining your employee manual and getting it to your employees.)

We firmly believe that your personnel policy is one area where leading by example is essential. For example, if you must take a day off because you're sick, hung over, or need a mental day off, do not broadcast it. Doing so gives your staff license to do the same. Our advice: Suck it up and show up for work!

Scheduling and attendance

If you write a schedule and no one shows up for work, you have a problem. Setting an effective attendance policy goes a long way toward minimizing employee problems. Figure 16-4 shows an example of an effective, comprehensive attendance policy.

Attendance Policy

Being on time and ready for work is part of good attendance. If you are late or plan on being absent, you place an extra burden on fellow employees. If unusual circumstances cause you to be late or absent, you must call your supervisor at least two hours in advance so that someone can be located to cover your shift until you arrive. If your supervisor isn't available, you should leave the following information with another manager:

- Name
- Reason for absence or lateness
- When you expect to be in
- Phone number where you can be reached

Leaving a message does not relieve you of the responsibility of speaking with your supervisor personally. You must continue to call until you make contact with your supervisor. Do not rely on friends, relatives, or fellow employees to report your absence or lateness.

Absences of more than one day must be reported daily, and a doctor's certificate of illness may be requested for any absence due to illness. Consecutive absences will require a doctor's note. Absences of more than four days due to illness or disability will require an approved medical leave of absence.

Failure to follow the proper call-in procedure may result in disciplinary action.

Figure 16-4:
Sample employee attendance policy.

Develop a policy for handling schedule changes. Generally speaking, employees are responsible for finding replacements to cover their shifts, but managers should approve replacements. Managers can refuse replacements for a variety of reasons, including performance difference between the two employees (if the replacement is a brand-new server, he probably can't handle the same workload as the ten-year veteran) or the fact that extra hours worked by the replacement will cause her to get overtime pay.

Post schedules at a consistent time each week. You set the standard for punctuality and respect by keeping this commitment to your employees.

Smoking

"Smoke 'em if you got 'em" is a common refrain among restaurant employees. But you need to create some boundaries for the sake of your business. Decide how you want to handle smoking by employees on company time and on company grounds to maintain your image. You need to tailor your policies to match your business philosophies and to your specific location, but here are some examples that we've seen:

- ✔ Don't allow any smoking at any time anywhere on your premises.

- ✔ Establish a nonsmoking restaurant, but allow employees to take smoke breaks outside your restaurant between shifts. Specify a smoking area away from the customers' entrance and require smokers to clean up the area on a regular basis.

- ✔ Provide a break room where smoking is permitted. Many old-school hotels use this model. But if you've ever smelled an employee break room where smoking is permitted, you realize what an eyesore (and nose sore) these rooms can be, especially to your nonsmoking employees.

No matter what your smoking policy, insist that employees don't smell like smoke when they return. Period.

Drinking or using illegal drugs

You should have a strong, clear, enforceable drug and alcohol policy that's in line with local laws. Figure 16-5 shows a good example of such a policy.

Figure 16-5: Sample drug and alcohol policy.

Drug and Alcohol Policy

The illegal use, consumption, possession, distribution, or dispensation of drugs or drug paraphernalia and the unauthorized use, possession, or being under the influence of alcohol, controlled substances, or inhalants on company premises, in company vehicles, or during work hours is prohibited.

Uniforms and grooming standards

A uniform of some kind is mandatory for most restaurants. Many places don't allow you to work in the clothes you came in, even if it is your uniform. You must change on site, leave your uniform for the company laundry, and pick up a clean, sanitary uniform at your next scheduled shift. This system works best for BOH employees who wear chef whites that are maintained by a laundry service. It can also work in large hotels, or very fine dining restaurants, with a large laundry budget. If you're not providing uniforms and their cleaning for your staff, managing this system is tough. You're probably better off requiring that they wear the accepted uniform during their shift and not worry about when they change.

Here are a few ideas to keep in mind as you choose uniforms for your employees:

✔ Uniforms for the wait staff, bussers, and bartenders should complement, enhance, and reinforce your concept. Hip, trendy restaurants demand hip, trendy servers with hip and trendy clothes. Other places can get by with more casual uniforms.

✔ Uniforms must be functional. Employees must be able to move freely and carry plates, trays, and the like. Don't attire your wait staff in high heels, particularly the men. Sure, stilettos look good, but they're tough to find in the largest sizes. Back-of-the-house (BOH) employees may have steel-toed nonslip shoes, but it may be appropriate for a host to wear strappy sandals.

✔ In most cases, the restaurant issues and maintains uniforms for dishwashers, cooks, and chefs. You should include a policy for handling the uniform that notes penalties for misuse or abuse.

Your concept and geographic location have lots to do with your grooming standards. You can limit jewelry to no rings except wedding or commitment rings. Decide on your policy for visible tattoos. Make some boundaries for facial hair. Many operations don't allow earrings for men and limit the number for women. Here are a few grooming standards that are nonnegotiable:

- ✔ Employees must restrain hair extending beyond the shoulders.
- ✔ Nails should be clean.
- ✔ Employees must not have noticeable body odor.
- ✔ Employees must not smell of smoke.
- ✔ Employees must not wear an excessive amount of cologne.

Customers see BOH employees from time to time, so hold BOH employees to the same grooming standards as the front-of-the-house (FOH) employees.

Social media policies

Social media is entrenched in every age group and socioeconomic set in the United States on some level. Your employees, customers, and vendors are paying attention to websites like LinkedIn, Twitter, Facebook, YouTube, Tumblr and whatever new services have popped up since we wrote this book. More and more businesses, universities, and government agencies are developing policies to help guide their employees and students in making decisions on what and how to share their opinions and experiences online. You should, too.

A social media policy should clearly establish guidelines for your employees to use when talking about your restaurant, your brand, your management team, and other employees online, in print, or in any other medium.

Start here when drafting your own social media policy:

- ✔ Identify who may speak to the media on behalf of the company. Typically, this is a very short list of people, likely the owner or the manager.
- ✔ Decide whether employees should identify themselves as part of your company. The concept of transparency is a hotly debated topic in the social media scene at the moment. Some companies absolutely require employees to identify their affiliation with the company so that all the facts are on the table, so to speak. Others don't allow people to identify themselves for fear their comments will be taken as the official company position. Make your position on the issue clear.

✔ Maintain that employees should not post anything that is false, obscene, defamatory, profane, harassing, abusive, hateful, or embarrassing to any other staff member, manager, or customer or even to a competitor. Insist that employees don't badmouth customers.

✔ Develop guidelines for how employees should respond if they see a negative post about the company.

✔ Insist that employees not share nonpublic, confidential company information.

✔ Recommend that if employees think posting something could get them into trouble, don't post it.

✔ Remind employees that even if their social media activities take place completely outside of work, if the posts are related to your business, they're covered by your policy.

✔ Acknowledge that the policy is a work in progress and will change as required to meet new situations as they arise.

✔ Clearly state the consequences for violating the policy.

Make sure to include personal blogs and websites in your policy. Giving employees clear guidelines can help them exercise good judgment when communicating about your business to the world.

Know that you can't, as an employer, control every online conversation related to your restaurant. Legally speaking, social media policies are still finding their footing. Courts seem to be taking the position that certain topics, like wages and working conditions, are protected speech, and employees must legally be allowed to discuss them without fear of losing their jobs. However, simply having a policy can discourage some employees from venting at will. Without a policy in place, it may not even occur to employees to keep some sorts of opinions to themselves.

Disciplinary measures

In some cases, despite your best attempts, rules do get broken. Here's the standard sequence of corrective action:

1. Verbal warning

2. Written warning

3. Suspension

4. Termination of employment

The window of time for a progressive discipline system should be very short. Move through the steps of your process if an employee doesn't respond to your progressive discipline system.

Place all written documentation regarding discipline measures in the employee's file. Documentation helps you establish patterns of behavior over an employee's tenure with your company. The more documentation you have to back you up in the case of a terminated employee who brings a suit against you or your company, the better.

Some offenses are cause for immediate termination and don't require progressive discipline. Poor service, violence, coming to work impaired by drugs or alcohol, or theft may demand immediate termination.

If you've built your organization right, no one is indispensable. And to an extent, your employees should know it. They should know that every single day, each person should do his or her job to the set standard or risk losing it. You've established goals, standards, policies, and so on. You've done the research and developed your concept, which you want your staff to help maintain. If you run into resistance to your standards and policies, eliminate the obstacles, even if that means firing an employee. Don't be afraid to fire employees who don't meet your standards.

If you terminate an employee, follow your written disciplinary policy to the letter. Your policy should include language stating that the employee must turn in all company property on his last day. Make sure that terminated employees know that if company property isn't returned in good condition, you may deduct the cost of it from their last paycheck.

Offering Benefits

Decide which benefits you can realistically afford to give to your staff. Each job benefit has options. Health insurance plans are available at a wide range of costs, with an equally wide range of coverage. Retirement plans and pension programs vary less, but they still have some flexibility. Consult your insurance agent to determine which benefits you can actually afford. We discuss health insurance and other benefits in the following sections.

Looking at health insurance

The right to affordable health insurance is a hotly debated political topic. Who's going to pay? How much will individuals pay? The list goes on. Keep your ears tuned to how the inevitable changes will affect your business.

At the moment, the government is looking to provide some tax rebates to help small businesses pay for insurance. If you have fewer than 25 full-time employees (or fewer than 50 part-time employees) and provide health insurance, you may qualify for a small-business tax credit of up to 35 percent to offset the cost of your insurance. This tax credit was set to increase to 50 percent on January 1, 2011. But this policy can change at any time, so keep the HealthCare.gov website (`www.healthcare.gov`) bookmarked so you can stay current with the requirements for your business.

From an employee's standpoint, your taking away or reducing benefits is never a good thing. Make sure you can afford what you're offering over an extended period of time, at least a year. When your premiums go up the following year (notice that we said *when,* not *if*), decide whether you'll pay the difference or pass along some of the cost to your employees. Breaking the news to employees that they'll have to contribute more out-of-pocket money is always tough, but with the rising costs of healthcare, it's the reality of every industry.

Considering other benefits

If you're a new or small business, you may not be able to afford health insurance or a pension plan. Don't forget the intangible benefits you can give your employees, such as preferred parking spots, preferred scheduling, birthdays off, long-term career planning, on-the-job training, and so on. They may not cost you much, but they matter to your employees. Even the prestige of working in a certain restaurant can be a benefit.

Free or reduced-cost shift meals are a fairly standard restaurant employee perk. Your meal program may be fairly complicated. Maybe employees get free meals when they're working but only a 50 percent discount when they're not. Often, the free shift meal is served at a specific time and is available to all employees. In other places, employees order off the menu at a discount before or after their shifts.

Here are a few other easy-to-implement perks:

- ✔ **Referral fees for bringing in quality new hires:** If you offer your employees $50 for a successful reference, you could pay them $25 when their referred employee is hired and the remaining $25 after the new hire celebrates 6 months of employment with you.

- ✔ **Attendance bonuses:** Offer employees an extra paid day off for perfect attendance and punctuality. You could set a policy that an employee can get half a day off with pay for every 3 months of perfect attendance, payable at the end of the year.

- ✔ **Paid bonus for successful completion of classes or training relevant to your business:** You can offer incentives for English classes, food safety training, or hospitality classes.

Chapter 17

Running a Safe and Clean Restaurant

Safety first! You hear that from the time you can walk (or run with scissors). The rule about safety is no different in the restaurant business. You just have to consider safety on a broader scale. As a restaurant owner or manager, you're responsible for the safety of everyone on your premises, including your diners, employees, and vendors. No small task! You can implement countless safety measures, but this chapter focuses on a few biggies: cleanliness, food safety, hand washing, and general safety precautions.

Making Sure Your Food Is Safe

Food safety is one of the most important aspects of running a restaurant. Constant attention to keeping your restaurant clean and organized is the best way to keep food safe. Cleanliness prevents other problems from developing (like vermin or bug infestations), and organization ensures that food is properly stored and your customers are gastronomically safe.

Some people approach food safety by trying to do the minimum and get away with what they can to avoid the hassle. But our view is simple: Always follow safety guidelines, exceeding them when possible, because it's the right thing to do — for you, your reputation, and your guests' health. If you have a passion for the business, you want only the best for your customers. Your reputation is reflected in how you treat your food and equipment and in the steps you take to maintain them. Plus, some health departments do use fines for violations as a big source of revenues. Follow their rules and don't give them a reason to fine you.

Although your local municipality *is* collecting money for fines, your real cost is the unrealized revenue from potential (or lost) customers who stay away because they find out about your infractions. Some health departments post their findings, and as unbelievable as it sounds, some (like New York City) don't remove their findings from their websites even if you're found "not guilty" of the charges! Rolling the dice isn't worth it.

Each state, county, and municipality has its own specific rules related to the type of establishment you run. Laws and ordinances may be different if you're running a free-standing restaurant, a café in a bookstore, or a taco truck in a parking lot. Contact your local health department for laws that apply to you. Check out the government section of your phone book and look for headings like "health department," "department of health," and "food safety." Or take a look online at www.cdc.gov/mmwr/international/relres.html to find your state health department.

Blaming bacteria and viruses

Bacteria and viruses are the main causes of foodborne illness. Two of the most common bacteria that cause foodborne illness are *Salmonella* and *Campylobacter.* Their symptoms include fever, abdominal cramping, and intestinal distress. If an individual already has a compromised immune system, is elderly, or is very young, the bacteria can cause a life-threatening infection. Both pathogens are almost always present in raw poultry, but you can easily kill them by

- ✔ Cooking poultry completely
- ✔ Avoiding *cross-contamination,* or spreading bacteria from one type of food to another through improper handling and storage (see the section "Preventing cross-contamination" later in this chapter)

Another common bacteria is *E. coli,* which lives in the intestines of cattle and makes its way to meat through improper handling. Symptoms (which can be life-threatening if the person isn't treated properly and promptly) usually don't include fever, but *E. coli* can cause vomiting, diarrhea, and possibly kidney failure, especially in children. *E. coli* infections are often traced back to beef products, most commonly ground beef. But remember that the bacteria can transfer to anything the raw meat comes into contact with, including foods that will never be cooked, such as lettuce.

Health departments are pushing to require restaurants to cook ground beef to well done. If *E. coli* is present on the surface of the steak, cooking the steak to medium or so is usually safe. But if you cook a burger to medium-rare, much of the burger is raw. The center of the burger may have been the surface of the meat at one point, but the grinding process has now made it the raw center.

Norovirus is the last major culprit in foodborne illness outbreaks. It's typically spread from human to food to human due to poor sanitation practices. This virus alone sickens more than 5 million people annually; symptoms include vomiting, diarrhea, fever, muscle aches, and headaches. Proper hand washing is the number-one defense against this nasty bug.

These are by no means the only pathogens you should be on the lookout for. Botulism can be present in canned goods. *Vibrio* is sometimes present in shellfish. And *Staphylococcus,* commonly called *Staph,* can contaminate prepared food in your coolers. Some bacteria, such as *Staph* and *Vibrio,* can't be killed in the cooking process. Check with your local health department for a complete list of organisms you should be aware of and how to avoid them.

Battling illness: Time and temperature

Your two biggest opponents in the war on foodborne illness are time and temperature. Watch out for the danger zone (the ideal temperature zone for bacterial growth): between 40 and 140 degrees Fahrenheit. Rapidly cool or heat foods so you can avoid this zone for prolonged periods — don't let foods stay in this zone for more than two to four hours. Hold your food at a temperature above or below this zone at all other times.

Some foods, such as raw chicken, arrive at your door contaminated. Count on it. How you handle the food after it enters your restaurant makes the biggest difference. A chicken breast mildly contaminated by *Salmonella* and left out at room temperature for 12 hours becomes highly contaminated and can cause illness. But even when contaminated food makes it into your restaurant, you can implement procedures to ensure that the illness doesn't make it to your customers. Here's a quick list of tips to keep your food safe:

- ✓ **Check food temperatures at every point in the production process.** Check temperatures using calibrated, sanitized thermometers.

- ✓ **Always store perishable foods at the proper temperature.** Store perishables below 40 degrees or above 140 degrees Fahrenheit, depending on the food.

- ✓ **Label and date all containers of perishable food and beverages.** Purchase labels specifically made for labeling food in restaurants (or print your own). They come in a pack, with a different-colored label for each day of the week. Make sure employees actually write the date the product was prepared on the label — doing so is more time-consuming, but it's the most effective system.

✔ **Practice FIFO (first in, first out).** Set up a rotation system so that you use the oldest products in your inventory first. This process cuts down on waste by reducing spoilage and ensures that you and your staff are in the know about what's on your shelf, how long it's been there, and what condition it's in.

✔ **Never leave food out at room temperature to thaw.** Always thaw food in a cooler or with a rapid-thaw process (such as under running water in a designated sink, if your local health department allows this method).

✔ **Always cook foods to the proper temperature (see your local health department's requirements for details) before holding.** *Holding* is keeping food at the proper temperature — above 140 degrees Fahrenheit or below 40 degrees — until service.

✔ **Cool cooked foods that won't be served immediately as quickly as possible.** In most areas, current laws require you to cool most foods to 70 degrees Fahrenheit within two hours and to 40 degrees within four hours (slightly lower temperatures usually apply to seafood).

Pay particular attention when cooling large quantities of food. Use ice wands and ice baths, and separate large quantities into smaller containers to cool foods quickly.

✔ **Reheat foods only once.** Toss the remainder. Some bacteria are *heat stable* (meaning heating doesn't kill them), so the more often you reheat foods, the more likely they are to be contaminated. If you're tossing a lot of food, heat smaller portions until you establish your *par levels,* or the amount of a supply (in this case, prepared food) you should have on hand for a given period of time (in this case, between prep periods). See Chapter 14 for details on establishing your pars.

You can also make sure that your staff isn't spreading diseases. Institute mandatory, consistent, and enforced hand-washing policies. See the later section "Implementing proper hand-washing procedures" for specifics. Have the kitchen staff use latex gloves whenever working with food. This step protects the food from the people (and their germs) and provides a first line of defense from burns, cuts, and similar boo-boos. Require your staff to change into work clothes at work to avoid bringing in contaminants from the outside.

Preventing cross-contamination

Contamination is the unintended presence of a harmful substance or organism in food. So cross-contamination occurs when bacteria (or another substance or organism) that's present in one food accidentally spreads to another food, usually through improper handling and storage. You're likely on the lookout for the usual suspects, such as ground beef and raw chicken. But cross-contamination is probably the single largest food safety problem because the contamination happens accidentally, so you may not even be aware of it.

Your best line of defense against cross-contamination is a good offense. Implement proper handling and storage practices, and you're on the road to a restaurant free of foodborne illness. Here are a few tips to get you started:

- Provide plenty of work space for staff working on a variety of foods at the same time.

- Clean and sanitize knives, utensils, and equipment before and after use.

- Provide sanitizer buckets with properly concentrated sanitizer solutions and clean towels. Check with your cleaning-product supplier for the details on how to use your particular products.

- Use hard plastic or rubber, nonabsorbing, food-grade cutting boards rather than ones made of wood. Clean and sanitize cutting boards after each and every use.

- Use separate cutting boards for raw foods, cooked foods, and foods you serve raw, such as fruits. Color-code the boards to keep them straight.

- Train all employees how to sneeze and cough properly. Specifically, they should sneeze and cough into the inside of their elbows rather than into their hands or worse, on food or prep surfaces. Make sure employees wash their hands immediately afterward.

Monitoring food safety outside the kitchen

Food safety isn't a concern that stops at the kitchen door. The way you and your front-of-the-house staff handle dishes after you leave the kitchen affects the safety of your food and your diners. In the front of the house, avoid these potential food safety hazards:

- **Waiters touching food or beverages with hands:** Waiters should touch only the plate or glassware, not the contents.

- **Waiters or bussers with dirty hands:** Some workers may clear dirty dishes and then not wash their hands before returning to the dining room. Effective hand-washing is a must for everyone in your organization.

- **Possible cross-contamination situations:** If a food server is slicing lemons, make sure he's not using a slicer that just sliced deli meats and wasn't cleaned and sanitized afterward.

- **Expired perishables in the wait station reach-in:** On a shift-to-shift basis, waiters should check milk, cream, and butter to confirm that the items have current use-by dates and don't smell bad. You especially need to do this check during slow business periods or when you've ignored the rotation schedule.

✔ **Dropped tongs or utensils on buffets:** Watch out for these germ carriers and replace them immediately with clean ones.

✔ **Improper stacking of food:** The bottoms of plates and containers may be contaminated. Create a barrier (a tray, plastic wrap, or the like) to keep bacteria from the bottom of one container from contaminating the top of another.

✔ **Dirty utensils at the dessert station:** Change the ice cream scoop, pie servers, and the like at the servers' dessert station once an hour, unless you keep the utensils inside the cooler.

Monitoring food safety outside the restaurant

Despite the efforts of the Food and Drug Administration (FDA) to ensure that the food coming in your doors with the FDA stamp on it is a safe, quality food product, problems can still occur between the time the food leaves the processing plant or farm and the time it gets to your cooler. Inspect your orders when they arrive to ensure proper product quality (greens and produce are fresh and free from rot and pests, for example). Demand the proper handling by your suppliers. Ensuring proper storage before the food gets to you is just as important as storing it properly in your possession.

Some shellfish, such as oysters, can contain illness-causing pathogens, such as *Vibrio,* that can make you sick if you eat them raw. If you're purchasing shellfish to serve in your restaurant, you must buy from a registered, authorized dealer and save all documentation related to the purchase, including invoices and tags from the individual shellfish bags. This information is critical in protecting you and your customers if someone traces an illness to your restaurant.

Critical control points: Following HACCP guidelines

Hazard Analysis Critical Control Points (HACCP) is a system of procedures, processes, and principles designed to help restaurants develop documented, effective food safety programs. The HACCP program focuses on the flow of food through your restaurant — from receiving to serving and beyond — identifying, monitoring, and removing potential hazards along the way.

In a nutshell, here's how you create your own plan:

1. **Track the flow of food products from delivery to diner.**

2. **Analyze that flow to identify food safety hazards associated with each food item and *critical control points,* or CCPs (points in the process where food safety hazards can be controlled, such as cooking and cooling times and holding temperatures).**

3. **Create and monitor protocols to make sure each CCP is addressed.**

4. **Document the process.**

Develop and document an effective HAACP plan for each potentially hazardous food product, beverage product, food-handling procedure, and storage protocol within your operation. It sounds time-consuming, and it is, but the development and proper implementation of HAACP within your operation will go a long way toward safeguarding your patrons and staff from foodborne illness and you, as an operator, from potentially devastating negative publicity and legal actions stemming from a foodborne illness outbreak.

Staff education: Picking up food safety tools

Your local health department can become your best partner in implementing food safety programs. Ask your inspector about programs that your staff can attend at the department's facility, such as SafeServe classes, or consider having a guest speaker at your next staff meeting. Health department staff can educate your staff on proper hand-washing practices by using cool visual tools like Glo Germ and UV lighting to spot — and stop — sloppy technique. Don't be afraid to ask the health department about its training services and facilities.

Implementing proper hand-washing procedures

From *Staph* infections to hepatitis A to the common cold, employees bring a variety of viruses, bacteria, and other potential pathogens to work with them every day. To reduce the risk of transferring any of these pesky organisms to your guests, facilities, and products, employees must wash their hands with hot water and soap before and after their shifts at designated hand sinks. Employees must also wash their hands at designated hand sinks during their shifts after doing any of the following:

- Using the restroom
- Touching the hair, mouth, nose, or other body parts
- Sneezing or coughing (even into their inner elbows)
- Tending to a wound
- Coming into contact with body fluids
- Eating, drinking, smoking, or using tobacco
- Handling raw food, dirty dishes, or trash
- Handling animals
- Cleaning restrooms
- Becoming contaminated in any way

Keeping the Restaurant Clean

Keeping your restaurant clean is the first step in maintaining food safety; it significantly decreases the threat of pests and vermin. Organizing your coolers helps keep foods from spilling, dripping, or falling into other foods. Regularly moving items to clean behind and under them helps keep your products rotated so that none expire and then get used in your menu items. And using fresh containers and pans ensures that you always know when the food was made and that it's safe to serve to your guests. Ultimately, you likely eat in your restaurant almost every day. Don't you want it to be clean?

Cleaning is only as good as your managers. They're ultimately responsible for the cleanliness, health inspection scores, and the processes that make it all work. Hold them to the highest possible standards.

Getting cleaning supplies

Get the right tools for the job. Buy cleaning products designed for cleaning commercial kitchens. These specialized products cut the kind of grease load a restaurant kitchen puts out, polish stainless steel as only a professional can, and truly sanitize the kind of bacteria and toxins that you find in a kitchen. The typical restaurant kitchen needs these cleaning supplies on hand:

- Soap for the hand sinks
- Hand sanitizer for the hand sinks
- Floor cleaner

- All-purpose cleaner
- Degreaser
- Glass cleaner
- Pot and pan soak

- ✔ Dish machine detergent

- ✔ Dish machine rinsing aid

- ✔ General sanitizer

- ✔ Silver, copper, or stainless steel polisher

- ✔ Oven cleaner

- ✔ Coffee pot and coffee machine cleaner

Cleaning chemicals can be very dangerous! Keep the following safety tips in mind as you educate your staff about cleaning supplies:

- ✔ **Keep the Material Safety Data Sheet (MSDS) paperwork for all these chemicals on file at all times.** That paperwork contains detailed information on safe handling procedures and instructions for dealing with accidental ingestion, exposure, and contact.

- ✔ **Never store chemicals near food, including the food in dry storage.** The fumes can permeate foods such as lettuce. And you run a tremendous contamination risk if something spills, sloshes, or sprays on any food products.

- ✔ **Observe your employees closely until you're comfortable with their use of chemicals.** You must use these chemicals in their proper ratios to maintain the safety of your staff and patrons (not to mention your wallet).

In addition to cleaners, you need the tools to use those cleaning products, including mops and mop buckets, a fresh supply of towels, small buckets for sanitizer solution, brooms, squeegees, scrubbing pads, and cleaning brushes.

And just to make sure that we cover everything, here are a few more tips:

- ✔ **Consider locking cleaning supplies.** Set up a requisition system, which can benefit you in a few ways:

  - • You can control the amount of chemicals in use at a given time.

  - • You create accountability for proper procedures. If someone has to ask a supervisor for the degreaser, you know who's accountable, and you can be reasonably sure they're using it (or not).

  - • You limit the opportunity for employees to supplement their home cleaning supplies by borrowing them from your restaurant.

- ✔ **Assign different towels different jobs.** You can use one stripe color for cleaning and dealing with any chemicals, another color for general kitchen use (such as wiping down surfaces), and a third type of towel — of the lint-free variety — solely for wiping down plates and stemware.

- ✔ **Never use steel wool or stainless steel scrubbing pads.** As they disintegrate with use, they leave behind bits that get into food.

- ✔ **Schedule cleaning for times other than at closing time.** When people are trying to get out after work, they tend to overlook things.

Scheduling your cleaning

The longer you let your restaurant go, the harder it is to clean, and the more likely that lack of cleanliness can develop into a bigger problem. Grease erodes paint. Uncovered food invites pests. Old food contaminates new food. Set the standard with exhaustive daily and shift-to-shift cleaning schedules.

Go through your restaurant, note everything that you need to clean, and then assign each item a schedule. Don't forget that many items need the occasional heavy-duty cleanup in addition to daily cleaning. Divide the duties by the employee or job title in a given area to begin to map out your schedule. Base your cleaning schedule on your type of operation. For example, a restaurant featuring fried foods has different cleaning needs than a sushi bar.

Your master cleaning schedule should be part of your operational manual (see Chapter 12). The *master cleaning schedule* explicitly states what to clean, who should clean it, when to clean it, and how to clean it. Create an elaborate cleaning schedule that covers every piece of equipment, every fixture, and every surface in your restaurant.

After putting together your list of things that need to be cleaned, decide when to have someone clean them. In the following subsections, we've put together suggested timelines for some common kitchen tasks.

Use this section to create your own schedule, but check your equipment for the manufacturer's cleaning recommendations. Some equipment (such as combination ovens) has a self-cleaning cycle and recommended cleaning schedule. Always follow the manufacturer's directions.

Must-do's several times each shift

Here are some things that need to be done several times each shift, as needed:

- ✔ Change water in the dish machine.
- ✔ Brush the grill between cooking vegetables, fish, and steak.
- ✔ Sweep the line and prep areas.
- ✔ Switch cutting boards.
- ✔ Change the sanitizer water.
- ✔ Empty the trash.
- ✔ Break down boxes.
- ✔ Change out ice wells.

Cleaning, shift after shift

You can have workers do these tasks on a shift-by-shift basis:

- ✔ Sweep the walk-in and dish area.
- ✔ Mop the entire kitchen.
- ✔ Clean the fryer.
- ✔ Filter the fryer oil.
- ✔ Send range grates to the dish machine.
- ✔ Change sanitizer solution in sanitizing buckets.
- ✔ Clean and sanitize all surfaces (reach-ins, prep tables, and so on).
- ✔ Hose down mats.
- ✔ Wipe down walls, surfaces, and hood vents behind the hot line.
- ✔ Empty the steam table. Clean, sanitize, and refill with fresh water.
- ✔ Clean the employee bathroom and locker room.

A cleaning a day . . .

Assign tasks like these on a daily basis:

- ✔ Empty equipment and hood grease traps.
- ✔ Change the foil linings on catch pans of grills, ranges, and flattops.
- ✔ Clean the can opener.
- ✔ Clean the soft-serve ice cream machine.
- ✔ Remove all the hood filters and run them through the dish machine.

Another good idea is to put in a rotating daily deep-cleaning and maintenance schedule. For example:

Day	Task
Monday	Sharpen knives.
Tuesday	Oil the omelet pans and cast-iron cookware.
Wednesday	Fill flour, sugar, and other bins in dry storage.
Thursday	Apply commercial drain cleaner to floor drains.

Restrict deep cleaning tasks to Monday through Thursday (or Sunday through Wednesday, depending on your restaurant) because typically the remaining days of the week are too busy, and your staff won't have time for extra cleaning tasks. Just keep up with your daily and shift cleaning on busy days and leave the heavy-duty chores for slower days.

Finally, create a list of requests for your maintenance staff. Try to assign at least one of these tasks each day during your slower times.

Week in, week out

Make quick work of these more intense weekly jobs with preventive maintenance throughout the week. Figure out your *down days* — days when you have the least amount of inventory in the coolers — and detail the coolers inside and out. Sunday or Monday is usually a great day for this process, because your stock is down from the busy weekend.

- ✔ Empty reach-ins and thoroughly clean and sanitize them. Judge the contents and keep or toss. Reorganize and replace items as needed.

- ✔ Pull the hot line out, if possible, and clean the walls and floor behind and below the line. This task helps you maintain cleanliness, sanitation, and safety. Grease can build up here and catch on fire.

- ✔ Delime the sinks, drains, and faucet heads.

- ✔ Clean the coffee machine.

- ✔ Deep-clean the ovens. Always follow your manufacturer's instructions for cleaning your particular kind of oven. Appropriate cleaning regimens vary greatly, so make sure you know how to clean yours safely.

That fun monthly cleaning

Break these jobs up among employees and spread them out over the month, doing yourself a favor in the labor category and staving off a mutiny:

- ✔ Turn the cooler fans off. Remove the covers. Wipe the fans. Clean the covers.

- ✔ Deep-clean the freezers.

- ✔ Empty and sanitize the ice machine.

- ✔ Check all filters on the reverse osmosis machine, water softeners, and the like.

- ✔ Calibrate ovens. Place an oven-safe thermometer in your oven; set your oven to 350 degrees. After the oven indicates it's reached the appropriate temperature, wait a few minutes for the thermometer to register the actual oven temperature. Make sure that both the oven and thermometer register 350 degrees. If not, repeat the test with a different thermometer. If you get similar results, your oven may not be calibrated properly. Call a technician to test the oven and adjust the temperature if necessary.

✔ Calibrate thermometers. Place stick thermometers in a full glass of ice filled with water for one minute to register the correct temperature, which is 32 degrees Fahrenheit. If the thermometer doesn't register 32 degrees, adjust the small dial under the head of the thermometer until the thermometer reaches 32 degrees. Some stick thermometers can't be calibrated. If you find that your thermometer isn't registering the correct temperature and you can't adjust it, toss it in the trash. We recommend that you only buy stick thermometers that can be calibrated.

✔ Prepare for "bug night" in conjunction with your exterminator. Bug night is the night that the exterminator comes to spray for pests. Your exterminator can provide you exact requirements based on what he's treating and the process he uses to treat it. The process you follow is specific to the process he uses. Basically, you need to protect your work areas and surfaces from any chemicals he may use. Examine walls, ceilings, and windows for possible pest entry points.

✔ Sharpen the slicer. You may have to do this sharpening weekly, depending on the volume of slicing.

✔ Deep-clean walls and ceilings.

✔ Pull everything from dry storage and wipe down the shelves. This cleaning usually coincides with inventory count. See Chapter 13 for info on inventory management.

✔ Change out any pest traps.

✔ Restock your first aid kit.

✔ Deep-clean kitchen floors with a motorized floor scrubber.

✔ Update MSDS (Material Safety Data Sheet) info you're missing. (See the earlier section "Getting cleaning supplies.")

Yearly safety stuff

You get to take care of the administration of safety stuff once a year. In most cases, you need to hire a professional to come in and do these jobs for you:

✔ Check fire suppression systems.

✔ Check fire extinguishers. (*Note:* This requirement can vary depending on where you live. Some states or cities may require that this job be done twice a year.)

✔ Clean hoods twice a year or more if you're putting out a lot of grease.

✔ Clean the pilot lights on all your gas equipment, such as your ovens, grills, and ranges. Refer to the cleaning instructions for your particular equipment.

✔ Call for service and maintenance on all your equipment.

✔ Update permits and licenses, as necessary. These documents validate your safety compliance.

Opening and closing procedures

Opening and closing procedures are an important part of cleanliness for several reasons. During opening, you confirm that everything is in tiptop shape and that the restaurant is ready to safely prepare meals for the day to come. During closing, you preserve any products for the next shift, get rid of vermin-attracting material from the previous shift, and make sure that all surfaces are free from grease to avoid slips and spills for the next shift.

The opening kitchen manager or chef makes sure that everything was cleaned the night before. She's also responsible for ensuring that all the food has made it through the night. And she must make sure that the opening staff is on board and knows how to start the restaurant day right.

Opening procedures

Here's the short version of the way a manager may start her day:

✔ Check temperatures to confirm that coolers and freezers are working properly and have been working properly overnight.

✔ Ensure that clean rags and aprons are available for the staff.

✔ Read log entries from the previous shift to check that equipment is working properly.

✔ Verify that equipment is working properly.

✔ Conduct a sweep of all vermin traps.

✔ Do a sweep of all food storage areas to make sure that all food is wholesome and that no stinkers are hiding anywhere.

Use this list as a starting point for creating your opening crew's duty list. Add your own food production requirements to round it out:

✔ Pre-clean any surfaces before food prep begins. This step ensures the surface is clean in case it didn't get sanitized the night before.

✔ Put out clean sanitizers, buckets, and rags.

✔ Verify that you have sufficient dish chemicals to get through the shift.

✔ Confirm that all ice bins and water wells are clean. Fill ice bins with fresh ice.

✔ Make sure that all pans and holding containers are clean. Always use fresh pans, not the ones the food was stored in overnight. If you don't change the pans every day, they become carriers of bacteria over a period of days.

✔ Clean and stock the bathrooms.

✔ Line all trash cans.

Closing procedures

A closing manager has the benefit of the cleaning schedule to keep everyone on track. But he should look for shortcuts that past shifts may have taken. Is the slicer clean underneath the guard? Does the top of the mixer have a dough farm on it? Is the can opener growing fungus? He should note any equipment problems or deep-cleaning required in the log book. Before he leaves, he makes sure that

✔ Doors are closed and locked.

✔ Coolers are sealed.

✔ All food is labeled and contained properly.

✔ Things that should be covered are covered.

✔ Nothing is improperly stored or dripping cross-contamination.

✔ The dish machine is empty and cleaned.

✔ All trash is appropriately disposed of.

✔ No one leaves without checking out with the manager or chef on duty.

Taking Precautions to Protect Your Customers and Staff

The following sections provide tips on a few of the big safety issues in the restaurant world, including first aid and emergency procedures. Check out Chapter 11 for info on responsible alcohol service.

Consider creating a policy that requires employees leaving after closing to walk out with a buddy. Walking around with a pocket full of tips or a bank drop bag can be an enticing target for criminals.

Food allergies and other dietary concerns

More Americans are afflicted by food allergies and intolerances today than ever before. Thoroughly educate your staff on all the ingredients in every dish (and the components of every dish) and your preparation methods. Be ready to answer detailed, specific questions from increasingly savvy diners; even people without allergies may have strict eating requirements for health or philosophical reasons.

In particular, pay attention to this list of the most common food allergies and intolerances:

- ✔ **Eggs:** Think outside the breakfast sandwich and consider eggs in baked goods, sauces, desserts, and more.

- ✔ **Peanuts:** You may not have an Indonesian peanut satay on your menu, but like many restaurants, you may fry items in peanut oil.

- ✔ **Tree nuts:** People often tolerate peanuts but not tree nuts (such as pine nuts, almonds, Brazil nuts, hazelnuts, and walnuts), or vice versa.

- ✔ **Fish:** Some customers may be able to handle white fish, and others can have anything but. Educate your employees so that they can speak to guests' concerns.

- ✔ **Shellfish:** Make sure that your staff knows that all crustaceans (lobsters, shrimp, prawns, langoustines, and crabs) are shellfish. All mollusks (including oysters, clams, mussels, scallops, abalone, cockles, and even snails) are considered shellfish.

    Even though it seems counterintuitive, allergenically speaking, some shell-less sea creatures such as octopus, squid, and sea urchin are lumped in with the shellfish group. Give the customer the information and let her decide.

- ✔ **Soy:** Soy is hidden in all kinds of processed food, and it's pretty tough to avoid. So if you're still using margarine, you likely have some soybean oil making its way into your menu items. And if you're using commercially prepared salad dressings, you also likely have soy.

- ✔ **Wheat:** Many people a serious sensitivity to *gluten,* a particular protein found in wheat; others are allergic to wheat in general. Remember that wheat (or its gluten) may be lurking in unexpected places, including soy sauce and thickeners for soups and sauces. People with celiac disease can't tolerate any gluten, so watch out for cross-contamination.

- ✔ **Dairy:** Some people have a dairy allergy, and others have an intolerance for *lactose,* a sugar found in dairy products. Consider unobvious ways dairy may be on your menu, such as through Parmesan cheese in your marinara sauce or milk solids in your canned chicken broth.

If you serve organic or vegan dishes, confirm that your purveyors meet the standards that you've promised to your diners. If the producer is using pesticides, your clientele probably considers that use a food safety issue. Likewise, if you're buying vegetarian veggie soup that has cream solids listed as an ingredient, your vegan patrons may be pretty upset.

First aid

With the number of sharp implements (from knives to slicers to can openers) and heating elements (including deep fryers, tilt skillets, and even coffee pots) found in restaurants, accidents are bound to happen. Your restaurant needs a basic first-aid kit with the following supplies:

- Assortment of adhesive bandages
- Gauze
- Assortment of nonstick pads
- Waterproof first aid tape
- Antibiotic ointment
- Antiseptic wipes
- Eyewash
- Sterile eye patches
- Burn gel
- Finger cots (latex gloves for one finger)

Some restaurants also include some over-the-counter medications, such as pain relievers, cold medicine, antihistamines, and antacids, in their kits or cabinets. These meds are helpful. You must weigh the cost of these supplies against the benefits you receive from them and make your own decision.

Never give any medication out of the first-aid kit to a guest. Giving guests aspirin or an antacid may seem like good customer service, but if someone has an allergic reaction to the medication, you can get into serious legal trouble.

Consider training your staff in CPR (cardiopulmonary resuscitation) in case a guest has a heart attack or stops breathing. The Heimlich maneuver (designed to help choking victims) is a must-know for restaurant employees. You can find people to provide training for these processes at your facility, or you can encourage your employees to get training on their own. Give employees a complimentary meal if they get certified. Go to the National Safety Council (www.nsc.org) or Red Cross (www.redcross.org) website to find training in your area.

Exits: In the event of an emergency

Your local fire marshal decides how many emergency exits you must have and where you have to put them. Your local codes tell you specifically what kind of doors you have to have, what kind of hardware you should put on the doors, which way the doors have to swing, and on and on. Very important stuff, but it varies from county to county and state to state. Check with your local office for the specific ordinances you may be subject to. Here's a general list of good tips to keep in mind regarding emergency exits:

- ✔ They should always be unlocked from the inside.

- ✔ You must clearly mark them. Make sure that you have lighted emergency exit signs.

- ✔ They must be accessible at all times. Never block an emergency exit, even with a movable barrier such as a trash can.

- ✔ If you install *panic hardware* (hardware that sounds an alarm when tripped), make sure that it's properly marked. Nothing is more embarrassing for a diner than accidentally tripping an emergency siren.

Make sure that all employees know the escape routes. Instruct your staff to help diners exit your restaurant in the event of an emergency. Conduct periodic reminders in staff meetings to ensure that everyone understands the plan and has the information top of mind.

Providing a Pest-Free Place

Restaurant pests include common critters (such as fruit flies and common houseflies) found in many homes, as well as more-concerning animals (such as all manner of insects or rodents). Some say that where there's food, there are pests, but we believe you can and should have a restaurant without critters, both in the front and the back of the house.

Before you open your doors, contract with an exterminator to regularly treat your restaurant for insects, vermin, and any other pests common to your area. Your pest-free process is only as good as your consistency, so get the exterminator on the payroll regularly and often.

In the event of an infestation, the best offense is a great defense. Every day, you defend your restaurant from potential pest attacks by keeping it clean and storing food properly. But if pests manage to get into your restaurant and do gain some ground, solve the long-term problem first and then address the short-term problem.

Working with your exterminator, here's how to get rid of unwanted guests (and we mean bugs and critters, not unruly diners):

1. **Look for and seal possible points of entry.**

   Just as you wouldn't plaster and paint a leaking interior ceiling until you'd repaired the actual leak in the exterior roof, you must find the entry points for the pests and close them up (contact a contractor to help you if necessary). Possible candidates include holes in the wall, floor, or ceiling. Often, rodents work their way in around pipes or other conduits. A lot of motivation (meaning food that they can get to) inspires critters to try to expand even small spaces to fit through.

   Examine your walls, ceilings, and floors during regularly scheduled cleaning sessions to identify any gaps that may one day allow pests in. Some preventive patching can go a long way.

2. **Find out what's attracting pests.**

   Likely candidates are improperly stored food, unemptied trash, and poorly sealed bottles. Remove the attractant(s).

3. **Neutralize any already-present pests.**

   Here's where your exterminator earns his money. He should have the right weapons to get rid of your particular problem.

Handling the Health Inspection

Unannounced visits from health inspectors are a fact of life in the restaurant business. An inspector walks around the restaurant, watches your staff, makes notes, and peruses your prepared foods, among other things. The inspection process is enough to make even the most-seasoned restaurant manager sweat, but your inspection will likely go well because you have consistently good sanitation practices, right?

Many municipalities offer letter grades (similar to those you received in school) to indicate how well a restaurant has done on its health inspections. Most managers intend to do well on health inspections, but with so many easily missed details, infractions can add up. If you fail your health inspection, you'll be closed down. Take this process seriously.

When the inspector arrives

When your inspector arrives, treat her like a VIP. You give everyone who walks through your doors good service, but you give an extra push when VIPs are in the house. When your health inspector shows up, do the following:

- ✓ **Remain calm.** Don't start scurrying around cleaning things up, shuffling papers, and the like. Take a deep breath and get down to business. See the next section for details on interacting with the health inspector.

- ✓ **Don't be intimidated.** Dial down your nervousness and amp up your confidence. You know what you're doing, and you fully expect to pass this inspection. If you don't believe that, at least make sure the inspector does.

- ✓ **Maintain a professional demeanor.** Don't get overly emotional or chummy or become a comedian. Be open and friendly, but maintain a professional distance.

Don't attempt to bribe the health inspector. In virtually any municipality, this act won't help you. Ever. In fact, you'll likely end up with a major fine or worse. You shouldn't even offer her a beverage.

During the inspection

You're designing the health inspector's experience in your establishment. Just as you'd walk the customer through the menu, walk the health inspector through your operation:

1. **Sit the inspector down, make her comfortable, and give her information.**

   Give the health inspector the info she needs to make sure she's in the right restaurant and can confirm you have your permits filed properly.

   By lucky coincidence, your initial sit-down with the inspector gives your employees time to peruse their areas and themselves to make sure everything is ready for the big event. They can double-check details such as making sure aprons are clean, ice scoops are handy, and sanitizer buckets are present. Note, though, that this opportunity isn't an all-out scurry to clean the restaurant. It's a 10-minute (max) window to confirm the most superficial of details. If you aren't making a consistent (daily, hourly, and minute-to-minute), full-scale effort to run your restaurant properly, this window won't save you.

2. Give the inspector a guided tour of your facility.

Choose a knowledgeable, even-tempered, trusted staff member for the tour guide. You need someone who can leave ego out of the inspection and won't become emotional with the inspector. Steer the inspector toward the highlights of the facility, but remember that you can't make her stay on a specific path. You have to be prepared for anything.

Be truthful with the health inspector. Answer questions as directly as possible, but don't offer extra information. If you give good, reasonable answers, then even if you do have some areas of concern, most inspectors will be lenient in giving you time to correct small infractions (as long as the restaurant is in good shape otherwise).

Avoiding a bad inspection

Here's our number-one recommendation to avoid a bad inspection: Always do the right thing. Use this chapter to keep your restaurant clean and your food stored properly so you don't have a problem.

If you're opening a new restaurant, invite the health department in for an initial inspection before you open your doors. If the inspector finds violations before you open, the department won't fine you. This is almost like a practice run. If the inspector comes in and finds violations after you've already opened, the health department will be much tougher on you.

You can take the additional step of hiring a health department consultant. Typically, these consultants were health inspectors themselves and know what to look for. They can come in and train your managers. Then you and your managers are in a better position to train staff and ensure your sanitation objectives are met. The consultant can conduct mock inspections of your restaurant to help you get ready for the big day.

How do you know whether you're doing a good job? If the health inspector leaves your restaurant after her inspection and then comes back in to eat right away, that's a very good sign that you're doing the right things.

Don't settle for the results of a negative inspection if you truly feel like you've been wrongly cited. On your citation, you get a hearing date for disputing the results (just as with a traffic ticket). Go to the hearing, prepared to argue your case. Even if you don't prevail across the board, you may get some of the infractions removed from your record. You can improve your overall grade and reduce your fines.

Chapter 18

Building a Clientele

*A*dvertising draws guests to your door. (In Chapter 15, we help you design and implement public relations and advertising strategies to get the word out and bring the customers in.) But customers are free agents. Just because they give your establishment a shot doesn't mean they'll return. How you deliver on your implicit or explicit promises to the customers after they're in their seats makes the difference between one-time customers and a regular *clientele* — patrons you want to have in your restaurant and who put money in your pocket by returning again and again with their friends, family, and colleagues. The best ad campaign in the world doesn't help you for long if you don't build a strong base of loyal customers by meeting and exceeding expectations.

Establishing a clientele transcends being popular. It's about being permanent. Just like doctors, lawyers, mechanics, and beauticians, you develop a loyal clientele based on how you deliver on people's wants, needs, and expectations. You won't survive for long by serving one-time-only customers.

A lot of clientele-building is common sense. Most people know the right things to do to make people feel special, important, and valuable. But few people actually do those things. That's where we come in. In this chapter, we remind you of the importance of exemplary customer service and outline practical strategies that you can use every day to begin building or expanding on your loyal customer base. We shed light on an often-overlooked opportunity to gain a loyal customer: customer complaints. And we outline some long-term clientele-building techniques to keep customers coming back.

Any successful restaurant has to evolve and innovate to continually bring new people in the door. The trick is to expand your base business to new customers while keeping your regulars.

Understanding Who Your Customer Is

After you've researched your target audience (see Chapter 3) and designed the appropriate marketing strategies (see Chapter 15), you get to turn your attention to actual human beings. In the same way that you have a few dates before you decide to marry someone, you have to get to know your customers and court them before they become your clientele. Understanding your customer begins with listening to what your customer has to say. Talk and *listen* to your guests. Ask the right questions, and your guests will give you the keys to their repeat business.

You must get to know your customers in order to figure out what motivates them to pick your restaurant over another one and how to encourage them to come back again and again (with friends). Discover what they want (or think they want) by watching their behavior, asking questions, and listening to what they have to say.

Consider your customers' wants and desires and incorporate them into your concept to help build a loyal customer base. Table 18-1 gives you an idea of how this approach works.

Table 18-1	Responding to Customers' Preferences
If Your Customers . . .	*You Can . . .*
Buy mixed drinks.	Offer a specialty cocktail menu.
Like live entertainment.	Offer live music one night a week.
Order salads and lighter items.	Offer more choices in this category and call attention to their healthful freshness.
Come in after a softball game.	Give them a team discount.
Read the paper while drinking their morning coffee.	Have newspapers available.
Ask for a particular kind of wine.	Order their favorite wine if they come in often enough.
Frequently post pictures of meals on their social media pages.	Give them something post-worthy when they come to your place.
Often special-order their breakfast.	Add a build-it-yourself menu option or even add their favorite custom preparation to the menu for others to enjoy.

If Your Customers . . .	You Can . . .
Use smartphones, tablets, or laptops in the restaurant.	Offer free Wi-Fi when they're in the restaurant.
Don't eat seafood, ever.	Educate them about your offerings, or dump them (the seafood, not the customers).
Don't like the far walk to the parking lot.	Offer valet service.
Like to watch sports.	Buy extra TVs and offer drink promotions during sporting events.
Drink lots of draft beer.	Expand your draft beer selection.

If you want more of a certain kind of diner, figure out what these types of diners want and give it to them. But you can't please everyone, so make changes to your business and your concept only as a concerted effort to gain the increased patronage of a certain type of diner. If you don't want more kids in your restaurant, don't make it especially kid-friendly.

Meeting and Exceeding Expectations

People come to restaurants ready to spend money. They're not simply browsing or window shopping. They're coming to your restaurant with an expectation of good, wholesome food; efficient service; and courteous treatment. Fewer places deliver those things than you may expect. Because restaurants regularly fall short of customers' expectations, a pleasant dining experience is often heralded as revolutionary when it does occur.

Diners have expectations, whether you're running the hot dog wagon outside the plant or the nameplate restaurant of a famous visionary chef. Coauthor Andy recalls a conversation with a world-class chef whose commitment to superlative guest service is legendary. The chef understood that guests come to his restaurant already expecting and demanding the finest foods, wines, and service in the world. Just delivering on that isn't enough. You have to look at each individual guest and figure out how to exceed his or her expectations, no matter how lofty. And every employee in the restaurant must be committed to delivering this level of customer service, to every diner, every day. If your employees aren't, your goals are at risk, and you need to make a change in your staff.

The minute customers walk in your door, they should experience the best you have to offer. Your host staff is your first exposure to the guest. If you frustrate diners here, it's tough to turn them around. You have to quote the right wait times and work the reservation system with enough padding in case you have guests who are lingering over coffee. In fact, you never know what may happen in a restaurant, so give yourself a little extra time. If you quote customers 15 minutes and you seat them in 5 minutes, they love it. But don't exaggerate the wait time just to exceed their expectations. If you tell them the wait will be an hour and then seat them in 5 minutes, you don't impress anyone. But remember, there's no reason to tell customers that the wait will be shorter than it is.

Chicago chef and restaurateur Gabriel Viti is a master of building a clientele at his nameplate restaurant, Gabriel's, in Highwood, Illinois. Not a single night goes by that he's not the first person you see when you walk in the door and the last hand you shake on the way out. He greets you by name and welcomes you into his restaurant as if he were inviting you into his home. He conveys a level of comfort and assurance that everything will be magnificent because he knows you and is personally committed to your individual dining enjoyment. He never gives off the vibe that you're lucky to be in his restaurant. Rather, he appears to be overjoyed that you have joined him this evening, and he'll see to your needs.

Good customer service is *not* a revolutionary concept — that's the way it should be everywhere, all the time. Here are some ways to exceed your customers' expectations:

✔ **Do the extras for people in your restaurant.** Don't just tell them where the restroom is; escort them discreetly. Entertain their kids. Slip a couple two forks when only the husband orders dessert.

✔ **Give them a story to tell.** Give them something positive to talk about the next day at work or online through their social networks. Table visits are important to get to know your customers, but move beyond "How is everything?" Join them in tasting the new port you just brought in. Talk to them about an upcoming wine dinner they may be interested in. Let them know about a cool food festival that's coming to town and give them tickets.

✔ **Find things that matter to them and capitalize.** Don't just serve people dinner. Find out what they enjoy and leverage that to form a relationship outside the restaurant. If they like hockey and you have season tickets, consider giving them tickets to a game. If a regular diner is into wine and you're going to tour a local vineyard, invite him to come along.

Tip: Most social media sites give information about what you have in common with your friends. For example, after a customer "Likes" your restaurant's Facebook page, you have access to his profile. In the top right corner of the profile, you can see a list of friends you have in common and things you both like. So the next time he comes in, you have the perfect conversation starter: "I see we both like Justin Bieber — who knew?"

✔ **Send cards to your regular clients.** Send them real, handwritten holiday cards. Reference specific conversations that you've had with those customers. Then build on the relationship over the next year. In a world of e-mail, a handwritten note goes a long way.

✔ **Show your customers that they're important to your success.** Invite them to participate in focus groups, sit on the advisory board for your restaurant, or be part of a VIP club. Make them feel like they have an ownership stake in your restaurant, and they'll share the experience with others, which likely will translate into more business for you.

Turning Unsatisfied Guests into Repeat Customers

Successful restaurateurs attempt to exceed guest expectations 100 percent of the time. *Attempt* is the key word here because, as hard as you may try, you won't walk away at the end of the day with an unblemished track record.

Every customer service situation is an opportunity to make a customer for life. People remember the bad. If you do something right nine times but mess it up the tenth time, that's what they remember. You need to make the problem go away. You want customers to remember that the tenth time, you fixed it. And they usually do.

Of course, avoiding problems in the first place is the best scenario. With fickle customers, shrinking margins, and limitless dining choices, you need to make it a priority to avoid doing things that result in unsatisfied customers. Here are a few basic things you can do to help ensure happy diners:

✔ Make sure that the restaurant temperature is right — not too hot and not too cold.

✔ Don't *auction* food (restaurant lingo for approaching the table with plate in hand, asking, "Who had the prosciutto and fig flatbread?" for example). Know what each guest ordered and deliver it to her correctly, just as she ordered it.

✔ Seat guests in the best possible place.

✔ Place clean menus, silverware, glassware, and tableware at every table every time.

✔ Make sure the music volume (and any other controllable sound) is at a pleasant level. You may need to make adjustments during a shift as your business levels increase and decrease.

✔ Keep your restrooms in tiptop shape.

✔ Quote accurate wait times and even err on the side of caution. Customers don't get mad if you seat them early.

But despite your best efforts, problems will occur. So in this section, we provide tips for staying alert and recognizing problems and show you how to turn an unsatisfied guest into a repeat customer.

Some guests walk into your restaurant unhappy. Other guests like to show off — they're in the business and want everyone to know it. And some people always complain, like to complain, or just can't help themselves. Whether the gripe is legitimate or not, you have to filter through *all* the complaints, both online and face-to-face, to get the opportunity to correct a real problem. One of the worst situations is failing to recognize a genuine problem that a customer is having. You never have the opportunity to correct it. You don't get a second chance; the customer just doesn't come back. And worse, given the prevalence of online forums for reviewing your restaurant, that customer's complaints can reach many potential customers before you have a chance to respond. Check out Chapter 15 for specific information on handling complaints and negative reviews online.

Recognizing unsatisfied guests

If every guest who had a problem said, "Hey, manager, I have a problem," you'd have no problem recognizing that message. But in the real world, many guests don't let you know, so you need to perform some detective work to make sure that all's well that seems well. If you see any of the following clues from your guests or on tabletops, investigate the problem. Check in with their server to get the whole story before you visit the table.

✔ **Human periscopes:** Look for people looking up and around and then back down. Typically, these folks don't have something they need. It may be a missing menu page, a refill on a soft drink, or extra napkins for a spilled drink. You want to get guests what they need as soon as possible so they can go back to enjoying their time in your restaurant.

✔ **Half-eaten food or food left on a plate:** Maybe the customer plans to box it up to go home, but be sure to confirm it. You want empty plates going back to the dish area.

✔ **Empty glasses:** People like full glasses of their beverages, especially non-alcoholic drinks, so replenish the water, soda, and iced tea regularly.

When asking guests about a refill on customers' alcoholic beverages, make it easy for them to say yes. Ask, "Would you like another glass of wine to go with your entree?" instead of "Do you have enough wine?" You can even take the next step and recommend a wine for their next course.

- ✔ **Watch-gazing:** Customers who keep looking at their watches may not be wondering where their food is, but investigate the situation anyway.

- ✔ **Waving, snapping, and other hand motions:** If you see customers making these gestures, it's not good. Hopefully, you can get to them quickly and fix the problem before they leave. Even if you feel attacked by someone in this agitated state, do your best to maintain your composure and resolve the situation. Also remember that even if you can't win back this customer, other customers are watching to see how you handle the situation. Don't risk losing them as well.

- ✔ **Aloofness:** If you see people who are laid back in their chairs and not looking happy and engaged, this behavior isn't an automatic problem. Some couples go out and never say a word to each other. Just because they don't appear to be enjoying each other doesn't mean you can do anything about it. As you gain experience, you'll be better able to judge the nuances of a diner's body language, but until then, consider stopping by the table to check in with these types of diners.

- ✔ **"Safe" orders:** If customers order chicken in your seafood restaurant, they may be afraid of the menu and simply need some educating. Don't let them miss what you do best.

Making things right

As corny as it sounds, the customer is always right. Resist the urge to reverse the blame on the customers because they were grumpy or petty. Accept the responsibility for their complaint. And remember, do your best from the start not to give them a reason to complain. Here are some steps for addressing problems:

1. **Listen to the guest.**

   Let your customer tell you what's wrong and even how he thinks you should fix it. Sometimes, just having an outlet to vent for a moment can start the process of resolution and calming down.

2. **Apologize or thank the guest, depending on the situation.**

   A sincere apology can go a long way toward resolving your long-term relationship with an unsatisfied customer. Sometimes guests may just have a recommendation or an idea that can really improve your business, not an actual problem. Thank them for their interest in your business and their patronage.

3. **Fix the current situation.**

   Figure out how you can correct the current problem. If a customer is completely dissatisfied with her entree or it isn't up to the usual standards, consider removing the item from her check. But giving a free dinner or dessert isn't always the answer. Do what you can to serve customers a quality meal before they leave. If a guest's steak is overdone, get her one that's cooked the way she likes it. If her pasta is cold, get her a fresh portion. Or ask her whether you can bring her something else.

   Remember, providing a quality meal and quality service in the face of a problem gives you a huge opportunity: Some of your best, most loyal clients come from what started as a bad situation. The way you handle the situation is what can make the difference in where the relationship goes from here.

4. **Rectify the long-term situation.**

   Don't patronize or placate your customers. They want to know that someone has heard their problem, fixed it, and will take steps to make sure that it doesn't happen again. If theirs is the fourteenth overcooked steak on the same shift, you probably have a problem with the grill (either the person manning the station or the equipment itself). Take the steps necessary to investigate what the true problem is and fix it. Customers hate for someone to listen but at the same time seem to blow them off. Give them your name and your card. Tell them to see you the next time they come in. Your sincerity and follow-through are essential in ensuring that they come back again.

Giving special treatment to big spenders

The diamond-crusted, jet-setting, super high rollers of the Las Vegas casinos — moguls, tycoons, robber barons, sheiks, and stars — are lavished with attention at every turn. They have their own attendants, concierges, shoppers, and chefs. They get the best tables at the restaurants, the finest seats at the shows, and unlimited access to the high-stakes tables. Why? Because they wager (and generally lose) more cash in one weekend than many restaurants gross all year.

You may not have guests in your restaurant tipping $600 for an espresso or $100 for prompt and courteous cocktail service, but the message is clear: Take care of those who take care of you. You need to treat your key regular clients with kid gloves, or they'll pack up their large wallets and go find someone who will. Remember our golden rule: Never make it hard for someone to give you money.

Making Social Media Work for You

Social media was made for connecting directly with people online. It may have started as a way for people to meet other like-minded individuals, but it's become an incredibly robust business platform as well. Websites like Facebook, foursquare, and Twitter allow you to set up official pages for your restaurant and begin collecting fans and followers (Chapter 15 can show you how). But turning those fans into dollars is up to you.

People are likely to connect with a brand online for one of four reasons: to get promotions or discounts, to get exclusive content not available elsewhere, to find out about new products or services, or to express their opinions. Give them what they want.

Here are your best bets for taking your social media fame and turning it into financial fortune:

- ✔ **Post updates regularly.** We recommend posting once a day. First off, updates keep you top of mind with your fans. People will come to expect a daily update about your drink specials, soup of the day, or details on who the guest bartender is that weekend. Second, posting daily builds content on your site for new fans. If someone eats at your place and then comes to your Facebook page and sees no activity, that person probably isn't going to "Like" you.

- ✔ **Reward loyalty.** Some sites, foursquare in particular, are designed to track the number of times a patron visits your establishment. They use apps on smartphones along with GPS features to allow users to "Check In" at your establishment. You can let them unlock a 25-percent-off coupon on their tenth visit or give them a logoed t-shirt on their fifth trip to your place.

- ✔ **Offer specials.** You can include a special code in your status update, Tweet, or other communication that your fans can use to get discounts, a free appetizer, or other perk. Foursquare allows you to input actual register codes, making redemption easy for your customers and your employees. Foursquare also has many specials built into its free toolset, including a Swarm Special that customers can unlock only if a certain number of members are in the restaurant. You set the parameters, and the only limit is your imagination.

- ✔ **Blow your own horn.** Let your fans know you've been voted best pizza in your town (and link to the publication that bestowed the award). Highlight the fact that your local restaurant critic just awarded you four out of five stars.

✔ **Share photos and details of events and day-to-day activities.** People love to get a glimpse behind the scenes. Who knows? If they missed your Cinco de Mayo party this year, the pictures may guarantee that they show up next year.

✔ **Respond to their comments and criticisms.** The world is watching you, so think before you respond to what may feel like unfair or meritless comments. Reflect on comments before blowing off anything as unfounded. All feedback is a gift. For tips on handling comments, see Chapter 15.

✔ **Promote scheduled events online.** An active event calendar is a draw to customers who like to have something special to look forward to. Many social media services give diners the ability to RSVP online to help you manage your numbers.

✔ **Ask fans what they want.** Facebook has a built-in poll feature. You can get customers' immediate feedback on new menu ideas or uniform ideas or theme dinners. If your customers feel like stakeholders, they're more likely to invest emotionally in your restaurant.

Take a look at Chapter 15 for help on setting up social media profiles and a website for your restaurant and linking them all together.

Chapter 19

Maintaining What You've Created

. . . .

In This Chapter

▶ Understanding your restaurant's financial performance

▶ Looking at restaurant operations

▶ Paying attention to feedback

. . . .

*W*hether you're considering opening a restaurant or you're already up and running, you have to understand how to read the financial numbers to figure out how your restaurant's doing. If you watch only the money coming in, you may have a very misleading perspective on how successful you truly are (or aren't). Many restaurants bring in lots of money in sales, only to watch it disappear in the trash cans (waste) or out the back door (theft) before it turns into a profit; others don't realize sales they could've had by implementing suggestions from their customers and staff.

In this chapter, we help you look at your current numbers and figure out what they mean. We show you how to listen to suggestions and complaints from all the well-meaning employees, diners, and professionals in and around your restaurant. And we help you figure out how to respond to keep your restaurant running smoothly and profitably.

Evaluating your company's financial performance doesn't just mean reading the numbers and looking for changes. Take the next step and figure out why numbers are changing, why they match (or don't match) your predictions, and how to get them all going in the right direction.

Evaluating Financial Performance

Using the numbers to analyze your restaurant's performance is critical. We don't mean for you to throw your common sense out the window. You have to have controls in place, do regular reviews of your numbers, and rely on your brain (and experience, if you have some) to dig deeper when the numbers aren't right.

Keep up with your business on a monthly, weekly, daily, and even shift-by-shift basis. Don't let the details sneak up and surprise you after it's too late. Don't miss the opportunity to make the corrections. Use the sample worksheets and the figures in this section and throughout the book to keep up with your numbers and the costs they represent.

Daily business review

Your *daily business review* is a report that you create by recording your sales figures, labor costs, and customer counts (and any other pertinent financial info or business conditions) every day. By recording this info in one place and every day, you build a history of your business that allows you to compare figures across previous days, months, and years to establish patterns and determine whether you've gained or lost ground in individual categories. Graphing this data and cataloging it over time are essential. You can find a sample review in Figure 19-1, but develop your own review that tracks data in the categories important to your particular business.

Your POS (point of sale) system (see Chapter 14) may already have a version of this report built into it. Check your system or check with your salesperson to take advantage of features you may not be using.

Build a history of your business, and you'll benefit in big ways. Here are a few things a daily business review can do for you:

- ✔ **Evaluate how various factors affect your business:** You can determine whether a current promotional event, the weather, or a holiday is affecting your sales compared to last year.

- ✔ **Confirm whether your overall volume is increasing over time:** Remember, if you want to grow 10 percent per year, you have to grow 10 percent each day. (Not literally, of course, but you get the picture.)

- ✔ **Alert you to the beginning of a problem but not necessarily to what the problem is:** For example, you may see that your liquor sales are down compared to the previous week's, but the report may not tell you why. You almost always need further investigation to get to the heart of the problem. If you dig deeper into other places, such as your logbook, your reservation book, and other appropriate resources, you discover that you had a large rehearsal dinner the previous week that accounts for a jump in your sales that week, and now you're actually back to normal.

- ✔ **Establish patterns:** Over time, you should start to see trends and patterns emerge in your sales figures. For example:

- Maybe your beverage-to-food mix is dropping on certain nights. Match it up with the staff schedules to see who's working and figure out whether someone's not selling or, worse, is pilfering your inventory.

- If your labor costs climb because a highly paid sauté cook is picking up shifts as a prep cook, talk to the chef about what's up.

- If your *cover count* (number of guests in the restaurant for a particular shift) is constant but your *check average* (the average amount each guest spends) plummets, did your chef put a bologna sandwich for $2.99 as the special?

- If cover counts remain the same at the bar but your beverage average takes a dip, look for drink giveaways.

Daily Business Review Week of								
	Monday	Tuesday	Wednesday	Thursday	Friday	Saturday	Sunday	Totals
Sales								
Sales (Previous Period)								
Food Sales								
Food Sales (Previous Period)								
Beverage Sales								
Beverage Sales (Previous Period)								
Labor Cost								
Labor Cost (Previous Period)								
Labor %								
Labor % (Previous Period)								
Food Cost % (Est.)								
Food Cost % (Previous Period)								
Cover Count								
Cover Count (Previous Period)								
Check Average								
Check Average (Previous Period)								
Food Ck Avg								
Food Ck Avg (Previous Period)								
Bev Ck Avg								
Bev Ck Avg (Previous Period)								
Food/Bev Mix								
Food/Bev Mix (Previous Period)								

Figure 19-1: Sample daily business review.

Make sure you understand how long a memory your POS system has. Some systems lose or overwrite data after three to five years. Discuss your needs with your salesperson (and his team of programmers) *before* purchasing a system; making changes later is expensive. Check out Chapter 14 for info on determining your POS needs.

Income statement

The *income statement* can also be called a *profit and loss* (P & L) statement. It summarizes your expenses and sales and gives you your bottom-line profit for the month. This statement doesn't diagnose your problems, but it identifies symptoms that can help you discover what's ailing you.

Many restaurants run monthly, quarterly, and annual statements. Some places use abbreviated, concise documents, and others create detailed documents with page after page showing every budget line in a category. Check out the income-statement figure in Chapter 4 for a sample 6-month income statement. Use one column of this statement to get a feel for what your monthly income statement may look like.

Our favorite income statement format provides comparative data in addition to the month's actual data. This type of income statement has three columns: the actual numbers, the numbers you projected you'd do, and the historical numbers from the same period last year.

Cash flow analysis

Keep a constant eye on your *cash flow,* the flow of money coming into (sales) and money going out of (expenses) your business. Prepare a report like the one in Chapter 4. Use as many real figures as you can (such as the invoices you know you need to pay next week) and forecast the rest (such as what your sales will likely be next weekend) as accurately as possible. In order to stay ahead, a restaurateur must know not only how much money he has at any given time but also how much he owes (or will owe very soon).

Keeping control of your cash, receivables, and payables is important. Don't expect to get credit extended to you, especially if you're new to the business. Here are some tips:

✔ **Weigh the benefits of discounts from suppliers for quick payment versus other uses for the cash.** If you're looking for the money to go out more slowly than it's coming in, for whatever reason, you may not be able to take advantage of some savings offered by suppliers. Many times, suppliers give, say, a 5-percent discount if you pay within 10 days rather than the standard 30 days. But some months require you to hold onto the cash for those extra 20 days instead of taking the discount. Maybe you need to pay your equipment service guy for 25 extra hours of labor to fix the range. Or maybe you need to upgrade the bathroom fixtures.

✔ **If your cash flow numbers aren't where you want them to be, reducing your inventory is a great place to start.** If your money is tied up in extra inventory you don't need, it's not working for you. Keep enough inventory to run your business efficiently. Keep the cash flowing your way and pay out as slowly as you can without incurring penalties.

✔ **Collect some payments for large parties or banquets in advance.** If you have to make large, expensive purchases for a party (such as cases of champagne or expensive cuts of meat), get at least part of your money in advance. Doing so can be a boon for your cash flow situation. But be careful: If you take in, say, a $5,000 deposit and count it as a sale two months before the event, make sure you spend the money on things for the party.

✔ **Beware of house accounts.** A *house account* allows individuals or businesses to run a tab and pay it at regular intervals, such as monthly, instead of paying each time they dine with you. House accounts can go sour quickly, especially as the charges add up. In this day of easy plastic money, no one needs a house account. Why wait until the end of the month to get paid (if you get paid at all)?

In Figure 19-2, we graph how your cash flow may look on each day of the month. We use several assumptions (we had to start somewhere), including the following:

✔ Your sales are constant at $5,000 each day.

✔ Half your diners pay in cash, and the other half pay with credit cards.

✔ Your credit card company charges you 3 percent of the total transaction as a fee. Credit card funds (less the transaction fees) are deposited into your account with a three-day lag time.

✔ Your operating expenses (including food costs, labor, and so on) are 88 percent of sales.

✔ Your rent is $5,000 per month and is paid on the 15th of the month.

✔ You're working on a 30-day month.

✔ You pay half your bills weekly and the other half on the last day of the month.

Your cash flow may look very different depending on things such as your sales (which usually fluctuate depending on the day of the week) and your bill payment schedule. But this figure shows you how quickly the money goes, even in an efficiently run restaurant.

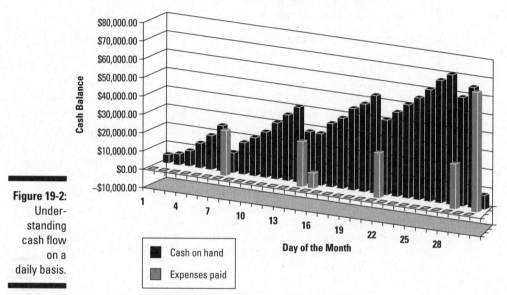

Understanding Cash Flow

Figure 19-2: Understanding cash flow on a daily basis.

Evaluating Operations

Operational reports show you factors that have an impact on your profitability. These reports aren't standard business reports, like the financial reports in the earlier section "Evaluating Financial Performance"; instead, they're specific to the restaurant business.

Menu mix analysis

A *menu mix analysis* (also known as *product mix analysis* in some systems) is a report used to evaluate the profitability of your menu on an item-by-item basis. It provides data on what's selling (and what's not) and, more importantly, how much money you're making off each item.

See the example menu mix analysis in Figure 19-3. The following are descriptions of the standard menu labels in the last column:

> ✔ **Star:** Profit is high and popularity is high
>
> ✔ **Workhorse:** Profit is low and popularity is high
>
> ✔ **Challenge:** Profit is high and popularity is low
>
> ✔ **Dog:** Profit is low and popularity is low

Typically, you decide what dollar amount determines high or low profit for your operation. In Figure 19-3, we use the average profit margin of our menu items, $15.02, as the cutoff, so anything above $15.02 is considered a high-profit item, and anything below that is a low-profit item. Ultimately, you need to set your own criteria for evaluating your menu mix.

You're looking for your menu to reflect a target overall food cost percentage. (You figure *food cost percentage* for individual dishes by taking the cost of all the ingredients used to make a dish and dividing it by the menu price.) To come up with the overall percentage, you have to take the overall cost of the food sold and divide it by the overall revenue you received from that food. (See Chapter 8 if you need more of an explanation on food cost and food cost percentage.)

Menu Item Name Dinner Items	Number Sold	Popularity %	Item Food Cost	Item Sell Price	Item Food Cost %	Item Profit Price-Cost	Total Cost Cost x # Sold	Total Revenue Price x # Sold	Total Profit Revenue -Cost	Profit Category	Popularity Category	Menu Label
Ribeye	47	15.1%	$4.82	$18.95	25.4%	$14.13	$226.54	$890.65	$664.11	Low	High	Workhorse
Pasta and Marinara	32	10.3%	$1.18	$9.95	11.9%	$8.77	$37.76	$318.40	$280.64	Low	High	Workhorse
Chicken Caesar Salad	14	4.5%	$2.13	$12.95	16.4%	$10.82	$29.82	$181.30	$151.48	Low	Low	Dog
Roasted Pork Loin	15	4.8%	$3.84	$18.95	20.3%	$15.11	$57.60	$284.25	$226.65	High	Low	Challenge
Cioppino	15	4.8%	$5.84	$24.95	23.4%	$19.11	$87.60	$374.25	$286.65	High	Low	Challenge
Mixed Grill	14	4.5%	$7.00	$29.95	23.4%	$22.95	$98.00	$419.30	$321.30	High	Low	Challenge
Grilled Salmon	23	7.4%	$3.25	$18.95	17.2%	$15.70	$74.75	$435.85	$361.10	High	High	Star
Shrimp Scampi	18	5.8%	$6.42	$24.95	25.7%	$18.53	$115.56	$449.10	$333.54	High	Low	Challenge
Filet Mignon	46	14.8%	$6.58	$21.95	30.0%	$15.37	$302.68	$1,009.70	$707.02	High	High	Star
Arrozo con Pollo	23	7.4%	$3.33	$17.95	18.6%	$14.62	$76.59	$412.85	$336.26	Low	High	Workhorse
Shrimp Diablo	26	8.4%	$6.42	$24.95	25.7%	$18.53	$166.92	$648.70	$481.78	High	High	Star
Sausage Pizza	38	12.2%	$2.32	$8.95	25.9%	$6.63	$88.16	$340.10	$251.94	Low	High	Workhorse
Total or Overall	311	100%					$1,361.98	$5,764.45	$4,402.47			
Average		8.3%	$4.43	$19.45	**20.0%**	$15.02						

Figure 19-3: Example of a menu mix analysis.

Use a computer to create your menu mix analysis. Many POS systems come with this functionality. If your system doesn't, create your own using a spreadsheet program. Automating this process saves you a ton of time in calculating the figures, leaving you more time to analyze them and make changes as appropriate. (Take a look at Chapter 21 for information on where to buy spreadsheets already created for this purpose.)

Tracking your menu

Use your own menu mix analysis to answer these questions (we use the example of Figure 19-3 in our discussion):

- **Which items are the most popular?** Our most popular items are our steaks. Both the ribeye and the filet are hot sellers, with 47 and 46, respectively, sold on the night we're looking at.

- **Which items bring in the most revenue dollars?** Notice that the high-revenue items usually aren't those that have a low food cost percentage. Pasta with marinara sauce has a low food cost percentage but also a comparatively low *profit margin*, the difference in the cost of the item and its price.

- **Which items have the highest and lowest profit margins?** Our highest margin item is the mixed grill at $22.95; our lowest is the sausage pizza at $6.63.

- **Are you maximizing your sales of your highest profit margin items?** Look at both the cioppino and the mixed grill. They're both high-profit items that are currently low in popularity ("Challenge" menu items). Think about ways to improve sales of these items to increase profit.

Working with the mix

Compare only similar items. For example, Figure 19-3 includes only dinner entrees. We don't include desserts, appetizers, or sandwiches, because not everyone orders one of these items. If you were to evaluate a dinner item compared to a dessert, you'd be comparing apples to oranges (or more accurately, pasta to cheesecake). Most people who come to your restaurant for dinner order a dinner entree. Sure, some people order an appetizer as an entree, others may split an entree, and someone else may want a sandwich from your lunch menu, but in most cases, people order dinner entrees. After dinner, some guests order desserts, and some don't.

Look at your menu mix over time. Figure 19-3 represents a single dinner shift, but the more info you get over a longer period of time, the more accurately you can view your data. Run menu mixes weekly, monthly, and at intervals that correspond to your business levels. If you have lots of traffic in the summer but not much in the winter, you may run menu mixes weekly, monthly, and seasonally. You may see that your summer customers eat very differently than your winter customers, so you may change your menu to match their preferences.

If you're changing your menu quarterly, seasonally, weekly, and so on, save a paper or electronic version of the menu so you can look back on preparation methods and side dishes. Your POS system may just tell you that you sold 18 orders of salmon in a day, but it won't necessarily tell you whether the salmon was grilled, sautéed, or roasted on a cedar plank unless you make each of these separate POS items. This system means more data entry, but the informational return is valuable in evaluating your menu mix. These menu details can complete the picture that your POS starts. Also, save special-occasion menus from holidays such as New Year's Eve, Valentine's Day, and Mother's Day. After you've been in business several years, the holidays blend together, so don't rely on your memory to keep track of it all.

If you run across items that aren't selling, consider the reasons before you decide how to adjust your plan. Here are some questions to get you started:

- **Are you charging too much?** Take a look at Chapter 8 for pricing your menu properly.

- **Is your menu description appealing?** See Chapter 8 for tips on making dishes sound like they're worth every penny and more.

- **Is the item ideally placed on the menu?** Chapter 8 gives you tips and tricks for placing your high-margin items where diners look most often.

- **Is the item intimidating to your diners?** Pushing the limits is okay if you have a core group of more-adventurous diners. Just keep in mind that the less-well-known items may take longer to catch on. Make sure you have the cash reserves to wait it out until they take off.

- **Is your staff educated about the item?** Maybe you can do additional training with your staff about these high-margin items and create an incentive program to sell them.

At times, raising the price of an item can actually improve its sales. Although you may cross a price barrier in the consumer's mind (some people won't pay more than $19.95), you may also create prestige and a market for the item (some people won't consider choosing something that isn't over the $20 mark). A price increase is also an incentive for wait staff that likes to *upsell* — encourage diners to choose higher quality (or additional) menu items.

Purchasing and inventory analysis

The true test of any purchasing and inventory program is how well it performs in the real world and brings you closer to your goal of profitability. You may be purchasing and pricing your menu right only to be giving food away because it's not prepared right, it ends up in the trash can, or it walks out the back door. Use a *cost of goods sold* (COGS) report (see Table 19-1) to help you figure out how your hard work in this area is really measuring up. In a nutshell, a COGS report measures your true and actual food cost percentage. It doesn't tell you why the number is too high or too low, however, so you need to dig deeper if it doesn't match your expectations.

Although you almost always write "COGS," you never say "cogs"; instead, you say "cost of goods sold."

Table 19-1	Sample Cost of Goods Sold (COGS) Report					
Product	Beginning Inventory (BI)	Purchases (P)	Ending Inventory (EI)	Cost of Goods Sold (COGS = BI + P – EI)	Sales	COGS/ Sales
Food	$2,800	$8,700	$2,700	$8,800	$29,678	29.65%
Liquor	1,345	750	1,296	799	4,120	19.39%
Beer	895	300	910	285	2,700	10.56%
Wine	3,200	350	2,100	1,450	6,800	21.32%
Total	$8,240	$10,100	$7,006	$11,334	$43,298	26.18%

Here's how to figure your COGS as a percentage of sales:

1. **Figure out your beginning inventory (BI).**

2. **Tally your invoices for the products you purchased (P) during the time period you're reporting on.**

   Create an *invoice log* to track your invoices and assign the invoices to categories that mirror your COGS categories.

3. **Figure out your ending inventory (EI).**

4. **Add your beginning inventory and your purchases and subtract your ending inventory from your invoices (BI + P – EI).**

   This calculation gives you the COGS in dollars.

5. **Divide that total by your sales and write that number as a percentage.**

   So here's the overall formula for the COGS percentage:

   COGS % = (BI + P – EI)/Sales

The more categorized your data is, the more easily you can spot problems, but the tougher it is to get an overall picture. Figure out what's best for your business. You may decide that you want all alcoholic beverages to be included in a single category rather than in three categories as in Figure 19-4. Most restaurants count nonalcoholic beverages, such as tea, coffee, and soda, in their food costs rather than in their beverage costs. But some restaurants count bottled water, juices, and so on with the beverage or bar costs because these items are often kept in the liquor storage area. There's no right way to count them, but be consistent no matter how you categorize. Mark the invoice for the item in the same category that you mark the sale.

The National Restaurant Association (www.restaurant.org) can help you find your local NRA office, which has norms and comparison data specific to concepts like yours in your local market.

Evaluating and Using Feedback

Feedback is a blessing and a curse. Every operation must continue to inno-vate or die, and some of the greatest opportunities for innovation come from feedback. Your employees and your customers are sources of feedback, both positive and negative. But figuring out what to do with the information you receive isn't always easy. Sometimes, the feedback represents a preference and doesn't shine light on an actual problem. You have to figure out how to sort through all the info and react appropriately.

If you ask for feedback but don't act on it, people may feel that you aren't listen-ing or don't care about their point of view. If possible, let them know that you considered their point of view and chose a different path. Choosing to make a different decision is way better than appearing to ignore your employees or cus-tomers. If you know that a recommendation won't work, let the person know, gently, during the same conversation. You may say something like, "I agree. The doorframe would look better if it were black. Unfortunately, our landlord requires that all tenants in this building keep the doorframes sea-foam green."

Paying attention to customer feedback

Customers provide feedback in all kinds of ways, some formal and some not-so-formal. Seek out every opportunity you can to get customers' feedback because, ultimately, their collective opinion matters. Your customers make the final decision on the success of your business.

Table talk

Visit guest tables informally as often as you can. Many guests won't stop you to let you know about something, but if you stop by their table, they may spew a fountain of feedback that you never anticipated.

Table chats are also a great way to get positive information. Too often, you're called to a table by a frazzled server or, even worse, an angry guest. Improve your odds by visiting tables of happy, smiling guests as well. Give your busi-ness card to happy people, who then can tell their friends they "know" the manager. (See Chapter 18 for more tips on building your clientele.)

Here are some tips for reading between the lines when you talk to tables of people:

- ✔ **Find ways to bring yourself into a conversation.** Pour a wine refill if you're passing by and ask how the guests like their food.

    Watch for signals that indicate a table doesn't want any attention, and don't bother those diners. Avoid tables where you notice private conversations (people talking quietly with their heads close together) or obvious signs of emotion — crying qualifies.

- ✔ **Keep the tone of your questions positive or at least neutral.** Ask, "Isn't that calamari delicious?" or "How is your filet mignon?" not, "Is everything okay?" The word *okay* isn't positive in this business. It's never a goal and shouldn't be an acceptable standard.

- ✔ **Ask open-ended rather than yes/no questions.** You're more likely to get helpful feedback than a polite, "Yes, thanks."

- ✔ **Be specific.** Know your menu well enough to recognize it half-eaten on a plate. People are impressed when you can ask, "How's your Arctic char tonight?" rather than "How's the fish?" Adding extra touches to the conversation helps: "The red and black caviar sauce is a home run. I had that for lunch. It was great."

    If you don't know what guests are eating, don't guess. Confusing two entrees can be embarrassing to you.

- ✔ **Remember names and faces.** Remembering regular customers can help build a rapport that can lead to some great specific feedback.

Comment cards and surveys

We recommend that you use some form of comment card or survey (printed or electronic) in your operation as a feedback tool. Figure 19-4 shows a sample guest survey. Your feedback form may be longer or shorter than the sample, depending on what you want to know about your guests' experience. You may prefer to have just general categories (food, service, atmosphere, and so on) rather than specific questions related to each category. Some restaurants add a space for the diner to compare the restaurant to similar restaurants.

Strike a balance between asking every possible thing you want to know and not getting specific, helpful info. People won't fill out a comment card if it's too long. And if people do fill out a long card or survey, they may just be going through the motions instead of providing good, relevant feedback. (For help with dealing with customer complaints, take a look at Chapter 18.)

To encourage feedback, consider offering respondents a freebie, such as dessert on their next visit or even a percentage off their next meal.

Don't get so desensitized to the feedback that you ignore people who are sincerely alerting you to an existing problem. Most people aren't trying to gouge you, take advantage of you, or get free stuff. Keep your cynicism in check. Look at each complaint independently and weigh its merits before dismissing it or acting on it.

Online customer reviews

Online customer reviews, at sites such as Yelp or Urbanspoon, are instantly available to a large number of potential customers.

If you choose to respond to negative reviews publicly, do so in a professional manner without launching into a personal attack. People may ignore an obviously mean-spirited negative review, but they typically have a tough time ignoring negativity from a business owner. Take a look at Chapter 15 for specific details on dealing with online customer feedback.

Guest Survey

We value your patronage and appreciate your valuable feedback on our service, our food quality, and your dining experience.

Please circle your rating on a scale of 1-10, 1 being the lowest, and 10 being the highest.

1. Reception

Courtesy & friendliness of door host	1 2 3 4 5 6 7 8 9 10
Accuracy of wait time	1 2 3 4 5 6 7 8 9 10
Service of bar staff	1 2 3 4 5 6 7 8 9 10
Overall Impression	1 2 3 4 5 6 7 8 9 10
Professionalism of phone respondent	1 2 3 4 5 6 7 8 9 10

2. Server

Courtesy	1 2 3 4 5 6 7 8 9 10
Speed	1 2 3 4 5 6 7 8 9 10
Attentiveness	1 2 3 4 5 6 7 8 9 10
Menu Knowledge	1 2 3 4 5 6 7 8 9 10
Overall Impression	1 2 3 4 5 6 7 8 9 10

3. Food

Presentation	1 2 3 4 5 6 7 8 9 10
Temperature	1 2 3 4 5 6 7 8 9 10
Taste	1 2 3 4 5 6 7 8 9 10
Overall Impression	1 2 3 4 5 6 7 8 9 10

4. Overall Dining Experience   1 2 3 4 5 6 7 8 9 10

_____

_____

_____

_____

_____

_____

5. How often do you frequent our restaurant?

First time ☐   1-4 times a year ☐   monthly ☐   more often ☐

6. What did you like best about our restaurant?

_____

_____

_____

7. Was there anything you didn't like?

_____

_____

_____

8. What could we do to make your dining experience better?

_____

_____

_____

Date _____   Number in Party _____

Occasion _____
(business, entertaining, celebration, etc.)

Server's Name _____

Your Name _____

Address _____

City _____ State _____ Zip _____

Telephone _____

Email address _____

Would you like to be on our contact list? ☐ Yes ☐ No

Figure 19-4: Sample guest survey.

Responding to professional criticism and praise

Professional critics take many forms, ranging from the local paper's restaurant critic to the colleague sitting next to you at a trade-show conference. You have to grow a thick skin to weather the constant commentary on your business, your lifeblood, your baby. But you can also use it to your advantage.

Reacting to negative reviews

Take all reviews and criticism with a grain of salt. If a critic praises you, treat it as reinforcement for doing things the right way. If the review is negative, evaluate it and formulate your reaction. But know that if the criticism is public, such as a published restaurant review, others will read it and form their own opinions.

You basically have six choices for dealing with negative professional criticism:

- ✔ **Ignore it.** Like Momma said, "If you can't say anything nice, don't say anything at all."

- ✔ **Acknowledge the feedback but don't make changes based on it.** If you've honestly evaluated the feedback and feel a problem doesn't exist, this option may be your best course of action. Note we said *honestly evaluated the feedback;* don't just shrug off something you don't want to hear. All feedback is a chance to review your operation through a fresh set of eyes.

- ✔ **Acknowledge it and pretend to act.** This strategy is possibly the riskiest. If you acknowledge a problem and say you're making changes, make changes. If a critic sees the same problems again, the next review may be worse.

- ✔ **Acknowledge it and act definitively.** Daniel Boulud's four-star restaurant bearing his name was cut down to three stars by a *New York Times* critic. Boulud took the review personally, but he also saw it as an opportunity to circle the wagons and reinvigorate his staff. When he felt he'd made all the necessary adjustments and improvements, he invited the critic back. Net result: back to four stars.

- ✔ **Acknowledge it and pretend not to act.** While boarding a plane from Tokyo, coauthor Mike was informed that his Grand Central Oyster Bar's review in the *New York Times* would be out before he landed in New York. His chef was in panic mode, but Mike told him, "If he reviews us for what we do, we'll be fine." Unfortunately, his restaurant was reviewed against some higher-end places that didn't match up fairly. Ultimately, the restaurant was given a less-than-stellar rating of "Fair," but the reviewer had many nice things to say, such as "Best Raw Bar in the City" and "The counter waitresses are goddesses."

Mike took out a full-page ad, but instead of publicly challenging the critic to an editorial duel, he thanked the critic, using full quotes directly from the review. Net result: GCOB had its highest grossing year ever, and behind the curtain, Mike used the review's negative points as constructive criticism, challenging his staff to do better and implementing improvements.

✔ **Counterattack.** Warner LeRoy, one of the most recognizable restaurateurs of his day, became incensed when the *New York Times* lambasted his resurrected Russian Tea Room in a review. In response, LeRoy took out full page ads opposite the ensuing weekly reviews for several weeks. The ads challenged and even ridiculed the critic. In the end, LeRoy's strategy came off looking angry and childish. It didn't help the restaurant, either: Ultimately, the Tea Room failed.

Don't react emotionally if you receive a negative review, as hard as that may be. Investigate the details in the review objectively to see whether the critique is valid. Use it as an opportunity to reevaluate your concept, menu, and processes. And you can always use it as a reason to rally the troops.

Using positive reviews

If you're lucky enough to get a good review, don't put everything on autopilot. Keep doing what got you there. A good review usually means an increase in business. Exceed the new diners' expectations, because the bar will be set high.

In politics, they call it the Big Mo — momentum. The increased business inspired by a good review can give your restaurant momentum, and you gotta take advantage of it. If your concept is based on a value-oriented promise, you may want to find a way to increase the number of diners you can seat. Some restaurateurs try to make the money while they're riding the wave by jacking up the prices. If exclusivity is essential to your concept, raising prices may be just the thing to do to capitalize on your newfound fame. Your approach is strictly a matter of personal choice and management style.

Make the most of any industry awards and distinctions — local or national — that you, your restaurant, or your employees receive. If your restaurant gets the vote for the "Best Taco under $3 in Town," let everyone know about it. If you win a Grand Award from *Wine Spectator* magazine, capitalize on it. Use any public praise or honors as an opportunity to praise yourself and your staff. Include newspaper and magazine clippings in your PR and advertising campaigns (see Chapter 15). Incorporate them into your décor by framing the actual award and displaying it for diners to see. Tastefully using this info somewhere on your menu or at your entrance (to give a potential patron that little extra nudge) is also a good idea.

Listening to employee feedback

Talk to your staff at all levels to get feedback. Find opportunities to regularly pick the brains of servers, bussers, line help, dishwashers, and the manager on duty. Use formal and informal opportunities to get the word on what's really going on from your employees' standpoint. Keep communication flowing through all the departments in your organization. Solutions sometimes come from unlikely places. Here are some ways to get the scoop:

- ✔ Use the manager's logbook to communicate problems with service, food, or employees. The more people who know what's going on, the more likely you are to be able to establish patterns and fix the problem. If you notice that server Brian constantly serves cold and overcooked food but no one else does, maybe the problem is really with Brian rather than the kitchen. Maybe he's ordering incorrectly or not running his food in a timely matter.

- ✔ Schedule regular staff meetings for the entire staff as well as departmental meetings. You may find that you get very different feedback at each meeting.

- ✔ Get a suggestion box. Some employees won't speak up in meetings or come to you directly with a suggestion. The anonymity of the suggestion box can be just the way to pull that next great idea out of them.

Your employees provide customer feedback that's somewhat filtered. It may not be the same information you'd get straight from the customers themselves. An employee, intentionally or not, puts his own spin on the situation and may offer solutions. It's up to you to decide which problems to respond to. If you're talking to different people and you're hearing the same things repeated, consider employees' input.

Part V
The Part of Tens

"I'm trying to remember the type of California white wine I like, but my mind keeps drawing a blanc."

In this part . . .

This wouldn't be a *For Dummies* book without a Part of Tens. Our take on this part includes ten or more myths about running a restaurant, resources for restaurant managers and owners, and our favorite stories that provide some insight into the strange world of restaurants.

Chapter 20

Ten Myths about Running a Restaurant

*O*ne of the biggest reasons people don't stay in the restaurant business is that they don't have realistic expectations of what the job is like. (The other heavy hitters are that it's really exhausting, time-consuming, unappreciated . . . but we digress.) In this chapter, we dispel some of the most common myths about running a restaurant while keeping our fingers crossed that we don't scare you away.

Running a Restaurant Is Easy

A typical chef's or restaurant manager's morning (we're talking before 11:00 a.m. here) may include all these activities: Getting in at 5:00 a.m. to inspect and accept deliveries. Starting soups and sauces at 6:00 a.m. Calling in last-minute orders for tonight's party of 50 that booked yesterday evening. Calling the equipment service technician about the steamer that went down in the middle of last night's shift. Creating a prep list. Supervising the staff. Finding replacement staff to fill in for late employees, call-offs, and no-shows. Ensuring that the dining room is ready to go before the restaurant opens. Performing a line check to confirm that all food is ready to go before the restaurant opens. Creating specials, such as a soup of the day and salad/sandwich combo. Fending off the persistent salesperson who has to talk to you this minute about the new glow-in-the-dark chicken tenders.

That's quite a to-do list to complete before 11:00 a.m., but that's not all. Then you push the paper to track sales, forecast revenue, and pay bills. If the liquor authority wants to know where you got a case of vodka, you have to be able to produce the receipt. If the health department is investigating a food-borne illness outbreak related to oysters, you better have the tags for your shellfish on file. If the state unemployment office needs confirmation that an employee quit and wasn't terminated, you need accurate employee files.

If you're building a new business or want to move beyond maintaining an existing one, you spend even more time developing marketing and PR strategies, looking for the best deals from your vendors while preserving the quality of your products, and recruiting a top-notch staff.

I'll Have a Place to Hang Out

Lots of people use this myth as one of the top reasons they should start a restaurant. They picture themselves hanging out and chatting with people at the bar or walking through a kitchen abuzz with cooks. They imagine getting paid while watching the World Series in a bar full of their friends. Whatever the specifics of your vision, if you're looking to own a place where you can hang out, you better be willing to pay other people to do the hard work.

It's essential for anyone running a restaurant, whether as the owner, chef, or manager, to be in the restaurant and watch what's actually happening. If you're hanging out, you're not seeing what's going on in the supply room, at Table 42, or out in the parking lot. Plus, hanging out socially in the restaurant can be a drain on your bottom line, especially if you're buying the drinks.

I Can Trust My Brother-in-Law

The dilemma over whether to include relatives in your business isn't unique to the restaurant business. Our general advice is "Don't get involved in business with your family, because it's hard to get out of business with your family." Many companies implement rules against hiring family members because it creates unnecessary complications.

The Neighbors Will Love Me

For reasons you may never know, your neighbors may have preconceived ideas of what you and your business are like. They may have had a bad experience with your predecessor. Maybe the place was a noisy bar, or maybe the previous tenant didn't maintain the exterior well. Other people are nasty as a way of entertaining themselves.

Get to know your neighborhood. People may already have allegiances that could be hurdles to your success. If there's already a favorite breakfast joint, winning people's loyalty to your pancake house may be hard. You need to know that going in and to make your point of difference clear (see Chapter 2 for details on points of difference).

I've Been to Culinary School, So I'm Ready to Run the Show

Attending culinary school is a great start, but it's just that — a start. Most schools accept students from all educational backgrounds, including recent high school graduates and people with advanced degrees in other subjects. But remember, graduation from culinary school marks the beginning of your restaurant career, not a shortcut to the top. Most kids fresh out of school have never hired or fired employees, negotiated with salespeople, placed orders, dealt with unions, or fixed equipment in the middle of a shift. You don't learn to deal with the controlled chaos of a restaurant in a classroom, not even one that looks like a restaurant.

I'm Going to Be a Celebrity Chef

The popular media has elevated many restaurant chefs to celebrity status. The work of celebrity chefs has gone a long way to shaping the culinary scene in this country and in the rest of the world. Having talked to many of these chefs, we've found that they think the idea of newfound fame is humorous, in the sense that for years they drove a stove for a living. Their careers haven't been all book signings, TV shows, and speaking engagements. People don't see the grueling hours they spent cleaning grease traps, being screamed at by pan-wielding European chefs of the previous generation, and mopping out coolers. These celebrities didn't attain their status overnight.

My Chili Rocks, So I Should Open a Place

Just because you're good at making chili (or anything else, for that matter) for two, four, or six people as a hobby, don't assume that you can turn it into a job. Running a restaurant is so much more than cooking well. It involves being a salesperson, host, purchasing agent, human resources manager, accountant, and efficiency expert all rolled into one. And few places succeed based on the power of a single dish, so it's a little risky to put all your beans in a single chili bowl. But with this warning in mind, remember that all is not lost for your dream of opening that little chili joint. Coffee bars, ice cream parlors, and hot dog carts can all do well, especially with a large population to draw from. Variety isn't always the spice of life. You may get lucky.

I Can Cut the Advertising Budget

In any business when sales are down, owners and managers naturally begin looking at places to cut the budget. All too often the advertising and marketing budgets are among the first to go. But when sales are down, you need more people coming in the door, and you need the people who are coming in the door to spend more money. Effective advertising can accomplish this goal and more than pay for itself.

Wraps Are Here to Stay

Trends, by definition, don't last. They're white-hot ideas, entrees, presentations, or whatever that capture the public's interest and then fade into the distance. Think wraps, frozen yogurt, merlot, and the $40 hamburger. All still have their place in the hearts of the dining public (except maybe the $40 burger), but they've settled into their proper places on menus everywhere. Wraps gave way to bowls. Frozen yogurt lost ground to its grandfather, frozen custard. Merlot at best shares the stage with red zinfandel, pinot noir, and shiraz. The list goes on. Don't invest yourself too much in the food equivalent of a one-hit wonder. It's great to get in at the beginning and ride the wave of a trend, but maintain your flexibility and be ready with Plan B when the bottom falls out — because it will.

I'll Be Home for the Holidays

Many restaurants, especially those close to retail areas, rely on the weeks between Thanksgiving and New Year's Day to turn in their biggest revenue. So if your wife's birthday falls on December 15, you can pretty much forget about taking the day off. You'll likely be working a banquet, catering an office party, or trying to keep the kitchen from crashing at the expo station.

Not only will you be working, but many of your key people likely won't be, so you'll be working even harder. Many of the folks whom you depend on throughout the year request time off during these busy times. You can't expect people to do what you're not willing to do yourself. And if several of your key people are missing, you need to be there to watch for disasters.

Chapter 21

Ten True Restaurant Stories That You Just Couldn't Make Up

*T*he restaurant business has no shortage of colorful characters. If you look around, you can always find something to smile about, whether it's customers, staff, suppliers, or colleagues. Here are a few of our favorite restaurant stories.

Déjà Vu All Over Again

A guy called a restaurant and said to the manager, "I'd like to confirm a reservation that was never made." The manager repeated what the caller said, just to make sure he'd heard it correctly. "That's right," the guy said. "I have a party of ten people coming in tonight at 7:30." The manager said, "We'd love to have you, but we can't guarantee that we can take ten of you at that time tonight." The guy said, "You have to. I'm confirming it." The manager said, "But you never made the reservation." The guy said, "That's what I'm doing now, confirming my reservation that wasn't made." The manager worked him in later that night, fairly close to 7:30.

Priceless

After eating his meal, a customer presented his waiter with what he said was his father's credit card. Despite the waiter's protest, the customer insisted that he could use this card. The manager got involved in the situation and suggested that the customer call his father and have him fax his authorization.

"He'll never authorize it," the customer said. "It'll get paid, but I can't ask permission." The manager let the customer leave but only after taking the customer's driver's license, which the manager said he would hold until the customer paid for his meal.

A month or so passed and the customer didn't return to pay. The manager received a phone call from a business owner in Texas, who begged, "Please, you gotta give the license back. This guy owes me money, and I need him to come back to Texas to work so he can pay me. He can't get on a plane without it." The manager and the business owner had extended conversations about the situation, and ultimately the business owner wired the money to the restaurant to free the license from limbo.

Free Pie Guy

A guy walked into a restaurant and helped himself to a piece of pie. The manager politely stopped the "customer" to ask what was up. The customer said, "I came for my free pie. The waitress told me to come back for a piece of pie whenever I want because mine was bad last time. You owe me a piece of pie." The manager said, "What was her name? What did she look like?" The customer said, "I don't know. She was old." The manager said, "Do you have any more info? A card? Something in writing from her? Can you give me a better description?" The customer said, "She had gray hair, I think." That cleared it right up.

Rat-atouille

A visiting restaurant manager elected himself to help an urban restaurant rid itself of a rodent problem — or more accurately, a problem rodent. The chef bragged that he was going to get it with a BB gun, but a couple of days later, the problem lingered. Around midnight one night, the visiting manager was coming out of the office and saw the rodent out of the corner of his eye. The manager, looking for anything to hit it with, grabbed a long stick with something heavy on the end. As the huge rat ran past him, it stepped on a glue trap and continued running down the hall with the glue trap stuck to its foot. The manager whacked the rat. It turned to him and hissed, going on the offensive. The manager pummeled the rat with his makeshift club, eventually killing it.

Still full of adrenaline, the manager decided to create a display worthy of his prize. He rigged up a hanger and some kitchen twine and then quickly ran to get a witness. He found the night-crew cook who always looked half asleep and usually gave the manager a hard time. The cook came around the corner and, to his bug-eyed surprise, saw a dead rat the size of a cat hanging from a rafter in the middle of the office by its tail.

Frosty the Newbie

A new manager was training in each of the various stations in the kitchen. After her kitchen training was complete, her line guys made her perform one last rite of passage. In their open kitchen concept, it was common to see the line cooks "flaming" the sauté pans to the delight of the diners. The sauté pans, with a bit of oil, would be heated in a line of gas burners. When the pans were hot, a cook would walk down the line and quickly pour water in the hot oil, causing large flames that burned out quickly. When the manager attempted to perform this traditional maneuver, she hesitated and let the oil get a little too hot. As the manager poured her water, the flames seemed higher than usual. Suddenly, the fire-suppression system over the range began pouring white puffs of dried chemicals over the range. The dining room was covered with harmless but annoying clouds of snowy white fire suppression chemicals. The entire restaurant had to be shut down and cleaned.

Drinks Are on Me

A waiter was preparing a tray full of drinks. A waitress working a nearby section asked him, "Hey, could you drop an OJ on Table 92 for me?" The waiter happily obliged. He got to her table, where about eleven people were sitting at a table for eight, and began to set down the juice. The guy across the table yelled, "Look out!" as the entire tray slowly and irretrievably tipped onto a customer. Each individual piece of stemware dumped its contents onto the customer before crashing directly on his head. As the waiter tried to help clean up the diner, he knocked over the glass of OJ that had started the avalanche and was the only glass left standing at that point. The table was in absolute hysterics before the last glass even fell. They became regulars and requested the waiter every time.

You Like My Tie?

Diners from around the world come to eat at a world-class restaurant in Chicago. Some wait for months to get a reservation and, as they wait, their anticipation builds. The owner takes the customers' expectations seriously and trains his staff to not only meet but exceed those expectations. But at a standard price of more than $500 per person, that's tough to do. The restaurant has an unwritten policy that if a guest compliments the waiter on his $100+ Armani tie, the guest will find that tie gift-wrapped for him at the end of his meal to take home as a gift, free of charge.

Chefs Behaving Badly

At a book signing at a gourmet shop owned by a world-renowned chef/restaurateur, an elderly woman pointed out that the black truffle butter was a bit cheaper at the gourmet shop down the street. The chef graciously set down his glass of wine, cleared his throat, and then recommended that she go buy it at the other store immediately. The lady, familiar with this chef's reputation as a tyrant, was flabbergasted and responded that she would tell all her friends how terribly he had treated her. He paused, looked her directly in the eyes, and calmly sneered, "Tell them *both* and get the hell out of my store."

Radio Fryer

In a very busy luxury restaurant in Denver, a cook considered it his right to blare music in the kitchen. He didn't even turn it down when the chef was in the kitchen trying to talk to the staff. Day after day, for close to a week, he and the chef had the same discussion about the loud radio. The next morning, on the chef's "day off," the cook turned the radio on once again. The chef walked in the door, looked the cook in the eye, and walked past. He grabbed the radio, placed it in a fry basket, and tossed it into the 350-degree fryer. Then he walked back to the cook and said, "When that's done, I need you to clean that fryer," and calmly walked to his office.

(Coat) Check, Please!

A guy walked up to a restaurant manager and proclaimed, "My coat's been stolen. My wallet, passport, everything was in it." The manager headed to the coat-check area to confer with the checker. The customer stopped him and said, "No, I hung it over there." The manager looked where the customer was pointing and saw the hooks by the counter-service area under a big sign that read, "Leave it at your own risk. We have a coat room. Check it in."

Index